MW00582307

DAILY DEVOT

WISDOM
HUNTERS

SEEKING
DAILY
THE
HEART
OF
GOD

VOLUME
II

BOYD BAILEY

DEDICATION

to the

Wisdom Hunters Board

Jonathan Bolden

Scott Melby

Deb Ochs

Your loving accountability keeps me focused on the Lord's best!

Copyright © 2012 by Boyd Bailey

All rights reserved.
No portion of this book may be reproduced, stored in a retrieval system, or transmitted in any form or
by any means—electronic, mechanical, photocopy, recording, scanning, or other—except for brief quotations
in critical reviews or articles, without the prior written permission of the publisher.

Published by Wisdom Hunters, LLC

Scripture taken from the Holy Bible, New International Version,® NIV®
Copyright © 1973, 1978, 1984 by International Bible Society.
Used by permission of Zondervan. All rights reserved.

Book design by truth in advertising; Atlanta GA (www.truthinadvertising.net)

Wisdom Hunters, LLC
1080 Holcomb Bridge Road
Building 200, Suite 140
Roswell, GA 30076
Visit us at www.WisdomHunters.com

The Wisdom Hunters name and logo are trademarks of Wisdom Hunters, LLC.

ISBN: 978-0615876443

TABLE OF MONTHS

ACKNOWLEDGEMENTS

Thanks to my wife **Rita,** *and our daughters,* **Rebekah, Rachel, Bethany,** *and* **Anna,**
and our three sons-in-laws, **Todd, Tripp,** *and* **J. T.,** *for letting me do life with you.*

Special thanks to our three grandchildren, **Lily, Hudson,** *and* **Emmeline,**
who give me a fresh understanding and appreciation for my heavenly Father's love for me.

Thanks to **Susan Fox, Lee McCutchan,** *and* **Donna Reed**
for your professional editing and proofing of these writings.

Thanks to **Ida Bell, Margaret Ann Martin,** *and* **Elizabeth Harris**
for making this book possible with your generous support.

Thanks to the **Wisdom Hunters staff** *for your selfless*
commitment to serve the Lord and His children.

Thanks to **Cliff Bartow** *and the* **Family Christian Store team**
for your ongoing encouragement and big vision for Wisdom Hunters.

Thanks to our pastor, **Andy Stanley,** *who consistently "rightly {divides} the word of truth"*
and who lives it out at work and home with the same consistency.

Thanks to the **Ministry Ventures staff** *who stays focused on Christ*
and serving people like no team I know. I so am proud to serve the Lord with you.

Thanks to the creative genius of **Mike and Sheila Dolinger**
who captured the heart of "Seeking God" in the look and the feel of the book.

Thanks to the **encouraging many** *who regularly write to tell us how the Lord*
has led you into a deeper walk with Him as a result of your regular time in His Word.

Thanks to my heavenly Father for loving me and extending His grace and blessing
through the power of the Holy Spirit and His inspired written Word, the Bible.

Boyd

INTRODUCTION

It is all about God—His will, His agenda, His affections, His grace, His forgiveness, His love, His power, His might, His glory, His honor, His holiness, His worship, His praise, His adoration, His justice, His Son, His gift, His wisdom, His patience, His judgment, His rewards, His Word, His revelation, His Spirit, His salvation, His peace, His security, His heaven, His earth, His return, His gifts, His joy, His mercy, His strength, His heart.

Because life is all about the Lord, we have the unique opportunity and real responsibility to daily seek His heart. When busyness blocks me from getting before God, I feel frustrated and alone. But when I block out the world's noise and shun shiny things, I feel His presence, believe His truth, and act accordingly. However, health issues, relational conflict, financial pressures, and inner turmoil still compete for Christ's peace. I desperately need a daily dose of spiritual courage. I simply need security in my Savior.

Are you trying to walk life's balance beam of expectations? If so, dismount and walk with Jesus on His patient path, which is not without pain but is peaceful and productive. Where the Lord leads is what you need. His light may only show one step at a time in your dark situation. That is okay because the next right thing is what faith requires. Do not stress over step ten in the future sequence of God's will. Each phase can patiently wait its turn.

Sometimes God's heart seems distant and detached. I do not feel or act spiritual. There is a drought in my soul, and I desperately need His rain of grace—just one cup of courage. Fortunately, this season of insecurity is usually temporary, as truth eventually triumphs over my distrust and discouragement. My emotions reengage with the Lord's eternal agenda. His patient prayers lead me back to belief. Jesus remains faithful when I am not.

"Be glad, people of Zion, rejoice in the LORD your God, for he has given you the autumn rains because he is faithful. He sends you abundant showers, both autumn and spring rains, as before" (Joel 2:23).

Furthermore, I am learning that seeking wisdom is not accidental but intentional. Knowledge and understanding come when my heart bows in humility, my spirit surrenders in submission, my soul rests in faith, and my will is bent on obedience. Disciplined devotion to my heavenly Father brings me back to be loved by Him.

So is it well with your soul? Are you running harder but getting nowhere fast? Your loving Lord Jesus offers a yoke of support that is easy, light, and restful. Clasp His compassionate hand, receive His kind words, look into His loving eyes, breathe in His fresh breath of peace, and receive His gift of grace. Lean into the Lord, and learn of Him.

"Come to me all you who are weary and burdened, and I will give you rest. Take my yoke upon you and learn from me, for I am gentle and humble in heart, and you will find rest for your souls. For my yoke is easy and my burden is light" (Matthew 11:28–30).

Boyd Bailey, Roswell, GA
Seeking to be a servant of Jesus, a support for saints, and a friend of sinners.

J1

GIANT OPPORTUNITIES

"The LORD said to Moses, 'Send some men to explore the land of Canaan, which I am giving to the Israelites....' Then Caleb silenced the people before Moses and said, 'We should go up and take possession of the land, for we can certainly do it.' But the men who had gone up with him said, 'We can't attack those people; they are stronger than we are.'" Numbers 13:1–2, 30–31

As we face life, we can be overwhelmed by its giant obstacles or be inspired by its giant opportunities. Challenges and uncertainty tend to corrode our confidence. It is in the face of the unknown that we can move forward by faith, or backward in disbelief. What giant obstacles are you facing? How can your obstacles be converted into opportunities? Obstacles are stepping-stones for obedient feet to follow.

Therefore, stay focused with aggressive patience, and you will eventually see some obstacles dissolve while others are transformed into treasures. Maybe a financial giant is looming large as an intimidating obstacle. If so, stay true to your integrity by not selectively suspending your core values for much needed results. Instead, remain faithful to wise stewardship and honesty. The right results will follow at the right time. Trust God to use scary giants for His glory.

God orchestrates giant opportunities for His greater good. He told Moses that He was giving His children the Promised Land; all they had to do was show up and receive His gift. Giant opportunities require faith, planning, perseverance, and hard work, as the reward of obedience and trust in the Lord is enough. So how are you facing the giants in your life— as obstacles or opportunities?

Leaders look and pray for opportunities, exploring them with energy and enthusiasm. Your relentless leadership inspires your family, friends, and work associates to remain faithful and not freak out. Therefore, take the land of opportunity the Lord has given you. Difficult days and economic challenges are greater opportunities for God to get the glory. So be aggressive, increase your efforts, pound heaven in prayer, and by faith receive what your Savior Jesus has already given you. Go after the giant opportunities with gusto and by grace.

The Bible says, "I can do all things through Him who strengthens me" (Philippians 4:13 NASB).

With what giant obstacle can I trust God to turn into an opportunity?

Related Readings: Joshua 14:6–8; Isaiah 41:10–16; Romans 8:31–37; Hebrews 11:33

GOD-SIZED GOALS

"Jesus replied, 'What is impossible with men is possible with God."
Luke 18:27

God-sized goals are meant to challenge our thinking and further our faith. These Holy Spirit-inspired big ideas are crafted by our Creator to spur us on to good works and transformational living. God-sized goals make us uncomfortable at times. They are not guaranteed to happen, but they position us to pray more and believe in God better.

It is through prayerful planning and implementation that gigantic goals move from mere possibility to a surer probability. Huge objectives are a hedge against mediocrity and a prod toward perfection. God-sized goals are given to govern your thinking and determine your time, so you are intentional and focused on His big picture. Otherwise, you can drift without a rudder of reality, destined for disappointment.

Best of all, God-sized goals get you to God. It is prayer and planning with significant progress that move you from the realm of possibility to the place of probability. In most cases, it is one man or woman's passion and focus that prove catalytic in the creation and execution of the goals. The leader looks failure in the eye and extinguishes it by faith, wisdom, and hard work, all wrapped around a skilled and unified team.

Christ-centered possibilities far outweigh man-centered probabilities. Perhaps you need to get away in solitude for several days, asking your Savior to sear your soul with His goals. Think outside the box of small belief, for the Lord is unlimited in His abilities and resources. God-sized goals arrest your attention, adjust your attitude, and accelerate your actions.

So, prayerfully set great goals, and He will grow your character in the process, while influencing others for His glory. Trust Him to teach you the way, to show you with eyes of faith way beyond the bounds of your experience, for His plan will prevail. The Bible says, "I know you can do all things; no plan of yours can be thwarted" (Job 42:2).

What goal is God giving me that needs to be accepted in faith, requiring hard work towards its accomplishment?

Related Readings: Genesis 18:14; Jeremiah 32:17; Matthew 19:26; Ephesians 1:19-20

J3

SIMPLE FAITH

"I tell you the truth, anyone who will not receive the kingdom of God
like a little child will never enter it." Mark 10:15

Simple faith does not mean simplistic faith. Christianity can be complex; for example, our full understanding of the three-in-one Godhead will not happen this side of heaven. There will always be a mysterious shroud around the gospel of Jesus Christ. This is why simple faith in Him is necessary to receive the revelation of His truth found in the Holy Bible.

Jesus made it simple when He described becoming like a little child in order to enter into His kingdom. Small children can clearly see simple truths because they are not encumbered by the complexities of adult living. Because of their humility and honesty, they are able to listen to the Lord's teaching about sinful man and his need for a Savior. For children, loving Jesus is an opportunity to be loved. They can easily accept God's gift of His only Son Jesus for their salvation. Thus childlike faith in Christ is your bridge to God.

"For God so loved the world that he gave his one and only Son, that whoever believes in him shall not perish but have eternal life. For God did not send his Son into the world to condemn the world, but to save the world through him" (John 3:16–17).

Do not miss meeting the Lord in simple faith because of the pain or problems you have encountered in this world. There is no lasting peace to be found on earth. Jesus said, "I have told you these things, so that in me you may have peace. In this world you will have trouble. But take heart! I have overcome the world" (John 16:33).

Your part is to confess faith in Jesus Christ, and His part is to forgive you of your sin and give you eternal life in heaven. The Bible teaches "that if you confess with your mouth, 'Jesus is Lord,' and believe in your heart that God raised him from the dead, you will be saved. For it is with your heart that you believe and are justified, and it is with your mouth that you confess and are saved" (Romans 10:9–10).

Have I simply placed my faith in Jesus Christ for the salvation of my sins? Have I made public my confession through baptism and engagement with a community of believers?

Related Readings: John 3:3; John 14:6; Romans 3:23; Romans 6:23

J4

WELL PLEASED

"And a voice from heaven said, 'This is my Son, whom I love; with him I am well pleased.'"
Matthew 3:17

Am I well pleasing to the Lord? Do I model a life of submission to my Savior? Do I defer all honor and glory to Him? For my heavenly Father to be well pleased with me is the heartbeat of humility. This means at times I displease others to please my Master Jesus. I will choose to embrace beliefs and behaviors that are otherworldly and can cause conflict.

A Christian pleasing to Christ first learns that to be raised high means to begin low. Jesus did not begin His ministry baptizing, but rather being baptized. He required of Himself everything expected from everyone else. Humble leaders do this; they follow the agreed-upon guidelines, realizing no one is above the rules. It is with a humble heart that a leader discerns the Lord's ways and then lives them out in front of the faithful and faithless.

Perhaps good-hearted people seek to place you on a pedestal of admiration and honor. It is at this point of recognition that you keep your spirit low, as your reputation is on the rise. The Lord sustains His blessing for those who defer honor back to Him. It pleases your heavenly Father to see you engage in humble acts, especially as your influence grows. The closer you grow to Christ, the more you see the need for His grace and forgiveness.

You can only deal with the soul of another if Jesus has dealt with your soul. It pleases Him when you first pronounce yourself needy before heaven, before you point out the needs of another. Humility looks inward at the heart before it outwardly observes the issues of another. The Lord is pleased when you take the lead to repent.

You go public with your faith after you have been private in prayer. This solemn preparation pleases your heavenly Father. Moreover, have you proclaimed your faith publically in baptism? It pleases God for you to go public for Him. It is an honor and becomes your sacred accountability. Private intimacy with your heavenly Father leads to a public inauguration of your faith. He is well pleased with you when you publically pronounce Him the Lord over your life. Humility pleases Him. Why? It listens and obeys.

"Then the LORD spoke to you out of the fire. You heard the sound of words but saw no form; there was only a voice. He declared to you his covenant, the Ten Commandments, which he commanded you to follow" (Deuteronomy 4:12–13).

Have I earned the right to publically declare my faith because of my private obedience? Does my Savior smile when He sees how I honor Him with my attitudes and actions?

Related Readings: Job 37:5; Haggai 1:12; John 5:25; Hebrews 4:7

MENTOR YOUNG PEOPLE

"At the window of my house I looked out through the lattice. I saw among the simple,
I noticed among the young men, a youth who lacked judgment." Proverbs 7:6–7

Most young people yearn for someone to invest time and wisdom in them. They know deep in their hearts they need help to handle heartaches. Their naïve knowledge has yet to graduate them from the school of hard knocks; so they need loving and wise instruction. Who in your circle of influence is a candidate for your caring attention?

It may be a son or daughter, a colleague at work, or a friend from church. God places people in our lives for a purpose. Perhaps you prayerfully pursue a mentor relationship with a teachable young person. He or she can learn from your mistakes as much or more as from your wise choices.

Mentors are not perfect, just wiser from failure and humbled by success. Look around and ask the Lord to lead you to a young person who may be edging in the wrong direction. Reach out to that young person. By doing so, you will have returned the favor to someone who loved you.

Indeed, mentors take time for others because they are eternally grateful for those who took time for them. Gratitude to God is a great reason to go the extra mile with someone younger. Read books together, maybe a book a month for a year. Meet over coffee to discuss how the book challenged your thinking and changed your behavior for the better.

A young leader can preclude problems when he or she is able to model the wise habits of his or her mentor. Always invite an older adult into your life who can educate you in the ways of God. Moreover, the mentor process is valuable to both parties. It provides accountability, encouragement, love, and obedience to Christ's commands. Mentor young people so they follow the right path, and in turn help someone else do the same.

The Bible says, "Encourage the young women to love their husbands, to love their children.... Likewise urge the young men to be sensible" (Titus 2:4, 6 NASB).

Who is the young person in my life in whom the Lord is leading me to invest time, wisdom, and resources?

Related Readings: Job 32:6; Psalm 119:9; Matthew 28:20; Titus 2:1–8

FALSE SPIRITUALITY

"She took hold of him and kissed him and with a brazen face she said:
'I have fellowship offerings at home; today I fulfilled my vows.'" Proverbs 7:13–14

Unfortunately, there are those who use religion to get their way. It may be a single adult who preys on an unsuspecting single adult at church. They attend church to take advantage of trusting souls. Some businessmen use the art of Christian conversation to give the appearance of values and principles based on the Bible.

However, once they make the sale or close the deal, their self-serving and dishonest ways reveal themselves. One of the worst types of deception is spiritual deception, because it uses God to get our way. In marriage it may be the husband who uses submission to control his wife, or a wife who uses grace to withhold from her husband.

Therefore, warn those who, like Simon in the early church, try to buy the Holy Spirit for their benefit, and cultivate authentic spirituality in your heart and mind through prayer, worship, and community.

True spirituality, on the other hand, is motivated and controlled by the Spirit of Christ. There is authenticity because almighty God is the initiator. True spirituality does not just look out for itself but is sincerely concerned with serving others. You are comfortable with those who have true spirituality because you know they care for you.

Integrity radiates from their business and religious activities. Their yes is their yes, and their no is their no. There are no surprises, because what you see is what you get. True spirituality comes over time, forged on the anvil of adversity, taught at the hearth of humility, and received at the gate of God's grace. You know your religion is real when you love others above your needs and when you care for the poor and needy.

The Bible says, "This is pure and undefiled religion in the sight of our God and Father, to visit orphans and widows in their distress, and to keep oneself unstained by the world" (James 1:27 NASB).

Whom do I need to confront in love about using their "Christianity" to take advantage of others?

Related Readings: Ecclesiastes 7:4; Matthew 25:36; Acts 8:19–20; 2 Corinthians 1:17

TRAVEL TEMPTATIONS

"My husband is not at home; he has gone on a long journey. He took his purse filled with money and will not be home till full moon." Proverbs 7:19–20

How do you deal with temptations when you travel? Conversely, what is your behavior when you are the spouse left at home? Is your house a palace of peace, or a prison of confinement? Not only must the weary traveler be wary of wrong behavior, but so must the one left holding down the fort at home.

Perhaps you craft together guidelines as a couple, defining what you will and will not do while separated by travel. Distance can grow the heart fonder and more faithful, or it can fire the flames of lust and infidelity. If you travel for your work, you most likely are motivated to meet the needs of your family.

However, every assignment is for a season; so maybe it is time to get off the road and reconnect with your child who is approaching the teenage years, or be there more often for your spouse who is starved for extra emotional support. Just be willing to adjust.

Moreover, do not drift into travel temptations that become divisive and deteriorate your marriage. One boundary may be to avoid bars and be back in your room soon after work and dinner. A righteous routine on the road gets the right results. Make it a priority, when at all possible, to travel with another person of similar values.

Be bold by becoming an influencer of integrity: good, clean fun without flirting with sin. On the other hand, your role in the marriage may be to support the children and manage the home daily. Take pride, not pity, during this season of unselfish service. By God's grace you are molding their minds to the things of Christ, influencing the culture with His kingdom priorities.

You are as valuable as the one out working to provide for the family as you are working to preserve the family. Stay occupied in prayer, Bible study, their schooling, and be available to those who need you. Marriage is a team effort that reaps outstanding outcomes when you are both on the same page of love and obedience to Christ. Travel temptations are terminated on both ends through trust in the Lord and trust in each other.

"He trusts in the LORD; let the LORD rescue him. Let him deliver him, since he delights in him" (Psalm 22:8).

What behavior boundaries do I need to cocreate with my spouse related to our time apart?

Related Readings: Numbers 5:11–15; Isaiah 46:6; Luke 12:39–46; 1 John 3:9

PAY ATTENTION

"Now then, my sons, listen to me; pay attention to what I say."
Proverbs 7:24

Pay attention, because there are some people who want to help you and some who want to hurt you. Pay special attention to those who seem to say the right things but have a hidden agenda in their heart. Everyone cannot be trusted, because not everyone is trustworthy.

The sooner you discern a man or women's motive, the quicker you will know how to manage your time. If their conversation is all about them, watch out for questionable behavior. Pay attention to the path people may want you to take, and so protect your reputation.

Moreover, you have limited emotional capacity and mind share; so make sure the Lord is leading you to get involved. Even good people and compelling causes can lead you astray. Pay attention, and learn to say no so you can say yes to God's best.

I struggle with saying no because I want to please people. However, pleasing people is not the best motivation. Faith in my heavenly Father is a much nobler goal. Learning to say no is how we gain peace and contentment over the long haul.

When you say no to someone or something, you can trust your Savior Jesus to take care of the need and you. Your no opens the door for someone else to be blessed by their yes. In some cases saying no requires more faith than saying yes. Therefore, pay attention and be prayerful before you commit time and resources.

Certainly, as you encounter temptation, do not entertain the slightest hint of yes. It is better to say no to his or her advances and lose a friendship than to say yes and lose your good name and gain regret. Pay attention and say no to earthly impulses so you can say yes to heaven's best.

The Bible says, "Set your minds on things above, not on earthly things" (Colossians 3:2).

In what area of my life do I need to pay more attention, saying no more often?

Related Readings: 2 Chronicles 20:15; Psalm 34:11; Mark 7:14; 1 Corinthians 4:14-15

WISDOM SPEAKS OUT

"Does not wisdom call out? Does not understanding raise her voice?
On the heights along the way, where the paths meet, she takes her stand." Proverbs 8:1–2

Wisdom is not shy; it proclaims itself and speaks out in public places. Like the Lord speaking to Moses on Mount Sinai, He spoke wisdom out loud with authority, clarity, and finality. John the Baptist boldly cried out repentance and faith in Christ to the crowds. Wisdom is not a secret secluded in solitary confinement waiting to be let out.

It calls out publically and openly. Because wisdom is so easily accessible, it is imperative we listen and learn from its instruction. Sunday morning teaching at your church should be a reservoir of wisdom. If not, consider transferring to a fellowship where access to truth is easily found. Wisdom drowns out the whispers of gossiping fools, because wisdom has the last word. Listen for wisdom, and you will learn how to follow the Lord.

The way of wisdom works because it invites God's blessing. For example, financial wisdom is to avoid debt, save, and pay cash. Relational wisdom is listening with understanding to another's needs, repeating what you heard to confirm your comprehension, and, if appropriate, offering ideas that may bring benefit.

Parenting wisdom is to find couples whose children are upright, learning from them. Business wisdom is to build your enterprise on honesty and integrity, not compromising your convictions for cash. Wisdom has worthy things to say; so each day listen for it and learn. Train your ears to listen for wisdom in sermons and everyday conversations.

Expose your eyes to wisdom in books and the Bible. Lastly, look for wise behavior to emulate from those who enjoy the fruit of faithful living. Wisdom speaks out so you can live it out. The Bible says, "Wisdom shouts in the street, she lifts her voice in the square" (Proverbs 1:20 NASB).

Where is wisdom trying to get my attention, and how can I apply its truth?

Related Readings: Exodus 19; Isaiah 58:1; Matthew 3:3; John 7:37; Hebrews 12:25

UNJUST TREATMENT

"When Jesus heard that John had been put in prison, he withdrew to Galilee."
Matthew 4:12

There are days of mistreatment that come from disloyal and jealous people. Sometimes good people experience bad consequences so the glory of God can be made known through their lives. John boldly took a public stand for his faith and was punished for his courageous obedience to God. Do you feel like you have been wronged for doing right? Has your faith been put on trial, and were you convicted for speaking the truth?

Your circumstance of ill treatment may not result in a physical rescue from Christ. It is in your trapped condition that He wants your intimacy with Him to grow deeper and sweeter. Your authorities at work may have broken a promise or used an unscrupulous process to get desired results. You feel used and abused. So how will your respond? Will you return evil for evil, or will you extend grace in the face of extreme frustration?

"Do not repay anyone evil for evil.... 'If your enemy is hungry, feed him; if he is thirsty, give him something to drink. In doing this, you will heap burning coals on his head'" (Romans 12:17, 20). A radical response of love is a remedy for being isolated by an unjust person.

What are you learning as a result of feeling rejected or misunderstood? Has your determination grown in its resolve, and do you have more focused attention on the mission of the organization? Loss of freedom and/or resources realigns us to the essentials of an effective strategy and efficient execution.

Use this time of limited options to build sustainable systems and productive process-es. Cling to your core values as your compass for behavior. Your optimism is an insurgent against others' insecurities. Lastly, let the Lord be your source of strength. Faith forged on the anvil of adversity becomes solid steel in mental toughness, emotional stability, and spiritual maturity.

When people see Jesus in your humble, non-defensive attitude, they hear His voice of truth. Learn your lessons from the Lord during stressful situations, and leave it with Him to educate others in what needs to be done. Perseverance pays with respect and results.

Am I consumed with trusting Christ or with my unjust treatment? How can I, by God's grace, love the unlovely?

Related Readings: Psalm 23; Psalm 109:5; 2 Timothy 3:2; Revelation 7:12

J11

CHRIST'S CALLING

"'Come follow me,' Jesus said, 'and I will make you fishers of men.'
At once they left their nets and followed him." Matthew 4:19–20

Disciples of Jesus are called by the Lord to minister in their homes and in the marketplace. However, Christ does call some of His followers to vocational ministry. It is a calling that many times comes to ordinary men and women who accomplish extraordinary results. Whom does He call? Christ's call comes to those who have a hungry heart for God.

Like Paul, you might have been suddenly smitten by a revelation of Jesus as Lord, or perhaps you were like David, who gradually went from feeding sheep what was perishable to feeding God's people the imperishable. Wherever Christ calls, His first command is to love God and people. A calling without love is like a car without gasoline. It may be attractive on the outside, but it is not going anywhere. Thus, love large where the Lord has called you.

Furthermore, He has called you to endure hardships. "You have persevered and have endured hardships for my name, and have not grown weary" (Revelation 2:3). Christians are not immune to conflict; in fact, your faith invites difficulty at times. So do not seek to shelter your life from adversity, but rather position yourself in obedience to Christ's calling. It is out of your regular routine of serving Him that you will see what He has in store next.

Make sure you minister first to your spouse and children. Do not be like the cobbler who has no shoes for his family. Your creditability for Christ is seeing your faith lived out with those who know you the best. What does it profit a man if he saves the whole world and loses his family? A calling to family first frees you to evangelize and disciple with God's favor. His calling aligns with His commands; so service for Him is seamless.

Above all, the Lord is looking for those already engaged in His Word, growing in their character, and active in sharing their faith. His calling comes to Christians who desire the Holy Spirit to conform them into the image of Christ. Your humble imitation of Jesus comes out of your intimate walk with Him. He calls those whom He can trust. So do not look for your calling. Look for Christ, and He will reveal His calling to you.

"I, even I, have spoken; yes, I have called him. I will bring him, and he will succeed in his mission" (Isaiah 48:15).

What is Christ's calling for my life? Am I steadfast in loving the Lord and people?

Related Readings: Acts 9:10; 1 Corinthians 7:17; Hebrews 5:4; Revelation 7:14

₁12

HATE EVIL

"To fear the Lord is to hate evil; I hate pride and arrogance, evil behavior and perverse speech."
Proverbs 8:13

The word hate makes us uncomfortable. It has a harsh and uncaring ring and reputation. However, there is a holy hatred of evil that is allowed and even expected by almighty God. Authentic Christianity is not easy on evil because it breaks the heart of God and destroys the soul of man. Evil is an encroachment by the enemy on eternity's agenda.

It takes down leaders who let pride and arrogance seep into their thick skulls and stay there. Indeed, if the rules apply to everyone but the leader, then it is just a matter of time before the fear of the Lord becomes a foreign concept. Sin is out of bounds for any child of God who abounds in His love and grace.

It is the wisdom of Christ that warms the heart, instructs the mind, and leads the way into behavior defined by truth. The Bible says, "God's mystery, that is, Christ Himself, in whom are hidden all the treasures of wisdom and knowledge" (Colossians 2:2–3 NASB).

Gossip, greed, jealousy, and lies are all evil intentions that corrupt a culture of transparency, generosity, contentment, and honesty. Stress can bring out the best and worst in others; so make sure, by the grace of God, you rise above the petty politics of blame.

Wisdom and maturity take responsibility and seek to lead the team in excellent execution of a proven strategy. If you do nothing, the naysayers will negotiate in fear and division. Furthermore, fight evil without fanfare, but by faith and wise work deliver constant and creditable results, and your antagonists will grow quiet.

It is the humility and wisdom of Christ that defeat evil initiatives. Therefore, give Him the glory, get the job done, and trust the Lord with the results. Hard times can produce hard hearts, unless you overcome evil with a humble heart of prayer and bold faith. Evil is extinguished through intense intercession of prayer from pure people.

The Bible says, "Make this your common practice: Confess your sins to each other and pray for each other so that you can live together whole and healed. The prayer of a person living right with God is something powerful to be reckoned with" (James 5:16–17 MSG).

What does a holy hatred of evil look like in my life?

Related Readings: Amos 5:15; Zechariah 8:17; Romans 12:9; 2 Timothy 2:19

J13

POLITICAL WISDOM

"By me [wisdom] kings reign and rulers make laws that are just;
by me princes govern, and all nobles who rule on earth." Proverbs 8:15–16

The wisdom of God overshadows the best and brightest thinking of man. This is why our ancestors accessed the Almighty for knowledge and understanding in crafting our constitution. Its remarkable effectiveness is contingent on faith: faith in God, faith in government, and faith in its citizens.

Indeed, politicians who plead with Providence for wisdom will become the wiser. Those rulers, who recognize their authority is from God, will rule for God. There is a humble ambition that escorts the most effective statesman into public service, as political pride is exchanged for humble wisdom.

Those rule wisely when religion rules in their conscience and character. Political wisdom is a prerequisite for those public servants who govern on behalf of the people and in alignment with the principles of Providence. These wise rulers are able to rest in peace in the middle of a storm.

A culture thrown into economic chaos especially needs principled men and women to step up, to sacrifice, and to make hard decisions. Wisdom in the middle of extreme uncertainty requires painful prescriptions to prevent further panic. Wise politicians face disastrous consequences and determine what is best for the whole in light of the long term.

Pray for political leaders to look beyond themselves and short-term relief into the perspective and principles of God found in Holy Scripture. Indeed, political wisdom prays for intervention by the Almighty and understanding from the Almighty. Perhaps during desperate days a filibuster of faith is first needed; so our leaders start by looking and listening to the Lord.

Just laws follow political wisdom because they do what is right, as Christ defines *right*. Wise politicians keep their hand of faithfulness on the Bible's principles and their hearts submitted under the Lord's authority. Presidents honor Him by never forgetting their sacred inaugural vow of "So help me God."

The Bible says, "Blessed be the LORD your God who delighted in you to set you on the throne of Israel; because the LORD loved Israel forever, therefore He made you king, to do justice and righteousness" (1 Kings 10:9 NASB).

How can I facilitate political wisdom with those public servants in my circle of influence?

Related Readings: Psalm 148:11–13; Daniel 2:21–47; Romans 13:1; Revelation 19:11–16

WISDOM CREATES

"The Lord brought me [wisdom] forth as the first of his works, before his deeds of old....
Then I was the craftsman at his side. I was filled with delight day after day,
rejoicing always in his presence." Proverbs 8:22, 30

Wisdom predates the creation. Like Jesus, it was with God from the beginning. Wisdom is the Lord's instrument of creativity and beauty. It stands by His side as a craftsman ever ready to create for the cause of Christ. Indeed, it is from heavenly inspired wisdom that we experience creative earthly results.

Wisdom longs for you to look for better ways to complement your calling, not limiting the Lord's resources. The creative energy of wisdom does not sit still but seeks out other meaningful methods and models. If how you did something in the past is not effective in the present, put it to rest and watch the Holy Spirit reengineer.

What will it take for you to let go of control and be creative? The best people leave entrenched environments lacking creativity; however, wise is the leader who invites innovation. Furthermore, there is a joy and an anticipation that accompany creativity. You feel fulfilled and significant when you create a product or process that achieves excellent results. Wisdom at work creates a system that rewards creative thinking around relationships and results.

Remain creative and live; lose creativity and die. Indeed, intense adversity invites lavish creativity; so be wise, and use hard times to harness ingenuity. Challenge team members to create compelling content rich in substance, affordable in price, and easily accessible. Above all else, tap into the wisdom and creativity of Christ.

Eternity explodes in colorful creativity that birthed the universe. Go to Jesus and seek His mind for new and imaginative thinking. Prayer gives you permission to invent and innovate. Unleash wisdom and experience the Technicolor creativity of Christ. Partner with your Creator, and by faith and wisdom create for the cause of Christ.

The Bible says, "O LORD, how many are Your works! In wisdom You have made them all; The earth is full of Your possessions" (Psalm 104:24 NASB).

What do I need to stop doing by faith, being more creative with a new and more affordable model?

Related Readings: Exodus 39:43; Proverbs 3:19; Hebrews 1:12; Colossians 1:16

GOD'S FAVOR

"Blessed is the man who listens to me [wisdom], watching daily at my doors, waiting at my doorway. For whoever find me finds life and receives favor from the Lord." Proverbs 8:34–35

God's favor is the fruit of friends who find wisdom. They seek wisdom by first watching at the doors of heaven, waiting patiently at the feet of their Savior Jesus. It is humbling to think each day almighty God is available to commission our cause for Christ. The wisdom of Jesus is what we pursue, because His is pure and profound.

As with Able, the Almighty looks for the best offering for blessing. Therefore, honor God by offering Him the first fruits of your day. Just as He deserves first dibs on your money, so He expects the beginning of your day. Get up and go to God first. There you discover a wealth of wisdom, and under the shadow of your Savior Jesus Christ you receive His favor.

Happiness happens to those who wait for wisdom. His blessing cannot be rushed; so rest in Him. The favor of God is well worth the wait; like with a newborn, the joy is unspeakable. How many times have we rushed ahead, outside the canopy of Christ's blessing? The Israelites, being led by faith, learned to stay under the cloud of God.

Indeed, there is no spiritual oxygen to sustain those in an out-of-favor environment. It is lifeless and lonely. However, for those on whom their heavenly Father's favor rests, there is rest. His blessing provides strength for the journey and perseverance to stay on the trail of trust.

Jesus experienced the favor of His heavenly Father when He submitted to public baptism—His confession of faith, His commitment to public service, and His commission to ministry. In what issue of obedience do you need wisdom to continually experience the favor of your heavenly Father? Your life is alive and vibrant because the Lord favors you. You are a favorite of your heavenly Father because you are learning to wait on Him and to walk humbly with the wise.

The Bible says, "He has told you, O man, what is good; And what does the LORD require of you But to do justice, to love kindness, And to walk humbly with your God?" (Micah 6:8 NASB).

How can I make sure I stay in a position to receive God's favor and blessing?

Related Readings: Genesis 4:4; Exodus 33:12; Luke 2:52; Philippians 3:8

RICH PROVISION

"Wisdom has built her house; she has hewn out its seven pillars.
She has prepared her meat and mixed her wine; she has also set her table."
Proverbs 9:1–2

Wisdom is the pathway to God's rich provision. His Holy Spirit allows you to see the common with uncommon eyes and thus come up with creative alternatives. Wisdom is the Lord's way of preparing plenty of resources and relationships for you to further His will. He is not stingy in sending forth His Holy Spirit for discernment and insight into people and situations.

Therefore, ask the Lord for understanding in what to do and what not to do. When God gives you the green light, go forward by faith, knowing He will provide. He has prepared a place for you, not only in heaven, but also on earth. Wisdom's preparations are plentiful and pretty. So be patient, do the next wise thing, and watch God work in ways you never imagined. Wisdom is at work on behalf of your work.

Could He be calling you to worship and community with different followers of Christ? A church built on the foundation of God's wisdom is the best preparation for your faith and family. Yes, you are best fed in a family of faith where the Word of God is given full attention and examination.

Like the Bereans in the early church, you are encouraged to ask bold questions - related to the meaning of Scripture. The church is God's house for prayer and the proclamation of His principles for the gaining of wisdom to live life.

Therefore, gather wisdom every chance you get and you will become rich indeed: rich in relationships, rich in character, rich in robust relationship with Jesus, and maybe rich in stuff. Wisdom is at work on your behalf; so tap into its rich provision. The Bible says, "For every house is built by someone, but the builder of all things is God" (Hebrews 3:4 NASB).

Where is the wisdom of God preparing His provision that I need to access by faith?

Related Readings: Genesis 43:16; Acts 17:10–12; 1 Timothy 3:15; 1 Corinthians 3:9–15

SETTLE MATTERS

"Settle matters quickly with your adversary who is taking you to court. Do it while
you are still with him on the way, or he may hand you over to the judge, and the judge
may hand you over to the officer, and you may be thrown into prison." Matthew 5:25

Settle matters sooner than later so all parties can focus on other significant issues.
Lawsuits drain the life from relationships and can easily bring long-term relational harm. It
is a financial, bottomless pit that throws stewardship to the wind. Check everyone's motives;
if fear, greed, or anger is driving the legal process, then it is unhealthy.

Why go through the emotional torture of a long, drawn-out, litigious process? A call for
justice is legitimate, but can't there be a fair settlement without having to drag the
relationship through an adversarial trial? Can't someone be the mature Christian adult and
bring a close to the conflict? Money can be made again, but broken relationships may not
be mended. Early Christians struggled with this issue of how to settle matters well.

"The very fact that you have lawsuits among you means you have been completely
defeated already. Why not rather be wronged? Why not rather be cheated? Instead, you
yourselves cheat and do wrong, and you do this to your brothers" (1 Corinthians 6:7–8).

Maybe you are in a legal contract that is onerous, even unbearable. Circumstances
have changed in your work environment, and you are straddled with a commitment you are
struggling to fulfill. Have you gone to the other party and explained your situation? Have
you asked him for concessions or a new contract? Perhaps there are other options that can
be worked out between you. Humble yourself and trust God to work it out.

"My son, if you have put up security for your neighbor, if you have struck hands in
pledge for another, if you have been trapped by what you said, ensnared by the words of
your mouth, then do this, my son, to free yourself, since you have fallen into your neighbor's
hands: Go and humble yourself; press your plea with your neighbor! Allow no sleep to your
eyes, no slumber to your eyelids. Free yourself, like a gazelle from the hand of the hunter,
like a bird from the snare of the fowler" (Proverbs 6:1–5).

Be honest, and from a prayerful position seek to understand the needs of the other,
offering reasonable solutions to the situation. Pray the Lord will open the heart of the other
party and bring creative alternatives to the table for discussion. Remember to keep your
Christian testimony pure and attractive. Your kingdom is not of this world; so bring honor
to King Jesus by doing the right thing in the right way. Settle matters soon.

How can I settle matters in a manner that honors the Lord and all parties?

Related Readings: Exodus 23:2–3; Hosea 10:4; 1 Corinthians 4:2–4; 1 Corinthians 6:1–6

J18

RACIAL RECONCILIATION

Then the Lord said to me, "'Go; I will send you far away to the Gentiles.'"
Acts 22:21

Race divides. Inherently it needs reconciliation. As followers of Jesus Christ, we are expected to be on the forefront of racial reconciliation. Christ is colorblind. There is no preference between Jew and Gentile, black or white, yellow or brown. They are all precious in His sight. Yet every day, millions are disenfranchised or killed because of their cultural heritage and skin color. Where pride and ego drive the human race into different geographical and racial directions, Christ reunites. He is the racial reconciler.

The feet of Jesus are on level ground for all races. Sin is the only explanation for one race's sense of superiority over another. It breaks the heart of God. Jesus went far out of His way to love a racial outcast in the Samaritan woman (John 4). He was compelled by the Holy Spirit to reach across class, cultural, and racial barriers.

In the same way and spirit, God is leading you to reach out to others different from you. He is calling on His disciples to be intentional in healing past hurts and serving current needs. Some will receive your sincere service, while others will question your motive. But when all is said and done, your part is to go and be a blessing. God's part is to facilitate trust and healing. You probably do not consider yourself a racist. That is, you do not feel or act better than another human being just because of your race.

However, to be silent or not intentionally reach out to another culture is passive racism. It is subtle, but the same ill effects occur. The offended or disillusioned ones are still stuck in their inferior state of mind, economics, and education. It is not the role of government to figure this out. Rather, it is the mandate of the church because Christians know better. We can model the way of racial reconciliation as did Jesus.

Consider a year-long, weekly, one-on-one study with someone of a different race. Learn about his or her culture, history, and hurts. Indeed, racial reconciliation happens one person at a time, and it happens relationally. Do not wait on someone to come to you. You go to that person. Yes, it is a little uncomfortable, and yes, there will be misunderstanding. But Jesus is the standard bearer and relational mediator.

Let the Bible be your foundational source of racial reconciliation. Start today on a cross-cultural mission. Is there someone at work or in your neighborhood? Invite the family into your home for a meal. Serve them every time you get a chance, and watch God work. Then the world will see—in Technicolor—that you are truly disciples of Christ because you love one another. Races will be reconciled, and God will be glorified. Jesus said, "By this all men will know that you are my disciples, if you love one another" (John 13:35).

Why is Christ color-blind? With whom can I build a relationship who is of a different race?

Related Readings: Genesis 11:1–8; John 4:1–42; Romans 10:12; Galatians 2:14

J19

RACIAL HEALING

"You are all sons of God through faith in Christ Jesus, for all of you who were baptized into Christ have clothed yourselves with Christ. There is neither Jew or Greek, slave nor free, male nor female, for you are all one in Christ Jesus." Galatians 3:26–28

Christianity is color-blind. The foot of the Cross is level and acceptable for all who embrace faith in Jesus Christ. Man erects barriers, but belief in Christ tears them down. Man makes himself superior and treats others as inferior. However, our superior Savior Jesus makes humble followers of the Lord significant.

Your devotion to Christ is meant to dissolve distrust toward those different from you. In fact, it is out of the beauty of diversity that your beliefs are made real. Faith untested by inclusiveness is indeed inferior. Belief in God equalizes egos and checks pride. Our Christian brand promise is love for one another, because He first loved us.

No race can escape the love of God and His children. Racial healing is a result of radical inclusiveness; so invite others inside. Oneness is the outcome of devotion to Christ. The free set others free, and all become bondservants of Christ. Those in bondage are set free to live life for the Lord and others.

Men and women become one in marriage and one in their love for the Lord. Races have no reason to boast over their lineage other than it is a gift from God. He determined when and where you where born. Your life was planned ahead by Providence. Therefore, thank God for giving you the family and the life He has given you.

Take responsibility for your actions, living life with gratitude and grace. Forgive freely, as Christ has forgiven you, and remove any race resentment with grace insistence. Heaven heals hearts on earth that are unified by faith in Christ Jesus.

His passionate prayer is, "I do not ask on behalf of these alone, but for those also who believe in Me through their word; that they may all be one; even as You, Father, are in Me and I in You, that they also may be in Us, so that the world may believe that You sent Me" (John 17:20–21 NASB).

How can I be a facilitator of race healing by the grace of God in Christ Jesus?

Related Readings: Exodus 12:48–49; Ezekiel 17:23; Matthew 23:8; Acts 10:28–47

KINGS AND PRESIDENTS

"I urge, then, first of all, that requests, prayers, intercession and thanksgiving
be made for everyone—for kings and all those in authority, that we may live
peaceful and quiet lives in all godliness and holiness." 1 Timothy 2:1–2

Kings and presidents come and go, but while in office they require much prayer. Public servants need sincere supplications from servants of the Lord. These leaders of nations have the power to inflict harm or uphold justice. They can pass laws that lead to fiscal irresponsibility or wisely legislate financial protection for the country.

It is God in response to our prayers, not pundits, who reveals the wisest choices. Our president is a mere man, but he is a man under the authority of almighty God. His mandate is not first from earthly man, but first and foremost from his Father in heaven. Rulers, who recognize and embrace their accountability of the temporal to the eternal, rule the wisest.

Pray our president will lead us to live faithful and content lives under Christ's lordship. Pray our commander in chief will receive inspiration and instruction from the Commander in Chief. Pray for our president to look into the future with eyes of faith and create a culture of character for our children and grandchildren.

Pray for our president to honor the sanctity of life in the womb. Pray for our leader of the free world to lead us into a high view of holy matrimony between a husband and wife. Pray for our president to pray. Pray for him to lead with conviction, courage of heart, and humility of mind.

Indeed, your prayers for the president are "good and acceptable in the sight of God our Savior, who desires all men to be saved and to come to the knowledge of the truth" (1 Timothy 2:3–4 NASB).

What day of the week can I take five minutes and pray for our president to have the wisdom to make the best decisions and the courage to follow through, regardless of the consequences?

Related Readings: Nehemiah 1:11; Ecclesiastes 3:12–13; Romans 13:1–7; 1 Peter 2:9–13

CHOOSE YOUR BATTLES

"Whoever corrects a mocker invites insult; whoever rebukes a wicked man incurs abuse."
Proverbs 9:7

We all have a limited amount of time and energy. Wisdom says to spend them both on productive people, not destructive ones. Verbal sparring with a proud person only invites insult. It is better to ignore their venomous venting than try to reason with them. Do your best, stay focused on the task, and trust your reputation with the giver of reputations—your Savior Jesus. Mockers only look to stir up things in the moment.

They have no long-term solutions; so avoid their cynical, crazy cycle. A mocker's mind is already made up and will not change, regardless of wise rationale. There are those who return evil for good; so do not go there, or you may end up in despair. Jesus says of caustic cynics who are full of pride, "Let them alone; they are blind guides of the blind. And if a blind man guides a blind man, both will fall into a pit" (Matthew 15:14 NASB).

Furthermore, what about family members who seem to be hurtling down a path of destruction? Specifically, you may have teenagers or adult children whose entire focus is friends and exercising their freedom. They seem to have rejected all common sense and Christlike influences. First of all, focus on their heart with love and acceptance.

If you battle over the external, it will be messy and costly. However, if they change from the inside out, their transformation will be beautiful and enduring. Ask them to pray, asking the Lord what He thinks about their decisions and choice of friends. Direct them back to Scripture as their Savior's standard for living.

Above all, pursue a peaceful and patient attitude in prayer. Our most significant battles are spiritual; they are won or lost on our knees. The Holy Spirit will lead you when to speak, what to say, and when to remain silent. Everyone wins when you value the relationship over winning the argument.

The Bible says, "Do not rebuke a mocker or he will hate you; rebuke a wise man and he will love you" (Proverbs 9:8).

What relationship do I need to quit striving over and give to the Lord?

Related Readings: 2 Chronicles 30:7–9; Proverbs 23:9; Matthew 7:6; Matthew 22:4–6

INVITE INSTRUCTION

"Rebuke a wise man and he will love you. Instruct a wise man and he will be wiser still; teach a righteous man and he will add to his learning." Proverbs 9:8-9

Wise people invite instruction. They understand that correction and rebuke are necessary to grow in wisdom and righteous behavior. Without well-meaning instructors who are willing to get in our faces, we only aspire to average at best. However, an invitation to mettle in my affairs defines authentic accountability.

Effective correction makes us uncomfortable at times, but we become all the wiser as a result. Indeed, conflict is inherent in accountability. So, if your relationships are conflict free, you can bet you are not being held accountable in the truest sense. Wisdom comes in the form of raw relationships that reek with loving reproof and the willingness to change.

It is out of a rebuke that you wake up and understand the realities you are facing. Your spouse is not nagging, just nudging you to act responsibly. Therefore, invite instruction, and you will increase in wisdom and understanding. There are no regrets from wise recipients of reproof.

Furthermore, be willing to be the bearer of bad news. With love and grace, go to your friend who has asked for your counsel, and give him or her truth. Pray first; then deliver the unpleasant news. It is much better for others to see the error of their ways before they reach a point of no return. Talk to them, not about them.

Pray for them privately, not publically with a pious prayer request. Love motivates a rebuke and then becomes a recipient of love. Your relationships will retreat in anger or rise to a higher level of respect through righteous rebuke. Take the time to prod another toward perfection because you care. Be respectful; instruct with patience, and one day the student may exceed the wisdom of the teacher.

Jesus said, "A student is not above his teacher, but everyone who is fully trained will be like his teacher" (Luke 6:40).

To whom do I need to listen, learning from their correction and rebuke?

Related Readings: Psalm 141:5; 2 Peter 3:18; 2 Timothy 4:2; Revelation 3:19

BEGINNING OF WISDOM

The fear of the LORD is the beginning of wisdom,
and knowledge of the Holy One is understanding." Proverbs 9:10

The fear of the Lord is fundamental to finding wisdom. Without awe of the Almighty, there is no access to His insights. Where reverence for His holiness is void, there is a lack of understanding into the ways of God. The first step in acquiring wisdom from almighty God is to fear Him. There is a worship of the Lord's majesty and a dread of His judgment.

His Holy Word—the Bible—is taken to heart as truth for the purpose of life transformation. At first, fear of the Lord may be so overwhelming that it casts out love and distracts our desire for intimacy. Anyone who has been broken understands this process. However, once a healthy fear of the Lord has been embraced, there is peace and knowledge of holy things, because there is submission to and love for the Holy One.

Moreover, we mock God when we move away from the language of fear, but He is not one to be mocked. So, as devoted followers of Christ, we sow the seeds of respect, reverence, and fear of the Lord. This discipline of faith results in a harvest of holiness, happiness, and wisdom. Fear of Him leads to knowledge of Him.

Therefore, bowing before Him on your knees in prayer, seek His face for forgiveness and relational restoration. Celebrate with Christ His conquest and ours over sin, sorrow, and death. What is counterintuitive on earth is intuitive in heaven. Listen to David admonish his son Solomon who became the wisest man in the world:

"As for you, my son Solomon, know the God of your father, and serve Him with a whole heart and a willing mind; for the LORD searches all hearts, and understands every intent of the thoughts. If you seek Him, He will let you find Him; but if you forsake Him, He will reject you forever" (1 Chronicles 28:9 NASB).

What area of my life lacks fear of the Lord, and how can I expose it to accountability?

Related Readings: Job 28:28; Psalm 111:10; Matthew 11:27; 1 John 5:20

DISCREET DEEDS

"Be careful not to do your 'acts of righteousness' before men, to be seen by them.
If you do, you will have no reward from your Father in heaven." Matthew 6:1

Discretion is the better part of doing good deeds. Why? One reason is that it does not bring attention to the giver but to the motive behind the gift. If I am the main attraction of a good act, then praise from men is my reward. But if I am serving others for an audience of One, then the Almighty's pleasure is my reward. His smile is enough remuneration for my good works. If not, I fall prey to the need for people's praise as fuel for my faith.

Hypocrites have to be stroked by someone other than their Savior Jesus. However, mature followers of Christ are satisfied to know their Lord is delighted with their discreet deeds. Jesus warns that our Christian duties of giving, praying, and fasting be done in secret so we do not become like those who wear their religion to impress others. Moreover, when your deeds are discreet, you do well for yourself, and you benefit. Your secret service serves your soul in prayer, your body in fasting, and your emotions in giving.

God's glory replaces vainglory as you venture into doing your acts of righteousness outside of the Lord's limelight. It is especially tempting for Christian celebrities to be lured into thinking they are the coming attraction, because they forget God's favor. The disciples must have struggled with this rock star complex as they traveled with the miracle-worker Jesus. One's pride in jockeying for the best position is spiritual hypocrisy.

Jesus addressed this attitude that craves attention. "Instead, whoever wants to become great among you must be your servant, and whoever wants to be first must be slave of all. For even the Son of Man did not come to be served, but to serve, and to give his life as a ransom for many" (Mark 10:43–45). Thus, our discreet service leads to greatness for God.

Therefore, be content, knowing your reward comes from Christ. Let sincere words of appreciation from others be an extra blessing you do not expect. Indeed, the accolades of others pale in comparison to the peace that comes in knowing you did your best for Jesus' sake. The satisfaction of serving secretly on behalf of your Lord is reward enough in this life. Pure religion privately reaches out to the least of these in love and gratitude to God.

"If anyone considers himself religious and yet does not keep a tight rein on his tongue, he deceives himself and his religion is worthless. Religion that God our Father accepts as pure and faultless is this: to look after orphans and widows in their distress and to keep oneself from being polluted by the world" (James 1:26–27).

How can I be discreet in doing good deeds? What is my motivation for my acts of kindness?

Related Readings: Genesis 15:1; Psalm 17:5; Luke 16:25; Hebrews 11:6

GOD'S SILENCE

"When Saul saw the Philistine army, he was afraid; terror filled his heart.
He inquired of the LORD, but the LORD did not answer him." 1 Samuel 28:5–6

Sometimes God is silent. He is silent in our prayers. He is silent in our circumstances. He is silent in our relationships, and He is silent in His Word. His silence can be deafening because it seems that His silence is ill-timed. In most cases, His silence revolves around a real need you are experiencing. You may feel that God is disinterested or that He does not care. The silence of God can be an overwhelming place to occupy and still trust Him.

Your predicament could be like a heavy bar bell on your chest with no spotter available to assist you. You feel all alone and unable to fix the problem or correct the issue. You do not even know where to start. You are in despair, at the tipping point of depression. Anger has clouded your reason, and heaven seems indifferent to your hurt.

Or, on the other hand, you are "suffering" from success and prosperity; yet God feels distant and disconnected. You have honored Him in the process, but He has not seemed to honor you with His warm and affirming presence. What is going on? What is God up to? What does He want you to do next for the good of His kingdom?

Indeed, God's silence is your opportunity to remain faithful, even when you are unsure of His intentions for your life. He is God and we are not; therefore, we do not have to pressure ourselves to figure out everything that is going on. Managing the big picture is in His job description, not yours; so rest in His silence. Refuse to become restless, resentful, or rebellious. But still you ask, "Why the silence?"

There may be two possible reasons for God's silence—sin or sanctification, or it may be a combination of both. When God withholds His blessing and direction for your life, it may be the direct consequence of the sin in your life. This is why regular confession and repentance of sin are critical for the follower of Christ. This is like breathing for your soul. Sin is like cotton in the ears of our heart; thus, God's voice becomes muffled, unclear, and eventually silent. Your removal of sin clears the wax from the ears of your heart.

God's silence may be used for your sanctification. He is in the process of making you more and more like His Son Jesus Christ. This is not always fun, though it is needed to learn God's ways and His purpose for your life. Even if He is silent, do what you know is right today, and trust Him with the next step for tomorrow. Do not let silence overwhelm you; rather, use it as a springboard to trust God's faithfulness.

"O God, whom I praise, do not remain silent" (Psalm 109:1).

What do I need to learn during my silent times with the Lord? Will I still trust Him?

Related Readings: Psalm 83:1; Isaiah 62:1; John 12:29; 2 Peter 1:18

FLIRTATIOUS FOLLY

"The woman Folly is loud; she is undisciplined and without knowledge."
Proverbs 9:13

What is flirtatious folly? It is enticement into reckless living. So you may ask, "What does it look like?" Its coyness is conceived in attractive idiots, as these disguised fools seek to lure naïve ones into their stupidity. Foolishness loves friends. It approaches in the form of a well-dressed, well-spoken man or woman. They draw you in with their looks and latch on to you with their words.

Folly can be found among the experienced and educated, or it can run rampant in lives of the young and simple. It forces itself on the middle-aged father who has grown discontent with his faith, family, and vocation. Instead of listening to the voice of reason, he socializes with silliness and invites irresponsibility. However, he does not harvest happiness, because the fruit of folly is death: relational, spiritual, and emotional.

Moreover, wise men and women recognize the futility of folly and flee from its influence. They avoid sexual folly by cultivating a caring marriage. A happy wife is a happy life, and a happy husband is a happy home. Furthermore, financial folly is fleeting for a family who lives well within their means, growing in generosity. Money becomes a means of honoring their Master Jesus (see Matthew 6:21).

What form of folly is staring you in the face? Wisdom is your warning to flee where good judgment is absent. It may require changing schools, breaking off a relationship, or moving to another neighborhood. Wisdom may not be sexy, but it brings success and satisfaction. Walk in wisdom and you will reap rich relationships, robust faith, and peace of mind.

The Bible says, "I will listen to what God the LORD will say; he promises peace to his people, his saints—but let them not return to folly" (Psalm 85:8).

Where do I need to force folly from my life and replace it with wisdom and discernment?

Related Readings: Job 2:9–10; Proverbs 21:9–19; James 1:13–15; 2 Peter 2:18–21

ILL-GOTTEN TREASURES

"Ill-gotten treasures are of no value, but righteousness delivers from death."
Proverbs 10:2

Ill-gotten treasures insult integrity in the process of procuring profit. It is money manipulated by man, rather than blessed by God. There is no profit for the soul, because the means by which the money was made centered on self, not the Savior Jesus. He clearly addresses this, "For what will it profit a man if he gains the whole world and forfeits his soul? Or what will a man give in exchange for his soul?" (Matthew 16:26 NASB).

Indeed, the methods and motives for making money matter. Can financial integrity be assured without transparency in our business dealings or personal financial management? Does God wink at our wrongs when we attach aggressive giving to ill-gotten gains? We need to be careful not to allow the ends of philanthropy to justify the means of dishonesty.

However, honestly earned treasures place the hand of heaven on your head. You can go to the bank and thank God along the way. So how do we know if our acquired treasures are legitimate, as the Lord defines *legitimate*? One indicator is the extent of His blessing, for God blesses benevolence birthed out of brokenness and honest work.

For example, you invite trustworthiness when there is full disclosure in financial reporting. It may mean losing a deal, but the Lord can lead you to better, even more lucrative, opportunities. Moreover, treat others as you want to be treated. Jesus said, "Do to others as you would have them do to you" (Luke 6:31). Thus, you avoid intimidation, fear tactics, and disrespectful attitudes. God blesses respect.

Lastly, a company with a Christlike culture is attractive. You do not have to look over your shoulder because you know other team members cover your back. Indeed, honesty is the best policy in producing profits. Untainted treasure comes from trusting God. It matters as much how you make it as how you give it away.

The Bible says, "Make sure that your character is free from the love of money" (Hebrews 13:5 NASB).

Where is my character being tempted to compromise for the sake of cash, and how can I make sure I behave correctly?

Related Readings: Job 36:19; Psalm 49:6–10; Luke 12:15–21; James 5:1–3

WALK WITH GOD

"Noah was a righteous man, blameless among the people of his time, and he walked with God."
Genesis 6:9

Noah's relationship with God was priority. He knew God was responsible for his life, liberty, and happiness. Simply put, Noah walked with God. He was not distracted by the chaos of the culture or soiled by society. So, what does it mean to walk with God? Walking is a beautiful word picture because it takes one of life's most basic acts and converts it into a supernatural relationship.

Walking implicates a relationship that is not hurried, that easily communicates, and that is invigorating. When we walk with God we are not rushed. We trust Him and are patient. Yes, there are seasons of life and cycles of time when we must be very deliberate and focused. A medical emergency causes us to rush for help, but overall, as we walk with God, we take life in stride.

We believe that any circumstance in life has to pass through God's protection, as He holds us in His hand (see John 10:28–30). So we stay close by Him as we walk, not rushing ahead in presumption, nor lagging behind in discouragement. Walking also implies communication. It is hard to communicate when you run. There are too many distractions.

However, a walk is disarming; eye contact is limited within a safe environment. A walk with the Lord can cover trivial pursuits, heartbreaking hurt, or the dreaming of God-sized dreams. Perhaps in your regular physical exercise, you can also stretch your spiritual muscles in conversation with your Master Trainer Jesus.

Lastly, a walk with God is invigorating. You are energized and ready to scale mountains. Your spiritual blood is pumping, and your heart is healthier. Your energy level is high because your God consciousness is elevated. Walk with God and you will survive, even thrive, within the challenges of life.

Have a little walk with Jesus, and tell Him all about your problems. He walks with you slowly through the valleys and supportively up the mountains. Grace is His guide to greater heights. How is your grace walk with Jesus?

He says, "My sheep listen to my voice; I know them, and they follow me" (John 10:27).

How can I walk with God, by the grace of God?

Related Readings: Genesis 48:15; 1 Kings 3:6; Luke 1:5–7; Hebrews 11:7

HURT HURTS

"He heals the brokenhearted and binds up their wounds."
Psalm 147:3

Hurting people hurt people. They have been wounded in the past and have not been healed in the present. It is very difficult for everyone, because the wounded ones simmer in silent suffering until they lash out at a loved one. Unless they are made whole by the grace of God, there will be no relational restoration with the Lord and others.

Do you or someone you love walk around with a wounded heart? Your hurt may be the result of extreme letdown from someone you trusted and admired, such as a parent or an abusive authority figure. This may explain your resistance to accountability and unwillingness to submit to authority. However, the gospel of Jesus Christ is all about binding up the brokenhearted. He came with healing in His wings for hurting hearts.

"But for you who revere my name, the sun of righteousness will rise with healing in its rays. And you will go out and frolic like well-fed calves" (Malachi 4:2).

Jesus says, "The Spirit of the Lord is upon Me, Because He has anointed Me to preach the gospel to the poor; He has sent Me to heal the brokenhearted" (Luke 4:18 NKJV). Hurt is healed when we let go of anger and allow the grace of God to replace it with forgiveness and peace.

If we remain immature and insist on our way, we will stay stuck in our childish cycle. But Jesus is calling us beyond adolescent attitudes. Paul struggled with this when he confessed, "I put childish ways behind me" (1 Corinthians 13:11). Lastly, when we cry out to Christ, He heals. Humility is an invitation to intimacy and healing.

You can love with a whole heart when the love of the Lord has mended your heart. Perhaps you seek out a biblically based Christian counselor, trusting him or her to lead you into God's grace and healing. Then, in humility, reach out to those you have wronged and watch relational healing take place. Honestly ask, "Has my heart been healed by heaven?"

The Bible says, "I will heal their waywardness and love them freely, for my anger has turned from them" (Hosea 14:4).

Is my heart healthy and whole? Whom can I ask to validate my diagnosis?

Related Readings: 2 Chronicles 7:14; Malachi 4:2; James 5:16; 1 Peter 2:24

LOVE FORGIVES

"Hatred stirs up dissension, but love covers over all wrongs."
Proverbs 10:12

True love forgives, regardless of the infraction, because it transcends mistreatment. So, what is your process for forgiveness? Is it conditional, based on the way you are treated, or is it unconditional? Hatred has no hope but to stir up dissension and rally a defense. However, love looks at being wronged as an opportunity to replace insult with encouragement. Love seeks to lead all parties to a place of health and happiness.

Indeed, hatred is not at home in a heart of love. It sows discord, while love plants peace. It embraces enmity, while love cuddles compassion. Hate stirs up, but love calms down. How do you handle those who are hard to be around? Perhaps out of love you serve them. Seek to serve, rather than be served. The Bible says, "Through love serve one another" (Galatians 5:13 NASB).

Furthermore, love forgives because you have been forgiven by the matchless love of God. It is the Lord's love toward you that empowers you to lovingly forgive another. Human love alone is unable to love without boundaries. Left to our own limited love, we only love those who love us. Jesus says, "If you love only those who love you, what reward is there for that? Even corrupt tax collectors do that much" (Matthew 5:46 NLT).

Therefore, look at love as an opportunity to give others what they do not deserve. Lean on the Lord as your source of unconditional love. Christ's love is all-inclusive and all-forgiving. In the same way, love those in your life actively and appropriately, with a kind word, a nice note of appreciation, a thoughtful gift, or a listening ear. How do you harness love into a habit of forgiveness?

The Bible says, "Most important of all, continue to show deep love for each other, for love covers a multitude of sins" (1 Peter 4:8 NLT).

Whom do I need to love, forgive, and serve in honor of God's great love?

Related Readings: Leviticus 19:17; Proverbs 17:9; Philippians 1:9; 1 John 4:20–21

FORGIVE FAST

"For if you forgive men when they sin against you, your heavenly Father
will also forgive you. But if you do not forgive men their sins,
your Father will not forgive your sins." Matthew 6:14–15

How do you respond when you have been wronged? How do you react to unrighteous behavior directed toward you? You can forgive fast and be freed from pride, pain, and anger, or you can stay mad and stew in your state of self-pity. Indeed, your forgiveness of others is evidence of your heavenly Father's forgiveness in your life.

Since God forgave you, you forgive others, and in turn He forgives you. This is Christ's cycle of forgiveness. If, however, we fail to forgive others, we place ourselves in an unforgivable position. Our unforgiving attitude invites unforgiveness from our heavenly Father; so those who find mercy with God are to show mercy on behalf of God.

Jesus not only came to reconcile us to His Father but also to one another. True worship is contingent on reconciliation with people. Jesus said, "Leave your gift there in front of the altar. First go and be reconciled to your brother; then come and offer your gift" (Matthew 5:24).

Who in your life requires you to let go of resentment? Who has distracted your authentic worship of Christ because of their hurtful words? By God's grace you can forgive them for Christ's sake, and then be liberated by the love of the Lord. You know you have truly forgiven when the joy of the Lord is once again your strength.

There is a song of salvation in your heart and a bounce of hope in your step. Forgiveness frees you to trust again. Love is the lever that turns on forgiveness in your heart. Allow the Lord to love you in this lonely place, and you will be able to love others authentically.

"Dear friends, since God so loved us, we also ought to love one another. No one has ever seen God; but if we love one another, God lives in us and his love is made complete in us" (1 John 4:11-12).

What does it mean for me to forgive others as God has forgiven me? How can I make love my motivation for forgiving my parents, friends, or foes?

Related Readings: Numbers 14:20; Psalm 32:1; Luke 6:37; 2 Corinthians 2:10

GOD OR MONEY

"No one can serve two masters. Either he will hate the one and love the other, or he will be devoted to the one and despise the other. You cannot serve both God and Money."
Matthew 6:24

How do you know if you love God or money more? Ask yourself if you worry more about missing your prayer time or missing your paycheck. Are you more anxious about what the Almighty thinks, or do you obsess over the opinion of others? Are you driven to seek God's kingdom first or to blindly build your own kingdom? Devotion to the eternal or the temporal is a choice. It cannot be to both. One really captures your worship.

Money makes promises it cannot keep, like security, peace, and prosperity. But the Lord makes promises He does keep, like grace, forgiveness, joy, and contentment. When the commands of these two contradict, will you follow Christ or cash? Decide now, so when you are in the emotion of the moment you do not give in to glittering gold.

What keeps you up at night? Is it how to make more money or how to make more of Jesus? Set your affections above, and you will be more effective below. The Lord is looking for His children with whom He can entrust more of His blessings. He longs for the faithful who use their finances to draw lost souls to salvation, hurting people to healing, and who boldly pray, "Your kingdom come…on earth as it is in heaven" (Matthew 6:10).

Perhaps you take your family on a mission trip to see how the masses live with little money but with a lot of the Lord. It is revolutionary for a soul that has been seduced by the mistress of money to see how believers without stuff affectionately embrace their Lord and Savior Jesus. Expose your faith to the poor, so you are liberated from wealth.

This is a heart issue. Who captures your affections—your Savior or your stuff? Money makes a poor master but a useful servant. Indeed, Jesus is the trustworthy Master with whom you can place your faith and devotion. Money tries to maneuver itself into a place of priority, but by faith you can relegate it to serve righteous causes. Love Him, not it.

"Do not love the world or anything in the world. If anyone loves the world, the love of the Father is not in him" (1 John 2:15).

What masters my mind and holds my heart—God or money? Who needs my money?

Related Readings: Malachi 3:8–10; Matthew 6:10; Colossians 3:1–10; 1 Timothy 6:6–10

RESPECTABLE LEADERS

"Now the overseer must be above reproach, the husband of but one wife, temperate, self-controlled, respectable, hospitable, able to teach, not given to drunkenness, not violent but gentle, not quarrelsome, not a lover of money." 1 Timothy 3:2–3

Respectability invites respect. You may say, "I cannot get any respect." If so, on what do you base your expectations? Is it your charm, charisma, or ability to converse well? None of these mean you are respectable; in fact, they can repel respect and garner disrespect. Your skills and gifts require character to convene the admiration of others.

Respect is earned, not demanded. It is sustained by influence, not position. Presidents, preachers, and parents are given respect by their position, but if they consistently underperform or lack integrity, respect is lost. It is not a right of the irresponsible but a privilege of the dependable. Respectable leaders get right results in the right way.

Respectable leaders also rise to the occasion and do the right things. They persevere and provide stability instead of panicking and creating chaos. They take responsibility by espousing the values of the organization and by not gossiping and blaming others. There is a depth of character that runs deep within their souls, not to be stolen by sin.

Lastly, respectable leaders are well-thought of when their track record is one of trustworthiness, honesty, and follow-through. However, the goal is not for people to like you. They may not like you when you lovingly hold them accountable, but they will respect you. They may not like your discipline, but they will respect your consistency. They may not embrace your beliefs, but if expressed in humility they will respect you. Perhaps you ask, "Am I respectable?" If so, you can expect respect.

The Bible says, "A sensible person wins admiration, but a warped mind is despised" (Proverbs 12:8 NLT).

What area of my character needs growth and transformation so as to solicit respect?

Related Readings: Exodus 18:21; Proverbs 15:27; John 10:12–13; Romans 16:18

TEMPERED TALK

"When words are many, sin is not absent, but he who holds his tongue is wise."
Proverbs 10:19

Tempered talk is evidence of wise conversation. It is when our words are many that we run the risk of soliciting sin. Too many words increase the probability of improper speech. For example, respectful conversation does not repeat the same words and phrases again and again in a confined period of time. This impatient cadence frustrates.

Perhaps a puzzled expression requires questioning for clarification or a definition for comprehension. Proud conversationalists can hijack a hearer's understanding with a hoard of words with no meaning. If your goal is to communicate, take the time to listen to the needs of your audience. People who feel cared for and understood have a keener sense of hearing and understanding. The Bible says, "Even a fool is thought wise if he keeps silent, and discerning if he holds his tongue" (Proverbs 17:28).

Wise people weigh their words before they speak. They allow their minds to catch up with their hearts. Furthermore, in the face of wrong behavior, emotions may need to express themselves. Let the other person know if you feel mistreated or misinformed. Concealed anger leads to living a lie (see Proverbs 10:18), but tempered talk is truthful and to the point.

Lastly, you reserve your words out of respect for the other person. If you do all the talking, you are the center of attention. This conversation is condescending because the other individual does not feel important enough to speak up. So you honor others when you speak less, listening more intently for how you can love them. Wisdom can be found in the words of each person you meet. Therefore, intentionally talk less and be wise.

The Bible says, "My dear brothers, take note of this: Everyone should be quick to listen, slow to speak and slow to become angry" (James 1:19).

Whom do I need to listen to more, while talking less?

Related Readings: Job 2:3; Amos 5:13; Titus 1:10; James 3:2

ECONOMIC STORM

"When the storm has swept by, the wicked are gone, but the righteous stand firm forever."
Proverbs 10:25

Economic storms expose evil, as when the ocean tide goes out, those naked in the water are exposed. Dead wood is swept away, to be seen no more. It may seem like the wicked are prospering, but eventually they will be found out. The Holy Spirit shakes out sin so it can be seen and judged. As the Lord promised His children in the past, "I will shake the house of Israel" (Amos 9:9).

What use is it to make a lot of noise and draw the attention of the elite and then lose your creditability under scrutiny? Economic storms collapse businesses and ministries that are dependent on debt and, conversely, cause good churches to increase in attendance. There is a purging of pride, and all manner of excess is exposed. What really matters in life becomes the priority: faith, family, friends, food, and shelter. Storms reveal worth.

Moreover, those who cling to Christ are not shaken. He is our cornerstone that no degree of chaos can challenge. The Bible says, "Those who trust in the LORD are like Mount Zion, which cannot be shaken but endures forever" (Psalm 125:1). The righteous cannot be moved, because their Master is immovable. Therefore, stand firm in the Lord.

Furthermore, your stability in your Savior is security for your family, friends, and work associates. Your unwavering faith during difficult days helps them replace panic with peace, fear with faith, and compromise with conviction. Indeed, if all you have left is a firm foundation of faith, begin rebuilding God's big vision. Are you a wise builder?

Jesus says, "Therefore everyone who hears these words of mine and puts them into practice is like a wise man who built his house on the rock" (Matthew 7:24).

How can I build my life, home, and work on the solid rock of Jesus?

Related Readings: Job 20:5; Psalm 37:10; Acts 2:25; Hebrews 12:28

RIGHTEOUS RESOLVE

"The righteous will never be uprooted, but the wicked will not remain in the land."
Proverbs 10:30

Resolve is the result of righteous living. There is a determination deep within a soul dependent on God. When you are established in faith, no one can move you away from Christ's call. He has appointed you to this post of service. Do not leave until the Lord reassigns you. Righteous resolve decides to stay put; so by faith keep on for Christ.

You may disappoint some but invigorate others. However, if your goal is to first trust and obey the Lord, you will be misunderstood by some and rejected by others. Friends may even urge you to move on, but you cannot because Christ has not released you. Your resolve is His resolve. Therefore, you persevere through pain, suffering, and uncertainty. Righteous resolve remains, regardless of the consequences, good or bad.

Moreover, there is a righteous resolve that remains in Christ (see John 15:5). Your conversion to Christianity was a resolution to abide under the influence of almighty God. You stay true to your commitment to Christ because of the joy that comes from following Jesus. "The meek…inherit the earth" (Matthew 5:5), while the wicked do not.

Lastly, you cannot lose what you give away, and you cannot keep what you will not release. Indeed, a righteous resolve has a relentless trust in the Lord. Obedience, generosity, and contentment all require tenacious trust. Therefore, resolve in your heart to go hard after God. Release your relentless pursuits only after He has released you. Perhaps you ask, "Is my resolve righteous, or is it contingent on circumstances?"

The Bible says, "Alarmed, Jehoshaphat resolved to inquire of the LORD" (2 Chronicles 20:3).

Where do I need a righteous resolve to remain true to my commitment and calling?

Related Readings: Psalm 15:5; Daniel 1:8; Romans 8:35–39; 1 Corinthians 2:2

POSSESSIONS COMPLICATE

"Their possessions were so great that they were not able to stay together.
And quarreling arose." Genesis 13:6–7

Abram and Lot had a lot of stuff. They were blessed with family, friends, and finances. However, things became complicated, and they were unable to coexist. Though they needed one another, they could not stay with one another.

The fear of losing their possessions superseded the joy of growing their relationship. So they divided, and as a result of their vulnerability, Lot lost everything. Jesus said, "[A] household divided against itself will not stand" (Matthew 12:25).

Possessions are not wrong in themselves. However, when the management of your wealth compromises your loyalty to people, there is a problem. Possessions should be subservient to people; otherwise, things get out of kilter. People know if you value your net worth over them. So how do we keep this balance between possessions and people?

Begin with an inventory of your time. How do you spend your time? Do you spend more time managing your stuff or loving people? You may need to sell some of your property, or, better yet, give it away. If your possessions have priority over people, there is a problem.

Ask yourself, "Does my stuff compete with my relationship with God?" Perhaps you downsize your stuff so you can upsize your focus on your Savior Jesus. By God's grace, use the material fortune He has entrusted to you as a magnet that draws you closer to God and people. Use your blessing of discretionary time to bless others.

The Bible says, "Command those who are rich in this present world not to be arrogant nor to put their hope in wealth, which is so uncertain, but to put their hope in God, who richly provides us with everything for our enjoyment. Command them to do good, to be rich in good deeds, and to be generous and willing to share. In this way they will lay up treasure for themselves as a firm foundation for the coming age, so that they may take hold of the life that is truly life" (1 Timothy 6:17–19).

How can I position my possessions so the Lord possesses more of me and my family?

Related Readings: Genesis 36:6-7; Ecclesiastes 5:10–11; Luke 3:11; 2 Corinthians 9:6–15

ROAD LESS TRAVELED

"Enter through the narrow gate. For wide is the gate and broad is the road that leads to destruction, and many enter through it. But small is the gate and narrow the road that leads to life, and only a few find it." Matthew 7:13–14

What road do you travel in life? Is it the narrow road of trust in God and others, or is it the wide road of trust in you alone? Do you briskly travel down the road of life with the masses, or is your trip more measured and prayerful with a few companions? The wide road may seem more exciting in the beginning, but it is the narrow road that leads to fulfillment.

You may have been on the road of righteousness with Christ for a long time. And now it seems like your Savior is directing you in a direction that is less familiar. The level of faith required to digest the risk is much higher and more daunting. Even within the family of faith there are not that many who have gone where your heavenly Father is asking you to go. How will you respond? Do not be so cautious that you miss Christ's new direction.

You first enter into the narrow gate of salvation in Jesus and then travel with Him down the fine line of faith and obedience. Those who go through the wide gate of disbelief experience destruction in their lives and souls. So make sure you have entered God's eternal entrance, and travel with Him deep into absolute abandonment of self.

The gate of grace leads to a road of forgiveness and mercy. You still encounter resistance; potholes of pride pop up, but avoid them by slowing down and reacting with humility and grace. People will come and go on your trip of trust; so enjoy them for this part of the journey. Do not remain disappointed when good people move on. The Lord will lead you to new travel companions required for your next assignment.

Above all, stay focused by faith on the Lord's leadership. Where He leads you, follow. Where He leads for the future will require more faith than the past. Sometimes He leads with a cloud of limited perception, and other times He gives you the fire of a long-term view. Whichever less traveled road you choose, make sure you journey with Jesus.

"By day the LORD went ahead of them in a pillar of cloud to guide them on their way and by night in a pillar of fire to give them light, so that they could travel by day or night" (Exodus 13:21).

What road am I currently traveling? What road is the Lord leading me to travel?

Related Readings: Genesis 41:45–47; Numbers 10:33; Luke 14:24–26; Acts 16:6

FALSE FAITH

"Not everyone who says to me, 'Lord, Lord,' will enter the kingdom of heaven, but only he who does the will of my Father who is in heaven. Many will say to me on that day, 'Lord, Lord, did we not prophesy in your name, and in your name drive out demons and perform many miracles?' Then I will tell them plainly, 'I never knew you. Away from me, you evildoers!'"
Matthew 7:21–23

There are those who claim to be Christians, but they are not. They fill the pulpits of churches, but they have not been filled with the Holy Spirit. They occupy pews, but Christ does not occupy their hearts. Jesus warned that there will be those who think their religious routines will redeem them, but in the end there will be a startling revelation.

Furthermore, a person is not a believer if in one breath he or she claims to be a Christian but in the next breath denies the historical fact of His resurrection. Those who do this offer a confusing blend of beliefs that in the end is a rejection of the long-held truths of the church. A false faith claims Christ was a good teacher but not a miracle worker. They deny His deity. "And if Christ has not been raised, your faith is futile; you are still in your sins. Then those also who have fallen asleep in Christ are lost" (1 Corinthians 15:17–18).

In the last days there will be those who use religion for their own ends. So beware not to waste time with counterfeit Christ followers. Their insincere efforts will only ensnare your time and money. Unfortunately, phony disciples easily dupe the weak in faith; when they finally wake up dazed and disillusioned, they walk away from God. So be wary of those who peddle prayer for their personal gain. Invest in the authentic.

"But know this, that in the last days perilous times will come: For men will be lovers of themselves, lovers of money, boasters, proud, blasphemers, disobedient to parents, unthankful, unholy, unloving, unforgiving, slanderers, without self-control, brutal, despisers of good, traitors, headstrong, haughty, lovers of pleasure rather than lovers of God, having a form of godliness but denying its power. And from such people turn away!" (2 Timothy 3:1–5 NKJV).

Above all, secure your salvation with genuine faith in Jesus Christ, using your - authentic influence to indoctrinate God's people in His ordinances found in the Bible. Disciple new Christians so they are not blown away by every new, attractive, but bogus belief. Followers of Jesus—grounded in the truth—are able to flee from a false faith.

"Then we will no longer be infants, tossed back and forth by the waves, and blown here and there by every wind of teaching and by the cunning and craftiness of men in their deceitful scheming. Instead, speaking the truth in love, we will in all things grow up into him who is the Head, that is, Christ" (Ephesians 4:14–15).

Is my faith in Jesus Christ personal and genuine? Whom can I help grow in their faith?

Related Readings: Jeremiah 14:14; Jeremiah 23:16; Matthew 24:24; 2 Peter 2:1

FAITHFUL GUIDE

"The integrity of the upright guides them, but the unfaithful are destroyed by their duplicity."
Proverbs 11:3

Integrity is an instrument of almighty God. He uses it to guide His children in the direction He desires for them. Have you ever wondered what God would have you do? Integrity is His directive to do the next right thing, trusting Him with the results. It is out of honesty we begin to comprehend Christ's desires. He delights in our uprightness.

For example, are you totally honest on your tax return? Is your tax preparer a person of unquestionable integrity? We can trust professionals to represent us well, but we are ultimately responsible for an honest outcome. Furthermore, is there anything you are doing, if printed as a newspaper headline, that would embarrass you and your family? Indeed, integrity brings joy to heaven and security on earth. It is your guide for godly living.

Moreover, the iniquity of the unfaithful destroys. The blessing of God is removed as it cannot be bought with bad behavior. Relationships are scarred and some even severed over dishonest dealings. Overnight, poor judgment can soil and potentially destroy a hard-earned reputation. Pride acts like integrity is only for others. It deceives itself and becomes a disgrace for its dishonest and duplicitous ways. Iniquity is an unfaithful guide.

"I put in charge of Jerusalem my brother Hanani, along with Hananiah the commander of the citadel, because he was a man of integrity and feared God more than most people do" (Nehemiah 7:2).

So we ask ourselves, "How can I be a man or woman of integrity over the balance of my life?" There is a simplicity about those who base their behavior on the principles of God's Word; nothing fancy, only faithful living in their daily routine. The grace of God governs their soul, the truth of God renews their mind, and accountability is an anchor for their actions. Honestly ask yourself, "Is integrity my faithful guide?"

The Bible says, "May integrity and uprightness protect me, because my hope is in you" (Psalm 25:21).

How can I better integrate integrity as a guide for my business dealings and behavior at home?

Related Readings: Genesis 20:4–7; Hosea 13:9; Matthew 7:13; Romans 7:9–12

FAITH STRETCHER

"Abraham fell facedown; he laughed and said to himself, 'Will a son be born to a man
a hundred years old? Will Sarah bear a child at the age of ninety?'"
Genesis 17:17

Sometimes God's will is not logical and does not even seem possible. Abraham certainly struggled with the idea of being a parent as a centenarian and his wife conceiving at ninety years of age. It was not possible; it did not make sense. Yet in reality all things are possible with God, and this was one of them.

The Lord made a promise that was out of the ordinary. He wanted to mark this occasion with an indelible stamp of a "God thing." Abraham tried to let God off the hook on this miraculous scheme by offering Him another plan. However, God was not interested in another plan; He was interested in setting the stage for a blessing that would validate His sovereignty, taking the faith of Abraham, Sarah, and an entire nation to a whole other level. God wants us, and He wants us to take Him at His Word.

Why is it hard to take God at His Word? Why do we struggle with believing in something that is not logical or takes us out of our comfort zone? One reason we struggle is our perception of God. We make Him so small. We bring Him down to our level rather than allowing Him to pull us up to His level! This is man-centered thinking; instead, let's allow God to be God.

Faith allows us to travel places with God that we would never experience otherwise. Would you not rather be in the middle of a lake in a storm with Jesus than on the calm shore around a warm fire without Him? This is where faith trumps logic. We trust Him when it does not make sense; we follow Him when we are not sure of the destination.

We believe the Lord when others think we are strange, too religious, or even fanatical. Let your Savior stretch your faith, trusting Him with the opportunity in front of you. Has your laughter turned to trust and awe in God and His accomplishments?

The Bible says, "Your father Abraham rejoiced to see My day, and he saw it and was glad" (John 8:56 NASB).

What impossibility am I facing but will trust that with God it is possible?

Related Readings: Deuteronomy 9:18–25; Psalm 126:1; Matthew 2:11; Romans 4:20

A CITY MOVEMENT

*"When the righteous prosper, the city rejoices; when the wicked perish,
there are shouts of joy. Through the blessing of the upright a city is exalted."*
Proverbs 11:10–11

How can we capture our cities for Christ? In the process, could our municipalities move more toward institutions of integrity? Perhaps it starts with each one of us who claims Jesus Christ as Savior. It is up to us to first get down on our knees and then get down to business with our heavenly Father. The people of God make up the city of God. It is through our confession and repentance of sin the city is set up for blessing from the Lord.

A city is not meant to be a passive party to the ways of wickedness. Daniel understood this, praying this passionate prayer for his city:

"O Lord, in keeping with all your righteous acts, turn away your anger and your wrath from Jerusalem, your city, your holy hill. Our sins and the iniquities of our fathers have made Jerusalem and your people an object of scorn to all those around us" (Daniel 9:16).

Indeed, a city movement for Christ is birthed out of passionate prayer and brokenness. Jesus cried out for His city. "As he approached Jerusalem and saw the city, he wept over it" (Luke 19:41). Our tears become a tool of the Holy Spirit to transform us and others. There is healing as sorrow turns to joy.

The early church rejoiced over this unleashing of the Lord's power. "So there was great joy in that city" (Acts 8:8). Lastly, a city moved along by the Holy Spirit becomes a shining light of its Savior Jesus. He exalts the community on His hill of hope for all to see, believe, and be saved.

Jesus says, "You are the light of the world. A city on a hill cannot be hidden" (Matthew 5:14). So we solemnly ask, "Have I claimed my city for Christ? Am I part of His movement?"

Whom can I invite to passionately pray with me over our city's movement toward God?

Related Readings: Genesis 41:38–42; Isaiah 16:5; Acts 13:44; Acts 16:13–15

BENEFITS OF KINDNESS

"A kindhearted woman gains respect, but ruthless men gain only wealth.
A kind man benefits himself, but a cruel man brings trouble on himself."
Proverbs 11:16–17

Kindness benefits everyone. It brings joy to the giver and peace to the receiver. The recipient reciprocates because respect is embedded in kindness. Kindheartedness facilitates respect as it treats others with dignity and honor. Even when offended or ostracized, a gracious heart takes the higher ground of humility and gentleness. It may not be liked, but it is respected. Kind actions attract the Almighty's approval.

What is kindness? At its core it is a reflection of Christ. It is what we expect of the Lord when we desire good things. Listen to the heart of this employee's prayer for his boss to experience God's kindness in marriage: "O LORD, God of my master Abraham, give me success today, and show kindness to my master Abraham" (Genesis 24:12). In the same way your Savior shows you kindness in salvation and His severe mercy.

Furthermore, because of Christ's great kindness, you are compelled to compassionate action. Ruthless men and women use whatever means of fear and intimidation necessary to gain wealth and power, but considerate adults do not compromise their character for cash or influence. Indeed, God's great kindness grants us the favor we need.

The Bible says, "The LORD was with him [Joseph]; he showed him kindness and granted him favor in the eyes of the prison warden" (Genesis 39:21).

Who does not need kindness? The undeserving especially need your kindness as a reminder of God's lasting love and infinite forgiveness. Be kind to the unkind, and they will see what really rests in your heart of hearts. Your kindheartedness will lead others to your source in Jesus Christ. Here the kindness of the Lord leads to repentance.

The Bible says, "Or do you show contempt for the riches of his kindness, tolerance and patience, not realizing that God's kindness leads you toward repentance?" (Romans 2:4).

To whom can I extend kindness who has been unkind to me?

Related Readings: Joshua 2:12; Ruth 3:10; Acts 4:9; Ephesians 2:6–8

A WORSHIPFUL WEDDING

"On the third day a wedding took place at Cana in Galilee. Jesus' mother was there,
and Jesus and his disciples had also been invited to the wedding."
John 2:1–2

What does it mean to have a worshipful wedding? For the follower of Jesus, it means that He is invited to the wedding. Not only is He invited, but He is also preeminent. Yes, the bride is the focus; however, faith in her Lord is more the focus. It is her day, but in honor of the bride and groom's commitment to Christ, His lordship overshadows them both.

His banner over them is love. "He has taken me to the banquet hall, and his banner over me is love" (Song of Songs 2:4). Where Jesus is invited, He comes with dignity, grace, and the object of worship. So we honor Him with music that is grateful praise to the One who brought together the couple in holy matrimony. The minister conducts a service that outlines Christ's expectations for the husband and wife. He expects holiness.

A wedding needs just enough informality to keep it personal, but not so much that it becomes irreverent. Just as Jesus gave Himself in unselfish sacrifice, so a Christian couple gives of themselves to see who can out serve the other. Couples who grow up get along. A mature marriage makes the most of how to love like the other wants to be loved.

"Do nothing out of selfish ambition or vain conceit, but in humility consider others better than yourselves. Each of you should look not only to your own interests, but also to the interests of others. Your attitude should be the same as that of Christ Jesus" (Philippians 2:3–5).

Indeed, a wedding is the celebration of God bringing together two lives under His lordship. But a wedding is also a declaration of commitment and fidelity, first to Christ and then to one another. It is the opening scene to a full-length film entitled "Marriage." Thus, make your wedding meaningful by planning it as your preparation for marriage.

How can I facilitate a worshipful wedding for friends, family, or myself? How can I stay true to my wedding vows with the goal of a Christ-centered marriage?

Related Readings: Psalm 45:1; Song of Songs 3:11; Matthew 25:10; Revelation 19:7–9

WEDDING ANNIVERSARY

"May your fountain be blessed, and may you rejoice in the wife of your youth."
Proverbs 5:18

There is something sacred and celebratory about another year of marriage. It is sacred because a covenant to God has been fulfilled. And it is celebratory because a man and woman have grown closer to Christ and to each other. This marriage milestone is meant to mean something. It is not just another day that comes and goes without recognition.

Wise are the husband and wife who make much over their wedding anniversary. It is a testimony to their commitment to Christ and His commitment to them. In a day when some men trade in their wives like a used car, and some women walk away from their husbands and children like a nuisance to their freedom, much needs to be made about marriages that achieve longevity. "Until death do us part" is not a trite saying but a bold declaration of life-long dedication. So be proud you have persevered and celebrate!

Plan ahead, spend some money, and invest in a long weekend away from home. Make sure you do not oversave for retirement and miss enjoying your marriage adventure now. The way to enjoy your spouse as your best friend in the future is to enjoy your spouse as your best friend now. "Hope deferred makes the heart sick, but a longing fulfilled is a tree of life" (Proverbs 13:12). Your wedding anniversary is a big deal; so make it a big deal.

Husbands, lead the way by talking with your wife about the best way to celebrate this year's anniversary. Perhaps you prearrange your favorite babysitter and work some extra hours so your wife is secure with the children's caregiver and at peace with the extra expenditures. If it is important, you will make it a priority that might even require a project plan. Give her a day at the spa in preparation for the second best celebration of the year.

The best celebration of the year is your union with Christ. Your relationship with Jesus is meant to be a mirror of your marriage. They are both by grace through faith. They both require focused attention and going deeper with each other; so hilariously celebrate your marriage anniversary. Enjoy the blessings of being together over time. It is something to be proud of, because God says marriage is meant to last a lifetime.

"Has not the LORD made them one? In flesh and spirit they are his. And why one? Because he was seeking godly offspring. So guard yourself in your spirit, and do not break faith with the wife of your youth" (Malachi 2:15).

How can I honor God and my spouse and have fun on our wedding anniversary?

Related Readings: Song of Songs 2:1–17; Romans 7:2; 1 Corinthians 7:2–3; Hebrews 13:4

INFLUENTIAL WIFE

"Listen to whatever Sarah tells you, because it is through Isaac
that your offspring will be reckoned." Genesis 21:12

Listen to your wife; she can be God's voice of wisdom and/or His heavenly sandpaper. Especially when you are in distress over a decision, she can bring perspective and calm to the situation. If you are tempted to make a dumb decision, she is there to remind you of your convictions. She is built-in accountability, even when you do not want to hear her voice. It may rub you the wrong way, but this irritation is how the Lord gets your attention.

Why does God frequently speak through your wife? One reason is that she has your best interest in mind. You became one in marriage; as your decisions go, so go your marriage and family. She wants you to be successful because your success or failure is a reflection of your relationship with her. Furthermore, she wants you to make wise decisions because she loves you. "Love...rejoices with the truth" (1 Corinthians 13:6).

Still it is sometimes hard to listen to your wife, even when you know it is God's desire, and the benefit it provides is obvious. Perhaps you question her motive, or her way of communicating is overbearing. If it is a question of motive, ask her why she is suggesting her advice. If her method of communication is harsh or untimely, address this with her, but still receive the truth. Suggest to her how and when to speak the truth in love.

You benefit by making wiser decisions, and she benefits by becoming a better communicator of truth. Value her objectivity, as she intuitively knows if someone or some situation does not feel right. God gives her uncanny discernment. So wives, share in love and in a timely fashion, and husbands, listen intently and respectfully with an eye toward implementation.

Are you listening to learn from your lover? "It [love] always protects, always trusts, always hopes, always perseveres" (1 Corinthians 13:7).

What wisdom is my wife imparting that I need to heed and follow?

Related Readings: 1 Samuel 8:7–9; Isaiah 46:10; Romans 9:7–8; Hebrews 11:17–18

FOLLOW JESUS FIRST

"When Jesus saw the crowd around him, he gave orders to cross to the other side of the lake. Then a teacher of the law came to him and said, 'Teacher, I will follow you wherever you go.'"
Matthew 8:18–19

Good leaders are first good followers. Do you follow the orders of Jesus? When He asks you to do the uncomfortable, do you move out of your comfort zone with confidence? Compelling Christian leaders have a focused following on their Master, the Lord Jesus. Where is He asking you to go that requires sacrifice and unconditional commitment? His orders do not always make sense, but they are totally trustworthy and helpful.

When He directs you to leave the noise of the crowds to the quietness of a few, do not delay. If you are obsessed by activity, you can easily lose your edge on energy and faith. When all my oomph is consumed by serving every request and answering every call, I have no time or concentration to hear from Christ. What is He saying? This is the most important inquiry I can make. What is Jesus telling me to do? When I listen, I learn.

You may be in the middle of a monster season of success; so make sure your achievements do not muffle the Lord's message. It is when we are fast and furious that our faith becomes perfunctory and predictable. Leadership requires alone time to retool and recalibrate our character. People follow when they know you have been with Jesus.

The most difficult part may be the transition from doing less to listening and thinking more. If you as the leader are not planning ahead, who is? Who has the best interest of the enterprise in mind? Who is defending the mission and vision of the organization so there is not a drift into competing strategies? Follow Jesus first; He frees you to see.

Where is the Lord leading you to go? Will you lag behind with excellent excuses, or will you make haste and move forward in faith? Go with God, and He will direct you through the storms of change. He may seem silent at times, but remember He led you to this place, and where He leads, He provides. Follow Jesus first, and go wherever He goes. You will lose people in the process, but you will gain better people for His next phase.

"Then Jesus said to his disciples, 'If anyone would come after me, he must deny himself and take up his cross and follow me'" (Matthew 16:24).

Where is Jesus leading me to go? Am I willing to let go and trust Him with what is next?

Related Readings: Numbers 32:11; Isaiah 8:10–12; 1 Corinthians 1:11–13; Revelation 14:4

STABILITY'S INFLUENCE

"Stay in this land for a while, and I will be with you and will bless you."
Genesis 26:3

Your investment in one geographical location compounds your influence over time. This is important because it affects your family, your community, and your career. It benefits your family to stay in one place because it gives them security and the opportunity to build lifelong friendships.

Over time the community around your family provides built-in accountability. You get to know the values and priorities of people, and they get to know yours. You watch out for each other's children, and you are more accountable. This high level of trust and expectation comes over time and is invaluable.

Your career creditability is enhanced if you stay in one place. People grow to love and trust you. They see you as reliable, someone they can go to with a need or question. They know you can get an answer or the referral of a helpful resource. So what type of location should you decide to put down roots with a goal to influence others for Christ?

Pray for an area where you and your family can grow spiritually. This means you have the opportunity to develop community, attending church with like-minded believers. This is critical; otherwise, you miss the opportunity for encouragement, mentorship, and accountability. This can happen in college, on your first work assignment, on the mission field, or in the area where you grew up. Early in life look for those who can become lifelong mentors for you; as you get older look for those you can mentor.

God blesses long-term, relational commitments. This takes trust. For example, it may mean turning down a raise or not moving, but you know in your heart by staying put your family and marriage will be stronger.

Yes, there is a time to move and a time to stay. Bridle your appetite for more and more material wealth, keep your life simple, and trust God in one location. Over time your influence will compound, and relationally you will become filthy rich. Are you content to leverage your influence for Christ?

The Bible says, "Remember your leaders, who spoke the word of God to you. Consider the outcome of their way of life and imitate their faith" (Hebrews 13:7).

Am I developing relationships for the long term so I earn the right to influence them for Christ?

Related Readings: Exodus 32:13; Psalm 37:1–6; Philippians 4:9; Hebrews 11:9–16

F18

BE A BLESSING

"So he [Jacob] went to him and kissed him. When Isaac caught
the smell of his clothes, he blessed him." Genesis 27:27

What is a blessing? It represents God's goodwill. Furthermore, He uses people as a channel for His blessing. They invoke divine favor, conferring well-being and prosperity to others. We all long for blessing. We desire blessing from God and blessing from those we love and respect. This high level of approval and support comes in a variety of forms.

It can be words of admonishment and instruction. Words may paint a larger context of God's overall will and purpose for your life. Blessings not only represent God's favor and direction but also sanction support from other servants of Christ. So where does this longing to be blessed lead? It means you first receive the blessing of God and others, so you in turn can be a blessing.

Think how you can be a blessing to another today. How can you give people a divine context so they recognize and enjoy God's purpose in their lives? Perhaps it is a quiet, private prayer for them. Or the Lord may lead you to publicly lay hands on someone, while asking for His blessing to reside on that person's life and work.

Your bold blessing may be just what others need as they continue in their faithfulness to their family and faith. It can be a simple word of encouragement or a letter of gratitude. Your blessing to others can be formal or informal. Think of creative ways to formally bless your children as they transition into adulthood, or how you can informally bless a friend launching a new career.

In Christ we bless others; without Christ we curse others. If we do nothing, people are prone to fill in the blanks with negative thoughts and feelings. What power you have through the power of a blessing. Use it prayerfully and happily. Have you been blessed so you can bless?

The Bible says, "Her children arise and call her blessed; her husband also, and he praises her" (Proverbs 31:28).

Whom can I bless today who may not feel worthy of blessing?

Related Readings: Genesis 5:2; 2 Samuel 6:20; 1 Peter 3:9; Revelation 1:3

F19

FORGIVENESS HEALS

"But Esau ran to meet Jacob and embraced him; he threw his arms around his neck
and kissed him. And they wept." Genesis 33:4

Just like the Prodigal Son Jesus describes in Luke 15 became broken and repentant, so Jacob does. As the loving father forgives, embraces, and weeps with the son, so Esau does with Jacob. It is a beautiful, beautiful picture of forgiveness. Deception was overcome by forgiveness. Stealing was overcome by forgiveness. Hurt was overcome by forgiveness. Anger was overcome by forgiveness. Pride was overcome by forgiveness.

Running away was overcome by forgiveness. Coming back together was facilitated by forgiveness. Forgiveness through Christ and toward each other is the great reconciler. Otherwise, we live life like most miserable men and women, still blaming others and lamenting over injustice inflicted on us and those we love. It is not fair because life hurts our idealism and optimism; however, to be healed is to forgive. So how do we forgive?

Forgiveness begins with an encounter with God, as the originator of forgiveness embraces us. He is the one with the limitless capacity to forgive. His forgiveness engulfs us with ability, a mandate, and a reservoir of forgiveness. Because He has thoroughly forgiven us through Christ, we can and will forgive others for Christ's sake. It is the essence of being a Christian. If you are a Christian, you forgive.

Why is forgiveness hard? One reason is our immature faith lacks a cure. Our focus is still on our needs and hurts, but God is calling us to forgive. It is from a faithful stance of loving Him and loving people. When you choose to live by faith, you forgive. When you forgive, you trust that God is working to make you and others more like Jesus. Begin today; let God embrace you, you embrace another, and then watch forgiveness do its work.

The Bible says, "Therefore confess your sins to each other and pray for each other so that you may be healed" (James 5:16).

Whom can I forgive today and begin the process of healing?

Related Readings: Psalm 30:2; Isaiah 53:5; Mark 5:34; 1 Peter 2:24

DESTRUCTIVE JEALOUSY

"His brothers were jealous of him."
Genesis 37:11

Jealousy bears the fruit of anger and criticism, as Joseph was the brunt of his brothers' envy. They did not appreciate his perceived disloyalty or his boastful attitude and actions. Joseph was very gifted and was held in high esteem by his father, but what should have worked to his advantage actually worked against him.

When another of greater influence likes you, you are set up to arouse the jealousy of others. If you are wise, you will discern this and seek to deflect unnecessary attention and accolades from a well-meaning leader. If you enjoy this attention, or take advantage of it by talking down to and/or behaving in a superior manner toward others, you will only enrage an already smoldering fire of jealousy. Instead, spread the compliments, giving the team credit.

A mature person will see jealousy coming and seek to preclude it by helping others be successful. For example, if you are given a position of influence, you will use this advantage for the benefit of others. Use your good will to spread the credit of success among the team. Downplay your accomplishments, and shine the spotlight on the character and accomplishments of others.

However, even when you practice discretion and seek to serve others, there will still be small room for jealousy. If someone chooses to reside in this small room, it is out of your control. Only small people live in small rooms.

Over time most people will recognize the smallness of others. It is a person's choice to grow up and join the team. Trust God with this person and situation. He will bring about His will, in His way, and in His time. Are you encouraging or discouraging jealousy?

The Bible says, "You are still worldly. For since there is jealousy and quarreling among you, are you not worldly? Are you not acting like mere men?" (1 Corinthians 3:3).

Do I need to let go of jealousy and replace it with gratitude?

Related Readings: 1 Samuel 18:1–3; Proverbs 27:4; Acts 13:45; 2 Corinthians 11:2

EXTRA FAITH REQUIRED

"Some men brought to him a paralytic, lying on a mat. When Jesus saw their faith,
he said to the paralytic, 'Take heart, son; your sins are forgiven.'" Matthew 9:2

Some situations call for the extra faith of others to get us through. It is okay to appropriate the faith of friends when you face a task that takes three people to tackle. You may have lost the confidence to carry on in your current condition, but faithful friends are willing to rally around you and help; so let them. Allow faithful friends to lift you to the Lord.

Invite the intimate concern of Christians who can lead you to Christ. When our faith is weak, the Lord places people in our path who can pick us up if necessary. Your emotions may be frazzled from overwork and underpay. You met the deadline, but it almost killed you in the process. Fatigue makes cowards of us all. Weak faith needs a faith infusion.

Furthermore, you may have strong faith, but to make it through this challenging season requires extra faith from family and friends. When was the last time you held hands and prayed together as a couple at home? Or are you so busy doing that you have neglected taking time together to go to Jesus?

The family unit, by God's design, allows an appropriation of faith for one another. One struggling family member has the support of other family members. A united family lifts one another to Christ's care and love.

The results of applying the faith of family and friends are extraordinary. Sins are forgiven, emotions are healed, bodies are made whole, life has a new lease, and Jesus becomes radically real. There is phenomenal encouragement when the body of Christ comes together to care for the wounded, the broken, and the lost. A full faith is freedom.

Therefore, seek out those who need our Savior Jesus, and do not be content until they come to Christ. If you are in need of extra faith, do not be shy in sharing your heart with those you trust and respect. When we all reach for Jesus together, He exceeds expectations.

"I long to see you so that I may impart to you some spiritual gift to make you strong— that is, that you and I may be mutually encouraged by each other's faith" (Romans 1:11– 12).

Who needs my faith to lift them to the Lord? Whom can I invite into my life for a fresh dose of faith?

Related Readings: Job 16:20–21; Psalm 85:10; 2 Thessalonians 1:3; 1 Peter 4:10

UNINTENTIONAL ARROGANCE

"But when his heart became arrogant and hardened with pride,
he was deposed from his royal throne and stripped of his glory." Daniel 5:20

Do you know anyone whose life ambition is to become arrogant? Probably not! Arrogance is like greed; it is easily seen in others but rarely seen in the mirror. It seeps its way into a man or woman's soul in the disguise of good ambition and healthy confidence. But power and problems expose it like gasoline on dormant embers. Left unchecked, arrogance implodes in a downward spiral of ruin. Its outcome is ugly.

Arrogance is indiscriminate in its influence of individuals. Fathers and mothers, husbands and wives, leaders and followers, brothers and sisters, parents and children, pastors and laymen, and entrepreneurs and institutions are all candidates for its crippling curse. The Lord is clear, as He is against the attitude and actions of the arrogant. And it is not good to be against God.

"'See, I am against you, O arrogant one,' declares the Lord, the LORD Almighty, 'for your day has come, the time for you to be punished'" (Jeremiah 50:31).

What incubates arrogance? Where does it come from? Like kudzu it takes over quickly and hangs on insidiously. It dwells deep within the hearts of extremely competent and confident people. Success feeds arrogance as you begin to believe you are the reason for your achievements instead of almighty God. There is an unholy hubris (excessive pride) that takes hold of the heart. It whispers thoughts like: "You are indispensable." "You are right and others are to blame." "You are superior because of your intellect and your net worth."

It is this bulletproof belief in one's own self that requires large doses of humility and teachability to keep us keen on instilling integrity and character into our language and life. Families, churches, businesses, universities, politicians, athletes, and individuals must guard against arrogance with gratitude and generosity. Gratitude to God gives Him the glory, and generosity frees us not to control but to share the fruits of success with others.

"Command those who are rich in this present world not to be arrogant nor to put their hope in wealth, which is so uncertain, but to put their hope in God, who richly provides us with everything for our enjoyment" (1 Timothy 6:17).

Am I drifting toward arrogance? Am I fully aware of my weaknesses and blind spots?

Related Readings: Isaiah 2:11; Zephaniah 3:4; 1 Corinthians 4:18–19; 2 Peter 2:11

TIME TO GO

"By faith Abraham, when called to go to a place he would later receive as his inheritance, obeyed and went, even though he did not know where he was going." Hebrews 11:8

It is time to go when God says so, even though you are not sure where you are going. Abraham was a "friend of God" (James 2:23 NASB) who trusted the heart of God. He was secure in his faith, knowing his heavenly Father would not lead him astray. Are you okay with only the call of Christ as your next step? Is He calling you out of your comfort zone to a new level of faith and obedience? It is here that you hear Him quite clearly.

Maybe He wants you to move with your company so your career can become the means of funding your passion for missions. Locals in foreign countries are keenly interested in teachers, housewives, doctors, bankers, and businessmen visiting their world. The marketplace is your ministry. It validates your value and confirms your character. The Lord will use your obedience to encourage the faith of others and especially the faith of your family.

The faith of parents often procures the blessing of obedience on their posterity. When your teenage son sees you say yes to Christ's challenge, he is more likely to say yes to wisdom when faced with issues of trust. Your daughter will not soon forget your family's earnest prayers as you sought to see God's best and to obey. Parents who obey God's call create the same expectation for their children; so follow the Lord for them.

Lastly, the call of Christ leads to His blessing on earth and in heaven. It may mean prosperity. It may mean poverty. Or it may mean somewhere in between. The most important reward is that of your eternal inheritance. Leave a legacy of loving the Lord, and you will have loved your children. Follow Him faithfully; there is a much higher probability they will as well. Is it time to go? Then go with your best friend Jesus.

The Bible says, "God's intimate friendship blessed my house" (Job 29:4).

Where is Christ calling me to a higher level of faith and obedience?

Related Readings: Nehemiah 9:7–8; Psalm 105:6–11; Acts 7:2–4; Galatians 3:6

REFRESHERS ARE REFRESHED

"A generous man will prosper; he who refreshes others will himself be refreshed."
Proverbs 11:25

What does it mean to be refreshed? It is to be made fresh, to revive, enliven, invigorate, rejuvenate, energize, restore, recharge, or revitalize. A meager cup of lukewarm coffee comes alive with taste and satisfaction when mixed with freshly brewed beans. A lukewarm life is warmed and encouraged when refreshed with words of encouragement and acts of kindness. Everyone we meet becomes a candidate for refreshment.

Our faith cools down when Christ seems silent and circumstances continue to crumble, but a sincere prayer from a righteous friend restores and warms our confidence. Our hope feels deferred in the face of disappointment and rejection, but we are energized by the acceptance and love of a community of believers in Jesus. Hope loves company. Seek refreshment from your Savior and His followers. Be refreshed so you can refresh others.

When your parched soul has been watered by dew from heaven, you can lead others to the Lord's watering hole. People are frantic from feeling robbed by insensitive institutions and greedy governments, but we can reconnect them to their generous God. Jesus gives us an abundant life to be shared with others who are absent of abundance. "I have come that they may have life, and that they may have it more abundantly" (John 10:10 NKJV).

Lastly, your refreshment reciprocates refreshment. When you refresh another financially, you are refreshed by faith and fulfillment. When you refresh another emotionally, you are refreshed by peace and contentment. When you refresh another spiritually, you are refreshed by the grace and love of God. Are you in need of refreshment? If so, receive Christ's full cup of joy. Drink often with the Lord so you can generously refresh friends.

The Bible says, "Taste and see that the LORD is good; blessed is the man who takes refuge in him" (Psalm 34:8).

How can I stay in a routine of refreshment so I in turn can refresh others?

Related Readings: Ruth 2:14; Psalm 41:1; Matthew 25:34–35; 2 Corinthians 9:6–7

FALSE TRUST

"Whoever trusts in his riches will fall, but the righteous will thrive like a green leaf."
Proverbs 11:28

Trust in stuff will cause you to stumble and eventually fall. Why? Why is money unfit for trust? It is unreliable because it cannot save us or bring us forgiveness, peace, or contentment. Money is an unemotional master that can trip you up if it becomes the basis for your security. It can be here today and gone tomorrow. Money moves around like a gypsy looking for the next place to live. Trust in riches fails to focus on Christ.

The Bible says, "Cast but a glance at riches, and they are gone, for they will surely sprout wings and fly off to the sky like an eagle" (Proverbs 23:5). Trust in riches causes some to fall from the faith, because they equate wealth with success. However, you can be faithful to the Lord and thus be successful whether rich or poor. It may take losing money to reveal our true motivation. Trust in riches is a recipe for false security, fear, and sadness.

However, the righteous understand the role of riches is to remind them of God's provision. The Bible says, "Moreover, when God gives any man wealth and possessions, and enables him to enjoy them, to accept his lot and be happy in his work—this is a gift of God" (Ecclesiastes 5:19). Are you struggling with the reduction of your wealth? Do you remember what really mattered when you were first married? Was it trust in the Lord, your spouse, and good health? The righteous thrive in trust and obedience to Christ.

Lastly, guard your good name during financial crisis. Character is of much greater value than cash. The Bible says, "A good name is more desirable than great riches; to be esteemed is better than silver or gold" (Proverbs 22:1). This means you do not fear and you follow through with your commitments. Faith grows in its giving during uncertain times. Am I thriving or surviving? Is my trust in gold or God?

Where does the Lord want me to aggressively give money, trusting in Him?

Related Readings: Deuteronomy 8:12–14; Job 31:24–25; Matthew 13:22; 1 Timothy 6:17

NOBLE WIFE

"A wife of noble character is her husband's crown, but a disgraceful wife is a decay in his bones."
Proverbs 12:4

Why are certain wives attractive and others unattractive? Why do you enjoy the company of some but avoid the company of others? A wife of noble character is attractive because she aspires to obey almighty God. She is a joy to be around as she enjoys being in the presence of the Lord. Her first allegiance is to her Savior Jesus Christ, exhibited by her regal appearance and respectful responses. God has first place in her heart.

Her husband takes pride in her because she can be trusted in all household matters and financial management. By faith she follows her husband's leadership. She entrusts him under the authority of God to hold him accountable. A wife of noble character knows how to prayerfully ask challenging questions of her husband without usurping his leadership. She is strong and gracious, bold and beautiful, firm and friendly, faithful and loving.

Her children are loved when they are unlovely and disciplined when they behave badly. They know their mom cares, even when she gets carried away in her correction. A wife of noble character is a model of motherhood for her daughters and an example of one her sons should marry. She is wise to honor her husband in front of their children, especially when they disagree. Her character is a compass for the actions of her kids.

Lastly, a wife of noble character is not afraid to mentor and encourage other wives; not with a superior spirit, but with an attitude of meekness and brokenness. She quickly admits to her past mistakes to save some young women from repeating the hurt and heartache. A student she remains, even while she endeavors to teach and train. Wisdom is worn around her words with humility and grace. Indeed, am I grateful, glad, and proud of my wife? The Bible says, "She is worth far more than rubies" (Proverbs 31:10).

How can I enjoy God's blessing of my husband and children?

Related Readings: Genesis 2:18–24; Ruth 3:11; 1 Corinthians 11:7–11; 1 Timothy 5:2

BAD NEWS

"'Lord, the one you love is sick.' When he heard this, Jesus said, 'This sickness will not
end in death. No, it is for God's glory so that God's Son may be glorified through it.'"
John 11:3-4

Are you the recent recipient of bad news? Is it cancer, job termination, financial free fall,
divorce, betrayal, or an accident? Bad news can cause you to blame others and remain mad
at God. It solicits sadness and assumes the worse. Bad news can break your heart, flood
your face with tears, and fill your heart with sorrow. It is a test of our trust and a revelation
of whom we really believe is in control.

Moreover, bad news is an invitation for God's good news. Bad news can bring out our
best. The gospel of Jesus Christ is our certainty when we are uncertain, our hope when we
are hopeless, and our salvation when we are sinful. It is our stability when we are out of control and our healing when we are hurting. The good news of God's sovereignty supersedes
the bad news of our sorrow and sickness. The Lord's dominion determines our destiny.

Furthermore, the affliction of your family is for the glory of God. The diseased body of
a believer is meant to point people toward their glorified body in glory. "But our citizenship
is in heaven. And we eagerly await a Savior from there, the Lord Jesus Christ, who, by the
power that enables him to bring everything under his control, will transform our lowly
bodies so that they will be like his glorious body" (Philippians 3:20–21).

Lastly, the affection of almighty God is the outcome of your adversity. His
trustworthiness transcends your troubles. The love of the Lord longs for you in your
lamentation. Circumstances brimming with bad news mean you are a prime candidate for
God's glorification. Be a secure son or daughter of your heavenly Father so others can see
God's Son in your life and glorify Him. Are you using bad news to bring glory to God?

"He who speaks from himself seeks his own glory; but He who is seeking the glory of
the One who sent Him, He is true, and there is no unrighteousness in Him" (John 7:18
NASB).

How can I best reflect Christ in my life when I receive bad news?

Related Readings: Genesis 22:2; Mark 5:39–42; Philippians 2:26–27; 1 Peter 1:21

COMPASSION BRIDGE

"When he saw the crowds, he had compassion on them, because they were
harassed and helpless, like sheep without a shepherd." Matthew 9:36

Where does compassion come from? Where do these deep feelings of sympathy and sorrow spring up? Compassion originates for Christians from the compassion they have experienced from Christ. He calls us by His grace to alleviate pain and suffering. The gospel is all about healing and making broken people whole in the name of Jesus.

"The Spirit of the LORD is upon Me, Because He has anointed Me To preach the gospel to the poor; He has sent Me to heal the brokenhearted, To proclaim liberty to the captives, And recovery of sight to the blind, To set at liberty those who are oppressed" (Luke 4:18 NKJV).

Compassion from Christ is a bridge to somewhere. It is a bridge to hope and happiness. It is a bridge to belief and blessing. It is a bridge to recovery and righteousness. It is a bridge to forgiveness and freedom. It is a bridge to peace and productivity. It is a bridge to heaven and healing. Compassion cuts into hard hearts and softens them for our Savior.

What is your perspective of people? Are you distant and aloof, or emotional and engaged? Yes, they can be cranky and quirky, but so can you. It is a shepherd's heart that summons us to empathy and kindness. Who in your life is EGR (extra grace required)? Extend grace to them, and watch God work through your compassionate care. It may be an unruly work associate, a loved one in hospice, or a prodigal child who needs your time.

Do not shy away from showing compassion. Partner with Christ, and you will have an unlimited supply from which to draw. A soul starves for want of a Savior; a body starves for want of sustenance. Compassionate Christians feed both in the name of Christ. Be a believer who builds bridges of compassion, and you will never lack for people who travel to the other side. See souls like your Savior, and you will be filled with His compassion.

Jesus was moved to tears for His city. "He saw the city and wept over it" (Luke 19:41 NASB).

Am I compelled by Christ's compassion to build bridges to men and women's souls?

Related Readings: 1 Kings 22:17; Ezekiel 34:2; Luke 15:20; Colossians 3:12

SHAME FROM DRUNKENNESS

"Noah, a man of the soil, proceeded to plant a vineyard. When he drank some of its wine, he became drunk and lay uncovered inside his tent." Genesis 9:20–21

What starts out as an innocent drink for relaxation can grow into an uninhibited attitude that leaves behind shame and regret. The conscience grows numb under the influence of too much alcohol. Noah, who had stayed sober in drunken company, was now drunk in sober company. What guidelines do you have in place to not drift into this embarrassing behavior? In a moment of exhilaration or despair, we can live to regret a drunken display.

"They grope in darkness with no light; he makes them stagger like drunkards" (Job 12:25). There is nothing appealing about a man or woman who loses his or her senses.

Yes, one consequence of drunkenness is shame—the feeling of embarrassment, humiliation, dishonor, and disgrace. A lifetime of faithfulness to the Lord can be soiled and even suffer a character court-martial in one irresponsible evening. Is an immature public display worth its consequences? We will feel naked and exposed before a holy God and those whom we admire. People will say and do things when they are drunk that would cause them to blush when sober. Drinking requires constraint by Christ's wise grace.

Thankfully, shame from sin can be caught quickly and put into check with confession and repentance, or it can linger on, seemly justified by irrational arguments. Indeed, we can be grateful for the Holy Spirit's conviction and for the accountability of those who love us. After all, it is those who know us the best whom we want to respect us the most.

Intoxication from the Holy Spirit is a sure remedy for resistance from other unseemly sources. A heart and mind full of God's Spirit have no room for shenanigans and rigmarole that bring remorse to the soul. Yes, the Lord's desire is for us to remain sober-minded, not thinking more highly or lowly of ourselves but in accordance with His ample grace.

"Therefore, with minds that are alert and fully sober, set your hope on the grace to be brought to you when Jesus Christ is revealed at his coming" (1 Peter 1:13).

What are my guidelines for accountability partners to protect me from shameful actions?

Related Readings: 1 Samuel 25:37; Romans 12:3; Ephesians 5:15–20; 1 Peter 4:7; 1 Peter 5:8

FREELY GIVE

"Freely you have received, freely give."
Matthew 10:8

What is your motivation for giving? Is it to freely give or to give expecting something in return? This is an ongoing tension for the generous giver. We give our time, our expertise, our money, our friendship, our commitment; we give our very life, with what expectation in mind? Disappointment follows gifts with strings attached, but gifts given freely lead to fulfillment. Can we be hilariously generous and still trust Christ?

You may ask, "What about my stewardship in giving gifts responsibly?" Wise givers give prayerfully and responsibly, but not to the exclusion of the Spirit's leading. If the Lord is leading you to invest time and money in a person, ministry, or church, then obey and trust Him with the outcome. Everything we have is His; so He is ultimately responsible for the fruit from generosity. He blesses His work, done His way.

Because Christ's gifts are not conditional, our gifts are not conditional. For example, at your conversion God freely gave you His Spirit for comfort, conviction, and direction. The Bible says, "We have not received the spirit of the world but the Spirit who is from God, that we may understand what God has freely given us" (1 Corinthians 2:12).

So, even when we grieve the Spirit with our disobedience, He still remains. The gift of the Holy Spirit does not come and go from our life; He is here to stay. His resolve to reside in our soul is reassurance that we are not alone. In the same way, when people you trust are in turmoil, stay with them through the rough ride until things smooth out. Anyone can give in the good times; so be there to give when they need you the most.

Faithfulness freely gives, not to gain, but to do good deeds. The Lord's freedom to extend goodness to you compels you to freely give back goodness. Grace is a gift to be received gratefully and given liberally. Give freely, and observe how much more is freely given to you. Your heavenly Father gave you His Son because He loves and forgives you freely.

"He predestined us to be adopted as his sons through Jesus Christ, in accordance with his pleasure and will—to the praise of his glorious grace, which he has freely given us in the One he loves. In him we have redemption through his blood, the forgiveness of sins, in accordance with the riches of God's grace" (Ephesians 1:5–7).

What are the Lord's expectations for His gifts to me? Am I freed up to give freely?

Related Readings: 1 Chronicles 29:9; Proverbs 11:24; Romans 3:24; 1 Corinthians 2:12

UNPRETENTIOUS LIVING

"Better to be a nobody and yet have a servant than pretend to be somebody and have no food."
Proverbs 12:9

Unpretentious living is an invitation to down-to-earth interaction with others. Rest and relaxation attend to those who are true to themselves without acting like someone they are not. However, pretentious speech and behavior require extra energy to engage with their environment. Contentment is illusive and intimacy is an illusion. I become the most stressful when I feel I have to live up to something or be someone I am not.

Moreover, when you are real, not fake, your friends feel the freedom to be the same. You give off energy instead of forever sucking it from others. In honesty I often ask myself, "Am I being myself, or am I trying to dress, talk, drive a certain car, or live in a high-status neighborhood that is motivated by a need to be somebody I am not?" Pretense is birthed out of pride, but humility is the fruit of unpretentious living.

Jesus is clear, "For everyone who exalts himself will be humbled, and he who humbles himself will be exalted" (Luke 14:11 NASB). In Christ you are somebody. High or low net worth, small or large home, new or used car, prestigious university or common college, in Him you are somebody. You are somebody to your Savior Jesus.

The Bible says, "Christ in you, the hope of glory" (Colossians 1:27). Out of your simple faith and modesty, the Lord takes center stage of your life. Humility positions you to point people to heaven. Therefore, keep your life unencumbered so people can see your Savior shine forth. Ask yourself, "Am I trying to impress people I really do not know or the lover of my soul, Jesus?"

The Bible says, "Those who want to make a good impression outwardly are trying to compel you to be circumcised. The only reason they do this is to avoid being persecuted for the cross of Christ" (Galatians 6:12).

How can I be more authentic and open with my spouse, children, and work associates?

Related Readings: 1 Samuel 16:7; Proverbs 13:7; Romans 2:28; 1 Peter 3:3

ROUTINE WORK

"He who works his land will have abundant food, but he who chases fantasies lacks judgment."
Proverbs 12:11

Routine work may not be sexy, but it is necessary. It is necessary to meet our needs and the needs of those who depend on us. The same work, day in and day out, can seem simple and even boring, but it is a test of our faithfulness. Will I continue to faithfully carry out uncomplicated responsibilities, even when my attention span is suffering? If so, this is God's path to blessing: "Steady plodding brings prosperity" (Proverbs 21:5 LB).

The contrast to routine work is chasing after phantom deals that are figments of our imagination. Be careful not to be led astray by fantasies that lead nowhere. It is false faith to think a gimmick or some conniving circumstance can replace hard work. Wisdom stops chasing after the next scheme and sticks instead to the certainty of available work. What does your spouse say is the smart thing to do? Give your spouse all the facts, and listen.

Furthermore, work is easily carried out when everything is going well and there are no indicators of job loss or an increase in responsibilities with less pay. However, it is during these uncertain times that Christ followers can step up and set the example. Your attitude of hope and hard work is a testimony of trust in the Lord. Stay engaged in executing your tasks with excellence, and you will inspire others to their labor of love.

Lastly, see routine work as your worship of the Lord. He is blessing your faithfulness to follow through with the smallest of details. Are you content to serve Christ in your current career?

The Bible says, "Whatever you do, work at it with all your heart, as working for the Lord, not for men, since you know that you will receive an inheritance from the Lord as a reward. It is the Lord Christ you are serving" (Colossians 3:23–24).

Is my work a compelling testimony to the excellence of God's gracious work?

Related Readings: Genesis 2:15; 1 Kings 19:19; Romans 12:11; 1 Timothy 4:11–12

PATIENT FORGIVENESS

"A fool shows his annoyance at once, but a prudent man overlooks an insult."
Proverbs 12:16

Fools are forever flailing away at an offense, while a prudent man or woman is patient to forgive. A fool is easily provoked to anger, always looking for an argument to win. He or she is combative with compassionless concern. However, prudence is careful in its response, not willing to be reckless, but just to be right. Wisdom employs forethought and prayer; so it answers with an attitude of respect. Prudence invokes patience.

Do you buckle under pressure and say things you later regret? It is better to keep quiet and cool down than to vent venomous words in the flesh. Make this a goal when disciplining your children. Avoid anger as the instructor of your punishment. We tend to speak harshly and act unreasonably when driven by anger. Wait prayerfully for twenty-four hours; then revisit the infraction with your child. Use cool correction.

Bridle your tongue by God's grace. The Bible says, "If anyone considers himself religious and yet does not keep a tight rein on his tongue, he deceives himself and his religion is worthless" (James 1:26). Your words can grieve another or give hope. They can hurt or heal. Therefore, submit to the Holy Spirit's control of your conversations.

Lastly, you are blessed if you are insulted for Christ's sake. "Blessed are you when people insult you, persecute you and falsely say all kinds of evil against you because of me" (Matthew 5:11). Reward awaits those rejected for righteousness sake.

In Christ we are dead to sin, and the dead are not insulted. "In the same way, count yourselves dead to sin but alive to God in Christ Jesus" (Romans 6:11).

Have you died to the right to be right? Do you hold a grudge or have to get even?

Related Readings: 1 Samuel 20:30–34; Esther 3:5; Matthew 27:39–40; James 1:19

DILIGENCE RULES

"Diligent hands will rule, but laziness ends in slave labor."
Proverbs 12:24

How hard do you work, or do you hardly work? God said to Adam, "Cursed is the ground because of you; through painful toil you will eat of it all the days of your life. By the sweat of your brow you will eat your food" (Genesis 3:17, 19). And He explained to Moses, "Six days you shall labor and do all your work, but the seventh day is a Sabbath to the LORD your God. On it you shall not do any work" (Exodus 20:9–10).

Has our culture become accustomed to receiving good things without great effort? Who is entitled to influence without being industrious? Perhaps there is a dearth of diligence that has depressed people and economies. Laziness leads to the control of others, while honest labor is given opportunities and advancement. Do not despair in your diligence, for you are set up for success. Mind your business meticulously, and you will enjoy the business.

Indeed, intense industry leads to preferment. The Bible says, "Now the man Jeroboam was a valiant warrior, and when Solomon saw that the young man was industrious, he appointed him over all the forced labor of the house of Joseph" (1 Kings 11:28 NASB). Your faithfulness to your work is not going unnoticed. Your diligence is a distinctive that separates you from the average or lazy laborer. Security comes with this level of service.

Lastly, the Lord blesses hands that are hard at work. He smiles when He sees your service exceeds expectations. You go the extra mile to make sure others are cared for, just as you would like to be. God knows through your thoroughness on the job and your integrity in its execution, you can be trusted with more.

The Bible says, "The elders who direct the affairs of the church well are worthy of double honor, especially those whose work is preaching and teaching" (1 Timothy 5:17).

Does my work honor the Lord with its focused diligence and commitment to quality?

Related Readings: 1 Kings 12:20; Proverbs 10:4; Romans 12:8; 1 Timothy 4:15

RIGHTEOUS HATRED

"The righteous hate what is false, but the wicked bring shame and disgrace."
Proverbs 13:5

There is a righteous hatred that rejects what is false. It might be false words, bogus behavior, a counterfeit countenance, a phony friendship, or deceptive dealings. The discernment of the Spirit-filled believer rises up to defend integrity. You cannot sit still to shenanigans when you know there is a violation of an agreed-upon code of ethics.

So how are we to respond to lies and liars? We first look in the mirror, making sure we are honest in our dealings and accurate with our words. Jesus said, "How can you say to your brother, 'Let me take the speck out of your eye,' when all the time there is a plank in your own eye?" (Matthew 7:4). It is required that I remove all self-deception before I can clearly see sin in another brother. Self-evaluation precedes confronting false conduct.

Furthermore, our heavenly Father expresses holy hatred over what is false. He hates "haughty eyes, a lying tongue…a heart that devises wicked schemes" (Proverbs 6:17–18). Because the Almighty abhors artificial acts, we must ask ourselves, "Do I take sin seriously, or do I casually flirt with it?" Loose lips lead to lies and deceit that bring shame and embarrassment. Avoid lies and liars, and you will live in peace and contentment.

Lastly, in your business, ministry, and testimony, remove all appearance of fraud and falsehood. Free yourself from image management with full disclosure and transparency. Create a culture that exposes any hint of a conflict of interest. Lies examined under light melt away. Hate dishonesty and reward honesty. Honesty is the only policy for the people of God.

"Therefore each of you must put off falsehood and speak truthfully to his neighbor, for we are all members of one body" (Ephesians 4:25).

Do I model honest words and boldly confront dishonesty in love?

Related Readings: Judges 16:11; Psalm 119:163; Colossians 3:9; Revelation 21:8

BRUTAL FACTS

"Then Joab went into the house of the king and said, 'Today you have humiliated all your men, who have just saved your life and the lives of your sons and daughters and the lives of your wives and concubines.'" 2 Samuel 19:5

Brutal facts are not always pretty or inviting, but they are reality. Initially, brutal news may take you aback and beat you up. But take heart; it is good for bad news to travel fast. You are better off to hear negative news first, before the information becomes filtered through other perspectives or the facts fester and become worse.

Brutal facts that are not given attention move from an inflamed infection to relational and organizational gangrene. Inevitably there follows an amputation; someone or something has be severed. This extreme action could have been avoided if the brutal facts had been revealed, recognized, and acted upon. Brutal facts are our friends; do not dismiss the messenger because the message is bad. He or she is just the delivery person.

Though the messenger's attitude and character may not always be stellar, the content of his or her words can be extremely accurate. The wise receiver of brutal facts will extract the chaff and keep the wheat. Brutal facts may mean you have lost touch with those who love you the most. In your zeal to provide for them, you have failed to get to know them.

A brutal fact may relate to your finances. What is the reality of your cash situation? Come clean with your spouse and seek accountability from a trusted third party. Or the state of your physical health may be a heart attack waiting to happen. Take care of your temple, or it will take care of you by tumbling down around you. Do you rationalize that all of your activity is for the Lord? The truth is that He can get by just fine without any of us.

So where can we find these brutal facts? Your spouse, parent, or friend is a good starting point. They have a vested interest in you; so normally their perception of the facts is fairly accurate. Listen with an ear to learn, but if you become defensive or argumentative, they will eventually shut down. Because they care, they want you to be aware.

Why not change on your own terms rather than being forced to change on another's? This is the essence of brutal facts: there are some things that need to change - you, the work culture, your family's state of flux. So use this as an opportunity to move from mediocrity to excellence. Embrace the brutal facts, learn from them, and become better.

"Then Nathan said to David, 'You are the man! This is what the LORD, the God of Israel, says'" (2 Samuel 12:7).

Who currently has concerns that I need to seriously consider? How do I need to change?

Related Readings: 2 Kings 5:10; Haggai 1:13; Romans 9:1; 3 John 1:12–13

WHEN IN DOUBT

"When John heard in prison what Christ was doing, he sent his disciples to ask him, 'Are you the one who was to come, or should we expect someone else?'" Matthew 11:2–3

Doubt seeks to destroy our faith. It is in our discouragement—even despair—that we begin to question God. "What did I do wrong?" "Lord, did you call me to this place of confusion?" "Where are my joy and hope?" "Are you even real or just a figment of my imagination?" Left to its natural conclusion, doubt crushes our faith in Christ.

Fortunately, faith does not have to take a furlough when we are frustrated and fatigued. It is in your confinement that Christ wants to remind you of His great power. So cry out to Him in your confused circumstances, and He will earnestly listen in love. "In my distress I called to the LORD; I called out to my God. From his temple he heard my voice; my cry came to his ears" (2 Samuel 22:7). He does not leave His loved ones alone and in doubt.

It is okay to be in doubt, but it is not okay to remain in doubt. What doubt challenges your faith in God? Is it His provision, His promises, His presence, His character, or His care? When these questions assault your confidence in Christ, take a step back and review His track record. The reality of your salvation sets you on the productive path of peace and forgiveness. Answered prayer over the years is proof enough of His love and concern.

Furthermore, use this temporary time of distrust to go deeper with Jesus. The pressure you feel on all sides is your Savior's way of soliciting your attention. When in doubt, seek out the Lord, learn to love Him completely, and discern more fully His profound promises. Use doubt to dig deeper into the truth of Scripture; marinate your mind. "Taste and see that the LORD is good; blessed is the man who takes refuge in him" (Psalm 34:8).

When in doubt, stay steadfast in seeking out your Savior. Wait on Him, especially when you wonder what is next. Where there is true faith there may be a mixture of unbelief; so remain faithful, even when questions manipulate your faith. Perseverance will one day free you as a stronger and more-committed follower of Christ. See Jesus for who He is. Doubt dissolves in His reassuring presence. Doubt starves to death when it is not fed.

"Blessed is he whose help is the God of Jacob, whose hope is in the LORD his God, the Maker of heaven and earth, the sea, and everything in them—the LORD, who remains faithful forever" (Psalm 146:5–6).

What doubts do I need to acknowledge and release to God? Is Christ trustworthy?

Related Readings: 2 Chronicles 33:12; Job 36:16–19; John 20:27; Jude 1:22

RIGHTEOUS LIGHT

"The light of the righteous shines brightly, but the lamp of the wicked is snuffed out."
Proverbs 13:9

Righteousness shines the brightest when dimming days become the darkest. We are called and compelled as Christians to glow for God during gloomy times. Are you caught up in our culture's chaos, or do you see it as a chance to burn brightly for Jesus? Hard times can harden our hearts or humble them, but it is a broken heart that burns the brightest.

Jesus said, "In the same way, let your light shine before men, that they may see your good deeds and praise your Father in heaven" (Matthew 5:16). Light left unattended extinguishes, but light exposed to the air of almighty God's love illuminates. Difficult days demand dependency on the Lord; so, in fact, your acts of service are fueled by faith. If you panic instead of praying, you will miss out on opportunities to love others.

I often ask, "Am I more worried about my stuff, or do I see uncertainty as a window of opportunity to serve others?" It may mean inviting someone to live in my home for a season, paying mortgage payments for three months for a friend, volunteering at a local shelter, or increasing my gifts to the church. Righteous light longs to love liberally.

Christ in us invites others to know Him, "For God, who said, 'Let light shine out of darkness,' made his light shine in our hearts to give us the light of the knowledge of the glory of God in the face of Christ" (2 Corinthians 4:6). Perhaps you invite some neighbors over for a six-week Bible study on money and see what God does.

"Do everything without complaining or arguing, so that you may become blameless and pure, children of God without fault in a crooked and depraved generation, in which you shine like stars in the universe" (Philippians 2:14–15).

How can I burn brighter as a light for my Lord at home and at work?

Related Readings: Job 18:5–6; Isaiah 50:10–11; Luke 11:36; Revelation 21:23

HEALTHY FEAR

"How then could I do such a wicked thing and sin against God?"
Genesis 39:9

The fear of God is healthy. Joseph understood this. Though he was in an environment where he could sin and nobody would know, he knew that most importantly God would know. This is healthy, because a respectful attitude toward God is accountability. No matter where we are or what we are doing, we know God is watching, and we know that He expects us to represent Him well. Wherever there is God, there is accountability.

We may be able to hide (for a time) our Internet probing of despicable sites, but God is not deceived. We may cover up (for a time) padded expense reports, but God is not fooled. Our flirtatious words and emotional attachment to someone other than our spouse disappoint and grieve our heavenly Father. Over time, all of these areas of sin will be exposed, and there will be tremendous hurt and disaster. However, when we fear Him we experience His accountability, and as we submit to Him there is obedience to do the right thing.

So where does fear of God come from? It comes from God. As a follower of Jesus Christ the Holy Spirit resides in you, and, among other things, He is there to convict you of sin. We have a God consciousness. His still, small voice (sometimes loud voice) is there to remind us of His expectations. He is jealous and wants us totally for Himself.

Lastly, the essence of fearing God is a reverential trust that compels you to love and obey Him. Ironclad faith in Jesus Christ as your Lord and Savior is foundational in your fear of God. The more you understand God's character through His Word, the more you grow to love and respect Him. Fear of God flows into a fervent faith that rejects sin and trusts Him.

"He put a new song in my mouth, a hymn of praise to our God. Many will see and fear and put their trust in the LORD" (Psalm 40:3).

Does my fear of God cause my behavior to change in my concern not to disappoint Jesus?

Related Readings: Numbers 32:23; Nehemiah 5:15; Acts 10:2; 2 Corinthians 5:11

M**11**

BUILD ON MOMENTUM

"Those who accepted his message were baptized, and about
three thousand were added to their number that day." Acts 2:41

Momentum makes progress, but lack of momentum loses ground. It is the impetus we need to ignite our life, work, ministry, or intimacy with the Lord. The early church experienced momentum at Pentecost. Jesus' death on the cross discouraged the masses from moving forward, but His resurrection thrust trust in Him back upon their hearts.

You may need an "upper room" prayer meeting to bolster your faith, seeking the Lord for wisdom on how to move forward with momentum. Your leadership may require transformation. New leaders may need to infuse life into the organization. Perhaps you replace old programs with newer exciting ones and let some initiatives mercifully die.

Be creative, for creativity flourishes in a climate of chaos. Limitations lead to innovations. Momentum makes you better because it builds your confidence and moves you toward more excellent outcomes. Athletic teams are familiar with this; whoever seizes the momentum in the game garners the advantage.

In the same way, the message of Jesus exploded in momentum after His resurrection, and it followed Peter's preaching Jesus to men and women from all nations. Therefore, keep Christ central as you advance boldly by grace. Harness trust in your Savor and Lord, and He will ignite forward motion.

Mostly, seek momentum in your walk with Christ. Is your intimacy stuck in inertia? If so, begin praying with intercessors, and ask God for the confidence to do the next right thing. Momentum builds on focus. Keep pushing the slow-moving flywheel of faith, and - eventually others will join you in advancing the mission.

Paul said, "I press on toward the goal for the prize of the upward call of God in Christ Jesus" (Philippians 3:14 NASB).

Where is God working? How can I build on His momentum?

Related Readings: Genesis 6:9; Psalm 119:40; Luke 9:51; Acts 20:24

FAITH VERSUS FEAR

"He replied, 'You of little faith, why are you so afraid?' Then he got up and
rebuked the winds and the waves, and it was completely calm." Matthew 8:26

Jesus responds to little faith or large faith. They are both important to Him. However, the larger your faith grows, the smaller your fears shrink. And the opposite is true. The smaller your faith is, the greater your fears will be. It may seem like Jesus is asleep as you are riding out this particular storm. He does not seem to care or be in control. However, during hard days like these, we ask ourselves, "Is God big enough to handle my greatest fear?"

Some of your peers may not believe like you believe, but they certainly need to believe that you really do believe in what you believe. It is during these adversarial times they see your faith validated. Your faith during this storm may be what draws someone to Jesus. Your peace and comfort are appealing and appetizing. This is what the human soul hungers and longs for. Your trust in God is required to calmly endure this crisis of belief.

Furthermore, untested faith can be weak underneath. A weak faith is a little faith. A new Christian may be passionate and on fire. Gratitude floods his or her soul, but this will be short-lived enthusiasm without shoring up a strong faith. Emotional faith can be a bridge to a closer walk with Jesus. Your feelings can stir your heart to receive eternal truth. A life storm awakens you to a fresh need for Jesus; so use this awareness to grow your faith.

Lastly, the stronger your faith grows, the weaker your fears become. It is imperative for you to feed your faith and starve your fears. Feast on the Bible, for a promise a day keeps fear away. Truth fosters faith. If the cancer of fear has infected the bone marrow of your faith, let the Lord do a truth transfusion. Jesus is here for you. He will calm the storm, but in the meantime trust Him. Watch your faith grow and your fears melt away.

"God is our refuge and strength, an ever-present help in trouble. Therefore we will not fear" (Psalm 46:1–2).

What fear on earth is eroding my faith in God? Can He be trusted with this concern?

Related Readings: Psalm 91:5; Isaiah 54:4; Romans 8:15; 1 Peter 3:6

SKILL AND ABILITY

"See I have chosen Bezalel…and I have filled him with the Spirit of God,
with skill, ability and knowledge in all kinds of crafts." Exodus 31:2-3

Our ability to work comes from God. Our ability to earn a degree and make money comes from God. Our ability to paint, sing, play a musical instrument, and execute a deal comes from God. He calls us and He equips us to carry out His will for our lives. Where He calls, He equips. And yes, if you do not use the God-given abilities you have, you could lose them.

You could lose them because of poor stewardship or a bad testimony. You could lose your skills because of atrophy. Just as muscle shrinks and becomes useless without use, so do the skills, abilities, gifts, and knowledge given to us by God. How are you doing in the management of your God-given abilities? His expectations are for you to continue to grow and improve. He wants you to focus on the things you do the very best.

"There are different kinds of gifts, but the same Spirit distributes them. There are different kinds of service, but the same Lord. There are different kinds of working, but in all of them and in everyone it is the same God at work" (1 Corinthians 12:4–6).

As we mature, ideally we narrow our focus to the one thing that is effortless for us. This is the thing that others say we do best and that blesses them when they are around us. Position your life to do the one thing at which you have become a genius by God's grace. It may be teaching; then focus on teaching. It may be leading; then focus on leading. It may be coaching; then focus on coaching. It may be singing; then focus on singing. It may be parenting; then focus on parenting. It may be writing; then focus on writing.

This requires discipline and, in some cases, sacrifice, but trust God with who you are. Serve out of your sweet spot, so you and everyone around you will be blessed. Yes, there are economic considerations, but each stage of life has its own opportunities. Stay nimble, and seize each opportunity in the context of what you do best, never forgetting to give God the credit for your abilities.

"Therefore I remind you to stir up the gift of God which is in you through the laying on of my hands" (2 Timothy 1:6 NKJV).

Related Readings: Deuteronomy 33:11; Proverbs 22:29; John 3:27; 1 Corinthians 12:4–11

PREPARATION PRECEDES POWER

"This is the one about whom it is written: 'I will send my messenger ahead of you, who will prepare your way before you.'" Matthew 11:10

Jesus spent thirty years in private preparation for three years of public service. He knew the necessary need to wait on His heavenly Father for the power of His blessing before He embarked on His eternal mission. What passionate desire has the Lord laid on your heart that awaits your thorough preparation? Like Elijah, you first prepare an altar of sacrifice by faith, and then wait on God to send forth His fire from heaven to ignite your work.

Similar to Jesus, you probably depend on others as part of your preparation process. The creditability of John the Baptist paved the way for the Lamb of God. In the same way, the good reputation of trusted friends can accelerate your success. This is why it is wise to wait on the endorsement of other trusted leaders. Pay the price of being mentored before you run ahead to your next assignment. New leaders need the approval of old leaders.

Pain is another product of preparation. Until your perspective has been seasoned by adversity, your confidence has not been tempered away from arrogance and toward humility. God does not waste pain as it produces the character required to represent Christ. It is in our hurt that we cry out in humble dependence, confession, and repentance. We learn the good and bad about ourselves in pain's process. Pain produces patience.

Are you expecting to receive the fruit of preparation without paying the price to prepare? Ministers who prepare are endowed with power from on high. Preparation precedes anointing. Parents who prepare learn from experienced parents. Preparation precedes obedient children. Students who prepare privately are recognized publically. Preparation precedes education. Leaders who prepare their minds and hearts feel God's favor.

What is your next step in the process of preparation? Is it to silently serve the poor or to boldly challenge the rich? Is it to earnestly work with your hands so you can better relate with your head? Do not dismiss thorough preparation in place of zealous shortcuts. Stay the course in Christ's school of learning submission, as His power rests on the prepared.

"'Answer me, O LORD, answer me, so these people will know that you, O LORD, are God, and that you are turning their hearts back again.' Then the fire of the LORD fell and burned up the sacrifice, the wood, the stones and the soil, and also licked up the water in the trench. When all the people saw this, they fell prostrate and cried, 'The LORD—he is God! The LORD—he is God!'" (1 Kings 18:37–39).

What patient preparation do I need to complete? Am I serving others in God's power?

Related Readings: Psalm 85:13; Amos 4:12; Ephesians 4:12; 2 Timothy 2:21

WILLING TO ACCEPT

"And if you are willing to accept it, he is the Elijah who was to come."
Matthew 11:14

Hard words, hard people, and hard situations are hard to accept. Do you or someone you know feel like you are between a rock and a hard place? Do your options seem like they have dried up? Is your energy to press forward depleted? Perhaps it is time to accept the cold, hard facts of where you find yourself. Reality has a way of catching up with our denial.

It is okay to be optimistic, but not to the peril of ignoring your predicament. Are emotional reactions driving your decisions, or do you prayerfully process the facts clearly and objectively with wise input from others you trust? Do you need to give up something—your house, your car, your career, your travel, or your expectations? What is the Lord asking you to give up so that you can gain Him and His peace? Acceptance requires action.

Furthermore, there are people who require additional patience and grace to accept. Have others wronged you to the point that your resentment is blocking your acceptance of them? You may justify your rejection of them because of their rejection of you. For example, children and parents can let us down and even devastate us, but Christians do not have the option of not accepting them for who they are. Love accepts even unworthy recipients.

Do you find yourself in a situation where you do not feel accepted—a new job, in-laws, a new school, a new city, a new relationship? You can stew in self-pity, or you can take the initiative to reach out to your rejecters. Kindness reaches out and rejects rejection. "A man who has friends must himself be friendly" (Proverbs 18:24 NKJV).

Above all, are you willing to accept God's call on your life? When His will is uncomfortable and uncertain, will you still go there in trust? Start by accepting Christ by faith as your Savior and Lord, and then continue to accept His commands as evidence that you are His disciple. Acceptance of the Lord allows you to love Him and other people. Acceptance cannot continue alone but is accelerated and accompanied by the Almighty's grace and love.

Do I wholeheartedly accept God's plan for my life? Whom do I need to accept in love?

Related Readings: Genesis 4:7; Ecclesiastes 5:19; Romans 11:15; 1 Timothy 1:15

DOLLAR COST AVERAGING

"Dishonest money dwindles away, but he who gathers money little by little makes it grow."
Proverbs 13:11

Is there a method to your money management? Do you have a process in place to - steadily save over time? If not, it is never too late to set up a system for saving. Some of us struggle with this because we bet on big returns, only to suffer loss. Steadily saving is not sexy but secure. Finances can be an elusive enemy or a friend who has our back.

Get-rich-quick schemes only feed greed. In God's economy, it is the one who diligently deposits smaller amounts in a secure place who reaps rewards. It is wise wealth that makes the first ten percent of their income a gift offering in the form of a tithe to their heavenly Father and the second ten percent an investment in their future. Money obtained by vanity is spent on vanity, but money gained by hard work and honesty is retained for growth.

It does take discipline not to spend all our earnings in an instant. Commercials and our obligation as consumers exploit our emotions. Culture sucks us in to spend not all we have but more than we have; so be on guard with a simple system for savings. For example, set up an automatic draft from each paycheck that goes straight into a savings account. Preserve this cash, and one day your financial fruit tree will become an orchard.

Lastly, look to the Lord as your provider, and see yourself as a steward of His stuff. The management of your Master's money requires savings. God's desire is growth in your financial security so you are free to give more and serve others. So we ask ourselves, "Am I frivolously spending just for today, or am I disciplined each day to deposit a dollar toward tomorrow?"

"The plans of the diligent lead to profit as surely as haste leads to poverty" (Proverbs 21:5).

What is a wise plan for me to systematically save as a responsible follower of Jesus?

Related Readings: Psalm 128:2; Jeremiah 17:11; Ephesians 4:28; James 5:1–5

WALKING WISELY

"He who walks with the wise grows wise, but a companion of fools suffers harm."
Proverbs 13:20

Do you have a wise woman or man in whom you confide? Is there someone- your dad, your mom, a business associate, or teacher- to whom you can go for objective advice based on the Bible? In our humility to learn, we harvest good sense and wisdom. Gaining God's perspective is not a onetime event but a lifetime of leaning on others to grow in our understanding. Wisdom comes from walking with the wise, not flirting with fools.

Good people engage with good company. There is not a separation of being influenced by skilled people with seedy morals during the week and hearing a sermon on Sunday. "Do not be misled: 'Bad company corrupts good character'" (1 Corinthians 15:33). Instead, there is intentionality toward integrity. You seek out a wise peer or ask a wise mom if you may call her for counsel. Wisdom walks with willing participants who obey.

Beware of fools who talk fast but do not follow through. They may be aware of what is right and can talk the talk, but they fail to walk the walk. They ignore integrity. Fools eventually damage relationships. Foolish behavior will come back to bite you; so avoid its influence. What seems like innocent fun eventually inflicts suffering and harms hearts. Fools are anti-wisdom. "Fools despise wisdom and discipline" (Proverbs 1:7).

So where can you find wise companions? Look for them in church or respected leadership roles in the community. Vet their resume of wise living by observing their spouse's countenance, watching how they love their children, and studying their financial management. Jettison foolish friends so you have the capacity to walk with the wise. Ask, "Am I growing in wisdom or floundering with fools?"

A wise ruler once said, "It is better to heed a wise man's rebuke than to listen to the song of fools" (Ecclesiastes 7:5).

Do I know a wise leader whose circle of influence I can join?

Related Readings: Genesis 13:12–13; Ruth 2:23; Acts 2:42; 2 Thessalonians 3:14

LOVE DISCIPLINES

"He who spares the rod hates his son, but he who loves him is careful to discipline him."
Proverbs 13:24

Love carefully disciplines; apathy silently ignores. Love looks for ways to instruct and improve, while busyness has no time for a tender touch of truth. Do you take the time to discipline your children? Do your offspring encounter your rebuke along with your encouragement? It is because we love them that we correct their attitudes and challenge them to better behavior. Rules restrain them from reacting foolishly or in the flesh.

How can our children learn to make wise decisions if we do not discipline them to love and obey God? Like a skilled artist with a warm lump of clay, our children are moldable; their character is pliable when crafted by Christ. We seek consistency in our own character so we have the moral authority and respect to lead them. Your children's first impression of the Lord is their father and mother; so be an authority who reveals His love.

The branch of a tree is easily bent when it is tender; so start when they are young with yielding to Christ's lordship. "Train a child in the way he should go, and when he is old he will not turn from it" (Proverbs 22:6). Foolishness flees from the faithful and prayerful punishment of loving parents. "Folly is bound up in the heart of a child, but the rod of discipline will drive it far from him" (Proverbs 22:15). Discipline leads to freedom.

You may lament the need for respect from your son or daughter. It is your consistent concern for their character growth that invites their respect. "Fathers...disciplined us and we respected them for it" (Hebrews 12:9). Moreover, loving parents honestly inquire, "How do I respond to the Lord's discipline?" My example of growth from my heavenly Father's discipline makes me an earthly father worth following.

"For whom the LORD loves He reproves, Even as a father corrects the son in whom he delights" (Proverbs 3:12 NASB).

Do I take the time to lovingly discipline my child with instruction and encouragement?

Related Readings: Proverbs 23:13–14; Proverbs 29:15–17; Hebrews 12:6–8; Ephesians 6:4

EMPTY NEST

"Where there are no oxen, the manager is empty, but from the
strength of an ox comes an abundant harvest." Proverbs 14:4

How do you feel since your home has emptied of children? Mad, sad, glad, lonely, without
purpose, or freed up may all be legitimate emotions you are processing. You have raised
them well, and now they are off on their own. You are proud of them, but you miss them.
They call from college (especially daughters), but it is not the same. It is not easy to export
your babies into adulthood; however, this is their faith walk to really know God.

We raise them the best we know how with love, discipline, and belief in Jesus Christ.
Sometimes they frustrate us by not cleaning their crib (room). Like an animal in a barn, they
can be messy and smelly. There are days you want a little peace and quiet, because they
are angry and loud when fighting with their siblings. But the empty nest is void of noise.
The kids are nowhere to be found; so enjoy them while you can.

"There is a time for everything, and a season for every activity under the heavens: a
time to be born and a time to die, a time to plant and a time to uproot, a time to kill and a
time to heal, a time to tear down and a time to build, a time to weep and a time to laugh,
a time to mourn and a time to dance" (Ecclesiastes 3:1–4).

You send them off to grow up and gain a heart of gratitude, and by God's grace they
will visit with a new sense of appreciation and maturity. Distance causes friendship with your
adult child to grow, not to be taken for granted. It is harder to keep up and communicate,
but in some ways it is more gratifying. You prepared them to leave so they can cleave to
the one the Lord has for them in marriage. Our empty nest is a test of trust in God's plan.

Lastly, engage with your spouse in your empty nest. Do you feel like you have drifted
apart over the years? If so, be intentional to regain the intense intimacy with your best
friend. Make these days of marriage your best, because you believe the Lord has given you
your lover to grow old together. Anticipate the gift of grandkids, as they will keep you busy
and alive. The empty nest is a season to enjoy the fruit of your family.

"A good man leaves an inheritance for his children's children"(Proverbs 13:22).

How can I invest in my spouse and children in this new season of life?

Related Readings: Genesis 7:1; Proverbs 31:15; Matthew 19:5; Acts 10:2

COMPROMISE CAN CORRUPT

"Look, I [Lot] have two daughters who have never slept with a man.
Let me bring them out to you, and you can do what you like with them." Genesis 19:8

Compromise can corrupt and destroy, especially moral compromise. Lot capitulated to the mores of society. He was more concerned with losing face to strangers than in the protection and purity of his own daughters. Though he did not know they were God's angels, it did not justify his wicked behavior. His moral compass was out of whack. He could see the wickedness in others but not recognize it in his own life.

The genesis of moral compromise is a blindness fueled by pride and fear. God's standards are desecrated, people's lives and eventually entire communities are in disarray, and even cultures are destroyed. We seek to meet the expectations of people over the Lord's. So how can we see compromise coming? How can we make sure in our business, home, and ministry we do not capitulate to compromise?

First understand, teach, cherish, celebrate, and live out God's standards. He is the absolute. He is equally as intolerant to sin as He is tolerant to those who walk in integrity. The Lord is intolerant of lying, stealing, adultery, and homosexuality. He is tolerant of truth, character, worship, love, and obedience. Model God's tolerance and intolerance.

A society that does not seek to establish laws based on divinely mandated morals will cease to be a thriving society. This is true throughout history and within all people groups. From families to government there must be a moral consciousness to survive. Otherwise, there is an implosion resulting from unrestrained immorality.

Humility asks, "Do I see the moral blind spots in my life?" "Have I asked friends to help me identify them?" "Do I hold high an uncompromising moral banner based on God's truth?"

Remove even the smallest carriers of compromise. "Catch for us the foxes, the little foxes that ruin the vineyards, our vineyards that are in bloom" (Song of Songs 2:15).

Are there any small compromises that I need to confess to the Lord and others?

Related Readings: Numbers 32:23; 1 Samuel 14:38; 2 Corinthians 10:5; Colossians 2:8

INVITATION TO INTIMACY

"Come to me, all you who are weary and burdened, and I will give you rest."
Matthew 11:28

Christ invites you to come to Him. Come to Him for care and compassion. Come to Him for understanding and acceptance. Come to Him for love and forgiveness. Come to Him for wisdom and discernment. Come to Him for energy and encouragement. Come to Him for confession and repentance. Come to Him for faith and patience. Come to Him for rest.

His invitation for intimacy is perpetual. You do not use up your allotted time and then move on to endure alone. You can engage with His eternal resources weekly, daily, hourly, and even moment by moment. Our Lord is a resource that never lacks resources. Do you respond to your invitation for intimacy, or do you later regret sending your regrets?

His revelation comes to those who choose to rest and reflect on Him. Jesus said, "No one knows the Father except the Son and those to whom the Son chooses to reveal him" (Matthew 11:27). So sit quietly at the feet of Jesus, and He will direct you in the way to go. Busyness tends to blur our course, but quietness before Christ brings clarity.

Job, in humble dependence on the Lord, said, "Teach me, and I will be quiet; show me where I have been wrong" (Job 6:24). David said, "He makes me lie down in green pastures, he leads me beside quiet waters" (Psalm 23:2). The Lord leads us to quietness.

What is Christ attempting to communicate, but in your hurriedness you cannot hear? Is rest a part of your routine? Do you take the time to listen to the Lord, or has He increased His interest from an invitation to insisting? Sometimes He uses sickness or injury to get our attention. When we are on our backs, we have to look up and see that Jesus offers rest.

Because the Son is intimate with His Father, He offers intimacy to you. You learn of Him when you long to love Him and know Him. There are no shortcuts with your Savior. He is the journey and the destination. Are you weary and worn out? If so, it is in your fatigue that He wants your faith to flourish. Be still, listen, and let Him love you and revive you.

"But I have stilled and quieted my soul; like a weaned child with its mother, like a weaned child is my soul within me" (Psalm 131:2).

What is Christ's invitation for me? Am I rested and resolved to walk in the Spirit?

Related Readings: Isaiah 30:15; Isaiah 32:17; Luke 23:56; Hebrews 4:1–3

PRACTICAL PROVISION

"At that time Jesus went through the grainfields on the Sabbath. His disciples
were hungry and began to pick some heads of grain and eat them." Matthew 12:1

The Lord's provision does not lack in practicality. What need do you have? Are you stressed out by striving, or have you looked around for a simple solution? It may take some creativity and risk, but if Christ has what you need in close proximity, do not be shy. Forgo ego and appropriate faith. Access His provision and let Him manage your image. His provision may not be positive for public relations, but He knows what is best.

Is your struggle over lack of work? Are you willing to work with your hands outside of your interests to provide for your family? Labor is labor; it can be toilsome and tiring at times. So even if your job is temporarily tedious, look at it as a gift from God. Be proud of your work, even when it is more transactional than relational. Our perspective becomes more grateful and realistic when work becomes a necessity, not an option.

Productive work keeps us focused on provision for those who depend on us, keeping us away from unproductive activities. Paul states it well, "For even when we were with you, we gave you this rule: 'If a man will not work, he shall not eat.' We hear that some among you are idle. They are not busy; they are busybodies'" (2 Thessalonians 3:10–11). Provision follows preparation; so prepare your heart in humility, your head in integrity, and your hands in diligence. God helps those who prepare, work hard, and trust Him.

It is bad theology to blame God, the church, and others for our needy situation. It is good theology to be resourceful and seek out solutions that require humility and focus. Whom have you invested in over the years who would be honored to give back to you? When you are transparent about your needs, you give other souls an opportunity to be blessed by blessing you. Honesty is a pure platform to invite God's provision through friends.

Lastly, do not allow religious restraints to rob you of receiving mercy and being served on the Christian Sabbath. Is there a better time for the body of Christ to care for one another than on our day of corporate worship and biblical teaching? Indeed, engage with believers when you are in need; each part of the body needs the other. If you remain silent, you deny others a blessing; when you speak up God practically provides.

"But God has combined the members of the body and has given greater honor to the parts that lacked it, so that there should be no division in the body, but that its parts should have equal concern for each other. If one part suffers, every part suffers with it; if one part is honored, every part rejoices with it" (1 Corinthians 12:24-26).

Have I recognized and received God's provision? Who needs my provision?

Related Readings: Joshua 9:14; Proverbs 6:8; Romans 5:17; 1 Timothy 6:17

SELF-DECEPTION

"There is a way that seems right to a man, but in the end it leads to death."
Proverbs 14:12

Self-deception is the worst kind of dishonesty because it is so convincing. Subtly it convenes our emotions and mind to ally around a lie. For example, self-deception whispers into the ear of our heart, "You are so smart and capable," but it forgets to include Christ's influence in its instruction. Then we wander down a prayerless path, forged in our own strength, only to discover we missed God's best by a mile.

In reality, we are only as prosperous as our Lord allows. He makes our path straight and successful as He defines *success*. "I guide you in the way of wisdom and lead you along straight paths" (Proverbs 4:11). To which voice do you adhere—your own or your Savior's? Perhaps His plan is for you to make less money and have more family time. Maybe you turn down this promotion and trust Him for a better one in a different season.

We can talk ourselves into anything, especially as it relates to money. I can easily justify a new house, car, kitchen, furniture, floors, or a grill. But do I really need to upgrade or just repair what I have? How can the Lord trust me with something newer if I have not been a good steward of what He has already given me? Trustworthy people can be trusted with more, but the untrustworthy lose opportunities. Thus manage well your present possessions.

Self-deceivers are self-destroyers; so avoid self-delusion by being accountable. Give others permission to ask you uncomfortable, even hard, questions. It is better to be -embarrassed sooner than humiliated later. Consider asking, "Am I transparent with my money and motives?" "What do God and godly advisors think?"

"The heart is hopelessly dark and deceitful, a puzzle that no one can figure out. But I, GOD, search the heart and examine the mind. I get to the heart of the human. I get to the root of things. I treat them as they really are, not as they pretend to be" (Jeremiah 17:9 MSG).

Am I talking myself into something that is a blind spot of self-deception?

Related Readings: Psalm 1:6; Isaiah 59:8; Matthew 7:13–14; Galatians 6:3

LEADERSHIP IN ADVERSITY

"After that, he poured water into a basin and began to wash his disciples' feet, drying them with the towel that was wrapped around him." John 13:5

Adversity invites leaders to lead. It is your time to trust the Lord and lead by faith, not fear. In hard times a leader asks, "Will I panic or pray?" "Will I stay calm or be sucked into the chaos?" "Will I serve the team or stay secluded in silence?" Jesus faced death, but He was determined to stay focused on His heavenly Father and the mission at hand. Adversity is an opportunity to prove the point of Providence. Christ is in control.

How can you use adversity to your advantage as a leader? One way is to unify the team around common objectives and goals. There is no better way to bring people together than in the fires of hardship and difficulty. In fact, you probably will not succeed without the team rising to its next level of leadership and team support. So reward creativity, because limitations lead to innovation. Lead the team to accomplish more with less. Paul said, "We put no stumbling block in anyone's path, so that our ministry will not be discredited. Rather, as servants of God we commend ourselves in every way: in great endurance; in troubles, hardships and distresses" (2 Corinthians 6:3–4).

Moreover, use hard times to create a culture of hard work and honesty. It may mean longer hours and less pay, but sacrifice is the price to be paid for productivity. Invite honest feedback so you accurately and effectively improve process and products. Raise team expectations beyond just surviving to thriving. They look to you for leadership; so lead.

Lastly, serve at home and work with appreciation. It is easy to demand more and more under pressure and forget to say "Thank you." Perhaps you give the team a day off, leave a grateful voicemail, buy everyone lunch, or send flowers. Wise leaders honestly inquire, "How can I out serve others, especially in the face of misfortune?" "Where do I need to take responsibility, not blaming outside forces?" Leaders model the way.

Jesus said, "I have set you an example that you should do as I have done for you" (John 13:15).

Related Readings: Exodus 4:28–30; 1 Samuel 17:22–24; Acts 10:4–8

KIND TO THE NEEDY

"He who despises his neighbor sins, but blessed is he who is kind to the needy."
Proverbs 14:21

The needy have unmet needs that cripple their ability to live life to its fullest. It may be the need for food, clothing, or a place to live. They may need a job, a car, or an opportunity to get ahead. The needy may be lost in their sins without Christ, which is the greatest of needs. Wherever or whatever their point of need is, our obligation is to kindly care for them.

"Give to the poor, and you will have treasure in heaven" (Matthew 19:21).

Evidence of our following Jesus is shown by our concern and care for the poor. Our kindness may require us to give up something so that another can gain something. Perhaps there is a fun trip you can give up so a poor person can obtain food for a month. What financial expenditure can you put on pause?

Whom do you know who could benefit from a car repair or a mortgage payment? Sacrifice solicits us most when the need of others is the highest. Furthermore, the best motivation for reaching out is kindness of heart, not guilt of mind. It is a kind word that lifts another person's spirit. It is a generous gratuity to a diligent server. It is a gentle response to a demanding spirit.

The needy are all around us, especially during economic downturns. Maybe there is an out-of-work neighbor you can invite into your home for dinner and encouragement. Kindness is a culprit of compassion and care. Look out for the needy because of the Lord's great love toward you.

Kindness asks, "Where would I be without God's grace?" "Where in my life can I extend His grace, love, and mercy?" Blessings await those who give and receive kindness. We are all needy, some more than others, but our provider is the same—Jesus Christ.

"Because of the LORD's great love we are not consumed, for his compassions never fail" (Lamentations 3:22).

Who in my life needs me to extend a kind word or deed all in the name of Jesus?

Related Readings: Deuteronomy 15:4; Isaiah 58:7–12; Luke 6:30–36; 1 John 3:17–22

AWARE OF REALITY

"But the Pharisees went out and plotted how they might kill Jesus. Aware of this,
Jesus withdrew from that place. Many followed him, and he healed all their sick."
Matthew 12:14–15

What is the reality of your situation? Are you aware of the good and the bad forces around you? How do you determine the wisest thing to do? We face questions of reality every day, and with the Lord's leading we can define and confront reality well. The gullible go ahead unconcerned, but the savvy seek the best way for the reality they face.

For example, has your health been compromised to the point of chronic pain? It may be time to take a step back and adjust your schedule so you can get the necessary rest to heal your body. Furthermore, have your relationships retreated to the point of nonexistence? Is it time to slow down and reengage with those who care about you?

If we ignore its instruction, reality is a painful teacher. We can do a reality check and become the better for it, or we can drive ahead oblivious to the consequences of our actions. Do you live in reality or in a world no one else recognizes as authentic? Seek the Lord, and you will see your situation more clearly. Christ is aware to help you beware.

Wise followers of Jesus learn to adjust to the reality of their circumstances. When your expectations become unrealistic, you adjust or you live in perpetual frustration. When your financial goals become unachievable, you adjust or you remain a slave to money. When your career only maintains, you adjust or you languish in unfulfilling work.

Lastly, ask Christ to create your own reality based on the Bible. Embrace your calling to serve people, and opportunities will arise to invest in individuals. It is your humble service that solicits the grace of God to generate a godly reality. Be aware of what is around you, adjusting toward giving God the glory in your new reality. Reality understood allows you to embrace change, reject fear, and trust Jesus in the process.

"Suddenly the fingers of a human hand appeared and wrote on the plaster of the wall, near the lampstand in the royal palace. The king watched the hand as it wrote. Then Daniel answered the king, 'You may keep your gifts for yourself and give your rewards to someone else. Nevertheless, I will read the writing for the king and tell him what it means'" (Daniel 5:5, 17). Daniel understood the writing on the wall. It defined reality.

What is my new reality? How can I honor God while facing the reality of my situation?

Related Readings: Genesis 13:7–11; Proverbs 22:3; John 3:3–9; Galatians 4:21

SUBMISSION SOLICITS SECURITY

"He who fears the LORD has a secure fortress, and for his children it will be a refuge."
Proverbs 14:26

Submission is a friend of the secure. Submitting to authority is the secret to securing peace of mind and protection. When we demand our own way and avoid authority, we expose ourselves to the enemy and his devices. "Submit yourselves, then, to God. Resist the devil, and he will flee from you" (James 4:7). Submission is a shield.

So submission begins by fearing the Lord. It is an attitude of humility, not pride; trust, not worry; respect, not lip service; and obedience, not foolishness. Our heart bows down in worship, and our head learns how to love and obey. Under the Almighty's authority, we are sheltered by His great grace. "He who dwells in the shelter of the Most High will rest in the shadow of the Almighty" (Psalm 91:1). Fear of God is where freedom is found.

Furthermore, our model of submission to our Savior is a template for our children, peers, and followers to apply. However, if they see us skirt around submission, they may secretly seek exceptions. Rebellion comes back to roost when we become selective in our obedience. What happens when your boss is unreasonable? Do you still submit to his authority? Yes, and let your excellent work become a testimony of trust in the Lord.

Lastly, what about a wife's submission to her husband? You submit to him and pray for him to understand his accountability to God, because he is accountable. A husband who comes under Christ's authority showers his bride with security, a gift she cherishes deeply. Therefore, build a firm fortress of faith.

"Submit to God and be at peace with him; in this way prosperity will come to you" (Job 22:21).

Am I under the authority of God and man? Does my submission result in service to others?

Related Readings: Genesis 16:9; 2 Chronicles 30:8; Romans 13:1–5; Ephesians 5:21–24

BOLD OBEDIENCE

"Asa did what was right in the eyes of the LORD, as his father David had done."
1 Kings 15:11

Bold obedience may be required for your current situation. Are you surrounded by those who are indifferent or disobedient to God's expectations? You may be the only dissenting voice to what is happening, but stick to your convictions. God's will for you is to do what is right, even if the majority disagrees. People are ultimately looking for leaders and other people who say what they believe and believe what they say.

Anybody can go along with the crowd or commit the sin of silence. Your inaction or quiet could validate the wrong side of the issue being debated. People need to know where you stand. Christ rewards followers who are willing to lose face, lose friends, lose finances, and even lose family if it comes down to choosing right or wrong.

"Peter said to him, 'We have left all we had to follow you!' 'I tell you the truth,' Jesus said to them, 'no one who has left home or wife or brothers or parents or children for the sake of the kingdom of God will fail to receive many times as much in this age and, in the age to come, eternal life'" (Luke 18:28–30).

Bold obedience is often what it takes to shake a nation, a family, a community, or even a church into the reality of God's expectations. If everyone just goes along as if nothing is wrong, then Satan lulls us into apathy and irresponsibility. So look around you, ask what needs to change, and let God use you as a catalyst for bold obedience. Your no may be the spark that lights the fire of courage in others who have been afraid to speak.

Are you a student? This could be a time for you to blend in with the crowd and float through your university days undetected. Or you can choose to use this most impression-able time of life as an excuse for bold obedience. Know what you believe, why you believe it, and live it! Live it in and out of class. Live it in the fraternity, the sorority, and at the ball games. College students are looking for something real and eternal.

Are you serving overseas in missions, work, or the military? This could be a time of temptation to capitulate to the mores of a foreign culture that are not honoring to Christ. However, you remain strong in the Lord, and with grace and humility live the Spirit-filled life. Be bold in your obedience and different to the point that others ask why you act like you act.

"I tell you, though he will not get up and give him the bread because he is his friend, yet because of the man's boldness he will get up and give him as much as he needs" (Luke 11:8).

What issue or person requires my boldness?

Related Readings: Genesis 4:7; Job 17:9; Acts 4:29; 2 Thessalonians 3:13

UNITED WE STAND

"Jesus knew their thoughts and said to them, 'Every kingdom divided against itself
will be ruined, and every city or household divided against itself will not stand.'"
Matthew 12:25

The church can be so diverse in its beliefs that it becomes divisive and ineffective. Thus, Jesus calls us to unify around the truth. He is the truth, and He states very clearly, "But I, when I am lifted up from the earth, will draw all men to myself" (John 12:32). Belief in the cross and resurrection of Jesus Christ brings Christians together in grateful worship.

Does your church believe in the basic tenets of the Christian faith? The inerrancy of the Bible, salvation by grace through faith, that heaven is real and hell is hot, the deity of Christ, and His second coming are all bedrock beliefs. Yes, there will be tangential issues that distract us from time to time, but we can learn to live with our differences and unite around the essentials—all with grace, love, patience, respect, and understanding.

"And over all these virtues put on love, which binds them all together in perfect unity" (Colossians 3:14).

What about governments that dispute to the point of irreconcilable differences? Can they divorce from the ideologies of each other and go on their merry ways? Of course not, but if they choose to abandon communication and respect for one another, they choose the chronic course of division and the ultimate demise of democracy's effectiveness.

Do your work and home have common values that are espoused and executed? When work associates and family members agree upon behaviors such as honesty, accountability, honor, teamwork, and transparency—all with a focus on Christ as the head—there is a high probability for unity. We cannot stand alone, but together we will conquer sin, sorrow, Satan, death, and hell as Christ did. Unify around what is right and watch God work.

"Though one may be overpowered, two can defend themselves. A cord of three strands is not quickly broken" (Ecclesiastes 4:12).

In what relationship do I need to find common ground? Is my church unified around Christ?

Related Readings: Judges 20:11; Psalm 133:1; John 17:23; Romans 15:5

ETERNAL OPTIMIST

"So we fix our eyes not on what is seen, but on what is unseen.
For what is seen is temporary, but what is unseen is eternal." 2 Corinthians 4:18

Eternal optimists base their optimism on the eternal, not the temporal. The temporal is consumed with current circumstances, while the eternal experiences eternal security. The temporal is anxious about another adverse event, while the eternal is at peace with Providence. The temporal trusts what it can see, while the eternal trusts in the unseen. Do you glance at the temporal and gaze on the eternal? If so, you are an eternal optimist.

By faith we see the Lord who is unseen, and this compels us to obey Christ. Moses experienced this during a time of transition. "By faith he left Egypt, not fearing the king's anger; he persevered because he saw him who is invisible" (Hebrews 11:27). Your eternal optimism is what gives you the courage to carry on; so do not let temporal pessimists persuade you to lose heart. Stay fixed on your Savior, the author of your faith.

Eternal optimism exits when fear gets the upper hand. Fear seeks to flush out your faith as irresponsible and irrelevant. However, it is faith that keeps you grounded in God, the definer of reality. The righteous learn to live in the reality of the Lord's love and leadership. Pain and striving are temporary, but healing and peace are eternal. You can be optimistic, knowing by faith you can be certain of the unseen.

"Now faith is being sure of what we hope for and certain of what we do not see" (Hebrews 11:1).

Lastly, are you a temporal pessimist or an eternal optimist? Are you striving to survive or thriving to succeed? Look to the unseen, and you will one day understand. Engage with the Almighty's agenda, and your focus will be forever and your results eternally significant. Can your family and friends depend on you to be an eternal optimist? Your hopeful attitude in the eternal gives them reason to be optimists.

Live and exclaim out loud: "There is surely a future hope for you, and your hope will not be cut off" (Proverbs 23:18).

Where is God calling me to see, with eyes of faith, the unseen, eternal optimism of Jesus?

Related Readings: Psalm 73:26; Isaiah 51:10–11; Matthew 6:21; John 6:27

PREPARATION'S PROVISION

"I will provide for you there, because five years of famine are still to come."
Genesis 45:11

Because Joseph prepared, he was able to provide. He provided for his family and for an entire nation. His preparations were very focused, deliberate, and timely. For seven years he was diligent to save during the days of abundance so there would be provision for all during the days of leanness. Yes, God provides, but usually through our wise decisions or someone else's. God does not operate in a vacuum. He works through people.

He wants us to prepare so we can be in a position to provide for others and for ourselves. Life is one big preparation. How are you doing in your preparations? How are your spiritual preparations? Are you prepared relationally? Do you currently spend time in your physical preparations? What are you doing about your career preparations? Are you preparing financially for the future?

"Finish your outdoor work and get your fields ready; after that, build your house" (Proverbs 24:27).

Consider your financial preparations. "The wise man saves for the future, but the foolish man spends whatever he gets" (Proverbs 21:20 LB). Consistent and steady saving prepares you for the future. Let a budget be your guide. Short-term restraint will allow you to enjoy long-term provision.

The day will come when your wise preparations will provide for you, possibly positioning you to provide for others. God does provide, but He usually works through wise preparation. "Righteousness goes before him and prepares the way for his steps" (Psalm 85:13).

Lastly, the focus of spiritual preparation is eternity. Your time, money, and resources are invested in the kingdom for the sake of eternity. The discipline of renewing our minds with God's Word, trusting in Him through prayer, giving generously, and loving others to Christ builds our spiritual muscles.

Relational preparation is investment in people. It is the ability to forgive fast and the unselfishness to freely connect others with your relationships and resources. Am I using my relational influence to point others to Christ? "A voice of one calling: 'In the desert prepare the way for the LORD; make straight in the wilderness a highway for our God'" (Isaiah 40:3).

What preparation is required before I take the next step of faith in the Lord's will?

Related Readings: Proverbs 6:6–8; Amos 4:12; 2 Timothy 2:21; Revelation 21:2

FOCUSED LEADERSHIP

"Brothers, I do not consider myself yet to have taken hold of it. But one thing I do:
Forgetting what is behind and straining toward what is ahead." Philippians 3:13

Paul understood and applied focused leadership. Under extreme conditions, he remained vigilant to plant churches and preach the gospel, even in the face of hostile resistance. So in uncertain times, I have to look into the mirror and ask, "Am I focused on the task at hand, or am I distracted by critics and circumstances?" Focused leadership finds a way.

Perhaps you take a more direct leadership role so the team can draft off your intensity. For example, consider attending or even leading the sales meetings for a season. Help the team discover creative ways to retain current customers and attract new ones. Be available to serve in ways and at times that will strategically create momentum and excel execution.

Focused leadership strips back to the essentials of getting right results. Focused leadership also applies at home. If finances have spiraled out of control, the husband is to take responsibility and lovingly lead his wife and children to frugally wise expenditures. Everyone sacrifices something during tight economic times. You may need to sell a car or explain to your teenager the only affordable option is in-state tuition. Above all, focused leadership stays focused by faith on Jesus Christ.

"Therefore, since we are surrounded by such a great cloud of witnesses, let us throw off everything that hinders and the sin that so easily entangles. And let us run with perseverance the race marked out for us, fixing our eyes on Jesus, the pioneer and perfecter of faith. For the joy set before him he endured the cross, scorning its shame, and sat down at the right hand of the throne of God. Consider him who endured such opposition from sinners, so that you will not grow weary and lose heart" (Hebrews 12:1–3).

Until you change, the organization or your family will not. Apathy and inertia are not options; the focused leader allows only intense interest and forward motion. Draw a circle around your feet, kneel down, and ask God for wisdom and discernment, starting with your own leadership transformation. Focus on your heavenly Father, and He will lead you to lead successfully. Prayerfully ask, "Is my heart on Him?"

"I consider everything a loss compared to the surpassing greatness of knowing Christ Jesus my Lord" (Philippians 3:8).

Related Readings: Joshua 1:7; 1 Kings 8:61; Luke 10:42; 1 Corinthians 9:24-27

DEPRESSION'S DESPAIR

"[Elijah]…went a day's journey into the desert. He came to a broom tree, sat down under it and prayed that he might die. 'I have had enough, LORD,' he said. 'Take my life; I am no better than my ancestors.' Then he lay down under the tree and fell asleep." 1 Kings 19:4–5

Depression strikes even the most spiritual of giants. In fact, those of spiritual stature are a target for depression, as it strikes indiscriminately and subtly. It attacks us when we are emotionally spent and physically fatigued. Many times after experiencing spiritual warfare, you are set up for depression. You can be on a spiritual mountaintop, but watch out; you are a candidate for the valley below.

There is a valley of despair between two mountains of God's faithfulness. One day you can feel and see the mighty hand of God on your life, and what seems like the next day, His favor is gone. You have been a humble servant in the hand of the Lord. He has used you to mentor and disciple others for His glory, but now people seem a burden. But be of good cheer, as you are blessed with spiritual grandchildren. Your faithfulness matters.

Sometimes unwittingly others put you on a pedestal, as they think you must be just fine because you are the mentor, the Bible teacher, and the more mature follower of Christ. Disarm them of this fantasy. Your confession of discouragement and depression will help those around you come out of their closet of depression and despair.

Depression could be a "thorn in your flesh" you will have all your life to keep you dependent on God, or it may be temporary. You may need professional help and medication to navigate through its immobilization of your life. But do not lose heart. God is just as real and faithful in the valley as He is on the mountaintop.

Get up and pursue God. The cloud of depression has a better chance of moving on when you get quiet before your heavenly Father. He wants you; so allow Him to love you. He loves you for who you are, His child, and not for what you do. Let Him love you unconditionally and freely, without reservation and limitation.

You may need to rearrange your schedule adding blocks of days for detoxification from busyness. Stay before the throne of grace, at a friend's lake house, or a quiet spot by the beach. Lastly, let the body of Christ love you. You have invested all these years in others, but now is the time to withdraw some of those relational dividends.

"My soul thirsts for God, for the living God. When can I go and meet with God? My tears have been my food day and night, while men say to me all day long, 'Where is your God?'" (Psalm 42:2–3).

Is my faith in a funk? How can I let the Lord love me right now? Whom can I serve?

Related Readings: Job 35:9–11; Psalm 115:1–3; Mark 15:34; Romans 7:21–25

A NATION EXALTED

"Righteousness exalts a nation, but sin is a disgrace to any people."
Proverbs 14:34

What makes a nation, any nation, great? Its goodness is what God blesses. Righteousness is the lever the Lord uses to lift a nation up as an example for other nations to follow. However, like people, a nation can fall from God's grace. His blessing is removed when a haughty country shows no remorse for sin and even sanctions its use. A blessed nation will cease to be great when it forgets where it came from by jettisoning Jesus.

It is when a nation is hurting that it needs healing most. The nation of Israel experienced this. "If my people, who are called by my name, will humble themselves and pray and seek my face and turn from their wicked ways, then will I hear from heaven and will forgive their sin and will heal their land" (2 Chronicles 7:14). Have we drifted as a nation to not needing God? Has our sin found us out? Are we reaping what we have sown?

The good news is that an exalted nation does not have people sneaking out but instead sneaking in. Peoples of the world clamor to a country Christ has blessed. The best and the brightest are drawn like a moth to a light to live somewhere they can chase their dreams. It is out of its goodness that a nation becomes a magnet for mankind. Righteousness reposes in the heart of great nations; it supports virtue and suppresses vice.

Lastly, a crippled country can come back, but not without consequences. It starts with individuals repenting and taking responsibility for their actions. "How can I come clean with Christ?" "Have I been financially irresponsible?" "Has greed governed my giving?" "Has fear frozen my faith?" "Have comfort and ease become my idols?"

"He has declared that he will set you in praise, fame and honor high above all the nations he has made and that you will be a people holy to the LORD your God, as he promised" (Deuteronomy 26:19).

How can I help God trust our nation with greatness again?

Related Readings: Proverbs 11:11; Jeremiah 22:2–25; Matthew 12:21; Romans 16:25–27

PITY PARTY

"Elijah was afraid…and prayed that he might die. 'I have had enough, LORD,' he said.'"
1 Kings 19:3–4

We can feel sorry for ourselves when our faith has been frazzled and fear intimidates us. I sometimes exclaim, "Lord, I have had enough!" I may even host a pity party in my heart; but, not so surprisingly, I am the only one who attends. Health issues, financial frustrations, relational conflict, spiritual disappointments, and circumstances out of our control all contribute to self-pity. Has your confidence been crushed? Have you gone from a spiritual high to a new low of anxiety? Have hope; there is a righteous road to relief.

Great men and women of God are not immune to severe insecurities. Elijah is calling down fire from heaven one day and is soon after huddled, frightened, and depressed in a cold cave. Isolation feeds our insecurities. It is in our struggles that we need the prayer and support of God's people. Maybe you have always been the one on the giving end, but now it is your opportunity to receive. You bless others when you accept their sincere love.

You can depend on God's protection when you do God's work. His resources are never reluctant to get involved with a humble heart. So lift your focus from yourself and your sorry situation and seek Him. He has the grace you need to get through tough times. "But he said to me, 'My grace is sufficient for you, for my power is made perfect in weakness'" (2 Corinthians 12:9). Your weakness is an opportunity for Christ's power to rest on you.

Moreover, make sure mental, emotional, or physical fatigue has not flattened your faith. Get away and rest in the Lord. Take long walks and take in the wonders of Christ's creation. You may need to play before you can pray. Perhaps you engage a Christ-centered counselor to help you process your angst and anguish. Lastly, reenlist in service for Jesus, and your self-pity will transition into love for others.

"Your love has given me great joy and encouragement, because you, brother, have refreshed the hearts of the saints" (Philemon 1:7).

How can I love my way out of my lamentations?

Related Readings: Numbers 20:16; Psalm 34:17; Acts 6:8; Romans 5:2

EMOTIONAL SUFFERING

"Then he said to them, 'My soul is overwhelmed with sorrow to the point of death. Stay here and keep watch with me.' Going a little farther, he fell with his face to the ground and prayed, 'My Father, if it is possible, may this cup be taken from me. Yet not as I will, but as you will.'"
Matthew 26:38–39

Jesus suffered emotionally and physically. Anguish welled up in His soul from betrayal, solitude, and the anticipation of a cruel death on a rugged cross. His righteous response was to cry out to His heavenly Father for relief—while trusting that His will be done. Do you find yourself in this tension of trust in God's will? Are your emotions ravished by the pain of conflicting desires? It is in our dark night of the soul that the Lord brings light.

Your emotions may be on the brink of brokenness from relationships that compete for your attention. You cannot please everyone all the time; your stomach is knotted up. Not sure what to do, you feel conflicted and confused. Maybe the loyalty of someone you thought valued your professional relationship has melted in the face of financial pressures. Solitude has diluted your confidence in your ability to understand what God wants.

It is during these times of emotional upheaval that we need to jettison feeling sorry for ourselves and determine not to give up on God and His game plan. Some people you thought would be there for you will wander away, but others you did not expect to show up will come forward with faith in you and hope in heaven. So wait; worry will pass.

"Have mercy on me, my God, have mercy on me, for in you I take refuge. I will take refuge in the shadow of your wings until the disaster has passed" (Psalm 57:1).

Be wise and avoid making life-altering decisions during times of extended, emotional experiences. If you vow to get someone back in passive defiance, it will eat away at the joy in your heart. If anger is driving your decision to fire someone at work or to file for divorce, then wait and let the Holy Spirit stabilize your stress and strengthen your faith.

Above all, seek the comfort of Christ during intense conflict and confusion. His warm embrace soothes your bruised feelings and heals your broken heart. Seek out friends whose acceptance, accountability, and prayers prove to be the hands and feet of Jesus. Alone you will simmer in sinful attitudes, but with God and godly company you will discover and follow His will. Emotional suffering is healed by heaven's hope.

"Faith and love…spring from the hope stored up for you in heaven" (Colossians 1:5).

What decision do I need to wait on until the Holy Spirit stabilizes my emotions?

Related Readings: 2 Samuel 22:23; Psalm 9:9; Nahum 1:7; Acts 28:27

ATTRACTIVE EVANGELISM

"A new command I give you: Love one another. As I have loved you, so you must love one another. By this everyone will know that you are my disciples, if you love one another."
John 13:34–35

Love is irresistible for those in search of a Savior. Everyone whose heart aches for authentic relationships will take notice when seeing Christians love one another. Parents who encourage and build up their sons and daughters are a magnet to their children's friends who live lonely lives in discouraging and disruptive home environments.

Have you thought of your home as a sanctuary for seeking souls? Every time a neighbor drops by, a friend stays overnight, or you host a party for your child's team, you have an opportunity to model the love of Jesus toward those you know and to those whom you meet for the first time. Leverage love for the Lord, and He will draw people to Himself.

"Share with the Lord's people who are in need. Practice hospitality" (Romans 12:13). Being a disciple of Jesus does have its benefits, and being loved is close to the top. When you placed your faith in Christ, you became a giver and receiver of Christian love. So do not resist the righteous care that Christ followers extend on your behalf. Be glad you model the love of God's children that can melt the hearts of outside observers. "Why," they ask, "do people give so much, expecting nothing in return?"

How do you intentionally love your brothers and sisters in Christ? Do you share relationships, money, your vacation home, your primary residence, or your car? It may be showing up during a health issue, praying for a job interview, babysitting their little one, or mowing their grass. Unbelievers take notice when believers lavishly love each other.

"You, my brothers and sisters, were called to be free. But do not use your freedom to indulge the flesh; rather, serve one another humbly in love" (Galatians 5:13).

Our capacity to love is limited only by the Lord's capacity to love us, to love in us, and to love through us. His love removes our insensitive heart and replaces it with sensitivity. The Almighty's agape love arranges our priorities around the needs of others first and ours second. His love first comforts pain in people and then waits for the appropriate time to administer truth. This level of unconditional love is a conduit for the lost to know Christ.

"Dear friends, since God so loved us, we also ought to love one another. No one has ever seen God; but if we love one another, God lives in us and his love is made complete in us" (1 John 4:11–12).

Am I receiving God's love? Whom do I know who needs my unselfish love and attention?

Related Readings: 2 Corinthians 13:11; 1 Thessalonians 4:9; 3 John 1:7-8

KNOWING GOD

"I want to know Christ—yes, to know the power of his resurrection and participation in his sufferings, becoming like him in his death, and so, somehow, attaining to the resurrection from the dead." Philippians 3:10–11

Knowing God is not for the casual Christian but for the committed one. This intimate relationship is forged on the anvil of adversity and expressed through the power of Christ's resurrected life. Knowing God requires dying to self and coming alive in Christ. Resurrected living is the fruit of a faith that is not satisfied with surface Christianity.

To know God is to be loved by Him, to love Him, and to love for Him. To know Him is to behold Him in the glory of His holiness and to bow down in humble worship. To know Christ is to receive His comfort and to carry on a caring conversation with Him. It is going deep in knowledge and understanding of God so we can carry His character and faith far and wide. Knowing God leads to making God known with our words and deeds.

"Know that the LORD is God. It is he who made us, and we are his; we are his people, the sheep of his pasture. Enter his gates with thanksgiving and his courts with praise; give thanks to him and praise his name" (Psalm 100:3–4).

Knowing God grows your character, as intimacy with Him influences you to be like Him. Christ's character begins to transform your character. His influence in your life broadens your influence in other lives. Indeed, your depth of character determines your breadth of influence. Grow in grace so you can export grace throughout your circle of influence. But be careful not to compare your character standard to that of others or even other Christians.

Comparison games are the enemy's game plan to get you off track in trusting Jesus. Pride will puncture your ballooning influence when you begin to take credit for what only the Lord can do. The more you know God, the less you see of yourself and the more you see of Him and others. You know Christ in His death, accompanied by a radical resurrection.

How do you grow to know Him better? It happens in the margins of life, not in a packed schedule with no room for interruptions. A frantic pace lacks grace. A hurried life is tired and unable to trust or give back. Start by slowing down and calendaring time with Christ. Be with Him so you can hear Him, get to know Him, and be changed by Him. Then the depth your character will grow the breadth of your influence—for His glory!

"For you are great and do marvelous deeds; you alone are God. Teach me your way, LORD, that I may rely on your faithfulness; give me an undivided heart, that I may fear your name" (Psalm 86:10–11).

How am I growing in my knowledge of God? How is He transforming my character and broadening my influence for Him?

Related Readings: 1 Chronicles 16:24; Isaiah 45:24; Isaiah 54:11; Matthew 21:42; John 5:29

HEART KNOWLEDGE

"If you declare with your mouth, 'Jesus is Lord,' and believe in your heart that God raised him from the dead, you will be saved. For it is with your heart that you believe and are justified, and it is with your mouth that you profess your faith and are saved." Romans 10:9–10

There is a very important distinction between heart knowledge and head knowledge. A person may know facts about God in his head without applying it to his heart by faith. A man or woman can hear all the right things, say the right things, attend church, and still be eighteen inches away from heaven—the distance between the head and the heart.

We can play church, masquerade our true hearts to others, and even fool ourselves, but God cannot be fooled. We can volunteer in ministry, give money, and receive accolades from genuine Christians, but has our heart truly been transformed by the grace of God? Evidence of conversion is a public declaration of Jesus as Lord and an internal confession that God raised Him from the dead. A heart engaged with eternity is saved from sin.

"The Lord says: 'These people come near to me with their mouth and honor me with their lips, but their hearts are far from me. Their worship of me is based on merely human rules they have been taught'" (Isaiah 29:13).

Where are you on the continuum of your commitment to Christ? Are you still seeking? Have you crossed over the line of belief by bowing in humble submission to your Savior and Lord Jesus? Be honest with yourself and God if you have not given your heart to heaven. Pray for the Lord to help your unbelief, and be bold to request prayer from others.

What life event will it take to lead you to authentic faith and repentance? Will it take marriage, the birth of a child, the loss of a child, the loss of a parent, health issues, or financial brokenness? When we are on our backs, our hearts look to heaven for help. When we drop to our knees in humble prayer, we see the Lord lifted up, and we invite His warm embrace.

Do not fight the hang-ups in your head—instead, surrender your heart to Jesus. The enemy will always find an excuse for your mind to excuse eternal life in heaven. Do not dismiss childlike faith in Jesus, for this is the entrance into His kingdom. We are first born again with an infant faith; then we mature by grace and the meat of God's Word. Have you made this initial move of heartfelt faith? Take this first step of trust, and start your walk with Jesus.

"But I trust in your unfailing love; my heart rejoices in your salvation" (Psalm 13:5).

What obstacle to faith do I need to lay at the feet of Jesus, trusting Him?

Related Readings: Job 33:3; Psalm 21:2; Mark 7:6; John 3:3; 2 Timothy 1:9

QUALITY LIVING

"Walk with the wise and become wise, for a companion of fools suffers harm."
Proverbs 13:20

What does quality living mean? Does it mean good health, harmony at home, a happy heart, financial security, freedom of speech and worship, a fulfilling career, grateful and content children, a meaningful marriage, a life of significance, or peace with God? In all probability, some of these elements and more make up a life worth living or quality living.

Moreover, quality living is determined by the quality of our relationships. We become like those with whom we spend time. If we spend time with those wise in their finances, and if we pay attention, we can become wise in our finances. If we are intentional in our faith, we will worship with those of great faith. Our life is a reflection of our relationships.

"Therefore I urge you to imitate me. For this reason I have sent to you Timothy, my son whom I love, who is faithful in the Lord. He will remind you of my way of life in Christ Jesus, which agrees with what I teach everywhere in every church" (1 Corinthians 4:16–17).

So how is your relational portfolio? Are you diversified with people who bring value to all aspects of your life? Conversely, are you intentionally investing time and interest in those who look to you for guidance? Quality living flows, not from just receiving wisdom, but from giving wisdom. Wisdom works in both directions for the good of the relationship.

Furthermore, be careful not to excuse bad behavior because you are trying to relate to questionable company. Draw a line far away from eroding your character's creditability. You can influence others for good without being bad. In some situations, what you do not do defines you more than what you do. Use business trips and vacations to model faithfulness, not foolishness. Stand for what is right when others agree to what is wrong.

"Do not be misled: 'Bad company corrupts good character'" (1 Corinthians 15:33).

Above all, quality living results from your relationship with Christ. He is life itself, and everything good in life flows from Him. When you grow in your personal relationship with Jesus, it affects the growth of your other relationships. Relationship building in heaven builds relationships on earth. Ultimately, Jesus is the life to model and follow. The resurrected life of Christ gives you the spiritual stamina to experience a quality life.

"Jesus said to her, 'I am the resurrection and the life. The one who believes in me will live, even though they die; and whoever lives by believing in me will never die. Do you believe this?' 'Yes, Lord,' she replied, 'I believe'" (John 11:25–27).

Who are the wise people with whom I spend time? Am I investing in quality relationships?

Related Readings: Psalm 56:13; 2 Corinthians 6:14; Philippians 2:1–4; 1 John 1:7

ALIVE AND WELL

"Later Jesus appeared to the Eleven as they were eating; he rebuked them for their lack of faith and their stubborn refusal to believe those who had seen him after he had risen." Mark 16:14

Jesus Christ is alive and well. His earlier followers, taken aback by His death, initially denied His resurrection. They rejected reliable testimonies and refused to receive the truth of Christ rising from the dead. However, when they encountered the risen Lord, He rebuked them and then loved them. Unbelievers can loathe the Lord. Deists can deny Christ's deity. Agnostics can be apathetic over His resurrection, but He is alive and well.

Contemporary Christless cultures could care less about Christ's resurrection, but it does not lessen His lordship over them. Everyone will one day confront Christ. "At the name of Jesus every knee should bow, in heaven and on earth and under the earth, and every tongue confess that Jesus Christ is Lord" (Philippians 2:10–11). Easter is an excuse for Jesus followers to celebrate His resurrection and His relevance.

The Lord is alive and well in your heart. His resurrection resulted in Christ taking residence in your soul and transforming your life. By faith you believed, and God gave you grace upon grace. Because He has risen from the grave, He has given all who confess Him as Lord abundant grace on earth and the promise of heaven with Him.

"For if, by the trespass of the one man, death reigned through that one man, how much more will those who receive God's abundant provision of grace and of the gift of righteousness reign in life through the one man, Jesus Christ" (Romans 5:17). He is all you need.

Lastly, you can live large for the Lord because He has triumphed over sin, sorrow, death, and hell. Easter is your eternal encouragement that He is alive and well. There will always be doubters, but do not dwell there. Focus on the undeniable force of faith that has captured you and millions before you. Because He has risen, you can rise above your circumstances, your hurt, and your fears.

"With great power the apostles continued to testify to the resurrection of the Lord Jesus, and much grace was upon them all" (Acts 4:33).

Am I a disciple who ignores His power or one who proclaims His power?

Related Readings: Numbers 14:11; Matthew 28:17; Acts 10:41; 1 Corinthians 15:1-58

HE IS ALIVE

"'Why do you look for the living among the dead? He is not here; he has risen! Remember how he told you, while he was still with you in Galilee: "The Son of Man must be delivered into the hands of sinful men, be crucified and on the third day be raised again"' Then they remembered his words." Luke 24:5–8

He is alive and I am forgiven and my soul has been set free. He is alive and I am forgiven and my joy I cannot contain. He is alive and I am forgiven and my faith is here to stay. He is alive and I am forgiven and my love flows deep and wide. He is alive and I am forgiven because He did what He promised—He arose after three days. He is alive! He is alive! He is alive!

What emotions did the friends and disciples of Jesus feel when they realized He was real? Certainly they were surprised by the joy of knowing Jesus was back, even larger than in life. Even though they had watched Him raise Lazarus after four days of death, their faith had forgotten. But now they were glad again because God raised His Son to life.

If you look for Jesus among the dead you will not find Him. He has left the cold cemetery and risen to be with the warm love of His Father. Dead churches cannot claim the calming presence of Christ because they have forsaken the faith required to recognize Him. Look for the Lord among the living, those who live out their faith with bold grace.

Remember the words of Jesus, and your faith will resound with reassurance. "I am the Living One; I was dead, and behold I am alive for ever and ever! And I hold the keys of death and Hades" (Revelation 1:18). You serve a risen Savior who lives in your life by faith. Take Him at His Word, and joy will fill your innermost being as you celebrate His appearance almost two thousand years ago. Enjoy Jesus, anticipating your Lord's second return.

"So Christ was sacrificed once to take away the sins of many people; and he will appear a second time, not to bear sin, but to bring salvation to those who are waiting for him" (Hebrews 9:28).

How can I reassure my faith with the reality of a risen Savior? Where are the places I can find Christ among the living? What words of Jesus do I need to constantly remember?

Related Readings: Matthew 24:30; Acts 1:3; 1 Thessalonians 4:17; 1 Peter 3:18

FRUITFUL FAITH

"Still other seed fell on good soil, where it produced a crop—
a hundred, sixty or thirty times what was sown." Matthew 13:8

How do I know my faith is fruitful? Am I producing fruit that is pleasing to my heavenly Father? I ask these questions often, as fruit is a reflection of a vibrant faith. So what is this fresh fruit of faith, and where does it germinate? It begins with the seed of God's Word being planted in the good soil of a teachable heart. So I ask myself, "Am I regularly receiving the Lord's truth and allowing it to deeply root in my soul?"

Our faith is like a field in constant need of clearing, plowing, planting, weeding, watering, and fertilizing. Our heavenly Father is the faithful farmer who is always ready to work the soil of our hearts with His loving care. So we are wise when we invite Him to break up the hardened areas of our hearts, to pull out the thorns of worry, and to remove the rocks of unbelief. Our Savior's seeds of truth transform fallow faith into faith of fruitful abundance.

"Sow for yourselves righteousness; Reap in mercy; Break up your fallow ground, For it is time to seek the LORD, Till He comes and rains righteousness on you" (Hosea 10:12 NKJV). Fruitful faith grows out of the ground where God has rained down righteousness. How is the soil of your heart? Is it good and soft, full of the needed nutrients of honesty and humility? Have you replaced the old dirt from your past with the new ground of gratitude to God? If seeds of truth remain on the surface of your heart, they may very well be snatched away by demonic distractions. Thus, daily invite God's Word to sink down deep into your soul, so the roots of righteousness are not threatened but blossom in belief.

"No discipline seems pleasant at the time, but painful. Later on, however, it produces a harvest of righteousness and peace for those who have been trained by it" (Hebrews 12:11). The regular discipline of watering with God's Word produces the fruit of faith.

Therefore, look to the Lord of the harvest in faith and perseverance. The fruit of character does not come overnight. There are no shortcuts in your Savior's ecosystem; so stay true to His process of prayer, study, and service that over time grows you into your Lord's likeness. Like a diligent farmer, see your soul sweat from spiritual discipline. Your heavenly Father is the gardener over the grounds of your life. His harvest is huge.

"Now he who supplies seed to the sower and bread for food will also supply and increase your store of seed and will enlarge the harvest of your righteousness" (2 Corinthians 9:10).

How can I cultivate my heart to be fertile with faith? Am I submitted to God as the gardener over the grounds of my life?

Related Readings: Jeremiah 4:3; Galatians 6:9; 2 Timothy 2:6; James 5:7

CARELESS WORDS

"But I tell you that men will have to give account on the day of judgment for every careless word they have spoken. For by your words you will be acquitted, and by your words you will be condemned." Matthew 12:36–37

My words are a reflection of my heart. When Christ captures my heart, my words are measured and meaningful. A heart pregnant with the Lord's purposes produces good fruit for its recipients. When my heart avoids the Almighty's instruction, my words become careless. They wound and bring harm to hearers who receive my insensitivity.

We communicate better when we understand the gravity of undisciplined speech. There is an accountability from God that one day gauges what we have said. No idle word will miss the microscope of our Master's judgment. "If anyone considers himself religious and yet does not keep a tight rein on his tongue, he deceives himself and his religion is worthless" (James 1:26). The Holy Spirit bridles our tongues with words of great worth.

So does your speech represent your Savior well? Do your words incubate in a heart of intimacy with God and accountability with man? Like a thoughtful and creative artist, use your words to paint a picture that provides understanding and instruction. Prepare your heart in prayer before you speak in a meeting or prior to a performance review. At home resolve to be respectful in all matters of conversation, and others will reciprocate.

Careless words are best corralled by Christ's calming presence. When He seasons our speech with grace, there is a gravitas that gains the attention of the most unsuspecting souls. It is when the Lord speaks through us that we experience the best communication. Indeed, a humble heart full of Christ's courage carries the right words at the right time. Speak with bold clarity, and trust God with the results. Convert careless words to kind ones.

"Let your speech always be with grace, seasoned with salt, that you may know how you ought to answer each one" (Colossians 4:6 NKJV).

Are my words measured in prayer? Do I speak with accountability to God in mind?

Related Readings: Psalm 139:4; Proverbs 18:21; Job 15:3; Ephesians 5:4

WORSHIP WHEN WORRIED

"Shout for joy to the LORD, all the earth. Worship the LORD with gladness; come before him with joyful songs. Know that the LORD is God. It is he who made us, and we are his; we are his people, the sheep of his pasture." Psalm 100:1-3

I cannot worship and worry at the same time. When Christ is my focus, they do not coexist, because worship pushes worry into its own wilderness. In my personal and corporate worship, almighty God becomes bigger than life. His holiness heals my heart, His beauty soothes my soul, His majesty humbles my pride, and His glory gets my full attention. Worship recalibrates my thinking to trust and my emotions to the eternal.

Our worship is meant to move us toward our Master in a manner that transforms our weak faith to a bold proclamation of His faithfulness. Music is a facilitator for our heart to lift itself out of the worries of this world to the calming presence of Christ. As Christ followers we are privileged to approach Him anytime in authentic adoration and praise. We shout with thanksgiving or quietly whisper words of gratitude to our King.

"Shout for joy to the LORD, all the earth, burst into jubilant song with music; make music to the LORD with the harp, with the harp and the sound of singing, with trumpets and the blast of the ram's horn—shout for joy before the LORD, the King" (Psalm 98:4–6).

How is your daily and weekly worship? Is it rote or radical? Is it fresh or perfunctory? Worship is a way to wrap your mind around what matters. The cares and competition of this world become strangely dim, as heaven comes into full focus in all its splendor. Like a giddy scientist peering through his Hubble telescope, your worship gives you glimpses into His glory. Your eyes of faith fall on the compassionate face of Christ.

Genuine worship focuses on your heavenly Father, but it changes you. You walk away wondering why you ever worried in the first place. You exit your place of worship having left the residue of your sin behind, because you came clean in confession and repentance. Sin cannot bow at the footstool of Holy God without melting away in fear.

Worship and worry no more, for this is your opportunity to engage God. Worship matters, because the Lord matters. Worship freely, and watch Him free you from worry. Like the sun cutting into a fog-covered bridge, He burns away your mind's clouded cares. Worship works, because worry cannot coexist in the presence of our King Jesus Christ.

"Therefore, since we are receiving a kingdom that cannot be shaken, let us be thankful, and so worship God acceptably with reverence and awe, for our 'God is a consuming fire'" (Hebrews 12:28–29).

Do I regularly replace my worry with worship? Do I authentically worship almighty God?

Related Readings: Nehemiah 9:3; Daniel 3:28; Matthew 28:17; Revelation 22:8-9

A15

FAMILY OF FAITH

*"For whoever does the will of my Father in heaven is my brother
and sister and mother." Matthew 12:50*

Sometimes I forget to thank the Lord for my brothers and sisters in Christ who are like family. They are there to check on me, pray for me, encourage me, and hold me accountable. Blood is thicker than water, but the bond around the blood of Christ can be even thicker. My family in the faith is a gift from God, not to be taken for granted.

Are you engaged with a community of Christ followers? Some of your family members may have forsaken you for your faith, but Jesus can more than compensate with those who love Him and His children. You have a family of faith that longs to love you. Have you initiated relationships at church or a Bible study? Look around you to love and be loved.

"They broke bread in their homes and ate together with glad and sincere hearts, praising God and enjoying the favor of all the people. And the Lord added to their number daily those who were being saved" (Acts 2:46-47).

Be with those who want to do the will of their heavenly Father, and you will want to do the will of your heavenly Father. The family of faith is contagious in its commitment to Christ. But how do you respond to relatives who want to pull you away from the presence of Jesus? How do you stay true to the Lord when there is tension over your trust in Him?

You cannot ignore them, even when they are unruly, because God has family in your life to be a reflection of Him. Your behavior may be the only Bible they read, and your words may be the only Jesus they hear. You know better, so you forgive and extend grace, while unbelieving family members do not know any better than to be harsh and hold grudges.

Lean into your family of faith so you in turn can lovingly serve your family outside the faith. Moreover, look for believers in your life who need family, and invite them into yours. We need each other, for the body of Christ is connected and sensitive to one another's needs. When you have Jesus as a friend, you have a family in the faith.

Paul said, "To Titus, my true son in our common faith: Grace and peace from God the Father and Christ Jesus our Savior" (Titus 1:4).

Whom do I count as family in the faith? How can I bless them? Who needs me to be - family for them?

Related Readings: Ruth 3:13; Matthew 19:29; Luke 2:49; 1 Timothy 5:8

GOOD GOVERNMENT

"Everyone must submit himself to the governing authorities, for there is no authority except
that which God has established. The authorities that exist have been established by God."
Romans 13:1

Good governments recognize almighty God as the ultimate authority. He is the One who establishes governments and gives them the power to preside over the people. Good governments are "of the people, by the people, for the people." When governments fail to serve the people on behalf of God, they ultimately fail. Wisdom is separation of church and state, but not separation of the church from the state.

A good government "of the people" is populated by good people. Its officials instruct and lead with integrity of heart and humility of mind. Moses modeled this when he chose leaders of character to help him manage the masses. "But select capable men from all the people—men who fear God, trustworthy men who hate dishonest gain—and appoint them as officials over thousands, hundreds, fifties and tens" (Exodus 18:21). It is integrity that infuses a country with common sense commands and laws based on the Lord.

A good government "by the people" means we are responsible to participate in the electoral process and pray for our elected officials. "I urge, then, first of all, that requests, prayers, intercession and thanksgiving be made for everyone—for kings and all those in authority, that we may live peaceful and quiet lives in all godliness and holiness. This is good, and pleases God our Savior" (1 Timothy 2:1–3). Our prayer for politicians pleases Jesus; so plead often on their behalf for wisdom and courage to do the right things.

Lastly, a good government "for the people" means the people are the recipients of its benefits. Good citizens pay taxes as Jesus commanded (see Luke 20:25), but good governments are faithful fiduciaries with the funds. They are wise overseers of free enterprise; so those who maliciously manipulate the markets are punished for their punitive acts. Creditable capitalism is based on character. A nation under God is a good government "of the people, by the people, for the people."

Am I a good citizen who contributes to good government?

Related Readings: Deuteronomy 17:15; Proverbs 8:15; John 19:11; 1 Peter 2:17

BLESSED TO UNDERSTAND

"But blessed are your eyes because they see, and your ears because they hear."
Matthew 13:16

Christ enters the life of a Christian at conversion. A divine exchange takes place that provides discernment and direction for the disciple. Because Jesus lives in me, I am able to learn and apply His ways. His Holy Spirit shows me His will through the eyes of my soul. Indeed, I hear His loving voice as I listen intently for His truth to me.

"My sheep listen to my voice; I know them, and they follow me" (John 10:27).

As a child of God, how do we know if the voice we hear is the voice of God? This is a fair question that brings us back to faith in the Lord to lead us in His path. As we grow in our understanding of Him, we better understand what He says in His Word. Like a child who trusts a parent who is consistent in character, so we freely follow what He says. Our Savior is selective and sensitive in what He says to us, but He expects us to follow Him.

What is Jesus seeking to show you or trying to tell you? You will be blessed with understanding by taking the time to know Him and His ways. Confusion comes from complex circumstances, but when you slow down and take a step back, clarity comes back. The Almighty gets your attention, allowing your head and heart to focus on Him.

Look around and see the Lord's order in His handiwork, like the structure of seasons and the cycle of life and death. His words are painted on the canvas of His creation for you to read with awe and appreciation. But you have to look and listen to understand. His sunshine says: I will warm you with My love. His rain says: I will refresh your thirsty soul. His wind says: I will cool your tired body. His moon shines hope onto our darkest days. You are blessed to understand when you seek to understand. So look, listen, and learn.

"For since the creation of the world God's invisible qualities—his eternal power and divine nature—have been clearly seen, being understood from what has been made, so that men are without excuse" (Romans 1:20).

What is the Lord trying to show me and tell me? Am I looking and listening by faith?

Related Readings: Isaiah 32:3; Proverbs 20:12; John 14:22

PHANTOM FEAR

"At dusk they got up and went to the camp of the Arameans.
When they reached the edge of the camp, not a man was there." 2 Kings 7:5

It is easy to build a case in our minds regarding why we need to be afraid of a situation or a person. But God is bigger than our fears. He does not want us to be fear driven. This is not healthy for us or those around us. We can replace fear with faith and recognize that He is at work. Sometimes what we create in our minds are just caricatures of fear.

Is the object of your fear real? Perhaps what was a legitimate fear in the past is no longer something to be feared. Yes, it was very real before, but today it is gone. There is no need to fret or lose sleep over the matter. It is a dead issue. It may have related to finances. Fear gripped your heart as you worried about having enough. But God has provided in ways you never dreamed. You are more than taken care of by Him.

Do not let money dupe you into embracing the false fear of needing just a little bit more. You can rest in God and trust Him with your finances. Or your struggle may be related to a harmful relationship from the past. You fear reprisal toward you and your children. He has threatened you in the past, and you know his capabilities.

However, time has passed, and he has really changed. There is no need to fear. God has sincerely changed his heart. A bold move on your part would be to reach out to him. His health may be failing, and he is more teachable than you have ever seen him. Forgive him and show him the love of Christ. Turn your fear into forgiveness.

What you see are remnants of fear, but they are not real. Do not be deceived. The phantom fears that haunt you can be exposed. Shed the light of God's Word and Christ's confidence on them, and they quickly evaporate. Pull back the curtain of fear, and it is gone.

We tend to fill in the unknown with fear and negativity. But you can choose by faith to fill in the unknown with peace and trust in God. Most circumstances are out of your control, but nothing sneaks up on God. He has it under control. The storm may be raging around you; however, focus on the captain of the ship—Jesus—rather than the hostile waves slapping against the sides of the boat. Dismiss fear and embrace Christ's comfort.

"Even though I walk through the valley of the shadow of death, I will fear no evil, for you are with me; your rod and your staff, they comfort me" (Psalm 23:4).

How can I recognize and dismiss false fears? Whom do I need to forgive and not fear?

Related Readings: Exodus 20:20; Job 39:22; John 12:42; Romans 8:15

ILLNESS IS PAINFUL

"Now Elisha was suffering from the illness from which he died.
Jehoash king of Israel went down to see him and wept over him." 2 Kings 13:14

Illness is painful to those who are sick and to the ones who love them. It is painful to experience and painful to watch. Illness does not discriminate. It afflicts the spiritual and the unspiritual, rich and poor, young and old. Sickness is a result of living in a sin-cursed world and occupying an environment that has been infiltrated by decay.

Some diseases can be treated with medicine, but others cannot. Medication may slow down the effects of illness, but some ailments cannot be stopped. They are terminal. You may be living on borrowed time. This is hard. I struggle with a young man in his prime with small children; he becomes stricken with a fatal illness. This does not seem right or even close to fair. Where is God? What is God up to? We are all terminal. We all will experience death. But why do some die much sooner than others?

I have to remember that this world is not our home. God has us here on temporary assignment. We are on earth to glorify our heavenly Father by doing His will. His will is clear. His passion is to make disciples. However, while we are in the process of making disciples, there is an enemy to contend with, and one of the enemy's weapons is illness.

His strategy is to sideline you from God's mission by using crippling, and even terminal, illness as a deterrent and a distraction. But God has a different plan. Because of, not in spite of your illness, God is drawing you and others closer to Christ. You are privileged to glory in the sufferings of Christ. "Now if we are children, then we are heirs—heirs of God and co-heirs with Christ, if indeed we share in his sufferings in order that we may also share in his glory" (Romans 8:17).

Your great faith in God in the middle of adversity is compelling. Your Savior's serenity challenges others to look again at this Jesus who is your rock and refuge in the middle of physical imperfection. The elevation of your faith lifts the faith of all those around you. God is drawing you and all those around you to Himself.

Dying can be a more powerful witness than living. Therefore, cling to Christ, love Him, and praise Him. He is the great physician who will give you the ultimate healing in His time. In the meantime, before you go home, invite as many people as possible to join you. They will listen because you have something they both need and want—peace with God and the peace of God. Illness is painful; however, it is not wasted pain but one of eternal purpose.

"I consider that our present sufferings are not worth comparing with the glory that will be revealed in us" (Romans 8:18).

Whom can I encourage who is entangled by illness? How can I use illness for His glory?

Related Readings: Ephesians 3:13; Philippians 3:10; Hebrews 2:10; 1 Peter 4:13

CAPACITY BUILDING

"To one he gave five talents of money, to another two talents,
and to another one talent, each according to his ability." Matthew 25:15

Capacity is the ability Christ gives me to carry out His commands. And capacity varies from person to person. Some people can get by on five to six hours of sleep while I require seven to eight. Where I get out of balance is when I compare my capacity with someone of greater capacity. Indeed, capacity is meant to provide guardrails, not guilt.

So how can we use capacity to our advantage instead of our disadvantage? How can we understand our limitations and trust the Lord with the results? It starts by being honest about how God has made us. If we can only execute one project with excellence, then we limit ourselves to one. If we only have the time, money, and love for two children, then we accept this as the responsible decision. Honesty about capacity is freeing for parents.

But isn't there a way to build capacity at work, at home, and in relationships? Yes, indeed! As you remain faithful with small responsibilities, the Lord and others can trust you with additional tasks. When you manage a small amount of money on a budget, you can be trusted with more resources to steward well. When you treat one individual with a full complement of grace and truth, you build relational capacity for more quality friendships.

Furthermore, you are over capacity when cash in your bank account is overdrawn or when you have written a relational check your emotions cannot cash. Therefore, monitor your capacity in prayer before Jesus. Ask Him for courage to say no to something new so you can say yes to current obligations. As in weight lifting, you can increase your mental, emotional, financial, and relational capacity, but it takes time, focus, and discipline.

The Lord has unlimited capacity for empathy, wisdom, and character. So go to Him for your character-capacity building. Make sure your character capacity keeps up with your success, and you will be able to handle success. Does your heart have the same capacity for humility as your mind does for truth? So build capacity around Christ's gifts to you.

"We do not dare to classify or compare ourselves with some who commend themselves. When they measure themselves by themselves and compare themselves with themselves, they are not wise. We, however, will not boast beyond proper limits, but will confine our boasting to the field God has assigned to us, a field that reaches even to you" (2 Corinthians 10:12–13).

What capacities do I have that Christ wants to grow? To whom do I need to say no?

Related Readings: Job 15:18; Psalm 147:5; John 3:34; 1 Corinthians 10:23

NUMBER ONE INFLUENCER

"Therefore do not be foolish, but understand what the Lord's will is. Do not get drunk on wine, which leads to debauchery. Instead, be filled with the Spirit." Ephesians 5:17–18

Who is my number one influencer? Is it my wife? Is it a friend? Is it my mom, brother, or mentor? All of these are important and influential, but I desire the number one influencer in my life to be the Holy Spirit. He is the one whose advice is always full of integrity. When I am Spirit led, I can be confident of an outcome that mirrors God's will.

It is easy to be influenced by a culture whose standards are below what is best. For example, the world may whine and say it is old-fashioned to have boundaries with the opposite sex. But, as believers in Jesus, we know it is wise to keep emotional distance from someone who is not our spouse. Spirit-led living does not linger long around unwise activities.

Who is your number one influencer? Perhaps it is a coach, colleague, or counselor who gives you good advice. All of these have their place, but never allow an individual to replace the Holy Spirit as your most important influencer. Sometimes a friend will suggest one thing and God's Spirit another. Go with God! His promptings are meant to triumph any attractive offer that may tease your emotions. Trust the Spirit's leading.

"Those who live according to the sinful nature have their minds set on what that nature desires; but those who live in accordance with the Spirit have their minds set on what the Spirit desires" (Romans 8:5).

It may be hard for you to follow the influence of your heavenly Father because your earthly father may have abandoned his responsibilities. However, the Spirit of your Father in heaven is trustworthy and true. He never leaves you or forsakes you. His Holy Spirit is sensitive to exactly what you need, when you need it. He is reliable.

So, once you have confessed and repented of your sin, ask Him for the fullness of His Spirit to flood your soul. The Spirit of God flushes out the foolishness of the flesh and fills it with wisdom from the Lord. The Holy Spirit brings wholeness to your heart and truth to your head. Be intoxicated by the Spirit's influence, and you will walk wisely.

"You, however, are controlled not by the sinful nature but by the Spirit, if the Spirit of God lives in you. And if anyone does not have the Spirit of Christ, he does not belong to Christ" (Romans 8:9).

Do I submit daily to the Holy Spirit's control? How do I know when the Spirit leads me?

Related Readings: Galatians 5:25; 2 Timothy 1:14; James 4:4; 1 John 3:24

TWO-WAY COMMUNICATION

"I must speak and find relief; I must open my lips and reply."
Job 32:20

Two-way communication is critical for the health of organizations and relationships. If I am so busy that I do not take time to talk through expectations, then I set up all parties for frustration. For example, I may expect a project to be due at a certain date, but if I do not monitor the progress along the way, then the deadline may come and go unaccomplished. If, however, a system is in place for ongoing feedback, then everyone is clear on where we are and where we need to go. Two-way communication brings clarity.

What about our most important relationships? Do we take the time to interact so there is authentic understanding of each other's needs? If we are not careful, we can take for granted the very ones we care for the most and, in a moment of misunderstanding, become angry in our disappointment. Two-way communication takes time to talk.

Communication that goes both ways requires knowledge and comprehension. If you speak out of emotion before you gain insight into the situation, then you only prolong a productive exchange. Suffering in adversity, Job struggled with this. "Job speaks without knowledge; his words lack insight" (Job 34:35). Two-way communication is a product of two people listening, understanding, and taking responsibility for the next steps.

Perhaps a weekly progress report on a present project at work is necessary to keep all team members accountable and up-to-date. At home you could incorporate a daily walk together just to catch up and hear each other's hearts. Quality communication flows from quantity time to hear and to be heard. Slow down and make sure you speak up.

Most importantly, communication with Christ is your greatest opportunity to gain insight and understanding into His heart. If you are too busy to pray, you are too busy. The Bible is His love letter to you. As you read Scripture, do you fill in your name as you read its admonishments? Two-way communication with Him means you desire to learn.

"Listen, my son, and be wise, and keep your heart on the right path" (Proverbs 23:19).

Do I honor others with constructive conversation? Do I listen intently to the Lord?

Related Readings: Psalm 15:1–3; Proverbs 8:6–7; Ephesians 4:25; Jude 1:10

DEATH WITH DIGNITY

"In those days Hezekiah became ill and was at the point of death. The prophet Isaiah son of Amoz went to him and said, 'This is what the LORD says: Put your house in order, because you are going to die; you will not recover.'" 2 Kings 20:1

Death is imminent, for some sooner than later. Have I put my house in order? He wants me to think through the needs of my family, the state of my soul, and how I can glorify God in the process. It is death with dignity. The process is not without hurt and pain, but it is thinking through the practical issues that affect my loved ones and me.

Death is a transition. It is the end of trusting the unseen and the beginning of resting in the seen. This is why Paul could say, "Where, O death is your victory? Where, O death is your sting? The sting of death is sin, and the power of sin is the law. But thanks be to God! He gives us the victory thorough our Lord Jesus Christ" (1 Corinthians 15:55–57).

Think about your relationships. Are you whole? Maybe you need to go to someone and ask his or her forgiveness, and/or you may need to forgive this person. Moreover, love your spouse and children by allowing God's Word to flow through you to them. Let them see your faith in action so their faith becomes galvanized and grounded in Christ. Allow them to love you as you love them back—freely and passionately. Love like the Lord—always.

Talk with those who care for you about your funeral. What Scripture do you want read? What praise songs and hymns do you want sung? Death is a celebration of life on earth and graduation to life eternal. Plan your funeral celebration as you graduate to glory. Prepare to die, and you are prepared to live. Use death as an excuse to point people to Jesus.

Most importantly, make right your relationship with God. Have you made peace with God? The foundation of your final preparation is your relationship with your heavenly Father. Let Him love and comfort you with His presence in your final preparation. Put your house in order with your finances, family, friends, and faith. Die with dignity. "Therefore, since we have been justified through faith, we have peace with God through our Lord Jesus Christ, through whom we have gained access by faith into this grace in which we now stand. And we rejoice in the hope of the glory of God" (Romans 5:1–2).

Is my house in order? What preparations do I need to make before I go to heaven?

Related Readings: Genesis 27:1–3; 2 Samuel 1:23; John 21:19; Romans 8:37–39

LACKING ONE THING

"Looking at him, Jesus felt a love for him and said to him, 'One thing you lack:
go and sell all you possess and give to the poor, and you will have treasure in heaven; and come,
follow Me.'" Mark 10:21

What one thing have I lacked letting loose of for the Lord? Is it my heart? Is it a house? Is it an automobile? Is it an attitude of pride in my good works? Is there a hidden sin of fraud that I have not faced up to? Or, do I justify my one holdout with the ninety-five percent I have surrendered? Idols have a way of subtly suffocating my unconditional surrender to my Savior Jesus.

Yet He loves us, even when we dismiss Him in disobedience or ignore His invitation to intimacy. Because He cares for His children, He raises His expectations for us to exceed what the world does. He looks at our inconsistencies and lovingly exposes our hypocrisies. Jesus knows it takes extreme measures to root out idols that have so deceived us we do not recognize their control. Like an addict who denies addiction, we act like things are all right when, in fact, we lack giving up the one thing that hurts Him.

Are you able to follow Him wholeheartedly, or is there a portion of your heart that has yet to feel the freedom of surrender? Has a child or a career garnered more of your attention than Christ and the poor? Once you surrender one hundred percent, Jesus has you in a position to receive His blessing. What you give over to Jesus qualifies to be given back by Jesus.

What you give up, He makes up exponentially. Like the fish and loaves (see Mark 8:4–9) that were given up on behalf of the masses, He multiplied their provision with providential care. Therefore, surrender your soul, your relationships, your opportunities, your finances, your job, your children, your thought life, your health, and your trust. Surrender to Jesus leads to sweet success in your Savior's eyes. Make your one thing His thing.

"Give to the one who asks you, and do not turn away from the one who wants to borrow from you" (Matthew 5:42). What is the one thing I lack giving up for the Lord?

How will my surrender bless others?

Related Readings: Genesis 42:34; 1 Samuel 1:27–28; Matthew 16:26; Acts 3:6

TRAINED AND MENTORED

"Then Paul said: 'I am a Jew, born in Tarsus of Cilicia, but brought up in this city.
Under Gamaliel I was thoroughly trained in the law of our fathers
and was just as zealous for God as any of you are today.'" Acts 22:2–3

What does it mean to be trained and mentored in the ways of Jesus? Over the years men and women invested in me by being my mentor. In one case it was a businessman who met me before sunrise. We steeped in the Scripture, and like the effects of a potent tea bag, Christ colored my heart. We prayed on our knees before the start of the day and stood up to walk with our Savior throughout the day. My mentor made time for me.

How can we be mentored or how can we train and mentor others? It may be a role model from a distance; however, virtual mentors have their limitations. We only see them at their best and rarely learn how to handle struggles and disappointments. Some others have influenced us through their writings and inspired us by their insightful biographies.

Do you have a seasoned saint up close and personal, one who can pray with you, instruct you, challenge you, encourage you, and give you wisdom for wise decision making? "My son, pay attention to my wisdom, listen well to my words of insight, that you may maintain discretion and your lips may preserve knowledge" (Proverbs 5:1–2).

Moreover, mentors alert you to sin crouching at the door of your heart and mind. Perhaps they nearly lost their marriage to avoidance of responsibility and being lured away by adultery's illusion. They can instruct you in what to do and what not to do. Paul, Moses, and David's horrific mistake of murder did not disqualify them from mentoring and training others out of their repentant hearts. Brokenness is required to mentor well.

However, it is not enough for us to just enjoy the benefits of mentoring without seeking out men and women to mentor. Jesus told His mentees, "The harvest is plentiful, but the workers are few. Ask the Lord of the harvest, therefore, to send out workers into his harvest field" (Luke 10:2). Then these reluctant and unproven disciples of Christ were empowered by the Holy Spirit to become workers for God. Pray to the Lord for a mentor, and He will lead and equip you to be an answered prayer.

"And the [instructions] which you have heard from me along with many witnesses, transmit and entrust [as a deposit] to reliable and faithful men who will be competent and qualified to teach others also" (2 Timothy 2:2 AMPLIFIED).

What profile of mentor makes sense for this season of my life? Whom can I mentor?

Related Readings: Exodus 18:1–27; Judges 4:4–28; 2 Kings 2:1–15; Acts 9:26–30

A GODLY LEGACY

"When Jacob had finished giving instructions to his sons, he drew his feet
up into the bed, breathed his last and was gathered to his people." Genesis 49:33

Jacob gave his dying instructions to his sons as they waited at his bedside. They lingered there out of love and respect. They had observed his life, not perfect by far, but overall a faithful life to God. The sons of the father wanted to receive his blessing, and they were proud of the legacy left to them, a legacy of faithfulness to God.

What legacy will you leave? If you died today, how would you be remembered? These are important questions for your children. Maybe your parents did not leave you a godly heritage; nevertheless, you have a wonderful opportunity to start a new tradition, one based on the principles of Scripture. Lord willing, your legacy will start a godly lineage that will reach across the future for generations to come. Yes, your name will probably be forgotten, but what you stand for will be held in high esteem for all to remember.

Perhaps you start by documenting your family vision and mission. Write down the outcomes you are praying for related to your family. Pray your parental example of character compels your children to walk with Christ. For example, hold the Bible with such high regard that its commands and principles are lived out in love and obedience.

Furthermore, love your children with acceptance, discipline, training, and kindness. Follow the ways of God, and your children will see and secure a clear path of purpose to pursue. Moreover, consider a family credo that defines what you value as a family. Character traits like humility, hard work, community, forgiveness, communication, and relationship can be woven throughout the language and behavior of your family. Challenge each child to be intoxicated by Scripture to the degree that God's Word is on their breath and behavior. Slow down and be intentional in legacy building; then your children and your children's children are more apt to love Christ. A godly legacy learns to love well.

"But from everlasting to everlasting the LORD's love is with those who fear him, and his righteousness with their children's children" (Psalm 103:17).

Do I live life with my legacy in mind, and do I bless each child uniquely and fully?

Related Readings: Daniel 10:19; Joshua 24:27–29; Luke 2:29; Hebrews 11:13–22

WORLDLY WISDOM

"Now this is our boast: Our conscience testifies that we have conducted ourselves in the world, and especially in our relations with you, with integrity and godly sincerity. We have done so, relying not on worldly wisdom but on God's grace." 2 Corinthians 1:12

Worldly wisdom has a way of reducing heaven's wisdom to an afterthought. Using our worldly wisdom, we pray and seek to discern the Lord's ways, only after our ways do not work. It is tempting to rely on what seems to work instead of asking what the principles to live by are, based on God's economy. Worldly wisdom is not only inferior but also competes with God's grace.

The Lord sees the world's wisdom as foolishness, and the world sees His wisdom as foolishness. Some who embrace the wisdom of the world say there is no personal God, but God says in His wisdom this thinking flows from a fool. "The fool says in his heart, 'There is no God'" (Psalm 14:1). Sadly, the world's wisdom has no room for Jesus.

"For since in the wisdom of God the world through its wisdom did not know him, God was pleased through the foolishness of what was preached to save those who believe" (1 Corinthians 1:21).

Worldly wisdom is flashier and sexier in its appeal. It invites pride to perch over those who have not yet achieved a superior standpoint. Ironically, the created dismisses the Creator as antiquated and out of touch. The traditional tenants of an all-knowing and ever-present Sovereign God are silly and irrational to this irreverent system of belief. But what worldly wisdom embraces as the truly enlightened, the Lord defines as educated fools.

"Where is the wise person? Where is the teacher of the law? Where is the philosopher of this age? Has not God made foolish the wisdom of the world?" (1 Corinthians 1:20).

Therefore, do not try to outsmart your Savior Jesus Christ with intelligence void of humility and the fear of God. Academics, without an infusion of faith in almighty God, lead down a reckless path of disconnection from Deity. However, wise is the man or woman who is full of the grace of God and studies truth long and hard for the glory of God.

Faith in Jesus Christ as the Son of God is not a leap into the dark; rather, it is a step into the light. Christian belief is based on the historical fact of His death on the cross and His resurrection from the dead. For some, the Lord's wisdom wins out over their own, and they begin to seek out those people and places that possess His knowledge. "I saw that wisdom is better than folly, just as light is better than darkness" (Ecclesiastes 2:13).

Am I embracing and believing the wisdom of the world or almighty God's wisdom?

Related Readings: Isaiah 29:14; Jeremiah 8:9; James 3:13–18

TRUTH APPLIED

"Do not merely listen to the word, and so deceive yourselves. Do what it says."
James 1:22

Truth applied makes us fully alive. Indeed, most people know enough truth to live a worthwhile life. They know to be honest and not lie. They know to be content and not covet another person's house, car, or spouse. They know to be patient and wait on the Lord to do a work of grace in a loved-one's life. They know to take responsibility and not blame someone else. They know to believe Jesus and trust Him with their life.

If we know the truth, why do we sometimes struggle with its application? Perhaps we are self-deceived to think the truth of Scripture is needed for someone else but not for us. Truth is right and good—just not right and good for me to practice, or worse, to think I am living it out when I am not. Feeling good or bad or being educated does not transform behavior. What alters our actions is an inward change expressed in outward obedience.

"If my people, who are called by my name, will humble themselves and pray and seek my face and turn from their wicked ways, then I will hear from heaven, and I will forgive their sin and will heal their land" (2 Chronicles 7:14).

Truth is like a vaccination that, when administered, prevents you from being infected with foolish living. It is like a lifesaving serum when applied to sin's poisonous snakebite, potentially healing you from relational, emotional, physical, and spiritual death. There is no downside to honestly gazing into the mirror of truth and assessing your life. Better yet, invite godly friends to look with you; then by God's grace apply truth for change.

"Godly sorrow brings repentance that leads to salvation and leaves no regret, but worldly sorrow brings death" (2 Corinthians 7:10).

Is there a dark area of your life that needs exposure to the bright light of truth? Are there bad attitudes and habits you blame on past pain and injustice? If so, lean into the truth, and do not be satisfied until truth's application frees you from mediocre living. Truth applied does make you fully alive. It is a dependable friend who walks with you through wise decision making. Dismiss dishonest living and invite freedom from honest living. Ask the Lord to reveal truth to you and empower you to live out the truth.

"You heard about Christ and were taught in him in accordance with the truth that is in Jesus. You were taught, with regard to your former way of life, to put off your old self, which is being corrupted by its deceitful desires; to be made new in the attitude of your minds; and to put on the new self, created to be like God in true righteousness and holiness" (Ephesians 4:21–24).

What truth do I need to embrace and celebrate in the transformation of my life?

Related Readings: Isaiah 1:19; Proverbs 23:22; Acts 6:7; Romans 6:16

WORK STRUGGLES

"To Adam he said, 'Because you listened to your wife and ate fruit from the tree about which I commanded you, "You must not eat from it," Cursed is the ground because of you; through painful toil you will eat food from it all the days of your life.'" Genesis 3:17

Work many times is work. Painful toil is a consequence of what happened in the beginning—God cursed the ground because of Adam and Eve's disobedience. Labor became laborious. Instead of paradise in the sinless garden of Eden, there were blood, sweat, and tears mingled with sin. Work is not meant to be ease, but intense effort.

"So the LORD God banished him from the Garden of Eden to work the ground from which he had been taken" (Genesis 3:23).

Is your work a struggle? Are you in one of the most stressful seasons of your career? If so, God does not waste pain. It is in your discomfort that He comforts and in your unease that He gives courage. If the Lord has your attention in an environment out of your control, stay true to what you can do, and leave the results with God. In stress seek Jesus. "So my heart began to despair over all my toilsome labor under the sun" (Ecclesiastes 2:20).

Furthermore, see work as worship to almighty God, a sacrifice of service you lay before Him for the Holy Spirit to ignite with power and effectiveness. Lift your heart and head in humility; present your hands and feet by faith—all for God's glory. Silently sing in sincere worship while you work. Worshipful music does for the ears what the Sistine Chapel does for the eyes. It is lovely to listen to for the glory of our Savior Jesus Christ.

Lastly, look at your work as a testament to excellence on behalf of Jesus. Your ministry is your work, and your work is your ministry. The days of the week, Monday through Saturday, are not secular days of service but a Christian's sacred obligation to model his or her faith with first-rate work. Perhaps you facilitate a Bible study at lunch or before or after hours. Your outstanding effort in the enterprise earns you the right to prayerfully and graciously share your faith.

So when job security is jittery and insecure, exhibit peace from God in the form of calm contentment and patient perseverance. Work struggles are the scenario in which others can see you act out what you say you believe. Perhaps your bold belief during adverse work conditions activates believers and leads unbelievers to begin their belief in Christ.

"Surely you remember, brothers and sisters, our toil and hardship; we worked night and day in order not to be a burden to anyone while we preached the gospel of God to you" (1 Thessalonians 2:9).

Do struggles at work lead me to worship my Savior Jesus and model excellent work?

Related Readings: Ecclesiastes 8:15; 2 Corinthians 11:26–31; Revelation 9:19–20

PEACEFUL PROTEST

"The king's heart is like channels of water in the hand of the LORD; He turns it wherever
He wishes. Every man's way is right in his own eyes, But the LORD weighs the hearts.
To do righteousness and justice Is desired by the LORD more than sacrifice."
Proverbs 21:1–3 NASB

There is a reaction associated with conflicting opinions—it can be a peaceful protest, or it can become a violent outburst. Mental illness can drive a man mad with murderous intent, but those of sound mind must not be driven by vicious rage. The most productive process in expressing disagreement initiates civil discourse and is redemptive in its motive.

For example, an unjust law denying a fellow countryman citizenship invites an honest debate from advocates who already enjoy this privilege. Furthermore, once established as a citizen in good standing, this person has the same equal rights of those who have enjoyed these advantages for generations. Good people stand up for those trampled underfoot.

"Our desire is not that others might be relieved while you are hard pressed, but that there might be equality. At the present time your plenty will supply what they need, so that in turn their plenty will supply what you need. The goal is equality" (2 Corinthians 8:13–14).

As followers of Jesus, we are wise to not take matters into our own hands but to leave them in the hands of our Lord. We appeal to a higher power—almighty God—to intervene in injustice. Like the king who gave Nehemiah everything he requested and more, so the Lord can direct the heart of authorities to change laws and resource righteous causes.

"The king said to me, 'What is it you want?' Then I prayed to the God of heaven, and I answered the king, 'If it pleases the king and if your servant has found favor in his sight, let him send me to the city in Judah where my ancestors are buried so that I can rebuild it'" (Nehemiah 2:4–5).

What just cause has Christ laid on your heart to facilitate a faith perspective? Many times people are just waiting for a voice of righteous reason to speak up for the unborn, the disabled, the deserted, the diseased, and those facing death. Quiet persistence pays off in a much wiser use of time than a brilliant flash in the pan that gives up after slim resistance. Productive prayer precedes a peaceful protest; so by grace stay humbly engaged in both.

"With this in mind, we constantly pray for you, that our God may make you worthy of his calling, and that by his power he may bring to fruition your every desire for goodness and your every deed prompted by faith" (2 Thessalonians 1:11).

Where is God leading me to peacefully protest as His prayer agent?

Related Readings: Isaiah 32:17; Psalm 35:20; Luke 6:29; 1 Timothy 2:2

RAISING TEENAGERS

*"Fathers, do not exasperate your children; instead, bring them up
in the training and instruction of the Lord." Ephesians 6:4*

It is hard not to be exasperated by a teenager, and it is hard not to exasperate a teenager. For those who think they know everything, it seems impossible to tell them anything. Yet God gives parents teenagers so they can learn laughter, wisdom, forgiveness, trust, and the grace of imposing guidelines. After all, the older teenagers become, the less a parent can control them—and more is their felt need to give them over to the Lord's accountability.

Indeed, tension arises in the transition from immaturity to maturity. It is during this avalanche of emotions that someone has to act like the adult. The parent is positioned by the Lord to be this voice of reason, as the transitioning teenager has yet to qualify. So persistent prayer, patience, and pardon go a long way in promoting peace in the home.

"Joseph, a young man of seventeen, was tending the flocks with his brothers, the sons of Bilhah and the sons of Zilpah, his father's wives, and he brought their father a bad report about them. Now Israel loved Joseph more than any of his other sons, because he had been born to him in his old age; and he made an ornate robe for him" (Genesis 37:2–3).

Fathers, these passionate preadults need your firm and loving leadership as they learn how to manage their freedoms. Mom is the gentle nurturer when they are in grade school, but as they acquire acne, you protect your wife from being taken advantage of with your wise and caring leadership. Most of all, remember to be intentional in your relational investment with your young person, as rules without relationship lead to rebellion.

Do you feel taken advantage of, lied to, and manipulated? If so, welcome to the world of hormones hijacking the heart of some self-absorbed teens. On the other hand, thank the Lord for those young people who, because of God's grace, have grown in character and their care for others. Make sure to give these models of faithfulness positive feedback. It is easy to only give attention to the troublemakers and take for granted the good kids.

Above all else, pray together as husband and wife for your teenagers to fear God, love Him, and obey Christ commands. Ask the Lord to fill you with the Holy Spirit so you can model for them what it means to be a loving disciple of Jesus. Confess your faults to the Lord and your child, and ask for their forgiveness. Teenagers trust transparency. Train and instruct them in worship, Bible study, service, faith, love, and grace-based living.

How can I model for my teenager trust in the Lord with my decision making?

Related Readings: Psalm 89:19; Proverbs 23:22; Lamentations 3:26–28; Matthew 18:21–22

COMFORT IN LOSS

"And many Jews had come to Martha and Mary to comfort them in the loss of their brother."
John 11:19

Have you lost someone or something close to your heart—a baby, a spouse, a friend, a job, or an opportunity? A great loss requires great grace, or the pain is unbearable. Why do some expecting mothers have a stillborn child and others do not? Can we truly understand these puzzling matters until we get to heaven and we are able to ask, "Why, Lord, why?"

Where is God when emotions run raw and a great hole of hurt embeds in the heart? We do not always understand the ways of God, but we can always count on Christ's comfort. The Lord lingers long, close to those caught in the pain of great loss. What others cannot totally understand, your heavenly Father fully comprehends. Grace soothes aching hearts. Christ's comfort nurses like cool cough syrup flowing down a swollen, enflamed throat.

"For just as we share abundantly in the sufferings of Christ, so also our comfort abounds through Christ" (2 Corinthians 1:5). The Lord's comfort is limitless in its capacity to cure.

Furthermore, Christ comforts us so we are able to extend His compelling comfort to others. Productive pain pays it forward in a faith-based solution to other sad souls. Giving is therapy in God's economy; so those of us saved by grace are not stingy with its application. Whom do you know who needs a listening ear, a silent prayer, or a caring visit?

If comfort is kept closed up in the closet of our busyness, then we miss out on one of life's great joys. There is shame on any servant of Jesus who only has time to hear the heart of the spiritually healthy. Be aware as tears hover under the surface of a tender heart in your circle of influence. Look around. Who are struggling with health, work, or relational issues? Comfort them, as your influence ripples like a rock slicing through a still body of water.

Noah was known as the comforter. "He named him Noah and said, 'He will comfort us in the labor and painful toil of our hands caused by the ground the LORD has cursed'" (Genesis 5:29). Comfort in Christ's name, and you will never lack candidates for comfort.

Say a prayer for someone in despair, send flowers to a young mom who just lost her little one after the first trimester of pregnancy, network for an acquaintance in career transition, pay the rent for a struggling relative, or introduce to someone who is broken the uplifting love and saving power of Jesus Christ. Comfort is your platform to proclaim God's grace. You cannot over comfort others; so join the body of Christ in loving on another hurting heart.

"Praise be to the God and Father of our Lord Jesus Christ, the Father of compassion and the God of all comfort, who comforts us in all our troubles, so that we can comfort those in any trouble with the comfort we ourselves receive from God" (2 Corinthians 1:3-4).

Where do I need Christ's comfort, and whom do I know who needs His comfort and joy?

Related Readings: Job 42:11; Psalm 86:17; Psalm 119:76; John 14:1; 2 Corinthians 7:6–7

DOUBT PARALYZES

"Moses answered, 'What if they do not believe me or listen to me and say,
"The Lord did not appear to you"?'" Exodus 4:1

Moses experienced the "what if" trap. "What if they do not believe me or listen to me?" And several thousand years later we struggle with the same doubts. What if they reject me? What if they say no? What if they say yes? What if I fail? What if I am hurt? What if they do not understand? If God has led us thus far and if His track record is one of faithfulness, are we not really saying, "What if God does not do what He said He will do?" Doubt detaches us from trust in the character of Christ.

If we are not careful, our beliefs and behavior can reflect this kind of irrational thinking about God. We really struggle at times (right before we take that step of faith) and wonder if God is really true to His Word and if He will come through for us. Yet we know that God has never failed us. His timing may have been different than we expected, but He has not failed us, and He will not fail us. Knowing this, we still struggle with doubt. Why is this?

"Then he [Jesus] said to Thomas, 'Put your finger here; see my hands. Reach out your hand and put it into my side. Stop doubting and believe'" (John 20:27).

Doubt is a normal part of the trust process. We go through doubt on the way to trust in the Lord. Even the most faithful followers of Jesus deal with doubt (see Matthew 11:2). However, the danger of doubt is to remain in doubt. Extended striving over doubt can paralyze you. It can paralyze your relationships, your finances, your career advancement, and, worst of all, your obedience to God. He is either trustworthy or He is not.

Lastly, the greatest difficulty is when we are in the middle of tremendous adversity or uncertainty. God's posture is one of continual compassion and sincere love. He is there to walk with you. He is leading you, and He will provide the needed skills, finances, health, and relationships for you to accomplish His will. Let Him use this time of trials to, once again, show that He is God.

"Now to him who is able to do immeasurably more than all we ask or imagine, according to his power that is at work within us, to him be glory"(Ephesians 3:20–21).

Lord, how do You want to empower me to face my doubts and fears by faith in You?

Related Readings: Jeremiah 1:6; Mark 11:23; James 1:6; Jude 1:22

A MOTHER'S PRAYER

"'I prayed for this child, and the LORD has granted me what I asked of him.
So now I give him to the LORD. For his whole life he will be given over to the LORD.'
And he worshiped the LORD there." 1 Samuel 1:27–28

A mother who prays causes Satan to shudder and his demons to take notice. It is her steady stream of supplications to her Savior Jesus that garners the attention of God. Dad may not be around, but her heavenly Father is there for wisdom and encouragement. She knows the Lord understands; so she seeks Him for grace and comfort. The prayer of a mom punctures the portals of heaven with passionate petitions that provide her peace.

She may aspire to be a mother but is struggling with the ability to conceive. Her heart breaks for the opportunity to be with child. Her prayers are pregnant with the desire to become pregnant, and Christ the giver of life listens compassionately and patiently to her pleas. A barren womb is meant to walk with the Lord during this time of feeling failure and rejection. So she prays for a child, and in the process He loves His child.

"Isaac prayed to the LORD on behalf of his wife, because she was childless. The LORD answered his prayer, and his wife Rebekah became pregnant" (Genesis 25:21).

A mother's prayers mark her family with faith and trust in God. Her overflow of mercy and grace is a reminder that Jesus is the "author and finisher" of the family's faith. The fruit from her prayers personify Christ's character, and hell clamors at the calm request from a mom who trusts God. She prays for her children to obey and worship the Lord and for her husband to fear God, hate sin, and love people. A mom's prayer matters.

Lastly, consider a prayer journal to capture Christ's faithfulness to your faith appeals. Pray for your children by name, and lift each of their unique needs to the Lord. Pray for your husband's submission to the accountability of almighty God. Indeed, a wise mother's first concern is prayer in Jesus' name.

"Do not be anxious about anything, but in everything, by prayer and petition, with thanksgiving, present your requests to God" (Philippians 4:6).

Lord, help me not to worry but to apply that same energy in passionate prayer.

Related Readings: Psalm 66:16–19; Isaiah 28:9; Luke 22:2–3; Acts 1:14

A MOTHER'S LOVE

"As apostles of Christ we could have been a burden to you, but we were gentle among you, like a mother caring for her little children." 1 Thessalonians 2:6-7

A mother's love reflects the love of the Lord, deep in its capacity and generous in its application. She awakes in the middle of the night to nurse a hungry infant or care for a sick child. Her intuition injects love at points of pain and in situations that require extensive encouragement. A mother's love lingers long in conversation and understands with her sensitive heart. She loves because Christ's love compels her to love as He does.

Moreover, a mother's love is loyal and longstanding. A child may be in trouble, but mom is always close by full of compassion and acceptance. Her love can be blind in its loyalty, but her offspring never doubt where they are welcome. Jesus was rejected by angry, jealous men and abandoned by His closest friends, but His mother was waiting with Him to the bitter end.

"Near the cross of Jesus stood his mother" (John 19:25).

A mother's love even has the capacity to be a mother to those who are not biologically her own. Amazingly she can informally "adopt" people for a season and love them emotionally, physically, spiritually, and relationally. She opens her home, shares her food, gives her time, dispenses her wisdom, and encourages obedience to follow Christ. Paul experienced this. "Greet Rufus, chosen in the Lord, and his mother, who has been a mother to me, too" (Romans 16:13). Moms sometime mother greatness who are not their own.

Lastly, a mother's love is gentle like God is gentle toward His children. He calls us to love and lead like Jesus. Love serves people and does not rule with rigor. Even when your children are cantankerous, you can calm them with your calm. Christ's love through you to your children models how they will one day mother their children.

"God's servant must not be argumentative, but a gentle listener and a teacher who keeps cool, working firmly but patiently with those who refuse to obey" (2 Timothy 2:24 TM).

Lord, how can I model gentle and patient love?

Related Readings: Genesis 47:12; Ruth 4:16; John 21:15–17; James 3:17

A MOTHER'S WORK

"She watches over the affairs of her household and does not eat the bread of idleness.
Her children arise and call her blessed; her husband also, and he praises her."
Proverbs 31:27–28

A mother's work is never done. There is always another meal to prepare, a face to wipe, clothes to wash, an errand to run, a room to clean, and a dollar to manage. She serves unselfishly like Jesus. "After that, he poured water into a basin and began to wash his disciples' feet, drying them with the towel that was wrapped around him" (John 13:5). A mother's work makes those around her look good. She is God's chosen one in the home.

The law of love and kindness is written on her heart, but some days it is hard to have the right attitude. The work can become laborious, monotonous, and taken for granted. It is at this point of feeling unappreciated that a wise mom reminds herself of heaven's applause. She is really serving for an audience of one, her loving Lord. Her Savior Jesus smiles at her service, and that is enough. The reward of doing right encourages her heart to do right.

"Then they can urge the younger women to love their husbands and children, to be self-controlled and pure, to be busy at home, to be kind, and to be subject to their husbands, so that no one will malign the word of God" (Titus 2:4–5).

In addition, there are the rewards of a child's smile and warm embrace and of hearing, "Thank you, mommy, for being my mommy." Or there are the rewards of a loving husband who genuinely thanks his wife and serves her by listening, serving, and giving praise. She takes pride in her work because she recognizes everything she has is a gift from God. Her home and family are a reflection of her and her heavenly Father. She manages the home for her Master's glory.

Lastly, your work is a model for your children to follow. Your actions become a teacher that prepares them for adulthood. Chores done well create children who work well. Assign them responsibilities so they learn thoroughness, cleanliness, and organization. Indeed, your work creates calm in the home like the Lord quiets your soul.

"But I have stilled and quieted my soul; like a weaned child with its mother, like a weaned child is my soul within me" (Psalm 131:2).

Lord, lead me to be content serving my family for Christ's sake.

Related Readings: Proverbs 4:3; Proverbs 31:10–31; 1 Timothy 5:14

A WORKING MOTHER

"She considers a field and buys it; out of her earnings she plants a vineyard.
She sets about her work vigorously; her arms are strong for her tasks."
Proverbs 31:16–17

Many moms work outside the home out of necessity, their choice, or a combination of both. God has gifted them to invest in the marketplace in a manner that is productive in business and that blesses their home. It is not easy to juggle two full-time jobs, but Christ gives them the grace to carry on. Single moms, in particular, face challenges most of us cannot understand. They need prayer, encouragement, strength, and support.

Whom do you know who is a single mom? How can you serve her? You might give an anonymous financial gift or involve your children in helping with her yard work. A woman who carries all the domestic and marketplace responsibilities needs a community of Christ followers as friends and confidants. If you are a child of a single mom, take the initiative to work around the house and outside the home. Support her with service.

Moreover, do you see your workplace as your ministry or just a way to make a living? Working moms have a unique opportunity to represent Christ in their careers. People will ask, "How do you balance work and home responsibilities?" This is an open door to brag about your husband's support and describe the importance of faith in the Lord. "If someone asks about your Christian hope, always be ready to explain it" (1 Peter 3:15 NLT).

Working mothers bring grace, wisdom, and stability to work environments. If you are an employer, encourage them with flexible time schedules and bonuses for a job well done. Facilitate for them a career culture that keeps family first when life and work priorities clash. Working moms deserve recognition and reward. Their Savior is smiling, and so should we.

"Finally, be strong in the Lord and in the strength of His might" (Ephesians 6:10 NASB).

Whom do I know whom I can encourage in her career by connecting her to a mentor?

Related Readings: Psalm 144:12; Jeremiah 32:9; Acts 16:11–40

VALUE CHURCH

"Let us rejoice and be glad and give him glory! For the wedding of the Lamb has come,
and his bride has made herself ready." Revelation 19:7

Why do we value church? We value church because God values church. The imagery He uses to illustrate its importance is stunning. It is the picture of a pure and prepared people approaching the Lord, as a bride ready to be received by her husband. The bride of Christ is the church, honored and loved deeply by Jesus. Yes, the church is made up of imperfect people who one day will be made perfect: "To present her to himself as a radiant church, without stain or wrinkle or any other blemish, but holy and blameless" (Ephesians 5:27).

You may say, "I do not need the church," but to say this is to say, "I do not value Jesus' relationships." We automatically care for the spouse of a friend because we honor our friend's relationships. In the same way, Christians who love the Lord love His bride. Furthermore, we need the church's prayers, accountability, community, fellowship, friendships, teaching, and worship. Pride resists the church, but humility engages with God's people. Investing time and money in the church is investing in eternal rewards.

Moreover, the church needs you. It needs your wisdom, your mentoring, your energy, your Bible knowledge, your experience, your service, your giving, and your influence. Involvement in church is a two-way street of giving and receiving. Mature followers of Jesus graduate from "sitting and soaking" to "serving and giving." Church is a conduit for sharing Christ and growing in God's grace. It is accountability to almighty God.

Lastly, Christ is ever building His church to overcome sin, Satan, sorrow, and death. Jesus said, "And I tell you that you are Peter, and on this rock I will build my church, and the gates of Hades will not overcome it" (Matthew 16:18). Meet God at church on Sunday to make Him known throughout the week.

"It [the church] was strengthened; and encouraged by the Holy Spirit, it grew in numbers, living in the fear of the Lord" (Acts 9:31).

Do I value the church as Jesus values the church? Is church engagement a regular part of my routine?

Related Readings: Psalm 45:9–16; Isaiah 25:1–9; John 3:29; 2 Corinthians 11:2

CONTENTMENT IS FREEING

"You shall not covet your neighbor's house."
Exodus 20:17

Moses needed a game plan. His job was more than one man could handle—managing a nation. It was God sized. So God gave him rules to facilitate the freedom desired by the people. He gave Moses and us these top ten rules so we could enjoy our freedom, not destroy our freedom. One of the rules relates to coveting. To covet means that I want what you have. I want your house, your car, your spouse, your health, or your bank account.

Instead of being grateful for what I have, I am discontent with what I do not have. To covet is to long and crave for something in an unhealthy manner. It is to lose perspective and do things you normally would not do in order to gain something you really do not need. Coveting creates expectations that cannot be met. To not covet is important, because it made God's top ten list of commandments. Indeed, coveting is tamed by contentment.

"Keep your lives free from the love of money and be content with what you have, because God has said, 'Never will I leave you; never will I forsake you'" (Hebrews 13:5).

Contentment is the opposite of coveting. It is not driven to have more but is motivated by giving more. Contentment is focused on what is best for others. How can I invest in you and serve you? It is also based on trust in the Lord. He knows exactly what I need. Ultimately it comes down to God and His sovereign choice in my life. Can He be trusted to provide just what I need and want? Or do I have to take matters into my own hands and go after things that will consume my time and money and wreck my home and health?

Do I go after things which, in the long run, take a lot of sideways energy and focus? Bigger and better is not always best. In fact, this is a trap. Bigger and better many times leads to bankruptcy; maybe not financially, but relationally, physically, and spiritually. Monitor your motives. Enjoy the freedom contentment brings, and avoid the snare of complication and bondage that covetousness invites.

"If they obey and serve him, they will spend the rest of their days in prosperity and their years in contentment" (Job 36:11).

Lord, does my lifestyle lend itself to contentment and service to others? How can I simplify my situation?

Related Readings: Joshua 7:7; Proverbs 19:23; Luke 3:14; 1 Timothy 6:6–8

COMPLETE OBEDIENCE

"Then he took the Book of the Covenant and read it to the people. They responded,
'We will do everything the LORD has said; we will obey.'" Exodus 24:7

Moses delivered in more detail God's expectations and rules. He gave the people very practical laws and instructions. His commands related to everything from how to deal with crimes like stealing and killing to how to take care of the poor, widows, and orphans. The attitude of the people was instant, total obedience. They had seen the disastrous consequences of halfhearted obedience and chose to avoid this foolish path.

When God speaks, does it settle the issue in your mind and heart? When He speaks to you through His Word in personal study, prayer, small group study, worship, through other people, or in biblical teaching by your pastor, how do you respond? Do you rationalize away His rules? Do you admit the teaching is true, but just for someone else rather than yourself? Do you ignore God when He is speaking? Or do you gladly and wholeheartedly embrace and obey God's Word? You believe in your head, but do you apply it to your heart, living it out in your behavior? Total and thorough obedience is important to God. Why?

"Jesus replied, 'Anyone who loves me will obey my teaching. My Father will love them, and we will come to them and make our home with them. Anyone who does not love me will not obey my teaching. These words you hear are not my own; they belong to the Father who sent me'" (John 14:23–24).

Obedience is important because it validates our trust in Him. We may not totally understand why at the moment, but we know in our hearts He can be trusted; so we obey Him, trusting that He knows what is best. You may be tempted to give partial or delayed obedience. You may say, "I'll obey the convenient part of His command but not the hard part because it does not apply to me." Or you may say, "I will do it later at a more opportune time." In both cases it is disobedience. Obedience that is not thorough and instant is disobedience.

Start with the obvious issues in your life. Do you owe her an apology? Give it. Do you owe money? Pay it back. Are you flirting with someone other than your spouse? Break it off. Where are you led to serve? Serve. Obedience is your friend. Invite it, embrace it, and then live it out instantly and thoroughly. Your love for Jesus compels you to obey.

"Whatever you have learned or received or heard from me, or seen in me—put it into practice. And the God of peace will be with you" (Philippians 4:9).

Lord, in what area of my life are you calling me to obedience that is complete and total?

Related Readings: Ezekiel 33:31–32; Luke 6:46–48; 1 Timothy 5:4

M11

QUALITY OF LIFE

"The thief does not come except to steal, and to kill, and to destroy. I have come that they may have life, and that they may have it more abundantly." John 10:10 NKJV

What is quality of life for the Christian? How does Christ define quality living? He gives abundant life, but what does this look like for those who love the Lord? Abundant life begins by receiving the gift of God in the life of Christ. "And this is the testimony: God has given us eternal life, and this life is in his Son" (1 John 5:11). Quality of life begins with eternal life as the end goal. God gives eternal life to be lived abundantly on earth.

Quality of life means we live life motivated by what outcomes will live on into eternity. Perhaps I get less and give more. By adjusting down my standard of living, I am able to give more toward what matters to Jesus. The Lord modeled well for us a life of quality. Service to others brings quality of life to all parties. Jesus modeled unselfish service.

"Each of you should look not only to your own interests, but also to the interests of others. Your attitude should be the same as that of Christ Jesus" (Philippians 2:4–5).

Quality of life may not lead to ease and comfort as our culture likes to advertise. Paul described his life of obedience to the Lord as a dangerous way: "I have been constantly on the move. I have been in danger from rivers, in danger from bandits, in danger from my own countrymen, in danger from Gentiles; in danger in the city, in danger in the country, in danger at sea; and in danger from false brothers" (2 Corinthians 11:26). You face danger by faith, but knowing you live for Christ's sake, you persevere and trust Him.

How is my quality of life? Is it abundant in its obedience to Christ? Is He my life to the point His priorities are my priorities? Do I let go of earthly indulgences so others can gain eternal rewards? The quality of my relationship with Jesus determines the quality of my relationships in life. Indeed, my quality of life flows from quantity time with Him.

"Since, then, you have been raised with Christ, set your hearts on things above, where Christ is seated at the right hand of God. Set your minds on things above, not on earthly things. For you died, and your life is now hidden with Christ in God" (Colossians 3:1–3).

How can Christ's life at work in and through me be experienced in the quality of my life?

Related Readings: Amos 6:1–7; Isaiah 54:2; 2 Peter 1:3; Revelation 2:7–10

HONOR, DUTY, COUNTRY

"All those gathered here will know that it is not by sword or spear that the LORD saves;
for the battle is the LORD's, and he will give all of you into our hands."
1 Samuel 17:47

Nations with effective armies are founded on honor, duty, and country. Honor is worship of the Creator and respect for His creation. Duty is obedience to God and His Word and the obligation to promote peace and tranquility. Country is a fierce loyalty to the home of the brave and land of the free. Honor, duty, and country promote a tenacious trust in the Lord, not arrogant reliance on our military might. "Some trust in chariots and some in horses, but we trust in the name of the LORD our God" (Psalm 20:7).

We honor God when we include Him and His principles in our conversation and in crafting our country's rule of law. We honor fellow citizens by providing an environment of life, liberty, and the pursuit of happiness. This is why our men and women die in defense of nations. Without faith, family, and freedom as compelling reasons for war, we will fail. Armies honor their own. They cover each other's backs, leaving no one behind.

"I will defend this city and save it, for my sake and for the sake of David my servant" (2 Kings 19:34).

Duty is a determination to do what is right for the benefit of the whole. You do what you have to do to engage and defeat the enemy. There is a relentless sense of duty that sets apart average armies from excellent armies. Cold and rain, guns and bullets, blood and injury, and illness and disease do not keep the determined defenders from persevering in pain. Responsibility to finish the drill drives those dogged by dignity and duty.

Lastly, the country communicates the courage to defend a nation's ideals. It is not a thirst for power but a trust in Providence. Men and women will die for a country of character, one rooted in righteous behavior. God and country go together like apple pie and ice cream. The integration of fidelity of faith and proud patriotism resists war, but when called upon to fight for freedom, finish the course.

"No king is saved by the size of his army; no warrior escapes by his great strength" (Psalm 33:16).

Am I grateful to God for our military? Do I pray for the Lord's peace and protection for them?

Related Readings: 1 Samuel 17:25–47; Psalm 20:9; Isaiah 31:1; Hebrews 11:33–35

м13

A MOM'S MOTHERING

"Near the cross of Jesus stood his mother, his mother's sister, Mary, the wife of Clopas, and Mary Magdalene. When Jesus saw his mother there, and the disciple whom he loved standing nearby, he said to his mother, 'Dear woman, here is your son,' and to the disciple, 'Here is your mother.' From that time on, this disciple took her into his home." John 19:25–27

Moms are magnificent, especially the ones placed in my life by the Lord. My mom and the mother of our children, in particular, are emissaries of encouragement. They are messengers of comfort and care. No one loves more unconditionally than mothers. They see only the good and forget the bad. A mother's love extends way beyond what is required into a reservoir of hope.

Furthermore, they are not afraid to speak the truth laced with an attractive attitude. It is not unusual for moms to become their child's best friend. This is a natural outcome to their acceptance and relational relentlessness. Because their emotional intelligence quotient is high, they are able to discern and remedy heartfelt needs in an instant. Indeed, they are compulsive givers with a propensity to out serve everyone. "Serve the LORD with gladness; Come before His presence with singing" (Psalm 100:2 NKJV).

This outlandish outpouring of love concerns me. It does not bother me that moms love so generously. What troubles me is their need for unconditional love. Are moms being mothered to the extent that their needs are being met? An unmothered mom is a good candidate for a miserable mom. If moms are not receiving what they need in emotional and spiritual support, they whither under the pressure. Like a flower in an arid climate, they need the saturating love, nurture, and security of their Savior Jesus.

Lastly, they value being valued and desire acceptance. They are secure, living in security, and long to be loved.

Lord, lead me to model this for my mom and the mother of our children. Show me how to shower on them what they have rained upon relationships, season after season, in unselfish service. I want to give back to them in the same way they have given to me and our children. I long for You to bless moms!

"Her children arise and call her blessed; her husband also, and he praises her" (Proverbs 31:28).

Lord, lead me to another mother whom I can mother on Your behalf.

Related Readings: Ruth 1:22; 1 Timothy 5:4; 2 Timothy 1:5; Titus 2:2–4

GOD'S NAME

GOD'S NAME

"You shall not misuse the name of the LORD your God, for the LORD will not hold anyone guiltless who misuses his name." Exodus 20:7

Be cautious how you use God's name. Using God's name with crude and obscene language is obviously inappropriate. This feeble attempt at dragging Deity down to the sewer of man's pathetic state is both ignorant and embarrassing for the offender. But there are more subtle uses of God's name that constitute misuse and mishandling of His name. It is taking the Lord's name in vain in a more sophisticated manner.

For example, be very careful what you ascribe to God and how you communicate this. Avoid the statement, "God wants me to quit my job. What do you think?" This may be true, but wouldn't a humble heart say something like, "I am praying about quitting my job. What do you think?" In this instance you are really seeking godly counsel, while in the first example you trumped any solid advice with the "God card." It is hard to question what you say God is telling you. Humility waits on prayerful validation from God and man.

"My mouth will speak in praise of the LORD. Let every creature praise His holy name for ever and ever" (Psalm 145:21).

It is tempting to drop God's name and credit Him with pending decisions. These are decisions in our heart of hearts we know need more prayer and counsel. But in our haste and impatience we blame God. Be careful. We can talk ourselves into anything and proxy God in along the way. What is He really saying? Should we think twice before we glibly say, "The Lord wants this or that, or the Lord is leading me to do this"? How do you know? What are your objective criteria? Are you just using God's name to justify and get something you want badly? Or is it spiritual pride? Honor His name with wise words.

With some of us it is a way to sound spiritual and attempt to gain the admiration and approval of others. Yes, use God's name very prayerfully, appropriately, and with respect and awe. His name is like an expensive and rare ointment, to be applied on occasion with a gentle and direct application. Use His name, but use it responsibly and with great humility.

"If anyone thinks himself to be religious, and yet does not bridle his tongue but deceives his own heart, this man's religion is worthless" (James 1:26 NASB).

Lord, how can I reverently speak Your name to ascribe honor and glory to You?

Related Readings: Deuteronomy 10:20; Numbers 30:2; Matthew 5:33; Galatians 6:7

PRIME OF LIFE

"A writing of Hezekiah king of Judah after his illness and recovery: I said, 'In the prime of my life must I go through the gates of death and be robbed of the rest of my years?'" Isaiah 38:9–10

Your prime of life is the time for God to shine the brightest through you. He has prepared for this purpose. It is during the prime of life that your understanding of God blossoms. Your love for people is robust. You are honest with your limitations and strengths. Your financial foundation is strong. Your family depends on God and loves you. Your experiences have caught up with your knowledge. You have become wise. Your character is Christlike. And you still have the energy to engage with others and execute kingdom initiatives. This has been your life preparation.

It is during the prime of your life that you can leverage the most for the kingdom of God. Your age is between forty-five and sixty-five. The age range may vary depending on your health, maturity, and circumstances. But you have made it to this point by the grace of God. Life is all about preparation, and you have faithfully prepared. The prime of your life is a time to give it everything you've got.

This is not the season to slow down for God. Rather it is time to kick it up a notch for Jesus. Crank it up for Christ. Do not hold back. Spend your influence, time, and money for Jesus' sake.

This is your prime time. Do not squander this window of opportunity. Be faithful, and watch Him do miraculous works through you. Your prime of life is like participating in the Olympic Games. He does not prepare you for life's olympics and expect you to coast. God's desire is for you to enjoy the ribbon wrapped "gold medal" of prayer for your intense intercession on the behalf of others at God's throne of grace. God's passion is for you to receive the "silver medal" of evangelism for your faithful sharing of the gospel. He wants to give you the "bronze medal" of discipleship for your effective teaching of the Word of God.

Indeed, there are other events for you to participate in during your prime of life—giving, mentoring, encouraging, rebuking, correcting, admonishing, leading, administering, mothering, fathering, grandparenting, and serving, to name a few more. Do not become idle for fear of failure. Failure is doing nothing. The Holy Spirit can better direct a moving object. Serve in the nursery at church, as an elder, parking attendant, or greeter. Join a ministry board of directors. Start a ministry. Serve overseas. Prepare for your prime of life, and engage in your prime of life.

"They will still bear fruit in old age, they will stay fresh and green" (Psalm 92:14).

Am I positioning my prime of life for the Lord's purposes?

Related Readings: Deuteronomy 1:36; Psalm 90:12; John 17:1–5

FAME AND FORTUNE

"King Solomon was greater in riches and wisdom than all the other kings of the earth."
1 Kings 10:23

Fame and fortune facilitate fear, greed, and discontentment. Unless you are intentional in your faith, generosity, and gratitude, you will become a culprit to casual Christianity. Affluence and comfort cause us to feel like we do not need Christ. So regardless of your level of success, stay desperately dependent on Jesus. Use fame and fortune for His kingdom's sake. He has blessed you mightily to bless others magnificently.

How are fame and fortune defined? It is relative to your situation and your socioeconomic standard of living. Fortune for you may be transitioning from a five-figure income to a six-figure income or from a six-figure salary to a seven-figure salary. Fame could be the experience of serving as parent-teacher association president, city councilman, or mayor. You may be the industry leader in your business or chairman of the board. People look up to you more than you realize; so use your authority and assets for the Lord.

"LORD, I have heard of your fame; I stand in awe of your deeds, LORD. Repeat them in our day, in our time make them known; in wrath remember mercy" (Habakkuk 3:2).

In whatever season you find yourself, God has blessed you with influence and resources. How are you leveraging them for the Lord? Are you intentional in using your influence for God's purposes? Do you have a plan to invest your riches in kingdom initiatives? Use fame and fortune for faith-motivated projects and people. Pray about how your notoriety can forward the cause of Christ. Success is a platform for your Savior's sake.

Furthermore, be aggressively accountable with your time and money. Give trusted friends permission to ask you the hard questions. Perhaps they review your annual tax returns and review your calendar quarterly to assess if you are doing what you set out to do. We all do better when others are watching our every move. Do not allow autonomy to isolate you from accountability. The more success you enjoy, the more accountability you require. Use your fame and fortune to influence others toward faith in Jesus Christ.

"Do not let this Book of the Law depart from your mouth; meditate on it day and night, so that you may be careful to do everything written in it. Then you will be prosperous and successful" (Joshua 1:8).

Are fame and fortune friends or foes to my faith?

Related Readings: 2 Chronicles 9:22–23; Psalm 89:27; Matthew 12:42; Colossians 2:2–3

A NEW BABY

"A woman giving birth to a child has pain because her time has come; but when her baby
is born she forgets the anguish because of her joy that a child is born into the world."
John 16:21

A new baby is a natural experience with a supernatural explanation. It is God's reminder of His incredible grace and gift of life. You cannot keep from staring at a new baby's little chubby fingers and pinkish back and belly. Babies have the scent of freshness straight from their heavenly Father's handiwork. A new baby brings joy and attention to Jesus.

New babies have the look of the Lord's love in their eyes. Their coos are the sounds of their Savior's caring communication. Their cries resound with a need for Christ. Their tender feet are a foreshadowing of walking with Jesus through the ups and downs of life. A new baby brings back memories of a mom in pain that is quickly overcome by joy. Mostly, an infant illustrates God's new birth of a soul delivered into eternal life.

A new baby points to the new birth. Just as the Lord delivers a physical life, so a spiritual birth is God's supernatural act of a soul's salvation. Jesus described it the best: "Unless a person submits to this original creation—the 'wind-hovering-over-the-water' creation, the invisible moving the visible, a baptism into a new life—it's not possible to enter God's kingdom. When you look at a baby, it's just that: a body you can look at and touch. But the person who takes shape within is formed by something you can't see and touch—the Spirit—and becomes a living spirit" (John 3:5–6 MSG).

Moreover, a new baby brings magnificent joy. The mom and dad are full of joy. The grandparents are teary eyed with joy, and the aunts and uncles are smitten by simple joy. Smiles cannot be contained around the mesmerizing effect of an infant. Prayers launch moment by moment from grateful hearts to heaven. Thank God for a new baby, and thank Him even more for those born into His kingdom.

Jesus said: "I tell you that in the same way there will be more rejoicing in heaven over one sinner who repents than over ninety-nine righteous persons who do not need to repent" (Luke 15:7).

Does my excitement for those born into God's family bring pure joy and praise to the Lord?

Related Readings: Genesis 3:16; Psalm 113:9; Luke 1:57–58; Galatians 4:27

THOROUGH WORK

"The Israelites had done all the work just as the LORD had commanded Moses.
Moses inspected the work and saw that they had done it just as the LORD had commanded.
So Moses blessed them." Exodus 39:42–43

We live in an instant society. We want relationships, money, and our eating experiences in an instant. In the process of making everything instantaneous, we have lost something. We have lost an appreciation for thoroughness in our work and in our relationships. We take shortcuts to finish on time, sacrificing quality, just to end up with an inferior outcome. Or even worse, we misrepresent the facts or lie outright to reach a goal because of the pressure we feel to produce. Thoroughness requires attention, trust, and tenacity.

Whatever happened to thoroughness—the discipline to plan ahead, provide accountability, cover the details, create a beautiful result, and celebrate the success? Instead, we plow ahead without proper understanding and procedures. Everyone does what is right in his own eyes, and we miss the opportunity to learn and benefit from one another. Indeed, thoroughness begins with a good example from the leader. Like Moses, Nehemiah stayed focused on the work at hand.

"So I sent messengers to them, saying, 'I am doing a great work and I cannot come down. Why should the work stop while I leave it and come down to you?' They sent messages to me four times in this manner, and I answered them in the same way" (Nehemiah 6:3–4 NASB).

Moses was a thorough leader. He listened patiently to God and then delivered in detail to the team what was expected and required to accomplish the project. He understood and applied wise management of people. He understood each of their individual gifts and skills. People who take pride in their work are the most thorough when they are competent in their area of responsibility and clear on expectations. They understand what is needed and when it is to be complete. Details and deadlines are friends of thoroughness.

Lastly, thoroughness is dependent on the needed resources and relationships to carry out the project. Do not be afraid to be resourceful. Seek out the people and information needed to carry out your job. Your thoroughness will speak volumes to your boss and to your peers. Your thorough and excellent work is the best testament to your trust in Christ. In the end you are blessed because of the quality product or service you created. God is glorified through thoroughness and the enduring influence of your work experiences.

"I have brought you glory on earth by finishing the work you gave me to do. And now, Father, glorify me in your presence with the glory I had with you before the world began" (John 17:4–5).

What current project requires my thorough attention to detailed implementation?

Related Readings: Genesis 7:5; Exodus 23:21–22; Matthew 28:20; 2 Timothy 2:15

SMART SILENCE

"Moses then said to Aaron, 'This is what the LORD spoke of when he said: "Among those who approach me I will show myself holy; in the sight of all the people I will be honored."' Aaron remained silent." Leviticus 10:3

Aaron lost two of his four sons because of their unwise decisions to disobey God. The emotions in Aaron's heart must have been racing. Just before the death of his sons, Aaron experienced the ultimate in ecstasy by luxuriating in the glory of the Lord with his best friend, family, and friends. He went from the mountaintop of celebration to the valley of death. He knew to speak in this state of emotion was risky, unwise, and fleshly.

As anger and humiliation boil, our words become ripe to lash out at God and others. It is wise to refrain in the face of raw emotion. There are times not to speak our minds, not spew our unguarded words and embarrass ourselves. Instead, by God's grace we can remain quiet, cool, and contemplative. Smart silence sends a message of maturity. Patience waits to speak guarded words full of grace and truth—those golden to God.

"Like an earring of gold or an ornament of fine gold is the rebuke of a wise judge to a listening ear" (Proverbs 25:12).

It is hard to remain silent when we feel hurt or disappointed. It is hard to harness our tongues when we see our children hurting and we feel incapacitated to help.It is hard to keep quiet and pray when we feel the Lord has let us down. Like an intravenous procedure in a fevered patient, smart silence requires extra doses of God's grace flooding our lives. His grace refrains us from speaking until a better time and day.

There are times to speak up in the heat of the emotion, but those situations are the exception. In most cases take a deep breath, send up a prayer to your heavenly Father, and wait before you speak. Wait until you are calm, and wait for others to cool down. At the appropriate time, make sure your words are birthed from a pure and prayerful heart. Silence is smart because it allows the Lord to soothe your soul.

"But I have stilled and quieted my soul; like a weaned child with its mother, like a weaned child is my soul within me" (Psalm 131:2).

In what relationship do I need to trust God and be silent?

Related Readings: Psalm 4:4; Isaiah 42:14; Mark 14:61; Acts 8:32

HUMILITY IS ATTRACTIVE

"Now Moses was a very humble man, more humble than anyone else on the face of the earth."
Numbers 12:3

Humility is attractive because it accepts others. You feel valued and important when you are in the presence of humility. Those who are humble are not pressing their agenda; rather, they are listening for your needs, dreams, and fears. Humility is other centric. It is also in position to trust God. You tend to trust those who trust God. They depend on their heavenly Father because they recognize their limitations without Him.

Humility also solicits followers. People want to follow a person of humility. They respect the honesty that travels with humility. This is vital to effective leadership. People will go the extra mile for an honest and humble leader. They serve with passion because they feel they are served and cared for by their humble leader. However, humility not only attracts positive reactions but negative ones as well.

"You armed me with strength for battle; you humbled my adversaries before me" (Psalm 18:39).

Critics can hound the humble. Some critics view those who are humble as weak; therefore, their humility is a target for criticism. The strategy of the critic is to wear down the humble one and force him or her to capitulate to the critic's claims. However, the critic may underestimate the resolve of the humble. A humble person submitted to the will of God will not wither under the critic's verbal firestorm. When there is a conflict between pleasing God or pleasing people, Christ is the choice.

There is a deep reservoir of stamina within the heart and mind of the humble to do what is right and trust God with the results. Over time the humble person will learn from his critics and become better because of them, but he will not compromise his core values and principles. Ultimately, the goal is to humbly love God and people. This is attractive.

"He has told you, O man, what is good; And what does the LORD require of you But to do justice, to love kindness, And to walk humbly with your God?" (Micah 6:8 NASB).

Do I walk humbly with the Lord my God? Are others attracted to humility in me?

Related Readings: Deuteronomy 33:1; Matthew 5:5; Acts 7:22; 2 Corinthians 10:1

RISKY COURAGE

"Then Caleb silenced the people before Moses and said, 'We should go up and take possession of the land, for we can certainly do it.'" Numbers 13:30

Courage is risky because it can be misunderstood and even rejected. The majority may dismiss your courage as unreasonable. You will not always have the majority on your side in decision making. This is a risk you may need to take. Just make sure it is the Lord leading you and not your stubborn pride. Fearful people sometimes reject courageous people because the pain of what could happen outweighs their present pain.

What about the pain that will occur if you do nothing and disobey God? This consequence can be dreadfully painful; yet many times this is overlooked, causing negative consequences to occur and placing blame on you. Look at it this way: in either case—the courageous choice or the do nothing choice—you will be given credit or blame. Thus, be guilty of the courageous choice and trust God with the outcome.

"Be strong and courageous. Do not be afraid or terrified because of them, for the LORD your God goes with you; he will never leave you nor forsake you" (Deuteronomy 31:6).

Courageous leaders have the ability to see the opportunities rather than the obstacles. Yes, the obstacles will be there but over time will fade into oblivion. As the old farmer once said about a large dead tree trunk in his field, "You can dynamite it out and make a mess, or you can plow around it. If you plow around it, over time it will decay and return to where it came from." This is true of obstacles; focus on your God-given opportunities, ignore the obstacles, and eventually the obstacles will decay for lack of attention.

Embrace and exploit your opportunities, and you will not have time to be distracted by the obstacles. The majority may be enamored and even paralyzed by the obstacles, but stay focused on the God-given goal, and He will overcome. Yes, courage and faith are first cousins. You need both, but fear is an evil uncle trying to distract you. Be courageous. God only gives you one life to live. Live it faithfully and aggressively for His glory.

Remember to draw your courage from the courageous one, the Lord Jesus Christ. His courage in you will conquer far beyond your ability to persevere. His daily infusion of courage through the Holy Spirit will defeat Satan's daily distractions of fear and blame. Courage moves forward; fear sits still. Courage is risky but ever so fulfilling.

"Be strong and courageous, because you will lead these people to inherit the land I swore to their forefathers to give them" (Joshua 1:6).

Where is Christ leading me to be courageous?

Related Readings: Joshua 10:25; Ezra 10:4; Mark 6:51; Acts 4:13

RESPECT THE ELDERLY

"Rise in the presence of the aged, show respect for the elderly and revere your God.
I am the LORD." Leviticus 19:32

Years can bring improvement in decision making, perspective, understanding of people, and our intimacy with God and those closest to us. The elderly represent a plethora of wisdom waiting to be tapped. They tell stories of real-life events that challenge, educate, and entertain. Those approaching their twilight years who love Jesus have an eternal perspective that is infectious. They see God for who He is.

Yet with all of these potential, positive traits, we stutter at spending time with the aged, even those who are own flesh and blood. Why is this so? Yes, some are hard to get along with; others reek of body staleness (having been trapped indoors), and others are very high maintenance. This is hard; yet it is temporary, and before you know it they will be gone. How many more days do you have with a parent, grandparent, or mentor?

"Teach the older men to be temperate, worthy of respect, self-controlled, and sound in faith, in love and in endurance" (Titus 2:2).

As the sand is rushing toward the bottom of the hourglass, what are some ways you can demonstrate respect toward the elderly? One way is to spend time with them. Perhaps it is a regular visit to the nursing home or retirement center. Love them by showing up with flowers and by reading an uplifting portion of Scripture. Listen to their hopes, dreams, and regrets. Throughout your conversation with the elderly, capture in your memory the nuggets of wisdom, thoughts, ideas, and places that resonate with how you do or do not want to live your life. Look for those life snapshots that you can emulate and pass down to your children and your children's children.

Respect for your elders may express itself with them visiting you rather than you visiting them. They may need to move in with you so you can love them twenty-four hours a day, seven days a week. Yes, this is a huge commitment. It is harder to "raise" your parents than it is to raise your children. Their needs are more complicated, and they certainly do not want to be told what to do, but you love them anyway.

You respect them, even when they are not respectable. Seize this time. Do not let it slip by in the abyss of busyness. It is an opportunity for your kids to experience how you would like for them to treat you one day. Your respect for the elderly is a reflection of your reverence for God. Love, serve, and respect them as if you were doing the same for Christ.

"Now Elihu had waited before speaking to Job because they were older than he" (Job 32:4).

How can I schedule regular time to learn from and love the elderly?

Related Readings: Job 32:4–6; Proverbs 16:31; Romans 13:7; 1 Timothy 5:1–2

REMEMBER THE POOR

"When you reap the harvest of your land, do not reap to the very edges of your field or gather the gleanings of your harvest. Leave them for the poor and the alien. I am the LORD your God."
Leviticus 23:22

God is passionate about the poor. Jesus died for the rich, the poor, and everyone in between. He downplayed our relationship with the poor only as it relates to our relationship with Him when he stated, "The poor you will always have with you" (Matthew 26:11). In reality, any relationship we have should pale in comparison to our relationship with Christ. But there is a special relationship with the poor that God expects of His children.

He is looking for intentionality in our attitude and actions toward those of much lesser means. How are we systematically and intentionally reaching out to the less fortunate? How are we investing in them socially, financially, educationally, vocationally, and spiritually? Investment in the poor is not an option or a nice gesture for the follower of Christ; it is a mandate and an expectation of God.

"You have been a refuge for the poor, a refuge for the needy in their distress, a shelter from the storm and a shade from the heat" (Isaiah 25:4).

Jesus made a bold statement to a young man who worshiped wealth: "If you want to be perfect, go, sell your possessions and give to the poor, and you will have treasure in heaven. Then come, follow me" (Matthew 19:21). We can start corporately to teach and preach about the biblical admonishments to remember and reach out to those of lesser means. Churches, organizations, and ministries focused on the poor are critical from the Christian's vantage point. Thus, how can we plan to serve the poor at their point of need?

Individually we have the opportunity to pray and provide for the down-and-out. Perhaps we seek out those who already effectively take the love of Jesus to the unfortunate, joining them in their established process and program. They have the credibility and trust of the community; so we can partner with them for the sake of the poor. Give directly to families who need to be taught life skills. In the process they can learn how much God loves and accepts them.

"The Spirit of the Lord is on me, because he has anointed me to preach good news to the poor" (Luke 4:18).

How can I follow the example of Jesus, spending more of my time with the poor?

Related Readings: Psalm 35:10; Mark 12:43; Luke 14:21; James 2:5–6

MANAGEMENT BY OBJECTIVES

"Aaron and his sons are to go into the sanctuary and assign to each man his work
and what he is to carry." Numbers 4:19

God believes in delegation and follow-through. He expects leaders to manage. This is the right and responsible thing to do. If a job is to be done well, you as the leader have to be a part of the process. Effective managers make expectations crystal clear. Clarity comes through repetition, hands on explanation, written instructions, and follow-up. It is important for team members to understand from different perspectives how their role is critical in accomplishing the overall vision. Inspect the results you expect from them.

On-the-job training is also important so team members have the opportunity to watch you or someone else complete the work with excellence. This gives the trainee opportunity to ask questions and interact with the trainer. Avoid the temptation to hurry and not be thorough in hands-on training. Ineffective training costs you in the long run. It costs you time, money, frustration, and personnel turnover. So how can you as a manager grow and improve your management skills? How can you be a good example for the team?

First of all, make sure you are managed well. Invite your supervisor or board of directors to hold you accountable. You have a much better chance to manage well if you are managed well. Then have regular performance reviews. We perform better when others are watching. The review needs to be relational, specific, and results focused. Next, walk around among your team. Seek to understand each person's role and what is expected, taking the time to follow up with tasks you have delegated. Follow through with your commitments, and you will maintain your moral authority to manage. Effective leaders manage in person, not in isolation. A recluse is a poor manager.

Lastly, challenge the management process. Do the systems of your enterprise facilitate or stifle management? In other words, do you get the proper data needed to evaluate a person or situation, or are you guessing and making assumptions not based on facts. Excellent managers produce processes that move toward the best results.

Paul instructed Timothy in this way, "Timothy, my dear son, be strong through the grace that God gives you in Christ Jesus. You have heard me teach things that have been confirmed by many reliable witnesses. Now teach these truths to other trustworthy people who will be able to pass them on to others" (2 Timothy 2:1–2 NLT).

How can I become a more effective manger and empower our team to manage well?

Related Readings: Exodus 18:17–26; Exodus 39:32; Matthew 28:19–20; Acts 6:1–7

TRUST ENOUGH

"But the LORD said to Moses and Aaron, 'Because you did not trust in me enough to honor me as holy in the sight of the Israelites, you will not bring this community into the land I give them.'"
Numbers 20:12

A mature and robust trust in God can open the door of opportunity; while a flippant, immature, or irreverent trust can slam shut the door of opportunity. I have to ask myself an honest question: "Do I trust God with my whole heart or only when it is convenient?" There is such a thing as not trusting in God enough to honor Him as holy. How can I make sure I trust in God enough? I can say I trust God, but do I really mean it?

Do I, deep in my heart of hearts, trust Him? Do I really trust Him with my job, my boyfriend or girlfriend, my future, my health, and my finances? If my trust is contingent on how I think things should go, then I really do not trust God. My trust has to be unconditional, good or bad, pretty or ugly. I will trust Him, even when I disagree or I am confused with my circumstances. Sometimes God tests you to authenticate your trust.

"Sovereign LORD, you are God! Your covenant is trustworthy, and you have promised these good things to your servant" (2 Samuel 7:28).

He wants you to know if He is sufficient or if you find Him lacking. The test is for your benefit because He already knows if you trust Him enough. You may be failing, just passing, average, or an honor student in God's school of faith. Are you convinced that you trust in God enough? Or is yours still an infant faith wrapped in insecurity?

Moving to the next level of trust is not always easy, but it is necessary for the maturing follower of Christ. The easy part is becoming a Christian; the hard part is being a Christian. This happens over time as God tests our trust to grow us up in Him. We can complain, or we can thank Him that He cares so much He does not want our trust to remain raw and disfigured. He is all about developing us into dedicated disciples of Jesus.

Even enemies of Jesus recognized His total trust in His heavenly Father. "He trusts in God" (Matthew 27:43).

Is my trust wholly dependent on the Lord alone plus nothing else?

Related Readings: Psalm 37:3–5; Isaiah 12:2; John 14:1; Titus 3:8

EMBRACE EXCELLENCE

"Be perfect, therefore, as your heavenly Father is perfect."
Matthew 5:48

We admire excellence in others. Professional athletes, attorneys, speakers, teachers, coaches, custodians, mothers, fathers, leaders, elected officials, and business men and women who excel motivate others to excel. Their commitment to thousands of hours in focused training and competition makes their flawless performance look easy. It is their obsession with perfection that leads them to excellence.

In Christ perfection is our position. Outside of Christ no one is perfect, but inside of Christ everyone is perfect. We are perfect because He is perfect. "So that we may present everyone perfect in Christ" (Colossians 1:28). The challenge lies in our living in a sinful world with sinful people; therefore, perfection is diluted. Nonetheless, Jesus commanded His children to be perfect on the same level as their heavenly Father. So as we seek perfection in this life, we see glimpses of glory, and we do capture excellence in the process.

What does excellence look like from the eyes of the eternal? Paul, a protagonist of perfection, describes our dilemma:

"Not that I have already obtained all this, or have already been made perfect, but I press on to take hold of that for which Christ Jesus took hold of me. Brothers, I do not consider myself yet to have taken hold of it. But one thing I do: Forgetting what is behind and straining toward what is ahead, I press on toward the goal to win the prize for which God has called me heavenward in Christ Jesus" (Philippians 3:12–14).

People with an eternal perspective promote perfection. Therefore, embrace excellence as a core value in your life and work. Because you represent the Lord Jesus, be an excellent example of a Christian. Be it ministry or business, your vocation is a vicarious look at our Lord. Talk about Jesus from a platform of perfection, and people will stop to listen. Excellence is your entrée into promoting a loving relationship with God.

"You are the most excellent of men and your lips have been anointed with grace, since God has blessed you forever" (Psalm 45:2).

Do I settle for mediocrity, or do I aspire to excellence? Are others attracted to the quality of my character, competence, and family?

Related Readings: Psalm 18:32; Isaiah 26:3; 2 Corinthians 7:1; Hebrews 10:14

MEANINGFUL MEMORIAL DAYS

"Cornelius stared at him in fear. 'What is it, Lord?' he asked. The angel answered,
'Your prayers and gifts to the poor have come up as a memorial offering before God.'"
Acts 10:4

Meaningful Memorial Days are meant to remember someone or something we hold in high esteem. We pause to reflect and honor their value to our lives and to our country. It is the memory of sacrifice, suffering, industriousness, and integrity that instills a humbling heritage. Men and women gave their lives in battle that we might gain our lives of freedom. Blood-soaked, foreign fields protected liberty at home—a grateful memory.

Memorial Days are the most meaningful when we take time to pause and pray. We thank God in sincere supplication for His favor in our engagement with the enemy, past and present. On our knees we acknowledge almighty God as the genesis for our great country. He led His people here to establish a nation founded on faith in Christ. If we fail to memorialize our Founding Fathers as figures of faith, then we fail as Christian citizens.

Moreover, your gifts to the poor and to all people are a memorial offering before God. Every gift is to be given in the name of Jesus. You give for the cause of Christ because of the great gift of salvation He has given you. Gifts given as a memorial to God gain His glory. You honor the Lord when you give on His behalf.

Lastly, His abundant grace is reason enough for righteous reflection. Is your salvation in Jesus still sweet and savory to your soul? Do you recount often the Lord's tender mercy toward you and your family? Remember how ecstatic you felt when Sovereign God engaged your soul with faith and forgiveness? Keep fresh your conversion experience.

Your testimony of trust in Jesus Christ—now and at your conversion—is a memorial to your Master's faithfulness. The death of Jesus for our soul's freedom and the death of men and women for our nation's soul are the most meaningful Memorial Days. Honor Him and honor them by promoting our liberties as a gift from almighty God and our faithful soldiers.

"For you know the grace of our Lord Jesus Christ, that though he was rich, yet for your sakes he became poor, so that you through his poverty might become rich" (2 Corinthians 8:9).

How can I make Memorial Days meaningful? Do I pray and give as a memorial to Jesus?

Related Readings: Exodus 20:8; Leviticus 2:9; Psalm 77:11; John 15:20–27

ABSOLUTE SURRENDER

"By faith Abraham, when God tested him, offered Isaac as a sacrifice.... Abraham reasoned
that God could raise the dead, and figuratively speaking, he did receive Isaac back from death."
Hebrews 11:17, 19

Absolute surrender is a prerequisite for the disciple of Jesus Christ. Like Abraham, we
have to lay anyone or anything that is precious and valuable on the altar of death. I
struggle with absolute surrender because it means giving over everything to God. I give
my spouse, my children, my career, my education, my health, and my finances. Once I offer
them to Him by faith, they become to me what they already are to Him—His.

Absolute surrender is a test of obedience that even those who are the stoutest of
heart have a hard time with. You can be a believer for a long period of time, and the Lord
still reminds you what is His. Have you left your home in the Lord's hands? His will may be
for you to sell it and enjoy a simpler lifestyle. Have you given your business or ministry over
to God's care? It may need to close down so Christ can raise up a new enterprise full of
energy and vision.

"Do not be stiff-necked, as your ancestors were; submit to the LORD. Come to his
sanctuary, which he has consecrated forever. Serve the LORD your God, so that his fierce
anger will turn away from you" (2 Chronicles 30:8).

Emotion causes our insides to churn when we absolutely surrender something we love
and are proud to have created. But it is out of our anguish that almighty God takes us
places where only trust in Him can provide an entry. His current command may seem to
contradict a past command; even so, you still let go and let God. Do not hang on so long
that the Lord removes it from you anyway. Present to Him a living sacrifice full of faith and
obedience. Whatever happens, He can bring it back to life even better.

What relationship or vision do I need to leave at the Lord's altar? Am I willing to walk
away and trust God will give me just what I need? Obedience is full of pleasant surprises;
so do not be afraid to go to that uncertain and uncomfortable place.

"He who had received the promises was about to sacrifice his one and only son, even
though God had said to him, 'It is through Isaac that your offspring will be reckoned'"
(Hebrews 11:17–18).

Have I absolutely surrendered to my heavenly Father who loves me supremely?

Related Readings: Genesis 22:1–14; Isaiah 41:8; Luke 20:36–38; Romans 4:1–19

NATIONAL DEBT DECEPTION

"If only you fully obey the LORD your God and are careful to follow all these commands I am giving you today. For the LORD your God will bless you as he has promised, and you will lend to many nations but will borrow from none. You will rule over many nations but none will rule over you. If there is a poor man among your brothers in any of the towns of the land that the LORD your God is giving you, do not be hardhearted or tightfisted toward your poor brother." Deuteronomy 15:5–7

National debt is deceptive and detrimental. It can even lead to the downfall of a once free and proud people. There is an articulate illusion that persuasively says we can mortgage our country's financial future on the backs of our children and grandchildren. Debt may be a quick fix, but left unchecked it is disastrous for those who are chained to its consequences. Indeed, God blesses nations responsible in the management of money.

Similar to personal debt, nations can become enslaved to countries that do not care about righteous rules and a Christian culture; in fact, their frame of reference may very well be a godless government. Do we want to answer to atheists known for religious intolerance and who initiate inhumane activity against their own citizens? If they treat their own unjustly and brutally, how will they treat their debtors opposed to their practices?

"Let no debt remain outstanding, except the continuing debt to love one another, for whoever loves others has fulfilled the law" (Romans 13:8).

Wisdom and common sense cry out for a cessation of a cavalier attitude that presumes on our country's future. God-fearing people cannot sit in silence as our country builds a house of credit cards. Economists may sign off on detrimental debt, but what does God think? Do we want to be ruled by unsympathetic nations and lose our incredible influence for goodness, decency, and generosity? Debt stunts our lending and giving to the poor.

Therefore, let's start by living within our own means and lowering our lifestyles. As we model the way personally, then we have the moral authority to vote for fiscally responsible men and women who will lead us into a world that looks to free nations for hope and help. Moreover, the Lord is looking for nations He can trust so He can bless with bountiful provision that is shared with the poor and needy at home and abroad.

"You will lend to many nations but will borrow from none. The LORD will make you the head, not the tail. If you pay attention to the commands of the LORD your God that I give you this day and carefully follow them, you will always be at the top, never at the bottom" (Deuteronomy 28:12–13).

Am I a good example of debt-restraint living? Am I free to give and loan to others liberally?

Related Readings: Leviticus 26:3–14; 1 Kings 4:21–24; Luke 6:35; 1 John 3:16–17

OBEY GOD

"Even if Balak gave me his palace filled with silver and gold, I could not do anything great or small to go beyond the command of the LORD my God." Numbers 22:18

The allure is to obey man rather than God. There will be occasions when we have to make this choice. People will use their position and wealth to sway us to use our influence for their purposes. This can get ugly when God specifically leads us not to bow to the wishes of powerful people with distorted motives. No amount of money or prestige should cause us not to follow and obey God. Obedience precludes powerful people.

One temptation is to feed our pride by pleasing people of power. But a fat ego always leads to a shriveled soul. Why would I ever gravitate to the spotlight while leaving God relegated to the dark corner of my life? Capitulation to the desires of man over the desires of the Lord leads to guilt and discontentment, while obedience to God leads to fulfillment and sweet communion with Christ.

"Obey me, and I will be your God and you will be my people. Walk in all the ways I command you, that it may go well with you" (Jeremiah 7:23).

Competition with devotion to Christ will happen, and when it does, the choice should have already been made. Great military leaders make their best choices before the war begins, not in the heat of the battle. So plan ahead your obedience; make it premeditated. No individual or circumstance should sway you into spiritual inertia. Partial or no obedience is disobedience. Indeed, you worship God when you obey His ways.

Obedience to Christ is freedom. You gain options through obedience and lose opportunities from disobedience. Obey God motivated by love and gratitude. You can trust that He knows what is best. Obey the Lord even when you do not understand why, because He can be trusted.

"Peter and the other apostles replied: 'We must obey God rather than men! The God of our fathers raised Jesus from the dead—whom you had killed by hanging him on a tree'" (Acts 5:29–30).

Do I obey Jesus when my emotions are conflicted? Am I willing to be misunderstood and mocked as a result of obedience?

Related Readings: Genesis 22:18; Joshua 5:6; John 14:23; Romans 15:18

TEACH YOUR GRANDCHILDREN

"Only be careful, and watch yourselves closely so that you do not forget the
things your eyes have seen or let them slip from your heart as long as you live.
Teach them to your children and to their children after them." Deuteronomy 4:9

Grandchildren really are exceptionally grand. You can spoil them and then send them home to their parents. But grandparents are grand to the grandchild as well. You are bigger than life. Your warm smile and gentleness provide a safe environment for their little personalities to cling. The grandchild cannot wait to eat your food, hear your stories, and be treated like a prince or princess. As a grandparent, it is almost like you have a second chance to parent without having the responsibility. Can you imagine that!

Though you do not have the direct responsibility to parent your precious little ones, you do have the responsibility to impart your wisdom and life experiences so they can learn from your mistakes and be inspired to follow God and do their very best in life. Your position of influence is staggering. Do not take it for granted. Use it to point these moldable hearts to Jesus. You are bigger than life to them; so point them beyond yourself to eternal life with God. So what does it look like to teach your grandchildren?

Be a babysitter, and you will never lack for opportunities to influence your grandchildren. Your children will rise up and call you blessed every time you give them a break from the kids. Or maybe you can be a surrogate grandparent for those who do not have grandparents. The safe environment you provide for your children to drop off their children is invaluable for both of you. Where else can you have this much fun?

Play games with them, explore, build a campfire, go shopping, play hide-and-seek, make-believe, and dress up. Trips are another fun teaching tool. Plan ahead and expose them to other people and places that will broaden their perception and give them a greater appreciation and understanding about different types of cultures. But all the time you are conscientiously weaving God's truth into the conversation and through your behavior.

Yes, this is the stage of life you find yourself winding down and you do not have as much energy as before, but what an opportunity. Regardless of their stage of life—pure preschoolers, energetic children, or idealistic teenagers—they will keep you young. Refuse to quietly slip away and do your own thing. Stay engaged in the lives of your grandkids for their sakes, but it is even more important to stay involved for the sake of God's glory.

"I have been reminded of your sincere faith, which first lived in your grandmother Lois and in your mother Eunice and, I am persuaded, now lives in you also" (2 Timothy 1:5).

Do I point my children and grandchildren beyond myself to the Lord, so our godly legacy will live on?

Related Readings: Psalm 103:17; Proverbs 13:22; Proverbs 17:6; 1 Timothy 5:4

SPIRITUAL RECEPTIVITY

"Then Jesus said, 'He who has ears to hear, let him hear.'"
Mark 4:9

Spiritual receptivity is necessary for the growing follower of Christ. Jesus knew that there had to be a willingness to want to know and understand before there could be any comprehension of His teachings. This hunger for God is an innate appetite that only He can satisfy. Even if you do not hear, you can want to hear. This is the attitude of a growing disciple of Jesus Christ. A willing heart is what the Holy Spirit infuses with insight.

Spiritual receptivity is born out of your attitude and validated by your actions. Actions are an indicator but not an initiator of openness to the Almighty's agenda. Have you ever grown weary working for the Lord, struggling to have a patient attitude? Yes, we all have from time to time, but it is a patient and grateful attitude that hears Christ communicate the most clearly. Gratitude for His grace, love, and forgiveness leads to hearing His voice.

His Word lodges alive and eventually bears fruit when the ears of your heart humbly listen to the Lord with an attitude of obedience. Jesus explained the results of a spiritually receptive heart; hearing and understanding His Word, thus finding faith and healing. Indeed, the comprehension of His ways is not limited to a select few "professional Christians." In fact, their ministry vocation can become a stumbling block to belief.

"'For this people's heart has become calloused; they hardly hear with their ears, and they have closed their eyes. Otherwise they might see with their eyes, hear with their ears, understand with their hearts and turn, and I would heal them.' But blessed are your eyes because they see, and your ears because they hear. For I tell you the truth, many prophets and righteous men longed to see what you see but did not see it, and to hear what you hear but did not hear it" (Matthew 13:15–17).

Spiritual receptivity means I submit to the Holy Spirit's prodding to preempt my pride. Instead of reacting to raw data, I wait and process with prayer so I am able to gain God's perspective and not be rushed by the world's way of doing things. Spiritual receptivity sees the face of God and hears the heart of heaven.

"Whether you turn to the right or to the left, your ears will hear a voice behind you, saying, 'This is the way; walk in it'" (Isaiah 30:21).

Do I hear with a heart toward hearing from heaven? Is my heart humbled to hear from the Holy Spirit?

Related Readings: 2 Samuel 7:22; Jeremiah 6:10; Romans 11:8; 2 Timothy 4:3

VOCATIONAL FULFILLMENT

"When his master saw that the LORD was with him and that the LORD gave him success in everything he did, Joseph found favor in his eyes and became his attendant. Potiphar put him in charge of his household, and he entrusted to his care everything he owned." Genesis 39:3–4

What brings you fulfillment in your work? Is it the sense of accomplishment? Is it the opportunity to encourage someone? Is it the satisfaction of caring for your family? Is it the sense of security from a steady income stream? Your vocational fulfillment flows from a combination of these characteristics and more. When you are fulfilled in your job, you are able to filter through the negatives on the way to the positives.

Be careful not to equate feeling passionate about your position with being fulfilled in your work. Passions ebb and flow around the excitement of a situation, like a start-up when everyone is thinking and working twenty-four hours a day, seven days a week. But this passionate breakneck pace is not sustainable. Your career is a marathon, not a sprint. Indeed, if you are absorbed in your work, not constantly glancing at the clock, then perhaps you are in a place of fulfillment.

"He named him Noah and said, 'He will comfort us in the labor and painful toil of our hands caused by the ground the LORD has cursed'" (Genesis 5:29).

Is it your sense of control over the outcome that draws you to serve where you work? You feel empowered, you are able to expand your skills, and you can make a meaningful contribution in your community as a parent or an employee. Vocational fulfillment flows from a heart engaged in a mission that means something to you and to the Lord.

If Christ has placed you where you are, can you be content to serve Him wholeheartedly? The Almighty's vocational assignment carries its own sense of satisfaction. Joseph found favor because God placed him in his leadership role. In the same way, use your workplace platform as a launching pad for the Lord. Your ability to support others, offer promotions, and create a caring culture facilitates fulfillment for everyone.

Vocational fulfillment is a faith journey that brings out the best in you and those around you. God blesses the work He assigns. Have you accepted the Lord's assignment? "From the time he put him in charge of his household and of all that he owned, the LORD blessed the household of the Egyptian because of Joseph" (Genesis 39:5).

What brings me fulfillment in my job? How can I help others find fulfillment in their work?

Related Readings: Genesis 6:22; Exodus 35:30–32; 1 Corinthians 12:28; 1 Peter 4:10–11

LOVE GOD

"Love the LORD your God with all your heart and with all your soul and with all your strength."
Deuteronomy 6:5

Why do we love God? We love Him because He commands us to love Him. We love Him because He first loved us. He loved us sacrificially with the death of His Son Jesus. He loves us unconditionally with the infinite depth of His grace. Comprehension of Christ's unfailing love compels us to love. "Live a life of love, just as Christ loved us and gave himself up for us as a fragrant offering and sacrifice to God" (Ephesians 5:2).

Love flows from our lips in praise and worship and from a heart of gratitude. Why do we love God? We love Him because we long to obey our Creator. Why do we love God? We love Him because we want to love the One who loves us. His love is irresistible. Like a child responds to a parent's love, so we long to love our Lord. God created us to love. So to love, begin by first loving Him. Your love for others flows from your love for God.

How do you love the Lord? First you give everything over to Him. "They gave themselves first to the Lord and then to us in keeping with God's will" (2 Corinthians 8:5). He desires all of you. This is the Lord's love language. Specifically, you give your heart, mind, will, emotions, and spirit to God. Because you love Him, you can trust Him.

You trust Him with your relationships, money, health, career, children, and future. When you give Him your worship and praise, you love Him. When you give to others, you love Him. When you give Him credit for your successes in life, you love Him. Love leads to giving. Your gifts to God invite others to want to understand God's gift of grace.

Indeed, your love of God is a catalyst to draw others to Him. Your love of God solicits questions from a searching world like "Why do you love so purely and passionately?" or "Why is your God worthy of such adoration and gratitude?" Let them in on your Savior's secret. You are able to love Him because He first loved you. Loving God is job one for the follower of Christ. He expects it, and He deserves it.

"Grace to all who love our Lord Jesus Christ with an undying love" (Ephesians 6:24).

Do I allow my heavenly Father to love me thoroughly so I can love others unconditionally?

Related Readings: 2 Chronicles 6:14; Psalm 86:15; 2 Thessalonians 2:16; 2 Thessalonians 3:5

SOURCE OF SUCCESS

"You may say to yourself, 'My power and the strength of my hands have produced this wealth for me.' But remember the LORD your God, for it is he who gives you the ability to produce wealth."
Deuteronomy 8:17–18

What is the source of your success? You may say that you worked hard to earn your good living. Yes, but God gave you the strength and energy to work hard. You may point out that you are smart and have been able to penetrate a market, meeting a unique need. This may be true, but God gave you the intelligence and the foresight to plan and create. He is the reason for your success, but it is easy to forget the source of your success.

Do you remember when you first started out how needy you were? You were needy for the right professional connections. You were needy for a career break. But most of all you were needy for God. There was a dependency on Him for everything. You would not have thought to go through a day without consulting and conversing with the Lord.

"For by the grace given me I say to every one of you: Do not think of yourself more highly than you ought, but rather think of yourself with sober judgment, in accordance with the faith God has distributed to each of you" (Romans 12:3).

But now since you have tasted success, you may not "feel" your need for God with the same intensity, though your need is even greater. Now that you are "successful," will you credit God with your success, managing your wealth from His perspective? Or maybe your success has slipped away and left you feeling average at best. Perhaps it is time to reemploy the tried and true trust in the Lord of hard work and abundant humility.

Have you become too busy to pray? Do you need more time to be still and sort out your options? Wealth creates choices, and without the wisdom of almighty God you choose poorly. Yes, God is very interested in how you deploy His stuff. Is your goal "bigger and better" or is it "giving and serving"? What a unique opportunity wealth has afforded you. As His steward, how are you investing your time and money in God's kingdom?

Your Savior Jesus is the originator and initiator of success. He gives you the ability to produce wealth and the biblical guidelines to manage wealth. Have you forgotten the source? One good way to be freed from the grip of pride that accompanies success is to give away your stuff to the extent that you are led to limit your lifestyle.

Walk in humility, and point to God as the source for your success and the reason for your generosity. "Yet for us there is but one God, the Father, from whom all things came and for whom we live; and there is but one Lord, Jesus Christ, through whom all things came and through whom we live" (1 Corinthians 8:6).

Do I glorify God with my life?

Related Readings: Joshua 1:8; Psalm 118:25; Daniel 4:30; 1 Corinthians 4:7

SERVE THE POOR

"There will always be poor people in the land. Therefore I command you to be openhanded toward your brothers and toward the poor and needy in your land."
Deuteronomy 15:11

What does it mean to be poor? Our basic needs of food, clothing, and shelter are a struggle for the poor. Life is on hold because they are not sure where their next meal is coming from or if what little they do eat has nutritional value. Their clothing is threadbare and insufficient to fight the elements of a blistering cold winter, or perhaps they have no home and are transient from one shelter to another. Indeed, God commands us to care for the poor.

However, those with abundance are tempted to judge the poor. They want to remind them that their disadvantages are due to poor choices. This may or may not be true, but they do not need sermonizing. What they need is their needs to be met. When we give bread to a growling stomach, we earn the right to offer the "Bread of Life" to their lean soul. Jesus said, "I tell you the truth, he who believes has everlasting life. I am the bread of life" (John 6:47–48). Food is a friendly facilitator of conversation about Christ.

So what are some ways we can be openhanded toward the poor? Intentionality is a key to effectively reaching out to the poor. Be intentional to schedule time with them. Perhaps you engage in an after-school reading program or sports activities. Your time is golden; so give some of your gold away by blocking out time to hang out with poor children.

When you wipe the nose of a child who lacks proper medicine or, more importantly, offer the love and security of a father, you become that child's friend and mentor. When you talk with a single mom who is weepy because of the physical and mental abuse she has received, your anger compels you to get her out by educating her regarding other options.

When a teenager is unable to have a well-balanced diet because his parents have spent the family's food money to buy drugs, your heart bleeds for him or her. These are the poor among you. We are insulated in our bubble of prosperity while the poor struggle in despair. Jesus walked among the poor. Do I? What can I do to serve just one who is poor?

"Do not go over your vineyard a second time or pick up the grapes that have fallen. Leave them for the poor and the alien. I am the LORD your God" (Leviticus 19:10).

Lord, whom do I need to serve in your name?

Related Readings: Exodus 23:11; Leviticus 25:25; Matthew 19:21; Luke 19:8

DEATH OF DISCOURAGEMENT

"Be strong and courageous.... The LORD himself goes before you and will be with you;
he will never leave you nor forsake you. Do not be afraid; do not be discouraged."
Deuteronomy 31:6, 8

God is with you; through faith in Jesus He is right here. If the Lord physically walked with you throughout the day, would you be afraid or discouraged? Of course you would be totally encouraged and secure. By faith your heavenly Father walks with you day in and day out. You are not left out in the cold. You have the resources of a child of God to be strong and courageous. Thus, rise up and receive the grace and strength of the Lord.

Yes, life does have its moments, and, yes, there are times of discouragement and fear, but you are not to dwell there. You can be confident because the Lord is preparing the way before you. He is executing the due diligence for your life's future. He is your advance man as you move forward. There will be bumps along the way, but as long as you follow the Lord, He will smooth the way, preparing your path.

Listen to what the Lord says: "I will lead the blind by ways they have not known, along unfamiliar paths I will guide them; I will turn the darkness into light before them and make the rough places smooth. These are the things I will do; I will not forsake them" (Isaiah 42:16). You can take courage because Christ is your compass and your companion.

Above all, He will never leave you or forsake you. Yes, you have and will face difficulties and heartache. Some of the adversity you encounter may feel insurmountable. But do not despair to the point of giving up. He has not left you. Even though it may not always feel like it, He is there. Like a child off at college for the first time, the security and support of his parents seems distant, but mom and dad still love him profusely though separated by distance.

When you blow it, He is there. When you succeed, He is there. When you are angry and fearful, He is there. He never leaves you. "I will never leave you nor forsake you" (Joshua 1:5). So maybe it is time to slow down and take an inventory of God's faithfulness over the years. It is at the point of your pain that others look to see if your Christianity works. Anybody can claim Christ when the road is smooth, but what if the bottom falls out and life stinks? Where do others see you turn? Do they see faith or fear?

When you fail and fall on your face, you will succeed if you fall on your knees in prayer and humbly depend on the Lord. When a fire breaks out we tell our kids to stop, drop, and roll. God gently encourages you in your fiery trial, reminding you to stop, drop to your knees, and pray. "But Jesus immediately said to them: 'Take courage! It is I. Don't be afraid'" (Matthew 14:27).

Have I prayerfully received the courage Christ offers?

Related Readings: Joshua 1:9; Psalm 9:9; 1 Corinthians 1:8; Ephesians 6:10

FOLLOW GOD'S WORD

"When he takes the throne of his kingdom, he is to write for himself on a scroll a copy
of this law.... He is to read it all the days of his life so that he may learn to revere the
LORD his God and follow carefully all the words of this law and these decrees."
Deuteronomy 17:18–19

No one is above the law, and no one is above God's law. From the earliest origins of government, God instructed the rulers to write, read, follow, and obey His Word. God knew the tremendous wisdom and character needed by a leader to govern fairly and effectively. Integration of God's principles is developed by a lifelong habit. The more you rise in power and responsibility, the more you need to understand the wisdom of God.

You cannot lead like Christ without comprehending and applying Scripture. Without the influence of the Bible, your decisions become shallow, sentimental, and self-serving. Decisions untethered from the truth contribute to moral decay and cultural confusion. You are on solid, historical ground in expecting a biblical worldview from your local, state, and national leaders. Do not expect a state church, but expect a state influenced by the church.

Our expectations of government leaders should be grounded in God's eternal Word. He is the gold standard for conduct and character. What do your state and national senators and representatives believe about the Word of God? Where do your mayor and councilmen stand? Your leaders are a reflection of you. The best minds our culture has to offer are anemic without the filter of faith on their thinking. Intelligence without intimacy with the Almighty leads to pride and self-rule. The Bible is our baseline for belief and behavior.

We are a government of the people, by the people, and for the people. Therefore, can we expect our political leaders to represent their people with a biblical understanding and to decree laws based on biblical standards? Yes, otherwise the logical conclusion to no biblical standard for belief is a messy morality.

We cease to be a God-fearing nation when everyone does what he or she thinks is right; someone has to be wrong for right to mean anything. May God save us from wisdom that leaves out instruction from the Lord's law.

"Jesus replied, 'Are you not in error because you do not know the Scriptures or the power of God?'" (Mark 12:24).

How can I be an exceptional student of Scripture? Whom can I elect to government whose heart is governed by God?

Related Readings: Joshua 1:8; Jeremiah 13:10; John 2:22; Acts 18:28

ACCURATE INFORMATION

"He [Apollos] was a learned man, with a thorough knowledge of the Scriptures.
He had been instructed in the way of the Lord, and he spoke with great fervor and taught
about Jesus accurately, though he knew only the baptism of John." Acts 18:24–25

Accurate information is an expression of integrity. It is the ability to gather all the pertinent facts and communicate them clearly to all necessary parties. It is when we get in a hurry that we distort data and forget details. We need to slow down and do an accuracy audit of our information. Are the dates right? Are the details precise? Does everyone affected understand? Accurate information and comprehension create creditability.

Accuracy begins by being properly schooled and instructed, so you become a subject matter expert in the material you manage. Apollos was a student of Scripture. He examined the mind and heart of God expressed in Holy Writ, and he allowed others to instruct him in the way of the Lord. He rightly divided the truth because he understood and applied the truth.

"Be diligent to present yourself approved to God, a worker who does not need to be ashamed, rightly dividing the word of truth" (2 Timothy 2:15 NKJV).

Have you gone to school on the subject you are seeking to master? Do you have a mentor to instruct you and hold you accountable? Excellent work requires you to be an apostle of accurate information. As you learn to love the details that matter, your work will matter more. Accurate information is extremely valuable because it is the foundation on which assumptions are built. Does your process protect you from displaying inaccurate information?

Confidence comes when there is clarity of facts and comprehension of the content. Doubt will dog you as long as the truth is tentative and details are left unaccounted for. It is better to work thoroughly on one project and get it right than to engage in a flurry of activity with only futility as its outcome.

"You must inquire, probe and investigate it thoroughly" (Deuteronomy 13:14).

*Do I take the proper time to gather, comprehend, and communicate accurate information?
Do I steward data precisely and accurately?*

Related Readings: Deuteronomy 25:15; Psalm 119:140; Acts 22:3; 2 Timothy 3:17

GOD BLESS YOU

"The LORD bless you and keep you; the LORD make his face shine upon you
and be gracious to you; the LORD turn his face toward you and give you peace."
Numbers 6:24–26

We have the opportunity to regularly encourage others with an admonishment for the Lord to bless them. This is the power of the spoken word. You can build up another by conferring upon them the favor of God. What a simple way to sincerely wish upon another the Lord's best with a kind "God bless you." We are not to say it glibly or just out of habit, but with deep feeling and a genuine desire for God's commendation.

We can also pray God's protection on others: their health, their travels, and their relationships. In any situation of uncertainty and/or danger, we can ask God to "keep them." Or maybe there are those who are in dire need of experiencing the fullness of God's grace. They are tired of "trying to live" the Christian life and need a fresh "baptism" of God's graciousness. You can see it in the hardness of their countenance or in the fatigue of their droopy posture. They are lacking in energy and drive. They need an outpouring of grace.

"May God Almighty bless you and make you fruitful and increase your numbers until you become a community of peoples" (Genesis 28:3).

God's grace is a safe environment to recover from rejection and hurt or to gain strength for the journey. Grace is inviting and invigorating. It is cool water for a thirsty soul. Life saps grace from our hearts while intimacy with Jesus infuses grace into our being. You can be a grace killer or a grace giver. People will flock to you because of your graciousness or avoid you like the plague because of your gracelessness.

The secret to giving God's grace is receiving God's grace. Each day ask God to renew your grace quota, filling your grace tank so you can bestow grace on others. What a joy to extend grace to the ungracious and to receive grace from the greatest grace giver, Jesus. Furthermore, our benediction and admonishment to others can be for them to experience God's peace. Once you discover peace with God, you have the peace of God.

His peace can lie dormant in our hearts, or it can flourish like kudzu on a hot summer day. Be a peacemaker. Yes, you can win the argument, but you may lose the relationship. Why not bless with peace rather than curse with contention? When you bless others, you too enjoy the blessings of God.

"Do not repay evil with evil or insult with insult, but with blessing, because to this you were called so that you may inherit a blessing" (1 Peter 3:9).

How can I boldly bestow the Lord's blessing? I want to receive His blessing so I can be a blessing.

Related Readings: Psalm 115:15; Isaiah 65:16; 1 Corinthians 4:12; Romans 12:14

FAITH FOCUS

"Love the LORD your God, listen to his voice, and hold fast to him. For the LORD is your life."
Deuteronomy 30:20

The Christian life is a matter of focus. Do I focus on my fears, my problems, and my needs, or I do I focus on God? Do I love Him, listen to Him, trust Him, and allow Him to consume my life, or am I wrapped up in myself? These are two very different perspectives. One takes life; the other gives life. One saps energy; the other gives energy. So how can we listen to God, trust God, and make God our life? It starts with love.

When we love God, our affections are heavenward. "Since, then, you have been raised with Christ, set your hearts on things above, where Christ is seated at the right hand of God. Set your minds on things above, not on earthly things" (Colossians 3:1–2). Love means we want to be with Him, understand Him, and please Him. Loving God means our love for others or things pales in comparison to our love for Him.

Others may become jealous because of the time and attention you give God. It may be hard for them to understand, but in reality, if your love of God is pure, those closest to you will be better off. Because the Lord loves you and you love Him, you cannot help but love those around you. "This is how we know what love is: Jesus Christ laid down his life for us. And we ought to lay down our lives for our brothers" (1 John 3:16).

Focus on God also means you listen to Him. Quietness and solitude become a part of who you are because God's voice is clear and crisp during stillness and reflection. Other competing noises are snuffed out when you take time to listen. Listen to Him in soft, contemplative worship music, listen to Him through mediation on His Word, or listen to Him beside a bubbling brook under the canopy of His creation. His voice is constant and soothing; He is everywhere, searching to communicate with and comfort His children.

How well do you listen to the Lord? Does it take a posture of desperation? Do the ears of your soul perk up in the presence of your Holy Creator? How can we not listen to the One who holds the world in His hands and who loves us beyond comprehension? Indeed, listen to Him, and do quickly what He says. Obedience acts on what it hears by faith.

Trust is also a part of our focus on God. He can be trusted because He is trustworthy. Others will let us down, but not God. He is always there to comfort us in our affliction and to convict us in our sin. Trust His flawless character; out of this trust flows peace that this life does not offer. Trust most especially during uncertain times; He will work it out for His glory. "The LORD's unfailing love surrounds the man who trusts in him" (Psalm 32:10).

Is my faith focused on receiving the love of my heavenly Father?

Related Readings: Psalm 115:15; Isaiah 65:16; 1 Corinthians 4:12; Romans 12:14

SEEK GOD FIRST

"The men of Israel sampled their provisions but did not inquire of the LORD."
Joshua 9:14

Seek God first, not as an afterthought or as a last resort. What may seem like an innocent decision may in reality be laced with deception. Yes, we need to give others the benefit of the doubt, but not to the exclusion of due diligence. This vetting process is the gathering of facts, their evaluation, and determination of what those facts mean. Wisdom verifies.

"What does the Lord think?" is the most strategic question you can ask. If you leave God out of the equation, you are almost guaranteed to have a flawed conclusion. Yes, He can still work through wrong assumptions, but He can accomplish much more through a prayerful decision-making process. So be careful. It is easy to get caught up in the emotion of the moment. Take time to ask yourself and the Lord pointed questions.

"Let the morning bring me word of your unfailing love, for I have put my trust in you. Show me the way I should go, for to you I entrust my life" (Psalm 143:8).

Perhaps you ask what the real motivation of this person is. What is my motivation? What are some other good options? Will this decision cause me to compromise my values or principles? Is the process respectful to the team? Does this attractive opportunity strategically align with our mission? What are objective and godly counselors telling me? Is this good stewardship? Will this outcome honor and glorify God?

Once you ask these questions or similar ones, be honest with their implications. What is your decision-making process? Be careful not to acquiesce to pressure in the moment. Feel totally free to "sleep on it" and allow time for God to speak to you in the quiet of the night. "I will praise the LORD, who counsels me; even at night my heart instructs me" (Psalm 16:7). It is of real concern if you are being pushed to make a decision. Most forced decisions are not good ones. Therefore, take your time, waiting on the Lord.

Certainly the promise that you will make fast money is suspect. "Steady plodding brings prosperity; hasty speculation brings poverty" (Proverbs 21:5 LB). If it is too good to be true, it is probably not. Wisdom makes friends with experts. Wise legal counsel, tax advisors, spiritual teachers, family counselors, financial planners, business mentors, and medical doctors can save you time and money in the long run.

"But seek first his kingdom and his righteousness, and all these things will be given to you as well" (Matthew 6:33).

Do I see due diligence as insurance? Do I first inquire of the Lord and listen to His voice?

Related Readings: Deuteronomy 4:29; 1 Kings 22:5; Acts 13:22; Acts 15:17

SAFE ENVIRONMENTS

"Then the LORD said to Joshua: 'Tell the Israelites to designate the cities of refuge, as I instructed you through Moses.'" Joshua 20:1–2

We all long for a place where we can be ourselves, where we can be understood and accepted. No one looks forward to a harsh environment of rejection. Rather, it is in those safe places that we find confidence, strength, and healing, especially when we have been deeply hurt, misunderstood, or ignored. God expects us to respect.

"Show proper respect to everyone: Love the brotherhood of believers, fear God, honor the king" (1 Peter 2:17).

You may be really struggling right now. It may be because of your bad choices, your good choices, or from the choices of another. Either way you are hurting. It is imperative that you find a safe place. You are not in a condition to continue by yourself. You need to talk through the issues, express your frustrations, and receive God's grace and understanding. Safe environments allow you to process pain. Who is safe to be around?

Perhaps it is your pastor, a trusted friend, a new employer, or a complete stranger. It may be a secluded trip to the mountains or the beach. Your soul is bleeding. It aches. Have you slipped into depression? Have you paused from the raging battle and let God and others help you heal? A sabbatical from service could give you the courage to carry on.

On the other hand, what are some ways for you to provide a safe environment for friends and family whose faith is faltering? One way is to forgive and accept as God forgives and accepts. "Now instead, you ought to forgive and comfort him, so that he will not be overwhelmed by excessive sorrow" (2 Corinthians 2:7). Let others know they are safe with you. You are not there to fix them or pronounce judgment. You are there to listen, understand, pray for them, and trust God with the needed heart change.

Furthermore, do not underestimate the power of your home environment. An invitation into your home automatically says "I care." Your home is a sanctuary of selfless love and service. The power of someone watching a healthy family experience life is healing in itself. If you allow your home to humbly serve another, it can drive out the infectious puss of pride and be an ointment of healing. A safe environment shows Jesus. Indeed, your Savior is the safest place for your soul.

"We know that anyone born of God does not continue to sin; the one who was born of God keeps him safe, and the evil one cannot harm him" (1 John 5:18).

Whom can I invite into a safe environment of acceptance and love?

Related Readings: Proverbs 29:25; Isaiah 14:30; John 17:12; 2 Timothy 4:18

DEPTH TO BREADTH

"Oh, the depth of the riches of the wisdom and knowledge of God!
How unsearchable his judgments, and his paths beyond tracing out!" Romans 11:33

God's ways require an understanding that is not shallow or unintentional but rather deep and deliberate. As a serious follower of my Savior Jesus I have to ask, "Am I delving deep into the heart and mind of God, or am I satisfied with a surface relationship?" The Almighty wants much more for His children than to be an acquaintance. His desire is an intense intimacy that engages and endures after our simple prayer of salvation to Jesus.

"Yet the LORD longs to be gracious to you; he rises to show you compassion. For the LORD is a God of justice. Blessed are all who wait for him!" (Isaiah 30:18). He longs to be gracious and give His sons and daughters good things. But are we so busy serving Him that we miss being with Him? Depth of relationship with Christ requires coming to His feet by faith and surrendering once again our self, our stuff, and our secrets.

If we take care of the depth, He will take of the breadth. If we make the effort to focus on internal intimacy, He will take care of our external influence. For example, take responsibility for being the spiritual leader in your home, and trust Him to open doors for you to be a spiritual leader outside your home. Focus on prayer with those you work with, and trust Him to open doors for you to pray with influencers outside of your work.

How do I know if I am going deeper with the Lord and not just enamored with theology in my holy huddle? Authentic intimacy with Christ is compelled to love, serve, and worship Him. Your motivation flows from the inside out. Instead of being driven by guilt, you are led by grace. You take yourself less seriously and Christ and His commands more seriously. There is a holy ambition to know God and to make Him known!

Indeed, a Holy Spirit exchange takes place. "God has revealed it to us by his Spirit. The Spirit searches all things, even the deep things of God" (1 Corinthians 2:10). His revelation shows us the way. However, as we dive deep into the riches of His wisdom, we are held hostage by humility. True depth with God honors Him and Him alone. Glory escapes from any self-promotion on earth and assigns itself to its true home in heaven.

As you go deep with the Lord, His affection captures your heart to pray for others like Paul: "God can testify how I long for all of you with the affection of Christ Jesus. And this is my prayer: that your love may abound more and more in knowledge and depth of insight, so that you may be able to discern what is best and may be pure and blameless until the day of Christ" (Philippians 1:8–10). Focus on the depth of relationship with Him, and He will take care of the breadth of relationship with others.

Am I focused on my depth of intimacy with God and trusting Him with my breadth of influence with others?

Related Readings: Psalm 63:1; Daniel 2:22; 2 Corinthians 2:4; 1 Timothy 3:9

PIONEER OR PROCRASTINATOR

"If the LORD is pleased with us, he will lead us into that land,
a land flowing with milk and honey, and will give it to us." Numbers 4:8

What is your picture of God's plan for your future? Is it full of possibilities and promise, or is it frightful and uncertain? Do you dwell on the disappointments of the past, or do you anticipate the blessings of the future? Are you a pioneer who is propelled forward by the prospects of good things, or are you a procrastinator paralyzed by doom and gloom?

The great news is that God has a hope and a future for His loved ones. "'For I know the plans I have for you,' declares the LORD, 'plans to prosper you and not to harm you, plans to give you hope and a future'" (Jeremiah 29:11). You can prayerfully plan and work hard because your Savior scripts your future. The Lord will lead you to His purposeful place.

Is moving forward with God's game plan without suffering and sacrifice? Of course not! Pioneers understand that conquering new horizons requires hardship and overcoming harsh conditions. Procrastinators, however, find excuses why taking new territory will not work. They are intimidated by the big boulders of unbelief that lie ahead on the trail of trust. But is God big enough to remove obstacles and clear the way? Yes, and He is waiting for you to walk with Him by grace. Pioneers are proactive to pray as they move ahead in faith.

Your heavenly Father will clear the way for you to travel to your next destination. Paul understood this. "Now may our God and Father himself and our Lord Jesus clear the way for us to come to you" (1 Thessalonians 3:11). Pioneers show up in the face of uncertainty and expect good things to happen, while procrastinators remain behind terrified by the prospects of bad things. Pioneers are at peace as they see God at work in the unseen.

Pioneers hope. Procrastinators fear. Pioneers encourage. Procrastinators complain. Pioneers support. Procrastinators tear down. Pioneers pray. Procrastinators worry. Pioneers are creative. Procrastinators are dull. Pioneers are determined. Procrastinators give up. Pioneers make progress. Procrastinators lose ground. Pioneers are leaders. Procrastinators were leaders. Pioneers serve a big God. Procrastinators serve a small god.

Are you a pioneer or a procrastinator? Where is the Lord leading you that requires great faith? Is your vision so compelling that unless God shows up it is doomed for failure? Keep pressing forward by faith, and by God's grace you will carry out His perfect plan.

"One thing I do: Forgetting what is behind and straining toward what is ahead" (Philippians 3:13).

Am I willing to release my fears and move forward by faith?

Related Readings: Numbers 20:12; Micah 4:13; Romans 15:23–24; 2 Corinthians 1:17

FAITHFUL FATHERS

"The living, the living—they praise you, as I am doing today;
fathers tell their children about your faithfulness." Isaiah 38:19

Where are the faithful fathers? Where can they be found? They can be found in church, on the little league ball fields, building sandcastles at the beach, and on their knees in prayer for their child's future spouse. They camp in the woods, buy ice cream, go shopping, teach the Bible to middle school youth, and coach high school athletes. They can be found in stable societies and in cultures that love Christ. Faithful fathers matter.

Faithful fathers are not a fantasy but a reality rooted in the fear of the Lord and care for their children. They are compelled by their heavenly Father to provide a home that nurtures, disciplines, accepts, and loves. Determined dads research and discover creative ways to win over their child's heart for Christ.

"Fathers, do not exasperate your children; instead, bring them up in the training and instruction of the Lord" (Ephesians 6:4).

Faithful fathers are friends with Jesus. They see Him as a model of unselfish service, generous giving, radical responsibility, and the ability to put the needs of others before His own needs. "Be devoted to one another in brotherly love. Honor one another above yourselves" (Romans 12:10). Dedicated dads find strength to carry on from Christ's affirmation and accolades. They father for the audience of their heavenly Father.

Lastly, faithful fathers lead their children to know, love, and obey their heavenly Father. This is your most vital role as a dad. Children learn from your life how to live, but they need to hear from your lips how to believe. Tell them the scriptural stories of salvation, sin, forgiveness, and faith. Joseph's perseverance, Esther's courage, Moses' leadership, David's repentance, and Ruth's encouragement are character qualities for them to emulate. Ask God for wisdom and grace to be a faithful father.

"Consequently, faith comes from hearing the message, and the message is heard through the word of Christ" (Romans 10:17).

How does my heavenly Father love me? How does He want me to love my children?

Related Readings: Psalm 44:1–2; Malachi 4:6; Luke 1:7; 1 Corinthians 4:15

EFFECTIVE FATHERS INSTRUCT

"Fathers, do not exasperate your children; instead, bring them up
in the training and instruction of the Lord." Ephesians 6:4

Men, it is not enough to just live right in front of your child; you must explain to them what is right. They need to know the "why" and the "how" behind what you do. Your words work wonders in their tender, teachable hearts. Your instruction means you care to coach and train them in truth. It is dad's tutoring of his tribe that empowers his little ones for life. They may not act like they are listening, but they are. Teaching truth transforms.

Truth leaves your lips and lodges in their hearts. When you take the time to transfer truth to your children, you are setting them up for success. Truth is transformational and freeing. It gives confidence, direction, and discernment. As they move into maturity, you will be missing at times, but truth will see them through.

"Instead, speaking the truth in love, we will in all things grow up into him who is the Head, that is, Christ" (Ephesians 4:15).

Instruct them in how to balance a checkbook, change a flat tire, mow the lawn, shoot a gun, dress appropriately, carry on a conversation, swim, fly a kite, book a plane ticket online, memorize poetry, journal, pray, study the Bible, grill burgers, and make homemade ice cream. Children crave being with their dad and learning his lessons from life. Tell them when you messed up, what you learned, and what you did right. Explain their best motivations are love of God and love for people. Teach lovingly and patiently.

Above all, teach them to know, understand, love, and fear Jesus. He is the truth. "I am the way and the truth and the life" (John 14:6). The more they go to Jesus, the more they will be educated in what matters most. He will reveal to them wisdom and understanding. Instruct your children in intimacy with the Almighty, and they will be inspired with a heart of humility, aspiring to know the mind of Christ. Lead them to sit at the feet of their Savior and learn from Him.

"Take my yoke upon you and learn from me" (Matthew 11:29). What type of instruction does my child respond to the best?

Lord, what is the best routine in this season of life to regularly teach our children Your works and Your ways?

Related Readings: Joshua 4:6–7; Proverbs 13:1; 1 Corinthians 2:13; 2 Timothy 3:15

MISSION ACCOMPLISHED

"For a long time now—to this very day—you have not deserted your brothers but have carried out the mission the LORD your God gave you." Joshua 22:3

What is your personal mission, and what is your professional mission? Are they clearly defined, and do they align? Your mission is your purpose in life; it is why you get up in the morning. Is yours compelling and Christ centric? Your mission flows from your heart, mind, and soul. It is who God made you to be and what He wants you to do. Are you on a mission from God? A life on purpose is able to produce lasting results blessed by the Lord.

Your mission keeps you honest and accountable. It is what God uses to measure the effectiveness of your life. He has created you for a specific purpose with a specific plan. You can rest assured that your mission involves loving Him and loving others, as these are His two greatest commandments. "'Love the Lord your God with all your heart and with all your soul and with all your strength and with all your mind'; and, 'Love your neighbor as yourself'" (Luke 10:27).

Your mission is a time-saver as it is a filter for decision making. It gives you permission to say no to many things and yes to a few things. Your mission is your friend, your motivator, and your protector. Embrace it and let it empower you; then you live life intentionally, rather than drifting and missing God's best. So how can you discover and live out God's mission for your life and work?

Your mining for your mission begins with God. How has He gifted you? What are your passions, and what do you do well? Will the mission you are considering be pleasing and acceptable to Him and those who care about you the most? What are your roles in life? You may be a son, a daughter, a brother, a sister, a parent, a friend, a leader, a husband, or a wife. Consider the influence of your life roles, and weave those into your purpose.

Your personal and professional missions should support alignment between the two. For example, if your personal mission is to be family friendly and your professional responsibilities require you to travel extensively, you may need to reevaluate. If your career is currently demanding an inordinate amount of time, make sure your family understands this is temporary so they can support your efforts.

Your mission should be a regular auditor of who you are and what you are doing. Start today and define who you are by God's definition. What would He have you do at this stage of life? Write it down or update it, and keep it in front of you. Then one day, like Jesus, you can say, "Mission accomplished." "I have brought you glory on earth by completing the work you gave me to do" (John 17:4).

What is God's purpose for my personal life, and am I on purpose for God?

Related Readings: Exodus 9:16; Psalm 57:2; 2 Thessalonians 1:11; Revelation 17:17
Note: *My personal mission is to glorify God by being a faithful husband, available father, loyal friend, and loving leader. My professional mission is to equip ministries for Christ!*

HOUSEHOLD OF FAITH

"Choose for yourselves this day whom you will serve.... But as for me and my household,
we will serve the LORD." Joshua 24:15

Is there enough evidence in your home for you to be convicted of following Jesus Christ? This is a choice that God gives us, a choice to center our home around faith or a facade. What happens behind the doors of your home? Is your home an incubator for faith? Indeed, your ministry begins at home. When your faith works at home, you have the creditability to export it to other environments. It is your laboratory for living.

This does not mean you are without problems, conflicts, and challenges at home. On the contrary, it is when your faith sustains you through family difficulties that it becomes a compelling reason for others to follow Christ. The question for the head of the home is, "Are you the spiritual leader?" As a single parent or father or mother in the home, do you model prayer and Bible study? Does the fruit of the Spirit flow from your character? Are you involved with a community of believers in a local church?

Belief in God is a choice; so what are some wise choices you can make to build your household of faith? Begin by developing an intimate relationship with Jesus Christ. Once you are born again, you have a tremendous opportunity and responsibility to grow in your faith. Learn the Bible, apply it to your life, and let God change you from the inside out.

Next, challenge your family to do the same. Create a culture of prayer that becomes a catalyst for their time with Christ. Family devotions, small groups with other believers, and journaling are a few ways to feed the faith appetite of your loved ones. Take your family to church. This sets the stage for a week of faith and obedience.

Perhaps you read a chapter in Proverbs over dinner. Pray with your spouse. Turn off the television one night a week for thirty minutes, and discuss God's Word. Or act out a Bible story in a play, and then pray for one another. Teach your children to pray for the sick, the lost, and the hurting. Model for them the joy of generous giving and serving.

Show them how to serve the homeless, the orphans, and the elderly. Allow your kids to experience summer camp. It will galvanize their faith. It is a financial sacrifice, but it is an investment that will keep on throwing off dividends throughout their lives.

Talk with your family about your own struggles and failures and God's faithfulness to answer prayer and take care of you in spite of your mistakes. Your family needs to see you as much vulnerable as they do confident. Indeed, facilitating faith in your home is a daily choice. This is one reason Jesus prayed, "Give us each day our daily bread" (Luke 11:3).

Am I a catalyst for Christ in my home? Do I serve the Lord with my family?

Related Readings: Genesis 18:19; 2 Kings 23:24; John 4:53; Acts 18:18

J19

TEST OF FAITH

They were left to test the Israelites to see whether they would obey the LORD's commands, which he had given their forefathers through Moses." Judges 3:4

It is easier to be a Christian when everything is going well. But what happens when things do not go your way? God sends a test or allows a test, and suddenly your faith has an opportunity to come alive and go to a deeper level of dependency. Perhaps you are experiencing disappointment from a friend, an unfaithful spouse, a rebellious child, the death of a loved one, a lost job, or your health is giving you fits.

You can rest assured a test is coming. You have either been through a test, are in a test, or are in between tests, but they are coming; so be ready. It may be a relational test, a financial test, a physical test, a family test, a career test, or a character test, but in God's school of faith, He gives regular exams with eternal consequences.

It may be a quick and unexpected pop quiz or an anticipated grueling final exam. The answer key is abandonment to almighty God. Your eternal instructor is trustworthy. Humbly learn what He is teaching you so you can teach others and become a better follower of Christ. "But what," you ask, "is the purpose of these tests of faith?"

Two possible reasons for God's test of faith are to teach you how to battle the enemy and to validate your obedience to God during difficult times. Your battle is not against a person or persons. It is spiritual warfare with an unseen enemy who lurks behind any and every opportunity he can to deceive, discourage, and destroy you.

Your protection against this spiritual enemy, Satan, is the belt of truth strapped around your waist, an armor of righteousness, your feet covered in peace, a shield of faith, a helmet of salvation, and the sword of the Spirit, God's Word (see Ephesians 6:13–18). Furthermore, engage a community of believers to cover your back with prayer. The believer's preparation and posture are what causes Satan to squirm and flee.

Another reason for your test of faith could be to validate your obedience to God. Will you remain faithful to Him, even when He seems very distant and uninterested? When life is hard, will you stay mad and blame others and God for your misfortune, or will you obey Him? Do the right thing, even when you do not feel like it, and God will honor your efforts.

He has a much bigger plan that does not waste pain. He is looking for trophies of grace to present to those in need of Christ and for those who may be stumbling and struggling in their faith. He is looking for men and women dead to themselves and their selfish desires but alive unto Christ. Pain positions you to be a product of the grace of God.

Yes, it may be very difficult right now, but stay true to God. He is bigger than anything or anyone who may have you down right now. Tests are temporary but trust is forever. "I served the Lord with great humility and with tears, although I was severely tested by the plots of the Jews" (Acts 20:19).

Am I trusting God with this test? Will I obey well?

Related Readings: Genesis 22:1; Deuteronomy 8:2; John 6:6; 2 Corinthians 2:9

GRACIOUS GOD

"But you are a forgiving God, gracious and compassionate, slow to anger
and abounding in love. Therefore you did not desert them." Nehemiah 9:17

We serve a gracious God who does not desert us in our time of need or reject us when we walk away. He knows our secret sins and still loves us in spite of our indiscretions. Our sin breaks His heart, but it does not disqualify us from His grace. David felt this when he prayed to his gracious God, "Turn to me and be gracious to me, for I am lonely and afflicted" (Psalm 25:16). Your need for grace is God's opportunity to extend you grace.

You may ask, "How do I qualify for God's grace?" Breathe. If you are alive, you qualify. His grace reaches a wife who feels worthless because of the verbal and physical lashes from her husband. The grace of God goes out to a brain cancer victim who waits in major uncertainty on an unproven clinical procedure. Your gracious God offers buckets of grace at your point of fear, rejection, anger, dismissal, job loss, divorce, and addiction.

Indeed, we are all candidates for God's grace daily; so take the time to appropriate His great gift. In prayer and by faith receive what your Sovereign Lord offers in abundance. Isaiah says it beautifully: "O LORD, be gracious to us; we long for you. Be our strength every morning, our salvation in time of distress" (Isaiah 33:2). In your bankrupt business and broken soul, His grace is sufficient to see you through. Gulp down gallons of grace.

Moreover, because you have the grace of God at your disposal, be a dispenser of grace. In the heat of relational conflict, it is not about you and your way. It is about the Lord's way. His remedy for relational angst is grace. Give grace to the ungracious, and God will bless your efforts with healing and understanding. People who live in fear have no concept or understanding of faith, but your gracious response gives them a glimpse into grace.

When they lash out, listen. When they accuse, forgive. When they are angry, stay calm. When they are critical, pray for them. When they give up, be there for them. "Each one should use whatever gift he has received to serve others, faithfully administering God's grace in its various forms" (1 Peter 4:10). Grace is the governor that keeps the relational engine running smoothly. Be a grace giver, and you will never lack people to love!

Do I regularly receive a fresh infusion of God's grace into my mind, soul, and spirit? Do I liberally live out grace and give grace to the ungracious and undeserving?

Related Readings: Proverbs 22:11; Joel 2:13; Ephesians 3:7; Philemon 1:25

J21

GENEROUS GOD

"Let them give thanks to the LORD for his unfailing love and his wonderful deeds for men, for he satisfies the thirsty and fills the hungry with good things." Psalm 107:8–9

The generosity of our God is unprecedented with His unfailing love and wonderful deeds. He gives rest when we are weary. He gives peace when we are fearful. He gives joy when we are sad. He gives comfort when we are sorrowful. He gives forgiveness when we are guilty. He gives hope when we are doubtful. He gives us His Son Jesus for salvation and His Holy Spirit for our comfort, conviction, and direction. He gives!

Why is the Lord so extremely charitable to His children? He gives because He loves. He loves you too much to leave you lost in your sins. This is why He gave Jesus as your gift of forgiveness. He loves you too much to leave you bound by lies. This is why He gave you the Holy Spirit to lead you in all truth. The revelation and understanding of truth is part of the Lord's abundant provision. His truth is your freedom to live well.

"He who forms the mountains, creates the wind, and reveals his thoughts to man" (Amos 4:13).

Moreover, it is God who gives you contentment in your work and wealth and possessions to enjoy. "When God gives any man wealth and possessions, and enables him to enjoy them, to accept his lot and be happy in his work—this is a gift of God" (Ecclesiastes 5:19). Therefore, thank Him for what you have, and trust Him for what you do not have.

Because God has been so generous to you, how can you be generous to others? Perhaps you give grace instead of judgment, forgiveness instead of resentment, transparency instead of deception, and freedom instead of control. Do you have family or friends who desperately need you to listen, offer advice, and provide financial assistance? Pray God's provision for people you know, and be available as an answer to your own prayer.

"I pray that out of his glorious riches he may strengthen you with power through his Spirit in your inner being, so that Christ may dwell in your hearts through faith. And I pray that you, being rooted and established in love, may have power...to grasp how wide and long and high and deep is the love of Christ" (Ephesians 3:16–18).

Am I grateful to God for His goodness and gifts to me? To whom can I offer generosity in Jesus name?

Related Readings: Deuteronomy 8:18; Job 33:4; Romans 15:5; 1 Corinthians 15:57

WISDOM WALK

He who walks with the wise grows wise, but a companion of fools suffers harm."
Proverbs 13:20

With whom do you walk (figuratively or literally) through life who offers you wisdom? Do you walk with your father or father-in-law, or mother or mother-in-law? When you walk with them are you slow to speak and quick to listen? Indeed, wisdom comes to those who listen more and talk less. Wisdom is a product of the people who pour into you.

Your wisdom walk may be over the phone with a mentor who lives in another city or a neighbor across the street who by God's grace has already raised God-fearing children. Look around you, and learn from those wise ones the Lord has placed in your life. Pray for a "Paul" who can be your spiritual instructor. "Timothy, my son whom I love, who is faithful in the Lord. He will remind you of my way of life in Christ Jesus, which agrees with what I teach everywhere in every church" (1 Corinthians 4:17).

No one is ever too old or too wise to need a regular wisdom walk. Perhaps you take the time to walk with your spouse after dinner or a coworker during the lunch hour. Vacations are ideal to walk with a wise family member. Walk while the brilliant sun arises or a majestic sunset kisses the horizon. A wisdom walk allows your soul to catch up with the hectic pace of your body. Indeed, walk with the wise, and you will grow wise.

Talk about topics that are relevant to your season of life. Maybe it is insight into parenting a teenager, financial management, decision making, how to love and respect your spouse, books to read, or devotion to Christ. Ask your wise walkers what mistakes they made and how you can learn from them. Listen to their ideas, process them in prayer, and apply them to your life. Otherwise, unused wisdom becomes fodder for foolishness!

Above all, have wisdom walks with almighty God. Unlike Adam and Eve, learn to live in the intimacy of the moment with your heavenly Father. "Then the man and his wife heard the sound of the LORD God as he was walking in the garden in the cool of the day, and they hid from the LORD God among the trees of the garden" (Genesis 3:8). Walk with Jesus, and you will become much the wiser. Keep Christ your closest companion.

Who are wise people in my life with whom I can enjoy regular wisdom walks? What does it look like for me to have wisdom walks with my heavenly Father?

Related Readings: Deuteronomy 8:7; Jeremiah 7:23; Luke 6:13–17; 1 Corinthians 15:33

ENGAGED TO MARRY

"This is how the birth of Jesus Christ came about: His mother Mary was pledged to be married to Joseph, but before they came together, she was found to be with child though the Holy Spirit."
Matthew 1:18

Marriage engagement is an exciting and sobering time. It is exciting anticipating being with the one you believe God has destined you to live life with. It is sobering because of the responsibility to love and care for another person in an unselfish and giving way. Indeed, the engagement period is preparation for marriage. For example, use this window of time to pay off debt and heal any fractured relationships.

Wise young couples are not just infatuated with each other and the upcoming wedding; they are also practical to prepare for marriage. They may enroll in classes on money management from a biblical perspective or invest in completing and discussing a marriage assessment around everyday issues like parenting, spiritual leadership, finances, conflict resolution, decision making, communication, and sex. Premarital instruction and application can save couples from unnecessary conflict down the marriage road.

"Listen, my son, to your father's instruction and do not forsake your mother's teaching" (Proverbs 1:8).

Furthermore, pray for a mentor couple who can shepherd your relationship during this engagement time. Meet with them over dinner or coffee, and listen to their lessons learned during their years of marriage and managing expectations. Be wise to spend much more time in marriage preparation than in wedding planning. One is an event that is over in a few hours, while the other is how you plan to spend the rest of your life together.

Lastly, Christ is the cornerstone of any engagement. Keep Him front and center in your conversation and decision making. Ask Him for the grace to communicate with people who have agendas different from your dream wedding. Make sure your wedding ceremony honors Jesus Christ by keeping the content grounded in Scripture and the look and the feel of the service honor the Lord. Marriage engagement is God's gift to prepare your heart, your mind, your soul, your relationships, your finances, and your faith.

"Righteousness goes before him and prepares the way for his steps" (Psalms 85:13).

How can I best prepare my heart, mind, and finances for marriage? Who is a mentor couple who can invest in us during our engagement and into our marriage?

Related Readings: Genesis 19:14; Deuteronomy 20:7; 1 Corinthians 7:36; Hebrews 13:4

A SENSITIVE HUSBAND

"Because Joseph her husband was a righteous man and did not want to expose
her to public disgrace, he had in mind to divorce her quietly." Matthew 1:19

Men in general and husbands in particular can lack sensitivity, unless the Holy Spirit tames them with truth. A husband can be so caught up in winning he loses the respect of his wife. Husbands have to work at being sensitive, while it comes more naturally to their wives. However, a husband who is sensitive to God learns sensitivity with his spouse. When the Holy Spirit harnesses a man's heart, sensitivity accompanies his actions.

Does sensitivity mean a passive and weak husband? On the contrary, it frees a man to hear from God and administer grace to his wife and children. "Each one should use whatever gift he has received to serve others, faithfully administering God's grace in its various forms" (1 Peter 4:10). Sensitivity means a husband prays for his wife, listens to her heart, offers gentle advice, values who she is, and encourages her with patient love.

A sensitive husband loves his wife in an understanding way. "In the same way, you husbands must give honor to your wives. Treat your wife with understanding as you live together" (1 Peter 3:7 NLT). A husband who walks in humility is a lifelong student of how to love his bride. He understands that her needs change with each season of life, and he is able to apply his understanding love at her point of need.

Therefore, husbands, speak privately to your wives with sensitivity and grace. Never publically disgrace or embarrass them. Learn from them the art of sensitive living. Moreover, wives, trust the Lord to mold your husbands into men of God. Win them over with character, not craftiness. "Your godly lives will speak to them without any words. They will be won over by observing your pure and reverent lives" (1 Peter 3:1–2 NLT).

Practice the presence of God in everyday life, and you will become sensitized by the Holy Spirit's calming effect. It is that gentle work of the Spirit in your soul that grows gentle giants for God. Sensitivity is strength, not weakness; wisdom, not foolishness; humility, not pride; and love, not judgment. Sensitive souls seek God first, before they react in anger.

Listen to Jesus respond to a hard heart with a sensitive spirit: "Jesus looked at him and loved him. 'One thing you lack,' he said. 'Go, sell everything you have and give to the poor, and you will have treasure in heaven. Then come, follow me'" (Mark 10:21).

How can I love and lead my wife with sensitivity and love? How can I model for my husband what it looks like to be sensitive and loving in an understanding way?

Related Readings: Genesis 19:14; Deuteronomy 20:7; 1 Corinthians 7:36; Hebrews 13:4

ANGEL OF GOD

"But after he had considered this, an angel of the Lord appeared to him in a dream and said, 'Joseph son of David, do not be afraid to take Mary home as your wife, because what is conceived in her is from the Holy Spirit.'" Matthew 1:20

There is angelic activity in the unseen world of spiritual activity. These creations of God carry spiritual significance in your life as they serve as God's messengers and His protectors. They helped Joseph overcome his fear by assuring him that the Holy Spirit was the creator of his circumstances; therefore, God had a greater purpose at work.

Do you look for evidence of angelic work around you? Have you considered that Christ has created your circumstances for His greater purpose? We know Jesus had thousands of angels at His side waiting to engage the enemy. "Do you think I cannot call on my Father, and he will at once put at my disposal more than twelve legions of angels?" (Matthew 26:53). Angels are at the Almighty's disposal to come to your aide.

Furthermore, there are good and bad angels that vie for your attention. Though once an angelic emissary presented to God, Satan is in the mix. "One day the angels came to present themselves before the LORD, and Satan also came with them" (Job 1:6). Demons seek to accuse and destroy you with lies, while angels from the Lord lace their language with truth and hope. What voice do you consider when you feel pressure and fear?

Thank God for your guardian angels, but do not take them for granted by using them as an excuse for foolish behavior. "For he will command his angels concerning you to guard you in all your ways" (Psalm 91:11). Reckless living is not an excuse for the deployment of heavenly help. The devil attempted to lure Jesus into presuming on His heavenly Father's favor during a time of weakness, but He resisted him with Scripture.

"Then the devil took him to the holy city and had him stand on the highest point of the temple. 'If you are the Son of God,' he said, 'throw yourself down. For it is written: "He will command his angels concerning you, and they will lift you up in their hands, so that you will not strike your foot against a stone."' Jesus answered him, 'It is also written: "Do not put the Lord your God to the test"'" (Matthew 4:5–7).

Angels are your confident security that Christ is in control. Take comfort in knowing that the enemy is being engaged on your behalf by a superior force and firepower. Use the Bible as your weapon of choice as Satan and His demons cringe and retreat at the sight of truth. Indeed, look out for and listen to the angelic voices in others.

Am I aware of and grateful to God for His angels who surround and protect my family and me? Do I lean into the Lord, His Word, and angelic support when confronting Satan?

Related Readings: Genesis 19:15; Psalm 78:49; Matthew 13:49; Acts 23:8

SAVIOR OF SINS

*"She will give birth to a son, and you are to give him the name Jesus,
because he will save his people from their sins." Matthew 1:21*

The birth of a child is extraordinary, but the birth of God's Son is incomprehensible for humans to fully process. Jesus the Son of God, embedded in the Holy Trinity, who enjoyed the glory of heaven, who has always been, came to earth to live and die for mankind. Christ's incarnation invaded earth in splendor for the salvation of sinful souls.

"In the beginning was the Word, and the Word was with God, and the Word was God. The Word became flesh and made his dwelling among us. We have seen his glory, the glory of the One and Only, who came from the Father, full of grace and truth" (John 1:1,14). Christ came to honor His heavenly Father by revealing His character. Jesus was God's heavenly solution for man's earthly problems of sin, sorrow, and suffering.

From what sins did He come to save us? Are they limited to the Ten Commandments? No, there is no sin that is beyond the forgiveness of your Savior Jesus. Unbelief is exonerated. Pride is pardoned. False humility is forgiven. Adultery is absolved. Lies are let off by the grace of God. Sinless Jesus lived among sinful men and then died for their sins. He said, "It is not the healthy who need a doctor, but the sick. I have not come to call the righteous, but sinners" (Mark 2:17). Sin is a sickness that only faith in Christ can cure.

Because we have all sinned, we all equally need a Savor. Small or large indiscretions require intervention from the grace of God. "For all have sinned and fall short of the glory of God, and are justified freely by his grace through the redemption that came by Christ Jesus" (Romans 3:23–24). You are saved from your sin by placing your faith in Jesus Christ. Halleluiah for the Lord's righteous remedy that covers all our sins!

Have you humbled yourself before Jesus Christ, repented of your sins, and placed your faith in Him as your Lord and Savior? Is there any downside to engaging in an intimate relationship with God through Jesus Christ? Few, if any, have regrets for falling in love with the Lord. So celebrate your salvation, whether your walk with God is infant, adolescent, teenager, young adult, adult, middle age, mature, or elderly. Praise Him!

Jesus died for you so He could work in you and love through you. "But the gift is not like the trespass. For if the many died by the trespass of the one man, how much more did God's grace and the gift that came by the grace of the one man, Jesus Christ, overflow to the many!" (Romans 5:15). When you receive the gift of God's grace, it keeps on giving.

Have I placed my trust in Christ for the forgiveness of my sin? Do I celebrate often His salvation? Am I compelled by love to let others know about His free gift of eternal life?

Related Readings: Psalm 14:7; Isaiah 25:9; 1 Thessalonians 5:9; Hebrews 2:3

DISCERNING GOD'S WILL

"Then Gideon said to God, 'Do not be angry with me. Let me make just one more request. Allow me one more test with the fleece.'" Judges 6:39

Understanding God's will is not always crystal clear, especially if you believe He is leading you to do something new. You may be approaching an initiative you have never tackled before, or you do not feel like you have the adequate faith or resources to accomplish the assignment. This type of questioning is wise. If your motive is to follow God, then the mature thing to do is seek confirmation of His will.

However, do not let fear keep you from taking a risk, and do not allow pride to rush you into the situation half-cocked. God is looking for people who will make hard decisions. Those decisions may cause disagreement or misunderstanding with family and friends, and if God is leading you in this direction, you have no other choice. Just make sure it is God leading you and not ego, anger, or greed.

He has prepared you for this next step of faith. Do not miss it. Most people, as they approach the end of this life on earth, do not regret taking too many risks. Just make sure you take Holy Spirit-led risks. So how can you discern God's best for your life? You may need to lay out a fleece, a test to see if God is in on the deal.

What does it mean to "lay out a fleece"? It does not mean you are tempting God, for this is sin, but it does mean you are trying to discern God's will through people, circumstances, or His Word. But do not be fooled. A fleece is not a magic wand to be used at your whim. Nor is a fleece something we hold over God to get Him to do our bidding.

A fleece is a sincere attempt from a pure heart to discern God's will. Sometimes it revolves around money. If money is not available, this is a very real indicator not to move forward. Sometimes it relates to the process itself. If you really have to force the issue, or if getting an answer from someone is difficult, if it is like "pushing a rope," then you need to be very cautious. If this side of the relationship is so hard and difficult, can you imagine what it will be like on the other side of the relationship?

Another important question is how this opportunity aligns with your principles and values. Will you be challenged spiritually, and will it be family friendly? Or will this new opportunity place you in a situation of compromise? On the other hand, do not hesitate to follow God into the battle. If He is with you, you are in good company.

The best indicator of God's will is the opportunity for Him to be glorified. If success depends on God and His coming through, not just your own ingenuity, then you are on the right track. Trust Him, watch Him work, and your faith and the faith of others will flourish.

Am I rushed, or do I trust the Lord to lead me through a prayerful process?

Related Readings: Exodus 18:15; Mark 3:35; John 11:4; Acts 18:21

THE LORD'S DEFENSE

"I have not wronged you, but you are doing me wrong by waging war against me. Let the LORD, the Judge, decide the dispute." Judges 11:27

People may accuse you of wrong when, in fact, they are wrong. You want to admit your mistakes and become a better person. If, however, the motive of your accuser is not right, if he or she is appealing to your guilt and emotions, then reject the false accusations. When the facts are on your side, be patient and wait on the Lord to defend you.

God would not have you caught up in a lot of sideways energy and activity, distracting you from the best use of your time. Some people are very persuasive and convincing with their words, but their character is lacking and their arguments do not add up. Do not lower yourself to their level and react to their lambasting with an equal fury of words. They do not deserve that much time, attention, and worry. Prayer is your posture.

It is like the bully on the playground trying to get your attention, getting others to cower to his intimidating ways. God is not intimidated by fear tactics, and neither should we. So how do we trust the Lord to defend us in difficult situations? How do we work with a caustic critic who is unreasonable? Seek to stay above the fray of angry arguments.

As you trust the Lord to defend what is right, keep your heart pure. You will be tempted to lash back with infuriating words or, at the other extreme, acquiesce to your critic's demands. Neither of these options is best. What is right is to stand your ground, involve other people as is appropriate to mediate, and remain friendly, firm, and fair. You may need to seek legal counsel to make sure you are following the due process of the law.

However, your ability to do what is right under a firestorm of criticism from someone you thought was a friend can be redemptive in the long run. Maybe your critic will wake up to the realities of what is right. Your short-term pain and patience will hopefully save another from long-term trials. God is the ultimate defender of you and His truth.

You cannot keep your reputation stellar and polished, but your Savior can cleanse your soiled status in the community. Submit to Him and trust Him during this lowly time of litigation, because God is the final say in what is right or wrong. He will judge fairly now and in eternity. You can sleep at night because God is in control of this situation. Your appeal is to almighty God.

"This is what your Sovereign LORD says, your God, who defends his people: 'See, I have taken out of your hand the cup that made you stagger; from that cup, the goblet of my wrath, you will never drink again'" (Isaiah 51:22).

Do I trust the Lord with my defense and my critics?

Related Readings: Psalm 68:5; Isaiah 19:20; 2 Timothy 4:16; 1 John 2:1

GOD'S DEPARTURE

"But he did not know that the LORD had left him."
Judges 16:20

God will never leave the follower of Jesus Christ, but His blessing, favor, and power can. In fact, His favor can leave you, while you are totally unaware of your loss. This is scary. To think that I can go through life believing I am okay with God when, in reality, I totally miss Him is a precarious position in which to live. It is lonely and dangerous to live outside the favor of God, and sometimes it leads to destruction.

Relationships, reputations, and finances can be obliterated when we choose to go our way and not God's way. Do not think you can ignore your spouse and children and think things are still okay with God. Exposure to online pornographic sites does not enhance God's power in your life. Seething anger and unresolved resentment do not cultivate a spirit of understanding God's wisdom and perspective; rather, they hinder your prayers. So how can you know if you are living with God's blessing, favor, and power or without it?

First of all, be honest with yourself. Are you running from God or toward God? Are you who He wants you to be, or are you masquerading, trying to be someone else? Is your anger out of bounds and out of control, or are you under the influence and forgiveness of the Holy Spirit? These are important questions for us to continually ask ourselves.

Then, it is important to be honest with others. We all have blind spots that stunt our spiritual growth. Look to others who truly love you, who can help you identify these sinful tendencies, and who will hold you accountable not to go there. Sin exposed to the light will dry up like a red worm on a hot July sidewalk, while sin concealed in the dark will flourish like rank mildew and mold in a cold, moist, infected cellar.

We do better when others are watching. It is better to be humbled before a small group that knows and loves us than to be humiliated before the masses which do not know us well or care as deeply. Lastly, remember your commitments to Christ, and fulfill them by His grace. Do not stray from your basic discipline of learning and applying God's Word and prayer. Wake up. Do not miss Him. His favor may have already left.

How do I best stay accountable to God and man? Am I experiencing the favor and blessing of the Lord? If not, what is hindering me?

Related Readings: Matthew 25:1–13; Hebrews 13:5; 1 Peter 3:7

ABSOLUTES ALLOW FREEDOM

"In those days Israel had no king; everyone did as he saw fit."
Judges 21:25

Spiritual and moral decline is the fruit of a nation or person who abandons absolutes. Once absolutes are dismissed, liberties are limited. A decline in spiritual fervor and moral purity always leads to the loss of freedom. For example, a home or car left unlocked in the past is locked today for fear of robbery. Indeed, small losses of freedom lead to larger losses of freedom. Without standards based on absolutes, absolutely anything can go.

The threat of stealing moves from your home to corporate America, where in some cases billions of dollars have been bilked to justify a short-term illusion of success to investors. Immoral and unspiritual individuals become deceptive and dishonest if allowed to do what is right in their own eyes. Without boundaries and absolutes, anything can go, and if anything can go, your freedom will deteriorate and eventually be destroyed.

The cultural battle that rages in our country is over the soul of our society. If absolutes win, then our children and grandchildren will see their cherished rights to life, liberty, and the pursuit of happiness extended. Therefore, will we bow to the false promise of freedom wrapped in the guise of no absolutes, or will we expose the lie and uphold God's standards and His definition of absolutes? People flourish where freedom loudly rings!

Yes, we lead out of love and compassion; however, there are behavioral boundaries to be guarded with vigilance. When the sanctity of life and the sanctity of marriage are under attack, we cannot sit passively by and just pray. As followers of Jesus Christ, we have a mandate to defend these bedrocks of civilization. Yes, we are busy, and yes, we have our own problems to deal with, but "you ain't seen nothing yet" if good people do nothing.

Your freedom will continue to deteriorate like the "frog in the kettle" that is unaware but slowly boiling to death. We should be the thermostats of society, not the barometers, and the influencers rather than the ones being influenced. Consider how you might get involved in the parent-teacher association at your child's school or the local government. Volunteer in church or ministries that need your skill set, gifts, and passion. Model the fruit of the Spirit (love, joy, peace, patience, kindness, goodness, faithfulness, gentleness, self-control) as you influence the culture for Christ.

Public policy is a reflection of private morality and spirituality. Absolutes abided by absolutely guarantee your freedom. So, by God's grace, continue to raise the bar of expectations and absolutes so that everyone is doing what is right in the Lord's eyes.

How can I best model and live out His absolutes in my life and in the life of my family? How would Christ have me engage in our cultural battle?

Related Readings: Genesis 4:7; Deuteronomy 6:18; Galatians 5:22; Hebrews 13:7–9

LOYALTY CREATES LOYALTY

"But Ruth replied, 'Don't urge me to leave you or to turn back from you. Where you go
I will go, and where you stay I will stay. Your people will be my people and your God my God.
Where you die I will die, and there I will be buried. May the LORD deal with me,
be it ever so severely, if anything but death separates you and me.'" Ruth 1:16–17

Most people long for loyalty in love, war, and work. You can require loyalty and you may see some response, or you can show loyalty and thus become attractive to loyalty. When you give loyalty, you have a much better chance of receiving loyalty. This is true in marriage, business, parenting, or friendship.

In marriage, how do you think unwavering loyalty makes your spouse feel? If your spouse knows you are loyal, no matter what, how will he or she respond? In most cases a spouse will return loyalty, and both of you will enjoy a tremendous amount of security and peace. Adversity or difficulties should not weaken your loyalty; rather, they should strengthen your resolve to be there for each other. Can you think of a better gift to give someone during difficult times? The quality of your relationship goes to a deeper level.

The work environment is another opportunity to exercise loyalty. A business owner or supervisor should first look at giving loyalty rather than demanding loyalty. Will you be there for the employee during the down business cycle as you have been when everything is going well? What can employees expect from you? Will you be consistently honest or only when it is expedient? Wise leaders create a culture of loyalty. It means you care. It is a two-way street that invites reciprocity. So where does loyalty begin?

Loyalty begins by recognizing, understanding, and receiving God's loving loyalty. Way beyond what we have asked for or deserve, He is loyal. The Lord's loyalty transcends my sin, my poor choices, and my pride. Like the father of the Prodigal Son, He is there. Even when I mope back to Him embarrassed and beaten down, Jesus remains loyal.

The intensity and thoroughness of God's loyalty makes the loyalty of a Saint Bernard or a golden retriever look shallow. He is there to receive you back even when you are - disloyal to Him. Once you recognize and understand the depth and breadth of God's loyalty to you, you cannot help but extend loyalty to others. You are secure in Jesus.

You are compelled to be loyal to another because of God's great loyalty to you! How can you do anything else? You become a loyalty maker rather than a loyalty breaker. People trust that you are with them, believe in them, and expect the best. You give them the benefit of the doubt. Be loyal, and there is a good chance you will receive loyalty, for loyalty creates loyalty.

Has God ever been disloyal to me? How can I remain loyal to the Lord and others?

Related Readings: Deuteronomy 31:6–8; 1 Samuel 22:14; Luke 15:11–32; Philippians 4:3

J2

DEVOTION OR DISCIPLINE

"His heart was devoted to the ways of the LORD."
2 Chronicles 17:6

What is the difference between devotion and discipline? Is one more valuable than the other? Devotion is an overriding commitment to Christ and to His way of doing things. It engages the heart and mind in learning the ways of the Lord and applying them. Devotion must be the driving force behind a disciple's faith to persevere in Christ's call on his or her life. Your devotion to God dictates how you will live your life.

Discipline, on the other hand, is the ability to stay focused on the task at hand. It finishes the assignment or completes the course. Those who are disciplined train to improve their strength or self-control. They are religious at carrying out routines, completing checklists, and getting things done. Discipline is designed to grow your faith with regular readings from God's Word and engaging prayers of praise, thanksgiving, confession, and repentance.

However, make sure your discipline is driven by your devotion, or you become judgmental and insensitive in your sense of accomplishment. Devotion to Christ first keeps your heart of faith full of grace and truth. Discipline without devotion is like a billowing cloud without refreshing rain. It can become so rigid in its rules that it runs off decent and devoted people. Devotion applies itself to God and man. "Be devoted to one another in brotherly love. Honor one another above yourselves" (Romans 12:10).

Furthermore, use your passionate devotion to focus solely on one thing. Like Paul, learn to channel all your energies into one endeavor, and see it through to the end. "Paul devoted himself exclusively to preaching, testifying to the Jews that Jesus was the Christ" (Acts 18:5). Better to complete one task than to start a dozen and leave some undone. Indeed, your devotion to Christ determines your discipline over the long term. So keep this your motivation, and discipline will follow. A heart devoted to the Lord's ways does not stray.

Is my heart devoted to the ways of the Lord? Does my discipline flow from my devotion to Christ?

Related Readings: Leviticus 27:28; Nehemiah 5:16; Matthew 6:24; Acts 2:42

CHRIST AND COUNTRY

"Blessed is the nation whose God is the LORD, the people he chose for his inheritance. From heaven the LORD looks down and sees all mankind." Psalm 33:12–13

God blesses a country that honors Him but brings down a country that dishonors Him. It honors Him for His people to pray in earnest for righteousness to reign in religion, the workplace, the seat of government, and the home. It dishonors the Lord when we behave like His commands are suggestions and we marginalize His mandates. Countries founded on Christ are blessed if they continue with Christ.

Where is our Christ-conscientiousness? Do our actions reflect accountability to almighty God and His ultimate judgment? Faith without the fear of God is weak and anemic in the face of moral relativism, academic attacks, and the indulgences of affluence. A nation that fears the Lord fears sin and its deadly consequences. Thus, Christians are called by Christ to engage in their communities with compassion and with a standard of right and wrong.

The law of the Lord is the basis of the law of the land in a country that honors Christ. The Bible is clear: "All who sin apart from the law will also perish apart from the law, and all who sin under the law will be judged by the law. For it is not those who hear the law who are righteous in God's sight, but it is those who obey the law who will be declared righteous" (Romans 2:12–13). God blesses a nation that obeys His laws.

Therefore, for our children's sake, let us raise our standards of acceptable actions for preachers, politicians, and parents. Let us return to public prayers of dependence on the Lord and private prayers of repentance from sin. Without God's blessing a country creeps into moral chaos, an economic meltdown, and institutional irrelevance, but with God's blessing a country thrives on trust in Him. We desperately need to stay in a position to receive God's blessing.

"If my people, who are called by my name, will humble themselves and pray and seek my face and turn from their wicked ways, then will I hear from heaven and will forgive their sin and will heal their land" (2 Chronicles 7:14).

Am I a citizen who unashamedly represents Christ in my community? Do I pray with persistence and humility for repentance among God's people?

Related Readings: Exodus 19:5–6; Psalm 144:15; Romans 12:14–15; 1 Peter 2:9

J4

AUTHENTIC INDEPENDENCE

"For the LORD your God will bless you as he has promised, and you will lend to many nations but will borrow from none. You will rule over many nations but none will rule over you."
Deuteronomy 15:6

The independence of a nation erodes under the heavy load of debt. As with personal debt, a nation in debt becomes a servant to its lender. "The rich rule over the poor, and the borrower is servant to the lender" (Proverbs 22:7). What happens when the lending nation becomes hostile, demanding, and controlling? It is perilous for a group of good people to become dependent on bad people who want to bring them down.

Where is our collective conscience as citizens over our government's credit abuse? Will we remain passive and silent as the future of our children is mortgaged overseas? We can continue to ignore the downside of our national debt and spend it all on ourselves. One day someone has to pay. Debt does not go away. It just entrenches its influence. Printing more money only compounds and extends the problem. Debt needs to die.

"Let no debt remain outstanding, except the continuing debt to love one another, for whoever loves others has fulfilled the law" (Romans 13:8).

There is a solution. It starts with individuals living within their means. We can eradicate our personal debt and demand the same of politicians and preachers. Authentic independence is achieved in households and halls of government by keeping a tight rein on debt. We do not spend our way out of a financial fiasco; we refrain from irrational expenditures, and we spend only what we can afford. Wisdom stops spending selfishly.

The Lord's command is to be a lender, not a borrower. The nation who lends has the leverage of influence, control, and economic benefit. Authentic independence is achieved by being on the lending side of the debt equation. Pride spends like a drunken sailor with no thought of tomorrow. However, humility saves today and pays off debt to obtain a safe and secure future. Authentic independence depends first on God and His laws.

"You were bought at a price; do not become slaves of men" (1 Corinthians 7:23).

How can I be a wise citizen who manages money responsibly?

Related Readings: Deuteronomy 28:15, 43–45; Proverbs 3:27–28; Romans 13:8

TRUST TRUSTWORTHY PEOPLE

*"'I will do whatever you say,' Ruth answered. So she went down to the threshing floor
and did everything her mother-in-law told her to do."*
Ruth 3:5–6

Sometimes we just do not know what to do, but God puts trustworthy people into our lives to guide us through the decision-making process. He speaks through trustworthy people. It is imperative to seek out trustworthy people so your emotions do not lead you astray. You can talk yourself into just about anything. One day you are convinced you need to move in one distinct direction, and the next day you feel the need to go in the opposite direction.

If you are not careful, you will fall into a pattern of using "rabbit ears." You default to the counsel of the last person who offered you advice. Yes, it is important to get input from a variety of people, but promise yourself and God that you will not commit to a decision until your counselors have properly weighed all the facts and you have prayerfully considered the various ideas offered by your trusting friends.

In some situations you are at a complete loss regarding what to do. You feel you have exhausted your options, and your emotional capacity is spent. You are at a crossroads and probably do not have the clarity of mind to make the best decision. This is where it is critical that you listen to trustworthy people. While you are in this funk or fog, look to them for guidance, and do what they say. Trust that God is speaking through them.

What do you look for in a trustworthy person? They could be your spouse, your pastor, a relative, a doctor, a lawyer, a coach, or a close friend. Pray for someone who has your best interests in mind. This person is not looking to get anything from you; rather, he or she wants to give you outstanding advice and help you through this trying transitional period in your life. A trustworthy person is someone who understands you and your situation and who perhaps experienced a similar situation in the past.

Traveling to an unfamiliar region of the United States or a foreign country can be disconcerting. Ideally, your preparations will include conversations with those who have been there. They recommend what to see and what not to see, what foods to enjoy and what to avoid. The best scenario is for the experienced traveler to accompany you on the trip and offer you trusted advice along the way.

In the same way, surround yourself with people who have been there, trustworthy individuals, a go-to person who will not lead you astray. If you currently are in the middle of an uncertainty, seek out three trusted people, discover the common theme in their counsel, and simply do what they say. God is probably speaking through them.

"The way of fools seems right to them, but the wise listen to advice" (Proverbs 12:13).

Who are three people I know who can offer trustworthy advice for a pending issue?

Related Readings: Nehemiah 13:13; Daniel 2:45; Luke 16:11–12; 1 Corinthians 7:25

J6

ATTENTIVE TO CHILDREN

"Samuel continued as judge over Israel all the days of his life. From year to year he went on
a circuit from Bethel to Gilgal to Mizpah, judging Israel in all those places." 1 Samuel 7:15–16
"But his sons did not walk in his ways. They turned aside after dishonest gain
and accepted bribes and perverted justice." 1 Samuel 8:3

Children need attention. They spell love T-I-M-E. We can be so busy, even busy doing good things, we miss out on God's best, which is spending time with our children. They need time to laugh and time to cry, time to run and jump, and time to be still and nap. Children need time to pray, go to the library, make snow angels, ski, play dolls, dress up, make believe, play in the dirt, climb trees, and play hide-and-seek.

Parents have the tremendous privilege of investing time in their children by having dates, hunting, and shopping together. You can take trips, run on the beach, chase sand crabs, swim, and watch the sun go down. You can eat a peanut butter sandwich and pretzels at their school, attend their sporting events, and proudly watch their school play or awards ceremony.

If we miss our children experiencing life, we neglect them. If we neglect our children, there is a high probability they will reject us and/or our faith. Indeed, their perception of dad and mom is their perception of God. If we are distant, uninvolved, and disengaged, so they will see their heavenly Father. Therefore, invest time, money, and love in your children.

Children require, and in some cases demand, a lot of attention. Your role is to be there for them, to be available. Your quality time with your children flows from your quantity time with them. You cannot stage or script quality time. It just happens, and you have to be around them to enjoy its benefit. When children are comfortable, they open up. Sometimes unexpectedly they begin to share their hearts. These spontaneous snippets of time become precious, teachable moments. Remember, quality time requires quantity time.

For example, after attending their sporting event, affirm and encourage them. They already know about their mistakes. They just need to know everything is okay and they will do better next time. The most important part is showing up. You are the first person they look for in the crowd. When you are there, it shows you care. You cannot make up for these childhood days, but there will be other deals, work projects, ministry roles, and business opportunities. Be careful not to let work or ministry compete with your family.

When at all possible, integrate two competing responsibilities. It may mean a family mission trip or serving together in the church nursery. If work requires travel, take a child with you. Make it a special trip with just the two of you. Let your children watch you "do life." Let them see you trusting God with a difficult situation or watch you give Him credit for a great success. Then as they mature into adults, your children feel accepted rather than neglected, they respect mom and dad, and they embrace faith in Jesus.

How does my child like to spend time with me?

Related Readings: Deuteronomy 6:6–7; Judges 14:3–4; Luke 2:41–52; Hebrews 11:23

INTELLIGENT DESIGN

"They lay their crowns before the throne and say: 'You are worthy, our Lord and God,
to receive glory and honor and power, for you created all things, and by your will they were
created and have their being.'" Revelation 4:10–11

God is the intelligence behind the design of creation and life. He is the architect of the universe and the engineer of eternal life. He is the wisdom behind the world. The soft, pinkish-blue sunset, He designed. The brilliant, bold and bright sunrise cascading over the treetops, He designed. The pure snow-capped mountains projecting toward heaven in reverence, He designed. The luscious green and gorgeous vegetation, He designed.

The deep blue seas and baby blue sky, He designed. The furry and sometimes ferocious predator-like animals, He designed. The multicolored bugs and beetles, He designed. The chirping sparrows, the clacking seagulls, and the hovering hummingbirds, He designed. Fish, shrimp, whales, and penguins, He designed. Most fascinating, the intricately designed makeup of water and flesh called the human body, He designed.

He is the Intelligent Designer of earth and mankind. It takes more arrogance than faith to believe otherwise. He gave us intelligence to understand that He is the Intelligent Designer. If we cannot accept that God is behind intelligent design, then we are not being intellectually honest. The evidence is overwhelming. Its affirmation quietly rests within our hearts, its confirmation floods our minds, and its declaration explodes from out of our mouths.

He cannot be ignored. Ironically, some who claim superior intelligence reject God as the Intelligent One. This is the pitfall of pride. Pride blinds us to the simple truth that we are not the smartest. Intellectual snobs conjecture, contrive, conjure up, complicate, and compromise Christ as creator God. This is easy to accept for Christians, since faith in Christ moves man from the center of the universe to worship the Creator of the universe.

Because of God's vast creation that is validated by His intelligent design, He deserves our utmost for His highest. It is no accident that heaven is full of hilarious hallelujahs on behalf of God the Father, God the Son, and God the Holy Spirit. Heaven is a raucous revival of real live worship for Christ who was slain for our sins.

Anything good that has been accomplished by God through you will be laid at the feet of Jesus. Your crown of rewards will not be proudly worn on your head; rather, it will be placed before the lowest spot in front of Christ. Heaven is all about Him.

Worship of Him on earth is but an appetizing morsel of what we will have to feast on when we gaze upon His face in glory. His design of you and creation is not only intelligent, it is good. Therefore, worship Him now in preparation of worshiping Him later. Praise, honor, all power, and all glory go to God! His intelligent design honors the Intelligent One.

Do I have an intelligent understanding of God's intelligent design? How can I grow my understanding of my Creator, so I can creatively communicate it to His creation?

Related Readings: Psalm 22:27–31; Psalm 36:6–7; Mark 10:10; Romans 1:18–23

PREPARE THE WAY

"This is he who was spoken of through the prophet Isaiah: 'A voice of one calling in the desert, "Prepare the way for the Lord, make straight paths for him."'" Matthew 3:3

There is a preparation of the heart that is needed to move from the wilderness of fear to the garden of God's grace. Outside of Christ we are all in our own wilderness, the feeling of detachment from God and His goodness. However, in His presence is a paradise of peace and comfort. So prayerful followers of Jesus continually prepare for the Lord to sup with them in the sanctuary of their souls. You prepare in anticipation of His presence.

How do you prepare for Christ's coming out in your life? For example, you may be in a financial wilderness. If so, seek the wisdom of the Bible regarding managing money. Perhaps you create a spending plan; if necessary, downsize your lifestyle to lower expenses; and maintain, even increase, giving. Sometimes it is necessary to seek help from a seasoned financial manager, one with objective advice and strategies for your season of life.

Your wilderness may be related to a hard issue that has been ignored but now needs addressing. Because communication has not been clear, each party has created his or her own reality around conflicting expectations. Take time to get everything out in the open, and talk through a process that works for everyone. A relational wilderness isolates you from the intimacy you need with others and with the Lord. Intimacy is united, not divided.

Most of all, make sure prayer has prepared a path for the Holy Spirit to lead and direct your life. Consider prayerful goals that can guide your life over the coming months. Collaborate with your spouse at home and your colleagues at work to come up with the best plan and a process for its ongoing implementation. For example, leave the wilderness of bad eating habits to the accountability of well-prepared meals of healthy foods. This takes time and money, but the dividends literally pay off for a lifetime.

Lastly, how is your heart? Is it tender to the things of God? Is the Scripture sustenance for your soul? The weeds of unbelief can create confusion, but the luscious, green grass of God's grace gives you an inviting place to practice His presence. His presence is your shelter in the wilderness of man's unseemly ways. Thus, prepare the way for the Lord, and you will travel well together.

"In the shelter of your presence you hide them from the intrigues of men; in your dwelling you keep them safe from accusing tongues" (Psalm 31:20).

Are my heart and life prepared to be blessed by God and to be a blessing to others? What preparation does the Lord require of me to carry out His calling on my life?

Related Readings: Psalm 50:23; Isaiah 40:3; Malachi 3:1; Luke 10:39–41; John 19:14

PLAIN LEADERS

"John's clothes were made of camel's hair, and he had a leather belt around his waist.
His food was locusts and wild honey." Matthew 3:4

Some leaders do not fit the mold of modern day leadership. Instead of dressing the part, they dress comfortably or more functionally for their job. They are not enamored with outward appearance; rather, they are consumed more with inward convictions. Leaders who do not look the part need time to make their message clear and gain trust from the team.

How do you measure the success of leaders? Is it their ability to appear confident and in control, or is it their inner resolve to do the right thing, as God defines *right*? Indeed, be suspect of charismatic leaders who lack the courage to be consistent in their character. Pray for your preacher to be himself and not a rookie replica of the popular preacher down the street or on television. We need men of God who are authentic and upright.

Plain leaders are plainspoken and do not unnecessarily draw attention to themselves. Their ordinary living gives over to extraordinary results. Because they do not desire attention, their principles and values have a lasting effect on individuals, the organization, and the community. Indeed, plain people are attracted to plain people for a purpose.

It is out of your ordinary leadership style that you have a platform to introduce others to your extraordinary Savior Jesus. Because you do not put on airs, almighty God has placed you in a position of trust; so use your influence for the Lord. Maybe the time is right to lead a Bible study at work or in your neighborhood. Have friends into your home so they can experience your authenticity. Plain leaders are content with modest and honest living. Therefore, seek to be a pure leader who perseveres because you have nothing to prove.

"But godliness with contentment is great gain. For we brought nothing into the world, and we can take nothing out of it. But if we have food and clothing, we will be content with that" (1 Timothy 6:6–8).

Am I content and at peace with the way the Lord has created me to lead? Is my number one goal to lead for His pleasure?

Related Readings: Exodus 4:13–15; 1 Timothy 3:1–12; 1 Timothy 6:3–5

FRUITFUL REPENTANCE

"Produce fruit in keeping with repentance."
Matthew 3:8

Authentic repentance is not perfunctory but fruitful in its follow-through. When the Holy Spirit arrests my heart and pricks my conscience about my behavior, I want to change. It may be a bold, loving friend who exposes my bad habit or unacceptable attitude. If so, will I change? Indeed, fruitful repentance is not just words of remorse but a change in the way I have been acting. It is the removal of my pride, an encounter with my blind spots.

Fruitful repentance may be the hardest for those of us who have been in the faith for a long time. We get settled on a track of thinking that quits learning and growing. We can become comfortable with Christ and forget to fear Him. We can take God for granted and go places in our minds that our newfound faith would have forbidden. Watch out that excuses or cover-ups do not become a default when you encounter a need for change.

For example, in our marriage we have opportunities to learn from each other every day. One spouse may be frugal in spending, while the other spends freely, becoming irresponsible with expenditures. So when liberal spenders become excessive, fruitful repentance may require them to discuss purchases with their spouse before they spend. Certainly do not hide any spending from your husband or wife, as this leads to great loss.

When you hear truth that is contrary to your living, how do you respond? If it remains a secret between you and God, it will worsen until you confess to others. Do not hide behind your teaching role in the church or your status with your family. People who love you will love you more when you come clean with judgmental attitudes, a flirtatious relationship, or an air of spiritual superiority. Penitent people invite forgiveness.

So what is some evidence of fruitful repentance? "But the fruit of the Spirit is love, joy, peace, patience, kindness, goodness, faithfulness, gentleness and self-control" (Galatians 5:22–23). Real repentance is not just embarrassed that it was caught but takes responsibility with positive and proactive change for the good. There is a transformation from haughtiness to humility, judgment to grace, fear to trust, and pride to penitence. Fruitful repentance fears the Lord and finds rest for its soul.

"This is what the Sovereign LORD, the Holy One of Israel, says: 'In repentance and rest is your salvation, in quietness and trust is your strength, but you would have none of it'" (Isaiah 30:15).

What attitude or actions of mine do I need to change? What positive fruit in my life is evidence of my repentance?

Related Readings: 2 Chronicles 32:26; Psalm 51:1–13; Matthew 21:32; Acts 3:19

SURROUNDED BY FAITH

*"And do not think you can say to yourselves, 'We have Abraham as our father.'
I tell you that out of these stones God can raise up children for Abraham." Matthew 3:9*

It is wise and good to be surrounded by those steeped in the faith. You are blessed if you come from a legacy that loves the Lord, a family of faith. However, do not depend on the faith of others as a substitute for your faith. God does not have grandchildren, only children. Let your faith be inspired by the faithfulness of your righteous relatives, make them proud of your wise choices, but avoid using them as a crutch for your convictions.

Have you been blessed with a Christian education? Are your parents in vocational ministry or highly committed volunteers in the church? If so, thank God every day for calling them to follow Christ wholeheartedly and for their obedience. But how do you define your faith? What do you believe about God your heavenly Father, Jesus the Savior of your sins, and the Holy Spirit your Comforter and Teacher? The faithfulness of others who surround you is meant to be a stepping-stone for your faith, not a surrogate.

The prayers of your parents, grandparents, and mentors are a motivation for you to pray and trust God. Be careful not to allow the prayers of those who love you to be your proxy for prayer to the Lord. Indeed, familiarity in the faith can breed contempt and apathy. Once you place your faith in Christ and allow Him to cleanse your life, make sure to refill with faithful living; otherwise, as Jesus says, "The final condition of that man is worse than the first" (Matthew 12:45). Fresh faith is kept alive by growing your own faith.

So how do you become a faith producer and faith reproducer? First of all, recognize Jesus Christ as the source of your faith. "Consequently, faith comes from hearing the message, and the message is heard through the word of Christ" (Romans 10:17). As you hear, understand, and apply the Word of Christ, your faith grows in grace, truth, and influence.

Lastly, when you commit to teach, train, disciple, or mentor others, you are accountable to live out the truth you are transferring to other faithful followers of Jesus. As Paul told Timothy, his son in the faith, "And the things you have heard me say in the presence of many witnesses entrust to reliable men who will also be qualified to teach others" (2 Timothy 2:2). Yes, it is smart to be surrounded by faith so you can then grow and share your faith.

How can I better steward my legacy of faith? Whom do I need to come around and encourage in the faith?

Related Readings: Genesis 12:1–3; Acts 16:29–35; 1 Corinthians 4:17; Ephesians 4:13

GRATITUDE TO GOD

"Yours, O LORD, is the greatness and the power and the glory and the majesty and splendor, for everything in heaven and earth is yours. Yours, O LORD, is the kingdom; you are exalted as head over all. Wealth and honor come from you; you are the ruler of all things. In your hands are strength and power to exalt and give strength to all. Now, our God, we give you thanks, and praise your glorious name." 1 Chronicles 29:11–13

Gratitude to God is a wellspring of living water. It roots out all kinds of evil. Discontent, self-pity, jealousy, and pride are no match for divine thankfulness. Gratitude to God is rooted in realization of His character and what He has done for us. Everything is God's, and everything comes from God. His majestic creation bows down and worships Him as a reflection of His glory. Nations and rulers, consciously or unconsciously, are under His authority. Moreover, money and respect come from God. He is the owner of all things.

Because He owns everything, He is ultimately responsible. And because He is responsible, He can be trusted. We can enjoy Him, His creation, His resources, His freedom, and each other. Christianity has its privileges for the follower of Jesus Christ. Heaven is sure, and sin has lost its grip. There is a glorious gratitude that erupts from our being when we reflect on God's glorious riches. "And my God will meet all your needs according to his glorious riches in Christ Jesus" (Philippians 4:19).

Gratitude to God is one of the secrets to living the Christian life. Glorious gratitude means we never get over what He has done for us, what He is doing for us, and what He will do for us. It is remembering His past, present, and future faithfulness. Glorious gratitude is transformational because it is God focused. The cares of this world melt like wax under the heat of heavenly appreciation. Have you thanked God for being God?

Godly gratitude understands what could have happened to you were it not for the grace of God. But, because of the Lord's intervention, He delivered you. It could have been a fatal car accident, but it was not. It could have been an immediate death, but it was not. It could have been a divorce, but it was not. It could have been a lifelong prodigal child, but it was not. It could have been a dead-end job, but it was not. It could have been a relational wreck, but it was not. You could still be lost in your sins, but you are not!

He is worthy of praise, gratitude, and adoration. What a great and mighty God we serve. So take a bath with the soap of gratitude to God every day. Your attitude and actions will become clean and fresh. People will run toward you with interest rather than avoiding you in your misery. Gratitude is a magnet for God and people. It makes you pleasant rather than distasteful. Wear it well, and wear it regularly. It is one fashion statement that never goes out of style. Gratitude to the Most High is attractive to the Lord and the lost.

"We give thanks to you, O God, we give thanks, for your Name is near; men tell of your wonderful deeds" (Psalm 75:1).

How has God protected and provided for me? How can gratitude to God guide my heart?

Related Readings: Daniel 2:23; Daniel 6:10; Acts 28:15; Romans 1:21

J13

WRITTEN AFFIRMATION

"Hiram king of Tyre replied by letter to Solomon: 'Because the LORD
loves his people, he has made you their king.'" 2 Chronicles 2:11

The written word is a life-changing medium of communication that never goes out of style. For example, Holy Scripture has been passed down through history. It relates God's heart and encourages people. Verbal communication can get lost over time, but the written word has the opportunity to persevere. So why not reach out and affirm with personal notes?

Yes, it takes time to arrange thoughts and piece sentences together, but what a fantastic way to show others you love and care about them. You say that you care when you take the time to write how you feel about someone. Maybe it is just a ten-minute handwritten note or a one-hour handwritten letter; either way, love on paper lasts. It is a gift that keeps giving.

God has written His love letter to you through the medium of the Bible. He has modeled the way. Indeed, people desperately need affirmation and care. Everyday life has the tendency to suck energy and hope from people, but we have the noble task of infusing courage and life through the written word. You do not have to be a gifted writer to write.

You simply need the heart; God will lead your hand. If your penmanship is unintelligible, use a keyboard. You have no excuse. It may be for someone's birthday (spiritual or physical), a job promotion, a school graduation, a thank you, a sickness, a death, a wedding anniversary, or for no special reason but to say, "I am thinking about you."

How does it make you feel when you receive an unexpected note of encouragement? Someone writes to affirm you as a mom, father, husband, wife, grandparent, Bible teacher, homemaker, friend, or a mentor. You probably feel undeserving; yet you are filled with gratitude. When you receive written affirmation, pay it forward to someone else.

Perhaps each time you receive an e-mail, note, or letter of affirmation, send one on to another needy soul. This is a gift that keeps on giving. Truth is stored in our hearts and minds with the ability to flush out lies of unworthiness and discouragement. It is not unusual for someone to physically file away written affirmation, only to taste its meaty morsels in future days of loneliness. Encouraging words transfer courage for living.

Written affirmation is not a test where you are graded for grammar, spelling, and style. Rather, it is a tool in the hand of God that offers hope, peace, love, and encouragement to His children. Share your heart with pen and paper, and the Lord will love through you.
"I write these things to you who believe in the name of the Son of God so that you may know that you have eternal life" (1 John 5:13).

What types of written words from others affirm me? On what occasion can I write to encourage friends and family?

Related Readings: Psalm 102:18; John 20:31; Hebrews 13:22; 1 John 1:4

J14

SURRENDER TO FIGHT

"For I am already being poured out like a drink offering, and the time has come for my departure. I have fought the good fight, I have finished the race, I have kept the faith." 2 Timothy 4:6–7

When I fight in the flesh I lose. When I fight in the Spirit I win. However, my spirit becomes enslaved unless I surrender to my Savior Jesus. Surrender is freedom—freedom to follow Christ in radical obedience. The Christian cause is a just battle against evil forces that is ensured victory as we remain faithful in service to our King of Kings.

Furthermore, our life battles are not with flesh and blood. "For our struggle is not against flesh and blood, but against the rulers, against the authorities, against the powers of this dark world and against the spiritual forces of evil in the heavenly realms" (Ephesians 6:12). When we engage the enemy with eternal forces, he flees in fear. We pour out our lives for the Lord in sweet surrender, and He fills us with His Spirit's fullness.

What are your weapons for spiritual warfare? Have you completely surrendered self? Do you take marching orders from your Master Christ Jesus only? Once you surrender, you are free by faith to fight the good fight by resisting resigning to the flesh where you will face certain defeat. You conquer your circumstances because Christ has overcome the world.

"I have told you these things, so that in me you may have peace. In this world you will have trouble. But take heart! I have overcome the world" (John 16:33).

Surrender leads to peace, and peace comes from surrender. Have you waved your white flag of faith in front of your heavenly Father? When you do, He graciously receives you. He promotes you and equips you with the full armor of God. Surrender brings you into the Lord's boot camp of belief. Like a good soldier, you are trained in the tactics of trust.

Daily surrender of self sets you free to follow Christ and fight the enemy. Jesus gave His life to you to do a work in you so He can live through you. Surrender so you can fight the good fight of faith in the strength of your Savior Jesus Christ. Yield and He fills!

"But you, man of God, flee from all this, and pursue righteousness, godliness, faith, love, endurance and gentleness. Fight the good fight of the faith. Take hold of the eternal life to which you were called when you made your good confession in the presence of many witnesses" (1 Timothy 6:11–12).

Do I recognize the spiritual battle that rages around me? Have I surrendered to Jesus so I am in the proper position of trust and obedience to put on the full armor of God?

Related Readings: Acts 20:24; Romans 8:37; Philippians 3:8; 1 Timothy 1:18

TOO BIG TO SUCCEED

"Then they said, 'Come, let us build ourselves a city, with a tower that reaches to the heavens,
so that we may make a name for ourselves and not be scattered over the face of the whole earth.'
So the LORD scattered them from there over all the earth, and they stopped building the city."
Genesis 11:4, 8

What is my motive for wanting bigger and better? Is it to make a name for myself or for
the glory of God? Indeed, bigger is not always better; in fact, bigger can get in the way of
what is best. When a bigger organization competes with being a better organization, I have
to ask, "What am I missing?" Has the transactional become priority over the relational?

We see this in churches when their primary goal becomes the building of buildings
over the building of disciples. Yes, there are plenty of good reasons to expand capacity,
such as the construction of educational facilities to teach God's Word. However, space
expansion is a means to an end, not an end in itself. Keep people the priority as you
produce more.

So we ask a sobering question. "Are we using debt or any other means of manipulation
just to become bigger but to miss God's best?" If becoming bigger drives your life, your
work, your home, or your church, then you are setting yourself up for failure. God is not
pleased when bigness overshadows the simple, like loving people in their sin. Love is large
to the Lord. His heart is for bigness to be a result, not a reason for your productive work.

Moreover, there are times that becoming bigger is not His will. In other words, growing larger is failure to follow God's best. It may mean giving away more instead of building
a bigger home that becomes a memorial to man. Scattering, not gathering, is God's way.
So let go of the good so God can make it His best. If you hold tight to control, then He will
pry open your hand of distrust and give to others He trusts.

Jesus gave us a clear warning to avoid building bigger buildings for our recognition:
"The ground of a certain rich man produced a good crop. He thought to himself, 'What shall
I do? I have no place to store my crops.' Then he said, 'This is what I'll do. I will tear down
my barns and build bigger ones, and there I will store all my grain and my goods. And I'll say
to myself, "You have plenty of good things laid up for many years. Take life easy; eat, drink
and be merry."' But God said to him, 'You fool! This very night your life will be demanded
from you. Then who will get what you have prepared for yourself?' This is how it will be with
anyone who stores up things for himself but is not rich toward God" (Luke 12:16–21).

Am I rich toward God over myself? Is bigness a result or a reason for my work?

Related Readings: Psalm 10:3; Ecclesiastes 5:10; 1 Corinthians 4:3–4; James 4:13–15

PRODUCTIVE LIVING

"But the one who received the seed that fell on good soil is the man who hears the word and understands it. He produces a crop, yielding a hundred, sixty or thirty times what was sown."
Matthew 13:23

Productive living comes from confidence in Christ, not from faith in the fleeting things of this world like health and wealth. Akin to a persistent farmer, I remain faithful to cultivate my heart in prayer and plant the seeds of Scripture deep down in my soul. Then the robust roots of righteousness cause my life to bear the fruit of Christ's character.

Indeed, many forces compete with our faith and cause us to flounder in fruitlessness. The deceitfulness of riches promises peace, only to deliver problems. The cares of this world, if left dormant in a hopeless condition, corrode our confidence in Christ. The enemy proactively seeks to snatch or distort truth so our thinking becomes unclear.

However, Jesus gives you a path for productive living. It begins with a teachable heart ever willing to receive His Word. You recognize the need to know more about what your Master requires of you, His servant. Regardless of His gracious past blessings, you look fresh in the face of Jesus for a new infusion of intimacy and understanding. His past favor is affirmation and encouragement, not for lazy living in the present. Grace taken for granted becomes license for loose living, but gratitude for grace gains favor from God.

"All this is for your benefit, so that the grace that is reaching more and more people may cause thanksgiving to overflow to the glory of God. Therefore we do not lose heart. Though outwardly we are wasting away, yet inwardly we are being renewed day by day" (2 Corinthians 4:15–16).

So stay productive on the path of faithful living. Thank Christ for the fruit-bearing capacity He has given you, and be content. Celebrate; do not compare with accomplishments of other saints in service for our Lord. Over time watch your capacity expand its productivity. Faithfulness compounds results like interest with money. So daily deposit God's Word in your life, and you will reap a huge harvest for Him. Productive living is peaceful living as it quietly grows your influence for God's glory.

"The fruit of righteousness will be peace; the effect of righteousness will be quietness and confidence forever" (Isaiah 32:17).

Is my life productive in the ways of God? Have I allowed Christ to fill me to capacity?

Related Readings: Genesis 26:12; John 15:8; Galatians 5:22–23; James 3:17

AUTHENTIC OR ARTIFICIAL

"But while everyone was sleeping, his enemy came and sowed weeds among the wheat,
and went away. When the wheat sprouted and formed heads, then the weeds also appeared."
Matthew 13:25–26

Is my faith genuine or only a replica of someone else's religion? I may look and smell like a Christian, but is my faith just a product of a conservative culture? Am I engaged from my heart in eternal matters? It haunts me to think that I may have fallen into a routine that has lost the freshness of a faith walk with Jesus. Am I authentic or artificial?

Artificial Christians speak religious rhetoric but act insensitively and harshly. Authentic Christians measure their words well, not to impress but to bring attention to Christ who lives His life through them. Artificial Christians look deceivingly like disciples of Jesus on the surface, but masked beneath their beliefs you find obsessive fear and faithlessness. Authentic Christians admit their fear and are motivated by faith.

As Jesus describes: Is your faith the real deal represented by wheat? Or is your faith only a shell of what is real represented by weeds? They grow together and both look the same, but one originates with the Almighty, while the other grows forth from the enemy's work.

On the day of Christ's judgment it will be made clear who really knows Jesus by faith. "Not everyone who says to me, 'Lord, Lord,' will enter the kingdom of heaven, but only he who does the will of my Father who is in heaven. Many will say to me on that day, 'Lord, Lord, did we not prophesy in your name, and in your name drive out demons and perform many miracles?' Then I will tell them plainly, 'I never knew you. Away from me, you evildoers!'" (Matthew 7:21–23).

So how can we know that we know Jesus? Scripture teaches, "He who has the Son has life; he who does not have the Son of God does not have life. I write these things to you who believe in the name of the Son of God so that you may know that you have eternal life" (1 John 5:12–13). Start with confession of Christ as your Savior.

Once you have by faith invited Jesus into your heart, the Holy Spirit will affirm His presence in your life. "The Spirit himself testifies with our spirit that we are God's children" (Romans 8:16). Also, you will bear good fruit that remains for the glory of God. The Lord is the fruit inspector, ever looking for the luscious and juicy harvest of authenticity, who in turn judges the hard plastic crop of artificial living.

"Every tree that does not bear good fruit is cut down and thrown into the fire. Thus, by their fruit you will recognize them" (Matthew 7:19–20).

Is my life an outflowing of a real and robust faith? Have I genuinely confessed Christ as the Lord and Savior of my life?

Related Readings: Proverbs 22:10; 1 Corinthians 11:31–32; James 2:12; 3 John 1:9–11

ORDINARY TO EXTRAORDINARY

*"Coming to his hometown, he began teaching the people in their synagogue, and they were
amazed. 'Where did this man get this wisdom and these miraculous powers?' they asked."*
Matthew 13:54

God uses the ordinary to accomplish the extraordinary. However, as an ordinary individual, at times I feel outmatched, underresourced, and overwhelmed. Sometimes those closest to my calling seem farthest away. Like a son who is still pictured in his adolescent charm, older family and friends are unable to understand the new adult child.

Jesus taught in His hometown, but His hometown did not receive His words; they were offended. It is an insult to those who are used to recognition and control when God uses the ordinary to get extraordinary results. Others may define you in a condescending way, but Christ's definition is what matters most. He makes you wise for His purposes.

Formal educational opportunities may not grace your résumé, but by God's grace you have learned more than most from self-study and divine revelation. You may have been born with a wooden spoon in your mouth, rather than silver, but the Lord gave you the gift of hard and smart work to rise above any adverse circumstance. The best option for the ordinary is forward by faith, while trusting Christ to orchestrate amazing outcomes.

"But God chose the foolish things of the world to shame the wise; God chose the weak things of the world to shame the strong. He chose the lowly things of this world and the despised things—and the things that are not—to nullify the things that are, so that no one may boast before him" (1 Corinthians 1:27–29).

What are you facing that makes you feel inadequate? Is it marriage, leadership, children, travel, reputation, or finances? Be encouraged. Where God calls, He equips. Where the Lord leads, He empowers the leader. You are not alone. Though some friends may forsake you and acquaintances criticize you from a distance, your confidence is in Christ. Your ordinary abilities in the hands of God become an extraordinary display of His handiwork.

As an ordinary follower of Jesus Christ, you have an extraordinary advantage. You are your heavenly Father's!

"Yet, O LORD, you are our Father. We are the clay, you are the potter; we are all the work of your hand" (Isaiah 64:8).

How can I submit my ordinary life for the Lord's extraordinary work?

Related Readings: Genesis 39:16; 1 Samuel 17:33–35; Matthew 4:18–19; Acts 4:13

SEEKING DAILY THE HEART OF GOD   VOLUME II

J19

MOTHERS SHOW UP

"Near the cross of Jesus stood his mother, his mother's sister, Mary the wife of Clopas, and Mary Magdalene. When Jesus saw his mother there, and the disciple whom he loved standing nearby, he said to his mother, 'Dear woman, here is your son,' and to the disciple, 'Here is your mother.' From that time on, this disciple took her into his home." John 19:25–27

Mothers show up. They show up at the birth of their child. They show up when the baby wakes up, cries, is hungry, or needs changing. Moms show up at the bus stop, in the car pool line, at teacher conferences, as homeroom moms, and at ball games. They show up to wash their children's clothes, clean their rooms, help with homework, and feed their bellies.

The Lord put relentless and forgiving love in the heart of mothers. Moms cannot not care for their children, because this is how Christ made them. Why does a godly mom show up in quiet supplication for the soul of her son or daughter? Why does a woman of God go to church faithfully with her children in tow so they can hear the truth about Jesus' love?

These women of faith keep showing up on behalf of their Savior because, like the mother of Jesus, they love Jesus. The love of Christian moms flows out of the love for their Lord. Their heavenly Father first loves them so they in turn can deeply love their loved ones with the Lord's everlasting love. Indeed, you show up to be loved by Jesus so you can show up to love for Jesus. Mothers who love their children best are first loved by Christ.

"I have been reminded of your sincere faith, which first lived in your grandmother Lois and in your mother Eunice and, I am persuaded, now lives in you also" (2 Timothy 1:5).

Lastly, loving moms show up during the darkest days of sorrow. They keep coming back to the bedside of their little one languishing with illness. The stamina of a mom over her sick child sometimes seems supernatural, and it is, because the Holy Spirit is her supply. He is there to give you the support you need to be the mom Christ has called you to be. Stay true to showing up with your Savior each day. He will equip and empower you to be the mom for your children. Show up for Jesus, and He will show up for you.

"'I prayed for this child, and the LORD has granted me what I asked of him. So now I give him to the LORD. For his whole life he will be given over to the LORD.' And he worshiped the LORD there" (1 Samuel 1:27–28).

Do I allow the Lord to love me so I can better love my child?

Related Readings: 1 Samuel 2:1–11; 2 Kings 4:29–30; Mark 3:31; 1 Thessalonians 2:7

BRAND INTEGRITY

"A good name is more desirable than great riches; to be esteemed is better than silver or gold."
Proverbs 22:1

What is my personal and professional brand? Are they the same? Do they align around the glory of God? My brand integrity is based on my promise to be who I claim to be. If I claim to be a person of compassion, do I show up when friends and family are suffering? If my ministry or business promises an excellent product, service, and delivery, do I stand by my professional guarantee? Brand integrity creates value, admiration, and loyalty.

However, if we overpromise and underdeliver, over time brand loyalty erodes, and once enthusiastic fans defect to a more effective service. For example, well-meaning leaders in the community can overcommit to serve on multiple boards. They then find themselves missing meetings and not engaging in the ethos of the organization. Their personal brand becomes tarnished, and it reflects badly on their professional brand.

"Then the LORD said to Satan, 'Have you considered my servant Job? There is no one on earth like him; he is blameless and upright, a man who fears God and shuns evil. And he still maintains his integrity, though you incited me against him to ruin him without any reason'" (Job 2:3).

So have you defined your personal and professional brand? How are you perceived, and does it align with how you see yourself? What is the Lord's desire for your branding? Your brand name is what distinguishes you from others who serve in your space. Is your distinctive relational care? If so, continue to build on this personal value with increased attention to those you serve. Do you withdraw emotional engagement from the content you create? Then perhaps you make it easier to access and organize your writings.

Lastly, look for brand integrity in those who represent you in the field, on your staff, and on your board of directors. Do they enhance your brand with their character and commitment, or do they dilute its reputation? It is better to have an empty role than to fill it with the wrong person. Do not be in a rush to grow your organization beyond its brand integrity. A good name at home and work is the brand that gives God the glory!

"Let love and faithfulness never leave you; bind them around your neck, write them on the tablet of your heart. Then you will win favor and a good name in the sight of God and man" (Proverbs 3:3–4).

What is my personal and professional brand? By God's grace do I deliver with integrity?

Related Readings: Psalm 52:9; Ecclesiastes 7:1; Acts 9:36; 1 Timothy 3:7; Revelation 3:1

THE GREAT ADVENTURE

"By faith Abraham, when called to go to a place he would later receive as his inheritance, obeyed and went, even though he did not know where he was going." Hebrews 11:8

God's will is a series of discoveries. And it is the transition between discoveries that tests the true nature of my faith. I can press forward by faith, or I can analyze the situation until I am paralyzed by uncertainty. Abraham continued toward the unknown because he was certain the Lord was leading him. Great adventure accompanies my obedience to God.

Believers who are bound and determined to obey Christ are not bored. We are compelled by the love for our Lord to conquer the next challenging circumstance and pioneer the unfamiliar in prayer. We become soft and satisfied when we stop seeking the next kingdom opportunity. Our Savior Jesus is our Sherpa (guide) as we traverse in trust.

"He guides the humble in what is right and teaches them his way" (Psalm 25:9).

Are you inspired or intimidated by your faith adventure? Do you anticipate or dread doing the next right thing as you fulfill God's calling on your life? Yes, Christ must come to you in clarity before you venture out for Him in obedience. But once you are sure of the Lord's leading, do not let up until you have arrived at His destination. Go on your great adventure with God, and, like a visit to a new country, enjoy the new sites and people.

The Holy Spirit directs a life on the move, not one that is stuck—preoccupied with either pleasure or pain. "A man's heart plans his way, But the LORD directs his steps" (Proverbs 16:9 NKJV). So make prayerful plans, but all the while remain nimble to the nudge of God's Spirit. If you fall in love with your plans, you may miss adjusting to the Almighty's way.

There is a reward to those who remain true to God's call. It may only be the satisfaction of knowing you faithfully followed the Lord, but this is all that matters in the end. As a pilgrim passing through this life, launch your next eternal endeavor and experience the righteous ride with Him. Nothing risked may mean nothing lost, but every journey for Jesus is great gain. Discover what He wants today, and it will lead to what He wants tomorrow.

"Lead me, LORD, in your righteousness because of my enemies— make your way straight before me" (Psalm 5:8).

What great adventure does God have for me? What can I do today to trust and obey?

Related Readings: Proverbs 11:3; Isaiah 48:17; Luke 4:1–3; Galatians 5:16–18

THE WHOLE GOSPEL

"The scroll of the prophet Isaiah was handed to him. Unrolling it, he found the place where it is written: 'The Spirit of the Lord is on me, because he has anointed me to preach good news to the poor. He has sent me to proclaim freedom for the prisoners and recovery of sight for the blind, to release the oppressed, to proclaim the year of the Lord's favor.'" Luke 4:17–19

The gospel is the good news of Jesus Christ. Paul preached it as salvation for all who believe. "By this gospel you are saved, if you hold firmly to the word I preached to you. Otherwise, you have believed in vain. For what I received I passed on to you as of first importance: that Christ died for our sins according to the Scriptures, that he was buried, that he was raised on the third day according to the Scriptures" (1 Corinthians 15:2–4).

But the good news of Jesus Christ is more than the salvation of our souls when we get to heaven; it is also freedom from bondage on earth. As followers of Jesus, we have the everyday opportunity to reach out to those displaced and ignored by society. Prisoners, the oppressed, the poor, and those suffering from injustice need our help and hope in Jesus' name. We do not just send the missionaries; we are also called to be His agents of grace and good deeds. The whole gospel of Jesus Christ is words and works for the deprived.

"Because of the service by which you have proved yourselves, men will praise God for the obedience that accompanies your confession of the gospel of Christ, and for your generosity in sharing with them and with everyone else" (2 Corinthians 9:13).

Whom do you know by first name who is poor and needy? Whose injustice has so gripped your heart that you will not sleep well until they are set free? Do your prayers extend beyond the Lord saving their souls to how you can serve their needs in Jesus name? The Lord's desire is mercy, justice, and humility—all for His glory. Like serving marathon runners from a water station with a smile and cup, you refresh them in their exhaustion.

"For I was hungry and you gave me something to eat, I was thirsty and you gave me something to drink, I was a stranger and you invited me in, I needed clothes and you clothed me, I was sick and you looked after me, I was in prison and you came to visit me" (Matthew 25:35–36).

Digging a ditch for the poor, so they can have water, is digging a ditch for Jesus. Giving clothes to the naked, so they can stay warm and grow in dignity, is clothing Jesus. Inviting strangers into your home, so they can sleep and be fed, is inviting Jesus into your home. Caring for the sick and visiting prisoners is caring for and visiting Jesus. The whole gospel is concerned about salvation for heaven and abundant life on earth.

Jesus prayed, "Your kingdom come, your will be done on earth as it is in heaven. Give us today our daily bread" (Matthew 6:10–11).

Where can I serve the poor and needy, the sick and oppressed? Do I see them as Jesus?

Related Readings: Isaiah 58:6–11; Micah 6:8; Galatians 2:14; Philippians 1:27

BATTLEFIELD PRAYING

"They were helped in fighting them, and God handed the Hagrites and all their allies over to them, because they cried out to him during the battle. He answered their prayers, because they trusted in him." 1 Chronicles 5:20

Battlefield praying is intense because your attention is divided between the battle you are waging and your dependence on God. This can be difficult, because the urgency of the battle compels you to engage while you feel the tension to depend on God. You can have the best training in the world, but without God you can lose the battle. It is a trust issue. Prayer is a reflection of my trust in God. It incubates trust with acceptance and intimacy.

We cannot allow the pressure of the battle to shift our focus from God to the enemy. This is fear. So we guard against taking matters into our own hands during the heat of the battle. It is prideful when we default to using the weapons of manipulation and a demanding spirit. Instead, prayer cuts through all these human shortcuts and reactions. It is patient.

Prayer keeps us focused on the winner of the war, Jesus. You may need a retreat from the battle to regroup and refresh. Rest is required, as it is a time for God's healing and for you to replenish your physical, emotional, and spiritual resources. If you fight the battle in your own strength, you will lose, but if you fight the battle in the Lord's strength, you will win. Adversity and uncertainty are your passport to prayerful intimacy with almighty God.

Your battle may be health related. It may be emotional lust or financial. It may be a relational conflict or the consequences of a bad decision. Wherever you find yourself, you can rest assured this is everyone's battle. You are not unique or different in this regard. You are not battling alone. Look around you, and pray for the walking wounded. They desperately need your prayers. They may be bleeding and do not even realize it.

"Never be lacking in zeal, but keep your spiritual fervor, serving the Lord. Be joyful in hope, patient in affliction, faithful in prayer. Share with God's people who are in need. Practice hospitality" (Romans 12:11–13).

God is looking for someone who will lead His people with a humble cry that moves them forward on their knees. You may have been given a battlefield promotion for such a time as this. Do not squander this opportunity and the influence God has given you. Engage in this prayer initiative for kingdom purposes. When you trust God, He trusts you.

It is His wisdom and the force of His character that ultimately win the war. So stay focused on your leader Jesus. Do not be enamored or distracted by the battle that is raging around you. Prayer keeps your perspective pure and focused on God's agenda. Stay engaged in prayer. There will be setbacks along the way, but do not lose heart. We know who wins the war!

In what battle do I need to prayerfully engage with the Lord's help? Whom can I support in prayer as they are engaged in a spiritual battle?

Related Readings: Ezra 10:1; Nehemiah 6:9; Hebrews 5:7; Jude 1:20

PASSIONATE WORK

"Remember the Sabbath day by keeping it holy. Six days you shall labor and do all your work, but the seventh day is a Sabbath to the LORD your God. On it you shall not do any work."
Exodus 20:8–10

Work loses its luster when its focus becomes twenty-four hours a day, seven days a week. Passion flies out the window of work when it consumes my thinking, with no break to refresh. Labor is laborious without a Sabbath to see how God's calling is much greater than a career. If money is my motivation, there is no rest, but Christ's call brings contentment.

How can passion and enthusiasm sustain us to serve at work? When the joy of the Lord is our strength, we work with unrelenting focus and follow-through. Joy comes from doing our job for Jesus. Then we love what we do, and we do what we love. His calling causes us to rise above our daily frustration and focus on His faithfulness.

"May God himself, the God of peace, sanctify you through and through. May your whole spirit, soul and body be kept blameless at the coming of our Lord Jesus Christ. The one who calls you is faithful and he will do it" (1 Thessalonians 5:23–25).

Do you see your work as a part of the Lord's greater calling on your life? Do you take time weekly to refresh and remember how He has used you in the marketplace and at home to be a mirror of His character? Passion is a product of a perspective that rises above transactional results to relational investments. People at work and family at home are not a means to an end; they are individuals who need the grace and love of God.

Indeed, productivity flows out of a passionate love for people, but it happens as you view work as an opportunity to reflect Christ in your contacts and in your contracts. Perhaps it starts by not working on the Sabbath. Give yourself and your team permission to recharge and reflect on the Lord's greater purposes. Celebration of Christ's calling is reason enough to rest your mind, body, and emotions so the other six days are fulfilling.

A weekly twenty-four-hour fast from our phone and computer contributes to passion at work. Instead of being drained with the dread of what needs to get done, we turn off man's machines and trust the Lord to take care of business in His timing. Passionate work is a product of peace that comes from being with Christ daily and weekly in Sabbath rest.

"Nehemiah said, 'Go and enjoy choice food and sweet drinks, and send some to those who have nothing prepared. This day is sacred to our Lord. Do not grieve, for the joy of the LORD is your strength'" (Nehemiah 8:10).

What do I need to trust the Lord with so I can truly rest on the Sabbath? Is my passion for work sustained by my Savior Jesus' greater call on my life?

Related Readings: Genesis 3:17–19; Deuteronomy 28:46–48; 1 Corinthians 1:9; Hebrews 4:1–11

OBJECTIVE ADVICE

"But Rehoboam rejected the advice the elders gave him and consulted
the young men who had grown up with him and were serving him."
2 Chronicles 10:8

Objective advice wants what is best for you and for those whom you influence. Objective advisors want God's will for your life. Sometimes it is not what you want to hear. It may not even be the easiest path to follow, but it is the right thing to do. There is only one agenda with objective advice: what is God's best and the right thing for you.

However, there will be other voices competing for your attention with their own agenda. You will not lack for biased advice. Their agenda includes what is in it for them. Biased advice favors a stronger position of power and financial gain for the advisor. It is tainted advice that needs to be avoided like sour milk. But objective advice is pure and healthy.

Your business or ministry will not go to the next level without your submission to wise and objective advice. Seek out older men and women and integrate them into your circle of influence. The same can be said of your family. Your spouse is on your side and has the purest objectives because he or she has the most to gain or lose by your decisions. Be humble, not harsh. Receive advice from your spouse and act upon it. Humility listens and learns.

Where do you find this quality of counsel? Seek out people who "have been there and done that." Experience educates beyond naïve idealism. So go after people with experience in the area you need advice. There is one caveat. Look for those who have learned from their experience. Experience without education is counterproductive.

Nevertheless, a good place to start for objective advice is with those who are older and more experienced. Ask them about their greatest successes and their greatest failures. As they talk, listen for humility, change, and the ability to take responsibility for their actions. Solicit objective advice from those who maintain your same values and principles.

These are people who will not compromise quality for quantity. They will not be enamored with short-term gain that dilutes long-term integrity. Objective advice does not depend on unnecessary persuasion. Rather, they trust God to lead you. They will speak the truth in love and leave the results to God. Ask for advice, filter it through prayer, and then do what they say. Godly, objective advice originates with the Lord!

"Listen to advice and accept instruction, and in the end you will be wise" (Proverbs 19:20).

Whom can I trust to give me objective advice? What area of my life needs their objective advice?

Related Readings: Proverbs 12:15; Isaiah 19:11; Romans 11:33–35; Acts 6:1–7

PEER PRESSURE

"The king was distressed, but because of his oaths and his dinner guests,
he ordered that her request be granted." Matthew 14:9

A public promise under the influence of alcohol can lead to a rash decision. This is the mindset of a person in power who is driven by pride and by pleasing people. Leaders without a divine moral compass will justify their decisions based solely on what others think. Negative peer pressure can persuade decision makers to make unwise decisions.

This happens at work when we want to please everyone and end up pleasing no one. It is futile to strive for outcomes that require consensuses one hundred percent of the time. As a leader, gather input and seek privately the buy in of influencers, but most of all ask, "What does Christ think?" The gentle pressure applied by the Holy Spirit leads to great gain in the long run.

However, there is positive peer pressure. After a process of prayer, planning, and testing assumptions, you and the team make a public declaration of a determined course. Those who trust you are looking for implementation of the agreed-upon strategic direction. If you deviate from the plan, you risk diluting your creditability. Positive peer pressure is accountability to follow through with collaborative goals and milestones.

Most importantly, positive peer pressure comes when you publically profess Jesus Christ as your Lord and Savior. A Christ-centered community creates a loving environment of accountability for those who are followers of Jesus. This is why you engage in church as a volunteer teacher, small group leader, parking attendant, worship leader, or greeter. Your private faith is meant to become a public expression that encourages others to be bold. Confess Christ with your lips, and let your life be evidence that what you say is true.

"That if you confess with your mouth, 'Jesus is Lord,' and believe in your heart that God raised him from the dead, you will be saved. For it is with your heart that you believe and are justified, and it is with your mouth that you confess and are saved. As the Scripture says, 'Anyone who trusts in him will never be put to shame'" (Romans 10:9–11).

What negative peer pressure do I need to avoid? What positive peer pressure do I need to embrace?

Related Readings: Job 2:9; Ruth 1:16–18; Acts 4:32–37; 1 Timothy 6:12–14

TIMELY TRANSITIONS

"The rest of their brothers (the priests and the Levites and all who had returned
from the captivity to Jerusalem) began the work, appointing Levites twenty years
of age and older to supervise the building of the house of the LORD." Ezra 3:8

Transitions are hard, even good ones. But sometimes it is time to move out and move on. God may be calling you back to a particular city or town for you to influence old and new friends for Christ. Or He may be calling you to a brand new endeavor full of wonder and risk. Either way, your transition is what is best for His kingdom and for your spiritual growth. Transitions are a time to trust totally and to live boldly.

The goal is to position yourself, with career and family, for the most impact on God's kingdom, placing you and your family in an environment that will challenge and nurture your spiritual growth. Yes, pray much and seek godly counsel, but do not let fear of the unknown stifle you. This life is your one opportunity to follow hard after God.

Do not let the things of this world paralyze you or cause you to pause. Hesitation can hurt. However, in your zeal, do be sensitive to your spouse. Make sure to nurture him or her through the process. Retain Christ as your compass through the transition. He will keep you honest and soften the hearts of those most affected by the move. Do not let the fear of man get you off mission. Rather, let the fear of God lead you to follow His call.

Transitions can be exciting. They can keep us young. They move our faith to a whole new level. You could have stayed in your comfort zone with a minimally felt need for God. But now your dependence on Him is daily, real time. You feel and know He is your loving heavenly Father. Your circumstances may or may not get better, but you will.

Is He leading you to a new city? Hire a realtor. Does He want you to downsize so you can simplify your life? Put up a for sale sign. Does He want you to cap your lifestyle so you can give away more money? Tell your financial advisor. Does He want you to move overseas and train national leaders? Get a passport. Does He want you to reach out to your neighbors? Invite them to dinner.

Divinely orchestrated transitions are like a loyal friend whom you totally trust. See this shift as an asset on heaven's balance sheet of your life. Ride change like the ocean waves. It may be a little scary or maybe a lot scary, but He is with you. You will crash occasionally, but He will buffer your fall, like resting on a soft, sandy sea bottom. Let this transition lead you closer to God and His will. You will never know exactly what you would have missed if you do not, and you will have few regrets if you do.

"Keep your lives free from the love of money and be content with what you have, because God has said, 'Never will I leave you; never will I forsake you.' So we say with confidence, 'The Lord is my helper; I will not be afraid. What can man do to me?'" (Hebrews 13:5–6).

What transition do I need to embrace, celebrate, and trust that the Lord is with me?

Related Readings: Psalm 66:6; Isaiah 43:2; Acts 12:10; Hebrew 11:29

DISCONNECT TO RECONNECT

"When Jesus heard what had happened, he withdrew by boat privately to a solitary place.
Hearing of this, the crowds followed him on foot from the towns." Matthew 14:13

There are times when the crowds crowd in on me. I need relief—relief from the routine, relief from responsibilities, relief from relationships, or relief from the raw pain of losing a loved one. Jesus felt this intense emotion as John the Baptist, His friend and spiritual confidant, was brutally beheaded. The pain of severe loss led Him to be alone.

Are you on the edge of complete exhaustion? Is your tolerance for any more trouble at the tipping point of chronic fatigue? If so, it is time to disconnect from distractions so you can reconnect to your relationship with the Lord. You preclude coming apart emotionally and physically when you come apart relationally with your Savior Jesus.

Our private investment in solitude gives our public service sustainability. If we are always available to everyone, then we are not effective with anyone. A soul that is always exposed to the light of life is unable to discern the desperate state of hurting humanity. So we schedule time on the calendar with Christ in seclusion, and He empowers us.

Your responsibilities will not rest while you rest, but trust the Lord to take care of any crisis that may arise. For you to disconnect from your duties means you prepare ahead of time to transition from your tasks while you are away. Do not be ensnared by your ego that always wants to be wanted. Let others learn what you know so you can go away and grow. We grow stale if we reject retreats, but we are energized when we engage them.

When we disconnect, we trust God to get things done through others in spite of our absence. Your break from work and home is an opportunity for a colleague to step up and be blessed with a new opportunity to be stretched. Why keep all the challenging circumstances to yourself? Let go so others can gain invaluable experience. Once you have truly disconnected from your phone, enjoy your soul reconnecting with Christ!

"The LORD your God is with you, he is mighty to save. He will take great delight in you, he will quiet you with his love, he will rejoice over you with singing" (Zephaniah 3:17).

What relationship or responsibility do I need to disconnect from for a season? When and where is the best place for me to reconnect with Christ?

Related Readings: 2 Chronicles 15:4; Daniel 9:3; Acts 17:27; Hebrews 11:6

COMPELLING COMPASSION

"When Jesus landed and saw a large crowd, he had compassion on them and healed their sick."
Matthew 14:14

Compelling compassion comes from a heart captured by Christ. It is the natural application of those who love the Lord. Love loves the object of affection of its lover; Jesus loves the unlovely. The compassion of Christ not only feels for the pitiful plight of hurting people, it helps. Compassion is the outcome of authentic and engaging faith.

"In all their distress he too was distressed, and the angel of his presence saved them. In his love and mercy he redeemed them; he lifted them up and carried them all the days of old" (Isaiah 63:9).

In solitude we are loved by our Savior, so when we return to society, we can love. Because of Christ's great compassion in our life, we are compelled to be compassionate. We were lost, but now we are found. We were blind, but now we see. We were sorrowful, but now we are joyful. We were condemned, but now we are redeemed. We were children of the devil, but now we are children of the Most High. Compassion loves.

Compelling compassion for you may mean weekend relief of a foster home parent, or giving the caregiver of an adult handicapped person a break. The special needs community has a compelling need for compassion, but they sit waiting for one of us to come. The elderly who are losing their faculties or who have lost their mind need a tender touch, a soothing smile, and a kind word. Your sympathy from your Savior is significant; so use it liberally. Compassion from a Christian points people to Christ in a compelling fashion.

"By this all men will know that you are my disciples, if you love one another" (John 13:35).

It is compassion, not criticism that draws loved ones to the Lord. Your son or daughter, brother or sister, or parent may be in the far country of faithlessness. Do they need you to point out what is painfully obvious, or do they need your healing touch for their hurting heart? At work, is the severance package for the departing employee generous or stingy? Prescribe compassion in significant doses, and watch God work in wonderful ways.

"They asked, and he brought them quail and satisfied them with the bread of heaven. He opened the rock, and water gushed out; like a river it flowed in the desert. For he remembered his holy promise" (Psalm 105:40–42).

What are the depths of Christ's compassion toward me? Whom do I need to show compelling compassion?

Related Readings: Psalm 86:15; Lamentation 3:21–23; Matthew 9:36; 1 Peter 3:8

SEEKING DAILY THE HEART OF GOD   VOLUME II

J30

LONELINESS IN ILLNESS

"As long as he has the infection he remains unclean. He must live alone;
he must live outside the camp." Leviticus 13:46

Leprosy was a dreaded disease much like AIDS is today. People were sent out of town into isolated colonies where they felt rejected and feared. This is the nature of illness, especially severe sickness. Those of us who are well either do not totally understand the condition of the sick or do not know what to say. However, we can still show up to love them and serve them during their time of struggle.

We do not want to feed the unhealthy person's feelings of rejection and fear. Illness can be dreadfully lonely. The emotional struggle is often harder than the physical pain. This is why we need each other in "sickness and in health." So what are some ways to reach out to those who are physically and emotionally hurting? How can we be intentional in our concern for them?

A first step is to put ourselves in their situation. If I were suffering from cancer, how would I want to be treated? Prayer and care would be high on the list. To be prayed for is the highest of privileges. Your prayers do make a difference. It is like adding additional supplies to hungry and fatigued troops on the front lines of battle.

God listens intently to your pleas for compassion and healing. "The prayer of a righteous man is powerful and effective" (James 5:16). Prayer makes a difference with God and the one for whom you are praying, and it makes a difference in you. Your prayers sensitize your heart toward the one you are lifting to God's throne of grace.

Care means you show up. This is ninety-nine percent of caring. You show up at the bedside, you show up at their home, and you show up at the funeral. When you take the time to show up, you provide a dose of medicine that cannot be prescribed by a physician. Your smile, warm touch, and listening ear refresh like a hot shower in the cold of winter. It may be a card, flowers, or a phone call; all of these add up to place the patient on the road to recovery or give him or her much needed peace of mind.

Yes, there are the "hard" elements of doctors, nurses, medicine, and therapy, but the "soft" elements of prayer and care provide a safe environment for the other to be more effective. Your caring connection in another's crisis creates communion and dismisses aloneness. Jesus illustrated the importance of loving the ill when He said about Himself: "I was sick and you looked after me" (Matthew 25:36).

Who is struggling with sickness whom I can love today? Who needs me to read Scripture and lift them to the Lord in prayer?

Related Readings: Exodus 23:25; Psalm 41:3; John 4:45–47; Acts 28:8–9

J31

NO GREATER LOVE

"My command is this: Love each other as I have loved you. Greater love has no one than this,
that he lay down his life for his friends. You are my friends if you do what I command."
John 15:12–14

There is no greater love than to give life in order to save life. In the case of war, the canvas of history is painted with good people who out of love for country and countrymen gave their lives to protect the lives of those they loved. The ultimate sacrifice of self is the giving of one's life on behalf of something of great value.

This pattern of Christ's love is proof of our love for people. Soldiers of faith who sacrifice their lives for people they have never met do so because of Christ's higher call of love. If we love liberty, if we love freedom, if we love democracy, if we love our inalienable rights, if we love each other, and if we love God, we honor those who went to war to extend these values at home and abroad. Love lays down its life for what is right.

"This is how we know what love is: Jesus Christ laid down his life for us. And we ought to lay down our lives for our brothers" (1 John 3:16).

This is why mothers are motivated to spend a lifetime giving a life of love for their families. They teach their children character and model its application for them. This is why fathers work as unto the Lord with passion and dedication so they can provide for their families. This is why some friends even sacrifice their health in order to serve the unhealthy. Christians give sacrificially because faith, hope, and love are their motivation.

Does our heart break for what breaks the heart of Jesus? Do we give up comfort in order to comfort? Do we die to self so we can give ourselves? If so, love will triumph and trump war at home, war at work, and war overseas. Love never fails to get the right results, the right way. Memorials are built where a greater love gave itself for a greater good. Remember the fallen who gave us freedom of religion. Thank God for their heroics.

However, the cross is the ultimate memorial to freedom. Thanks be to God that His great love came to us even when we were enemies of His. "For if, when we were God's enemies, we were reconciled to him through the death of his Son, how much more, having been reconciled, shall we be saved through his life!" (Romans 5:10).

Where is the Lord calling me to give my life? Whom can I honor who gave themselves so I can enjoy my freedom?

Related Readings: 2 Samuel 10:12; Romans 5:7; Galatians 4:15; Philippians 2:15

BLESSED TO BLESS

"And he directed the people to sit down on the grass. Taking the five loaves and the two fish and looking up to heaven, he gave thanks and broke the loaves. Then he gave them to the disciples, and the disciples gave them to the people." Matthew 14:19

Jesus takes the little I have to accomplish much for His purposes. What I give to Him in faith, He gives back to me having multiplied, so in turn I can pass on to people in need. Christ's cycle of blessing is simple but profound: give—receive—give. Five loaves of bread and two fish consecrated by Christ become a feast that feeds at least ten thousand including the women and children. Almighty God does not hold back His blessings.

A small portion of passionate prayer produces a prayer pregnant with results. A little bit of money leverages a large kingdom return at home and around the world. A normal life broken by Jesus is one He makes whole and uses to bring healing to other hurting hearts. A relationship left at the Lord's altar He revives with the ability to give love and forgiveness. Give what you have to Jesus, and He will give it back to you much better.

"Restore to me the joy of your salvation and grant me a willing spirit, to sustain me. Then I will teach transgressors your ways, and sinners will turn back to you" (Psalm 51:12–13).

Furthermore, Jesus modeled thanking His heavenly Father before eating the meal. This is why we give thanks to God before we partake of breakfast, lunch, or dinner. Whether in the privacy of our homes or in the public's eye, we close our eyes and give gratitude to the Provider of our provision, all in Jesus' name. A public blessing will bless some and offend others, but God is glorified. Look for other believers, and bless them by paying their bill.

"For I received from the Lord what I also passed on to you: The Lord Jesus, on the night he was betrayed, took bread, and when he had given thanks, he broke it and said, 'This is my body, which is for you; do this in remembrance of me'" (1 Corinthians 11:23–24).

Lastly, the Lord often chooses to deliver His blessings through His available and trustworthy disciples. Stay close to Christ, and He will empower you with resources and instruct you how to distribute His blessings to individuals, even the masses. Give your raw realities to Jesus. He transforms them and entrusts you with their deployment to the needy. God has blessed you so you can be a blessing; therefore, remain in a position to be blessed.

"As you know, we consider blessed those who have persevered. You have heard of Job's perseverance and have seen what the Lord finally brought about. The Lord is full of compassion and mercy" (James 5:11).

What do I need to surrender to Christ for His blessing? How can I bless others with what God has blessed me?

Related Readings: Romans 14:6; 1 Corinthians 10:31; 2 Corinthians 9:10; 1 Timothy 4:4

OBEY WHEN AFRAID

"'Lord, if it's you,' Peter replied, 'tell me to come to you on the water.' 'Come,' he said. Then Peter got down out of the boat, walked on the water and came toward Jesus." Matthew 14:28–29

Sometimes Jesus sends us ahead in our boat of faith while He prays for us from a distance. We feel alone at times because He is not physically beside us to provide reassurance that we are on the right course. Then global uncertainty or storms of sickness strike our core beliefs, and we become fearful. In our crisis of faith, we can get out of our boat of fear and walk on the water toward Jesus, or we can sink in unbelief.

"Because Jesus lives forever, he has a permanent priesthood. Therefore he is able to save completely those who come to God through him, because he always lives to intercede for them" (Hebrews 7:24–25).

Where does the Lord have you? Are you waiting to launch out in faith? Are you in the middle of a storm anticipating His reassurance any minute? Or has He asked you to get out of the boat toward a major faith-stretching goal? Wherever you are in your continuum of faith in Christ, trust Him in the transition. If you are on the shore, get in the boat of belief. If you are in the middle a fearful storm of life, look for Christ coming toward you. If He is asking you to get out of the boat and walk on water, trust Him.

What seems unnatural or impossible to you may be reasonable to Him. It is not a blind leap of faith, for you are fixing your eyes on Jesus. Keep your eyes on Jesus. Do not look to the left at the storm, to the right at the still shore, or down at the uncertain water. Look straight ahead into the confident eyes of Christ. Watch Him as you walk on water in faith.

"Let us fix our eyes on Jesus, the author and perfecter of our faith, who for the joy set before him endured the cross, scorning its shame, and sat down at the right hand of the throne of God. Consider him who endured such opposition from sinful men, so that you will not grow weary and lose heart" (Hebrews 12:2–3).

We walk on water not to be seen but to see Him. There is a depth of trust and love for the Lord that only comes from walking toward Him with virgin legs. Like a child learning to walk looks toward his or her loving parent with outstretched arms, so we wobble toward our smiling Savior. Go with God and experience great gain, or stay where you are and suffer great loss. Move out of your comfort zone so Christ can be your sole comfort. Stay in the boat and see your limited work. Walk on water and watch His unlimited work.

"Now to him who is able to do immeasurably more than all we ask or imagine, according to his power that is at work within us, to him be glory in the church and in Christ Jesus throughout all generations, for ever and ever! Amen" (Ephesians 3:20–21).

Where is the Lord asking me to get out of my comfort zone and go with Him?

Related Readings: Genesis 12:4; Numbers 14:8; Acts 9:17; Revelation 17:14

BREAK BAD TRADITIONS

"'Why do your disciples break the tradition of the elders? They don't wash their hands before they eat!' Jesus replied, 'And why do you break the command of God for the sake of your tradition?'" Matthew 15:2–3

There are good traditions, and there are bad traditions. A good tradition aligns with God's expectations and honors Him and others in the process. A bad tradition benefits man and breaks Christ's command. Indeed, it is wise to take an inventory of our current traditions and make sure they are grounded in God and not made up by man. Is there any habit, belief, or assumption you give credence to that may be undermining your family or faith?

For example, a good tradition is routinely giving ten percent of our income to the Lord's work, beginning with the local church and expanding to support ministries. However, a bad tradition is when a Christian leader tries to control the conscience of a person's giving through guilt and intimidation. It is Spirit-led giving, not man's manipulation, that gains the best outcome. Tried and true traditions are anchored by trust in the Lord's control.

You may face a colleague at work or a strong-willed person in your extended family who has his or her way of doing things. This person's tradition worked well in the past but is inefficient in the present. How do you break bad habits of another for the good of the company or for what is best for the family? Prayer, patience, and a plan are your best change management tools.

Prayerfully come up with alternatives that honor the old but give preference to the new. Be bold to ask challenging questions in a spirit of humility. Why are we doing it this way? Is there a better way? How can we improve the process to make the best progress? Are you called to do this? Do you have the gifts and experience required for this project?

Good traditions gain God's favor over time; bad traditions struggle to survive. What project or program needs to be taken off life support so other resources can be freed up to further the mission? Some traditional strategies suffer from fatigue and need to be put to rest. Other new ones need focused support to execute with excellence. Be honest about your spiritual life and strategic direction. Are your traditions truly from God and for God? And are you trying to change the unchangeable, or are you trusting Christ with change?

"See, the former things have taken place, and new things I declare; before they spring into being I announce them to you" (Isaiah 42:9).

"And no one pours new wine into old wineskins. If he does, the wine will burst the skins, and both the wine and the wineskins will be ruined. No, he pours new wine into new wineskins" (Mark 2:22).

What accepted traditions do I need to respectfully reject? What new traditions do I need to embrace by faith?

Related Readings: 2 Chronicles 35:25; Micah 6:16; Mark 7:4–9; Galatians 1:14

LOVINGLY LEAVE THEM

"Leave them; they are blind guides. If a blind man leads a blind man, both will fall into a pit."
Matthew 15:14

There comes a time when an individual Christian is led by the Lord to leave his or her church because the church has left its convictions in Christ's teachings. Sadly, there are times when a Christian congregation is led by the Lord to leave its denomination because the denomination has left its belief in the Bible. Staying is a sin, if the Lord leads to leave.

Why is it important for us to separate ourselves from false teachers who are offended by the truth of Jesus' teaching? One major reason is that this path of apostasy leads to spiritual death. Do you want to follow a shepherd who denies the deity of the Great Shepherd Jesus? Do you want to associate with a church that denies that Jesus is coming back for His bride—the church? Spiritual life comes from embracing all of Christ's commands.

"The shepherds are senseless and do not inquire of the LORD; so they do not prosper and all their flock is scattered" (Jeremiah 10:21).

Christianity is not a menu of beliefs that is itemized and selected only as it fits into the mainstream acceptance of the culture. On the contrary, Christianity is meant to transform the culture with its conviction in Christ's death for our sins and His resurrection to give us His life, all by grace through faith. Spiritual guides who define God in their trivial terms are blind and lead other blind followers into a pit of pride and eternal entrapment.

If you are hiking rough terrain, is it wise and responsible to follow a knowledgeable, well-spoken, but blindfolded guide? Of course it is not. Neither do you blindly follow a spiritual leader, church, or denomination that cannot see spiritually because of their blindfold of unbelief. You leave them because you love them too much to stay, and you pray that by leaving you can one day lead them into the light of spiritual sight.

Lastly, leave well, not maliciously but motivated by loving malcontent. Transition out in the Holy Spirit's strength, seasoned with a life of grace and humility. Make your leaving an illustration of why you are not staying—faith and obedience to Christ's commands. Leaving is not easy, but leaving as the Lord leads opens up eternal opportunities.

"Then I will give you shepherds after my own heart, who will lead you with knowledge and understanding" (Jeremiah 3:15).

How will my leaving affect the faith of my family and friends? Is love my motivation?

Related Readings: Jeremiah 50:6; Ezekiel 34:1–23; Matthew 23:16–24; 1 Peter 5:2–4

A CLEAN HEART

"But the things that come out of the mouth come from the heart, and these make a man 'unclean.' For out of the heart come evil thoughts, murder, adultery, sexual immorality, theft, false testimony, slander. These are what make a man 'unclean.'" Matthew 15:18-20

Maintaining a clean heart is a daily choice, one that has a multitude of options. Intellectual images bombard our beliefs like England's blitzkrieg. Good and bad thoughts compete for our heart's affection. It is a haven for hellish or heavenly deliberation. If I give in to stinking thinking, I soil my soul with unsavory influence and miss my sweet Savior's soothing protection. A heart given to heaven keeps the hounds of hell away.

It is contemplation on Christ and His character that flushes out unseemly fantasy and fills my mind with the realities of His righteousness. Yes, there is a struggle to keep a clean heart until we see Jesus face-to-face; however, in the interim it is intimacy with our Lord that invites integrity of heart. "May integrity and uprightness protect me, because my hope is in you" (Psalm 25:21). Intimacy leads to integrity, which creates a clean heart.

One strategy of Satan is for Christians to compartmentalize their hearts between good and bad, sacred and secular, clean and unclean. This is deceptive because clean and unclean do not mix any more than oil and water blend together. The black oil of an impure heart contaminates a heart cleansed by the saving grace of Christ. Only the power of almighty God can cap the spewing influence of sin deep in the depths of our hearts.

"Be self-controlled and alert. Your enemy the devil prowls around like a roaring lion looking for someone to devour. Resist him, standing firm in the faith" (1 Peter 5:8–9).

So as a follower of Jesus, how do you keep the barnacles of bad behavior from the hull of your heart? Daily surrender and submission to God is an exceptional governor for good behavior. This allows you to harness humility, receive the grace of God, and defeat the devil. Battle bad behavior alone and you are overwhelmed, but by grace you overcome.

"All of you, clothe yourselves with humility toward one another, because, 'God opposes the proud but gives grace to the humble.' Humble yourselves, therefore, under God's mighty hand, that he may lift you up in due time" (1 Peter 5:5–6).

Keeping a clean heart is everyone's battle; so stay accountable to God and people. Perhaps you give permission to a small group that examines your heart with loving questions like: "Are you filling your mind with clean images?" "Are you harboring any anger in your heart?" "Is your heart hurting and in need of healing?" A clean heart comes as we submit to Christ, invite accountability from others, and confess our sins.

"Let us draw near to God with a sincere heart in full assurance of faith, having our hearts sprinkled to cleanse us from a guilty conscience and having our bodies washed with pure water" (Hebrews 10:22).

Do I have a regular routine of allowing Christ to cleanse my heart? Am I accountable?

Related Readings: Psalm 24:3–5; Proverbs 20:7–11; Matthew 22:16; Titus 2:6–8

CRY OUT FOR CHILDREN

"A Canaanite woman from that vicinity came to him, crying out, 'Lord, Son of David, have mercy on me! My daughter is suffering terribly from demon-possession.' [She] came and knelt before Him. 'Lord, help me!' she said." Matthew 15:22, 25

Life circumstances can crush our faith or cause us to pray more earnestly. Especially when it involves our children, our resolve ratchets up more intensely. When we see our little one languishing in illness, we cry out to Christ for mercy. When our grown children reel from unwise decisions, our hearts break as we bring their needs before our Lord daily. Offspring caught in adversity involve intense intercession.

Great trials require great faith; so prayerful parents kneel before their Savior Jesus and solicit mercy on behalf of their son or daughter. Because the pain of watching a child suffer is overwhelming for the mom or dad, they need grace and mercy for their own emotional stability and peace of mind. Faithful parents offer prayers and need prayer.

But what happens when nothing happens? When Jesus is silent about your son's alternate lifestyle or drug abuse, do you stop soliciting heaven for help? When nothing changes with your daughter's promiscuity or pattern of lies, do you quit loving her? Grace does not give up but doubles down in determination to plead with Christ for help and healing.

"Be joyful in hope, patient in affliction, faithful in prayer" (Romans 12:12).

Children or grandchildren caught in Satan's scheme of deception and irresponsible living need prayers flung to heaven with fervent entreaty. Jesus is listening. He cares. He can mend a broken heart and make it much better than before. The crumbs of mercy from Christ's table of trust feed hungry souls who never stop worshiping their Lord.

So in your trial, or in your support of a loved one who is under severe affliction, stay true to pray and trust Jesus. Cry out to Christ for healing and relief. Receive His reassurance; resolve not to give up going to God for grace and mercy in your time of need. Great faith gets great results because you serve a great and compassionate God.

"Let us then approach the throne of grace with confidence, so that we may receive mercy and find grace to help us in our time of need" (Hebrews 4:16).

How much does the Lord love my child? Have I given over my child to His care?

Related Readings: Isaiah 38:19; Matthew 19:13; Luke 15:20; John 11:4

LIVE YOUR PASSION

"For this reason I remind you to fan into flame the gift of God, which is in you through the laying on of my hands. For God did not give us a spirit of timidity, but a spirit of power, of love and of self-discipline." 2 Timothy 1:6–7

Am I living my passion? Do I tolerate my daily tasks, or am I compelled to complete my checklist? Am I motivated by passion or by a paycheck? It is in this tension of wanting to engage in activities that align with my giftedness that I need to trust the Lord. Life is too short for me to grind out good results when I can enjoy the best outcome in my area of passion. Why settle for less than the Lord's very best? He gifts me where He calls me.

However, the gift of God in the heart of His children can become dormant and underutilized. Like an unused arm or leg, it can atrophy and become unusable. God's gifts need the flame of faith to ignite their potential much like oxygen gives life to fire. The Holy Spirit is blowing across the ship of your sanctification, but is your sail hoisted up toward heaven to capture His power? God's gifts are given for His glory and your enjoyment.

What is your gift that needs clear definition and focused development? Is it writing? Is Christ calling you to romance pen with paper to create a clear, concise, and compelling message of faith, hope, and love? Is it music? Is the Lord leading you to a daily routine of practice with a musical instrument or the creation of beauty with a paintbrush?

Maybe in your heart you are a woodworker, a seamstress, a teacher, a coach, a cop, or a counselor. You may ask, "How can I make a living around my passion?" Money will follow the life motivated by passionate work. Work hard and smart; trust the Lord for provision. You will never lack for opportunity when God's gift is your guiding force.

Live out your passion before you run out of passion. Passion produces ongoing - energy. When you focus on your strengths you become strong. When you focus on your weaknesses you become weak. God's will is for you to work in your strengths so you can be a blessing to those you influence. Your influence will expand exponentially when it - launches from a heart empowered by its passionate desires.

Ask the Almighty to align your heart desires with His desires, and enjoy this - combustion for Christ. Live out your passion so you die with no dread. Passion lived out is powerful in God's hand. By faith unleash the passionate gift the Lord has put in your heart.

"May he give you the desire of your heart and make all your plans succeed" (Psalm 20:4).

Am I living out my passions with my God-given purpose? If not, when can I start?

Related Readings: Psalm 21:2; Matthew 25:25; 1 Timothy 4:14; 1 Peter 4:10

HUMBLE YOURSELF

"Humble yourselves, therefore, under God's mighty hand, that he may lift you up in due time."
1 Peter 5:6

Christ's command is clear to His children: "Humble yourselves." What He requires is a volitional and willful act of humility. Just like I choose to love, I choose to humble myself. I can be humble like I can be compassionate, forgiving, and gentle. Humility is not an outside force waiting to have its way; it indwells the believer waiting for action.

So how do we humble ourselves? It is submission to God and others that unleashes humility. It will lie dormant and a doormat to pride unless we surrender to our Savior Jesus. We give up our right to be right so we can walk in humility. It is taking the low place that gains the high ground of grace. Humility is the preserver of peace, while pride is the disturber of peace. We first humble ourselves and then trust God to do what is right.

Are you at enmity with the Lord? If so, humble yourself. Are you at odds with an individual? If so, humble yourself. Did you mess up at work? If so, humble yourself and take responsibility for your poor performance. Did you speak harsh and hurtful words? If so, humble yourself and ask for forgiveness. Humility heals, while pride prolongs pain.

It is the proactive process of humbling ourselves that keeps power from feeding our pride and fame from deflating our faith. Success is an enemy to humility because it tries to move us from submission to self-sufficiency. Leaders, do not let the accolades of man soften your submission to God. If you act like you do not need the Almighty, He will allow you to fall on your face in forced submission. It is better to voluntarily submit to authorities in heaven and on earth than to be made to surrender and be humiliated.

Grace is the gift you receive from God when you humble yourself. Grace is the gasoline that runs the engine of an eternal and abundant life. Humble yourself and watch the Lord lift you up in His timing. Self-exaltation is not sustainable; eternity's exaltation is forever. Submit under His mighty hand, and you will decrease, while He increases.

"He must become greater; I must become less" (John 3:30).

Do I humble myself daily by submitting to almighty God and to authority in my life?

Related Readings: Proverbs 3:34; Proverbs 16:18; Ephesians 5:21; James 4:7–10

THE SPIRITUAL LEADER

"But if serving the Lord seems undesirable to you, then choose for yourselves this day whom you will serve, whether the gods your forefathers served beyond the River, or the gods of the Amorites, in whose land you are living. But as for me and my household, we will serve the Lord."
Joshua 24:15

What does it mean to be the spiritual leader of my home? Do I have to reach a level of spiritual maturity before I qualify? What if my wife is more spiritual than I am? Should she be the spiritual leader? Spiritual leadership is determined by position, not knowledge. God places a man in the role of spiritual leader to lead his wife and children in faith.

Our wives and children may know more of the Bible, but the Lord still holds us responsible for their spiritual well-being. So as husbands and fathers, we have to ask ourselves, "What are we doing to lead our families spiritually?" This non-optional assignment from almighty God forces us into faith-based behavior. We want to model daily time in Bible reading and prayer. Spiritual leaders show the way to knowing God.

"The jailer brought them into his house and set a meal before them; he was filled with joy because he had come to believe in God—he and his whole family" (Acts 16:34). Spiritual leadership does not require a graduate degree in theology, but it does require a degree of planning and preparation. Spiritual leaders create a prayerful plan of intentional action that exposes their families to faith opportunities. You spend time looking for houses of worship that meet the needs of your wife and child, much like you would want them to live in the right home or attend the right school. Spiritual leadership seeks out a church.

"Let us go to his dwelling place; let us worship at his footstool" (Psalm 132:7).

Men who make it a big deal to lead their family spiritually make the most difference at home and in the community. Your investment in family Bible study, your example of faith under fire, and your Christlike character are living testaments to the truth of God. Talk about the Lord when you linger in traffic with your children, pray with them when they are fearful and upset, hold your wives hand and listen to her heart, sign up for the next marriage retreat, and serve others unselfishly. You cannot control the culture, but you and your house can serve the Lord. Spiritual leaders lead their family to love God.

"For the husband is the head of the wife as Christ is the head of the church, his body, of which he is the Savior. Now as the church submits to Christ, so also wives should submit to their husbands in everything" (Ephesians 5:23–24).

How can I take responsibility to lead my family spiritually? How can I leave a legacy for the Lord?

Related Readings: 2 Samuel 12:20; Psalm 100:4; Acts 18:7; 2 Timothy 1:16

JOIN GOD

"God is with us; he is our leader. His priests with their trumpets will sound the battle cry against you. Men of Israel, do not fight against the LORD, the God of your fathers, for you will not succeed." 2 Chronicles 13:12

I am either for God or against God. There is no in-between. If I ignore God, I am against Him. If my words honor God but my actions do not follow, I am against Him. If I am against those whom God is with, I am against God. Resisting God is not a smart place to be. It is much wiser to join God than to resist God. Joining Jesus brings joy!

We prayerfully discover where God is working and join Him. We resign ourselves from resistance to God and instead align with His will. There is no better place than to be partnered with God and His people. He is the pilot, and we are the copilots. He is the owner, and we are the managers. He is the King, and we are His servants. He is our heavenly Father, and we are His children. He is with us as He sends us out on His behalf.

"After Paul had seen the vision, we got ready at once to leave for Macedonia, concluding that God had called us to preach the gospel to them" (Acts 16:10).

Join Him at church and worship Him with his people. Saints and sinners alike will welcome you. We are all fellow strugglers on a joint mission with Jesus. Join Him in your marriage. No marriage has ever regretted placing Christ as the focal point. He is the stabilizer and perspective needed for a husband, wife, and child to flourish.

Join Him while you are stretching your mind in college. As you love Him with your mind, His wisdom will impregnate your thinking with good, pure, and productive thoughts. You will be wise beyond your years for His purposes. Join Him in your business pursuits. You will be surprised how He can lead you to the right deal and help you craft and execute the perfect plan. Join Him in a vision much bigger than yourself. Pray for a vision that unless God pulls it off, it certainly will not happen. Joint venture with Jesus.

Stop meddling with mediocre projects that man can pull off without the Lord. Ask instead, "Where is He working?" Join Him. By faith you can ride the wave of His wonder. Wake up and do not waste His precious time. You may be fighting a battle He has already won. Or you may be laboring in a field He has already left. Boldly go where no man has gone but where God is gathering a critical mass of like-minded disciples.

Our prayer is not for God to be on our side but for us to be on His. He is working in ways far beyond what we could envision, imagine, or figure out. Through intense prayer and with His faithful followers, let's join together and watch Him work. Otherwise, we are sleeping with the enemy and messing around biding our time. Seek out divine endeavors, join Him, and hang on for the ride. There is nothing like the Lord's leverage—one hundred fold who can influence an entire world for Jesus Christ. So by faith join Him today!

Where is the Lord calling me to leave my comfort zone for Christ's sake and join Him?

Related Readings: 1 Chronicles 16:10–11; Matthew 8:22; Acts 12:8; 1 Timothy 1:3

A11

BEAUTIFUL SAVIOR

"How beautiful on the mountains are the feet of those who bring good news, who proclaim peace, who bring good tidings, who proclaim salvation, who say to Zion, 'Your God reigns!'" Isaiah 52:7

Jesus is beautiful! He is the Lily of the Valley and the Bright and Morning Star. He is the Rose of Sharon and Immanuel: God with us. Our strong Savior is a tower of refuge, a secure cleft in the rock, and the solid rock of our salvation. "For you have been my refuge, a strong tower against the foe" (Psalm 61:3). Jesus protects His precious progeny.

Christ is a suffering servant, an unselfish servant, a humble servant, and a sacrificial servant. He is the Son of Man, the Son of God, the Lamb of God, and Lord of all. Jesus is our Emancipator, our Deliverer, our God, and a light to our dark path. "I am the light of the world. Whoever follows me will never walk in darkness, but will have the light of life" (John 8:12). He is a beautiful Savior who brings direction to His disciples.

He is "I am," the Great Shepherd, the Lion of Judah, our Kinsman Redeemer, the Bread of Life, and Living Water. Jesus is the mediator between God and man, the final Judge, our Advocate, and He is Mighty God and Prince of Peace. "And he will be called Wonderful Counselor, Mighty God, Everlasting Father, Prince of Peace" (Isaiah 9:6).

Christ is the scapegoat for our sin and the final sacrificial lamb for the sins of mankind. He is the resurrected Lord, the returning Lord, and the Lord of all. He is the King of Kings and Lord of Lords. Our beautiful Savior is the Alpha and Omega. He is the Word made flesh, the door, the gate, the way, the truth, the life, and the lover of your soul. He is holy, gentle, and meek in spirit. He defeats the enemy and casts Satan into hell for eternity.

He is Messiah, the miracle worker, healer, preacher, teacher, and friend. He forgives sin, judges sin, and loves sinners. He is love. He is God. So adore your beautiful Savior in majestic worship and praise. Enjoy the beauty of His compassionate countenance. Jesus Christ is your beautiful Savior, ready to save to the uttermost all who believe. Embrace the beauty of your Savior; He will make something beautiful of your life. Behold Jesus!

"Therefore He is also able to save to the uttermost those who come to God through Him, since He always lives to make intercession for them" (Hebrews 7:25 NKJV).

Have I received Jesus as my Savior through repentance and faith? Do I worship Him in the beauty of His holiness?

Related Readings: Song of Songs 2:1; Ruth 4:1–14; 1 Timothy 2:5; Revelation 21:6

JUDICIAL ACCOUNTABILITY

"He appointed judges in the land, in each of the fortified cities of Judah. He told them,
'Consider carefully what you do, because you are not judging for man but for the LORD, who is
with you whenever you give a verdict. Now let the fear of the LORD be upon you. Judge carefully,
for with the LORD our God there is not injustice or partiality or bribery.'" 2 Chronicles 19:5–7

Judges are first accountable to God. Even if they do not believe in God, they are accountable to God. Our rule of law is based on God's law. They are intertwined like salt and water in the sea. You cannot have one without the other. The ocean would not be the ocean if it were not filled with salty water. Our law is like water salted with God's truth.

America will cease to be America if law based on the Word of God does not govern her. A judge can recognize this historical fact and reality, or he can ignore it and even attempt to overturn it. However, his choice to create a new standard based on man's relevant wisdom will not be without consequences. Who defines truth when you marginalize God's law? Who is capable of defining right and wrong other than the Lord?

It is the pinnacle of pride to think that man can replace God. Yet this is where we find ourselves. We are bored with the obvious. God is not good enough for us anymore. We desire something more compliant with our selfish and man-centered behavior. So-called enlightened, intellectual progressives are leading us down a slippery slope to perdition. A man-centered judicial system leads to an inconsistent mess with a society out of control.

So what does a follower of Christ do? Do we have recourse? Yes, we train up children who fear God. We challenge them to study law, political science, philosophy, theology, and history. We provide environments for them that will produce judicial giants grounded in the law of God. Education is our friend. Some great educational institutions founded by faith have left their roots, but there are others who stand on the solid rock of Scripture.

Do not let the status of the world relegate you to irreverence and moral ambiguity. Partner with educational institutions that will produce judges who fear God and abhor sin. Pray for men and women who will judge justly and under His authority. Pseudo intelligence seeks to leave out God, when in reality true wisdom comes from God. This is why the Ten Commandments are displayed in the highest court of our land.

Lastly, support our political process of judicial elections and appointments. Your involvement makes a difference. The character and moral judgment of our judges are value reflections of those who have participated in the process. The appointment of God-fearing judges will not happen by accident. It will happen as God-fearing people get involved with their time and money. We are all accountable to God. Let's judge right now with God's standard, knowing that one day we will be judged by His standards.

Do I live uprightly under the law of the land? Do I expect judges to judge according to God's standards?

Related Readings: Genesis 18:25–26; Psalm 51:4; John 18:31–32; Romans 3:3–8

IGNORING GOD

"The LORD spoke to Manasseh and his people, but they paid no attention."
2 Chronicles 33:10

None of us like to be ignored, especially God. When we ignore someone, we communicate disrespect. Can you imagine the president of your country visiting your home? As he enters your foyer you escort him into the sitting room. There you have a long talk and really begin to get to know one another. Amazingly, he gives you permission for unlimited visits to his office or home over your lifetime.

Yet after our initial start with Christ, some of us have ignored His invitation to get to know one another. "Here I am! I stand at the door and knock. If anyone hears my voice and opens the door, I will come in and eat with him and he with me" (Revelation 3:20). We have ignored God. Maybe your reasons are noble. You have been busy providing for your family, pursing your career, or helping people. But where is God in the process? Love does not ignore.

If I love you, I want time with you. I listen to you and pray for you. I return your calls, write you encouraging e-mails, and check on you. Indeed, ignoring melts like butter under the hot light of love. Love and disregard cannot coexist. Jesus said, "If you love me, you will feed my sheep." (See John 21:15.) Love pays attention; it engages, teaches, and shepherds.

Also, as you pay attention to God, you become passionate about His interests. People become precious, not a distraction. The international community becomes your congregation. You see those of diverse cultures as sheep without a shepherd. Your heart bleeds for them, because the heart of God bleeds over their need for Him and His truth.

Take a spiritual audit of your Christianity. Better yet, engage with an "outside auditor" to give you an objective opinion of your compliance to God's standards for you. Will he or she discover you blasé, just running with the crowd, or find you hard after God? Do your calendar and checkbook reflect what the Lord cannot ignore: injustice, poverty, abandoned children, the lost, those who are brokenhearted, and all who are ensnared by sin?

Enthusiastically connect with our Creator. Pursue a friendship with Jesus. Take the time to be still, listen to the Lord, and do His will. Intimacy does not ignore the agenda of almighty God; it embraces eternity and ignores the diversions of this world.

"I have told you these things, so that in me you may have peace. In this world you will have trouble. But take heart! I have overcome the world" (John 16:33).

Do I inadvertently ignore God with my busy schedule, or do I pursue intimacy with Christ?

Related Readings: 1 Chronicles 22:19; Psalm 63:1; Acts 24:16; 1 Timothy 4:10

REMEMBER GOD'S FAITHFULNESS

"Aware of their discussion, Jesus asked, 'You of little faith, why are you talking among yourselves about having no bread? Do you still not understand? Don't you remember the five loaves for the five thousand, and how many basketfuls you gathered?'" Matthew 16:8–9

Temporary amnesia over almighty God's faithfulness can strike the most faithful. Jesus can heal and provide one day, and by the next day those who witnessed His miraculous provision act like He is unable to repeat His resourcefulness. The spiritual nature of Christ's work can be forgotten or dismissed by human nature's frail and finicky faith.

"But they soon forgot what he had done and did not wait for his counsel" (Psalm 106:13).

We can see Him answer prayer one day and by the next day grow impatient in the need for more prayer. The Lord led our troubled teenager through a selfish season, and then we stress out when the younger sibling starts to show signs of self-centeredness. God provided when financial fatigue almost caused us to collapse; so He can provide again.

"They forgot the God who saved them, who had done great things in Egypt, miracles in the land of Ham and awesome deeds by the Red Sea" (Psalm 106:21–22).

God's track record of faithfulness can be trusted. His reoccurring acts of righteousness show up in just the right time. There is no need for you to strive or stress over the next steps He has for you. Yes, seek godly advice and receive daily the counsel of Christ through His Holy Word, the Bible. But rest in and be reassured that the Lord is faithful.

When you forget, He reminds you. When you are weak, He is strong. When you fall down, He lifts you up. When you are afraid, He reassures you. When you are hungry, He feeds you. When you are tired, He gives you rest. When you are in trouble, He forgives and loves you. When you are in doubt, He reminds you that Christ is in you. Thus, teach and tell others of His provision. Trust His track record of faithfulness.

"He decreed statutes for Jacob and established the law in Israel, which he commanded our forefathers to teach their children, so the next generation would know them, even the children yet to be born, and they in turn would tell their children. Then they would put their trust in God and would not forget his deeds but would keep his commands" (Psalm 78:5–7).

How has the Lord shown His faithful provision in my life, work, and family?

Related Readings: Psalm 86:2; Isaiah 12:2; John 14:1; Romans 15:13

IDOL OF APPROVAL

"Am I now trying to win the approval of men, or of God? Or am I trying to please men?
If I were still trying to please men, I would not be a servant of Christ." Galatians 1:10

I struggle with needing the approval of people. These questions assault my identity: Do they accept me? Do they trust me? Do they believe in me? Am I good enough for them? How can I make them feel good or happy? Do they respect and value me? Worldly approval seeks to gain affection or avoid resentment at the expense of my identity in Christ.

Approval is not bad in itself. Wise children want their parents' approval. It is respectful and job security for an employee to seek the approval of his or her boss. It is healthy to win the approval of friends and family members you love and who love you. But approval becomes ugly when it defines who you are. Unrestrained accommodation leads to idolatry. Thus, the Lord's approval may dismiss men's approval for their own protection.

"They set up kings without my consent; they choose princes without my approval. With their silver and gold they make idols for themselves to their own destruction" (Hosea 8:4).

God disapproves when we are driven by approval outside of His influence. If approval from people is required for me to be happy and content, I am set up for frustration and discontentment. Sanction from people can compete with sanction from the Spirit. This happens when I replace my identity in Christ with my identity in consent from others.

Therefore, it is imperative that the Lord's approval becomes our motivation above seeking anyone else's approval. For example, this may mean saying no to accompanying a friend to a place God disapproves. So seeking Christ's approval first means you can relax, be yourself, and not have to prove yourself to people who are impossible to please anyway.

You avoid the idol of approval when you worship God alone and accept who He says you are in Christ. You are a child of your heavenly Father, accepted in the Beloved (Jesus), and sealed by the Holy Spirit. Approval from the Almighty gives you confidence to be who you are and leave the results to God. We will never please all the people all the time.

In Christ you are approved by God and extremely valuable as His incredible creation. When the Lord approves of you, you do not have to prove yourself to others. Ignore the idol of approval by first pleasing and worshiping Jesus Christ. His approval matters most.

"While he was still speaking, a bright cloud enveloped them, and a voice from the cloud said, 'This is my Son, whom I love; with him I am well pleased. Listen to him!'" (Matthew 17:5).

Whose approval do I need to give to the Lord and trust Him with their reactions?

Related Readings: Judges 18:6; Esther 2:17; John 6:27; 1 Corinthians 11:19

WHO IS JESUS?

"'But what about you?' he asked. 'Who do you say I am?' Simon Peter answered, 'You are the Christ, the Son of the living God.'" Matthew 16:15–16

There will always be those who deny the deity of Christ. They try to dilute His status as Savior by relegating Him to just a healer, like a medical practitioner of today with no supernatural intervention. Or other skeptics seek to corral Christ into a group of good moral teachers who had good things to say, but He certainly was not the Son of God.

However, God reveals to those who believe that the Son of Man was also the Son of God. John the Baptist was humble and bold, but only a man. Elijah was a prophet called by the Lord, but a man nonetheless. Jeremiah was full of passion and love for his people, but he was a man and not the Messiah Christ who was to come. Jesus is the Son of the living God. When asked if He was the One, Jesus did not stutter. He offered evidence for this fact: "The Jews gathered around him, saying, 'How long will you keep us in suspense? If you are the Christ, tell us plainly.' Jesus answered, 'I did tell you, but you do not believe. The miracles I do in my Father's name speak for me'" (John 10:24–25).

Faith is the first step to accepting the fact of Jesus Christ as the Son of God, who died on the cross for your sins and rose from the dead to give you life eternal. Because you base your belief on the historical knowledge of Christ's claim to be God, you are in good company with the thousands of His contemporaries who also believed based on His words and deeds. Facts become understanding when you apply faith and trust in Jesus.

Therefore, do not allow the diversity of opinions to cause you to doubt Christ's claims. He is either Lord of your life—or not. He is either the Savior of your soul—or not. He is Creator of all celestial beauty, planet earth's mountains, oceans, animals, and plants, and your body, mind, and soul—or not. Settle today who Jesus is, and do not sway from your belief.

He is the living Lord who knows our every thought, action, and motivation. God is nowhere close to being dead; He is only dead to those whose faith has died. We serve a living Savior who is on the move to expand His kingdom on earth. Jesus is alive!

When you walk closely with Christ, you confess with conviction that He is the Son of the living God. You are blessed when you are bold in your belief because you bolster the faith of others in Jesus. Do not be shy about your Savior. When people ask, "Who is Jesus?", tell them that He is the way to God, the truth of God, and the life of God.

"Jesus answered, 'I am the way and the truth and the life. No one comes to the Father except through me'" (John 14:6).

Can Christ count on me to give a clear account of who He is and what He expects?

Related Readings: Isaiah 53:1–12; Jeremiah 10:10; John 1:29; Hebrews 3:12–13

GIFTED BIBLE TEACHERS

"Ezra had devoted himself to the study and observance of the Law of the LORD, and to teaching its decrees and laws in Israel." Ezra 7:10

A gifted Bible teacher is a gift from God. He equips them with the discernment of His Word and the ability to apply it to everyday life. Gifted teachers dissect facts from Holy Scripture and then bridge their relevance into contemporary society. This requires - prayerful preparation. Biblical facts without application become dry, dusty, and boring. Indeed, factual information without individual life change facilitates our pride.

"Knowledge puffs up, but love builds up. The man who thinks he knows something does not yet know as he ought to know" (1 Corinthians 8:1-2).

The danger is to fill our minds without a change of heart; so the gifted Bible teacher presents his message to both mind and heart. Of course, the other extreme is a potential problem. Bible teachers who attempt to apply the Scripture without proper biblical context and grounding in God's Word run the risk of sharing opinion rather than absolutes and Scriptural principles. Truth needs to be released, not watered down or overexplained.

"Be diligent to present yourself approved to God, a worker who does not need to be ashamed, rightly dividing the word of truth" (2 Timothy 2:15 NKJV).

The teacher's role is to harvest God's truth and humbly deliver it to the sheep of his flock. Like a seasoned chef, he wants the delivery to invite interest. The presentation of a delicious meal is inviting to the eye and stomach; so the proper presentation of God's Word is to the head and heart. One quality of an effective delivery is a humble spirit.

People do not want to be talked down to. They want to be taught by a fellow learner and struggler. People respect you for your strengths but connect with you for your weaknesses. "Perfect" Bible teachers build walls between the people, while "imperfect" ones build bridges to the people.

Another good quality of a compelling presentation is stories. Jesus told stories. Stories illustrate truth with clarity. Like the sun shining through a freshly cleaned window, you can see much better. Interesting storytellers are students of people who understand their hopes and fears. Gifted Bible teachers comfort the afflicted and afflict the comfortable.

Lastly, the gifted Bible teacher loves to read, research, and engraft God's Word into his own soul. The Bible oozes from his being. Scripture is not just a source for sermon preparation, but first a source for heart preparation. He opens the Word of God and asks God to speak to him and to change him.

God, change me first, so I can present your truth to others in need of You. Pour me out as a broken vessel to others who are hungry and thirsty for Your truth!

Do I allow the Word of God to change me first, before I teach it to others?

Related Readings: Ezra 7:6; Ecclesiastes 12:9–11; Hebrews 5:12; James 3:1

FITLY JOINED TOGETHER

"From whom the whole body fitly joined together and compacted by that which
every joint supplieth, according to the effectual working in the measure of every part,
maketh increase of the body unto the edifying of itself in love." Ephesians 4:16 KJV

What does it mean to be fitly joined together? Like a hand in a well-fit glove, there is a comfort and ease of use. When people are in their proper positions and understand their roles, there is not a lot of inefficiency. A good fit means everyone on the team is excelling and no one is worried about the follow-through of a fellow worker.

There is an ease that comes in relationships and work when we are fitly joined together. There is a chemistry and connection that happens when we complement one another's gifts. For instance, a visionary needs process thinkers and project managers around him or her. The chief executive is responsible for execution through complementary skilled team members. Alignment around implementation brings agreed-upon results.

When the body of Christ works together, there is mutual love and unity. This is why it is wise to engage partners and people in your business or ministry who have the same values and priorities in life. A very competent team member without depth of character can cannibalize your culture. Furthermore, a person of character without consistent competence can bruise your brand promise. Fitly joined together requires trustworthiness.

Ultimately, we are united around Christ who is the Head. Whether it is marriage, business, or ministry, focus on Jesus keeps our perspective bigger than ourselves. He is the One who empowers and equips His children with wisdom, strength, and skills. Be bold to move someone out of a role that is not a good fit so the whole team becomes healthy and fit.

Keep your company and home Christ centered. Receive God's gifts and graces for the sake of the whole body of Christ, and you will experience the fruit of being fitly joined together. Love and respect among believers facilitate unity and spiritual growth. You know you fit together by faith when excellence is the outcome of each one's work.

"And in him you too are being built together to become a dwelling in which God lives by his Spirit" (Ephesians 2:22).

Is my marriage jointly fit together in Christ? Who at work is not the right fit?

Related Readings: Ezra 3:9; Matthew 19:6; Acts 1:14; Ephesians 2:21

TRUST IN MONEY

"Do not store up for yourselves treasures on earth, where moth and rust destroy, and where thieves break in and steal. But store up for yourselves treasures in heaven, where moth and rust do not destroy, and where thieves do not break in and steal. For where your treasure is, there your heart will be also." Matthew 6:19–21

My biggest temptation may be to trust in money more than I trust in my Master Jesus. Cash is constantly bidding for my allegiance over my commitment to Christ. I know the Lord takes care of His children, but don't I have to save enough money to be secure? Financial planning is prudent and wise, but not to the point of replacing my dependence on God. When I obsess about the need for more money, I am totally trusting in money.

Ironically, our currency carries the not-so-subtle reminder, "In God We Trust," perhaps engraved by our faith-filled Founding Fathers as a warning not to waste our energy engaging money as the source of our security. Can we trust money and trust God at the same time? No, Jesus is very clear about the status of stuff in relation to God's devotion:

"No one can serve two masters. Either he will hate the one and love the other, or he will be devoted to the one and despise the other. You cannot serve both God and Money" (Matthew 6:24).

You cannot trust cash and Christ simultaneously. Money is not trustworthy. So honestly ask, "Is my future secured by my savings or by my Savior?" It is impossible to obtain a one hundred percent secured financial future. God knows we need this uncertainty to stay dependent on Him. Frustration and fear become the pattern of those who focus on finances over faith.

"Whoever loves money never has money enough; whoever loves wealth is never satisfied with his income. This too is meaningless. As goods increase, so do those who consume them. And what benefit are they to the owner except to feast his eyes on them?" (Ecclesiastes 5:10–11).

The love of money and trust in money are both sins. So how can we responsibly prepare for the future and remain loyal to the Lord? Start with gratitude to God for His daily provision, be a joyful and generous giver, and submit moment by moment to the Lord's ownership. You know you trust in the Lord alone when your treasures in heaven far exceed your treasures on earth. Treasures left with Jesus produce a peaceful heart.

"And the peace of God, which transcends all understanding, will guard your hearts and your minds in Christ Jesus" (Philippians 4:7).

Does cash compete with my trust in Christ? How can I aggressively store up treasure in heaven?

Related Readings: Proverbs 23:5; Luke 19:8–10; 2 Corinthians 8:9; Colossians 3:5

CHRIST'S CHURCH

"And I tell you that you are Peter, and on this rock I will build my church,
and the gates of Hades will not overcome it." Matthew 16:18

The church is Christ's. He bought her with His blood. He married her with His everlasting covenant, and He is coming back to take her and present her in all His glory. Because He owns the church, hell cannot highjack it, and man cannot mitigate its mission. His church has survived and thrived for almost two thousand years and will until He comes back for His bride. But aren't some churches ineffective? Yes, there are some in name only, but the true church of Christ is being built by its founder—the Lord Jesus Christ.

"Christ loved the church and gave himself up for her to make her holy, cleansing her by the washing with water through the word, and to present her to himself as a radiant church, without stain or wrinkle or any other blemish, but holy and blameless" (Ephesians 5:25–27).

Jesus builds the church by growing His followers into dedicated and mature disciples who are full of the fruit of the Spirit. His eternal plan is for His disciples to fall deeper in love with Him and with each other. Nothing or no one can stop Christ's construction of His church. Sin cannot, because He has the power to forgive. Satan cannot, because He conquered him at the cross. Death cannot, because He overcame death's sting. Persecution cannot, because the church thrives when under pressure. He is building His church—now.

"And God placed all things under his feet and appointed him to be head over everything for the church, which is his body, the fullness of him who fills everything in every way" (Ephesians 1:22–23).

Furthermore, Christ builds His church upon the confession of His children: "He is Christ, Son of the living God." When we confess Christ with our words, backed by our life, we partner with the Holy Spirit in erecting the Lord's eternal edifice, His church. His dwelling is not captured by church buildings. His dwelling is in the hearts of men, women, boys, and girls who, empowered by His grace, give others the opportunity to hear the old, old story of Jesus' love for them. He is building His church for His glory!

"His intent was that now, through the church, the manifold wisdom of God should be made known to the rulers and authorities in the heavenly realms, according to his eternal purpose which he accomplished in Christ Jesus our Lord" (Ephesians 3:10–11).

Am I engaged with Christ in building His church by confessing Him as God's Son?

Related Readings: Acts 16:5; Romans 8:9–11; Colossians 1:18; Revelation 2:1–29

SUFFERING SERVANT

"From that time on Jesus began to explain to his disciples that he must go to Jerusalem and suffer many things at the hands of the elders, chief priests and teachers of the law, and that he must be killed and on the third day be raised to life." Matthew 16:21

Suffering matures our faith and is for the mature of faith. How can it be that suffering is the path of perfecting my faith? Why do good people have to suffer for the sins of others? Like Peter, "Never, Lord!…This shall never happen to you!" (Matthew 16:22), our humanness wants to protect loved ones from suffering, when this may be God's will. He strips away my man-centered motives, leaving me exposed to the raw reality of dependence on Him.

"Therefore, leaving the discussion of the elementary principles of Christ, let us go on to perfection, not laying again the foundation of repentance from dead works and of faith toward God" (Hebrews 6:1 NKJV).

It is otherworldly to experience joy in the middle of adversity; yet this is what Christ-centered living does. It is in our suffering that we see a glimpse of our Savior's suffering. The sight of His unjust suffering soothes my soul with sweet surrender to Jesus. His afflictions show me how to suffer with faith, grace, patience, and joy deep in my heart.

"Consider it pure joy, my brothers, whenever you face trials of many kinds, because you know that the testing of your faith develops perseverance. Perseverance must finish its work so that you may be mature and complete, not lacking anything" (James 1:2–4).

God may reveal gradually the purpose of your suffering, or you may only know that it is to display His glory. Therefore, do not lament to the Lord your suffering and miss Him; rather, give it over to Him to know Him and to learn from Him how to suffer well.

Suffering is not secluded to a select people group. It cuts across all cultures—the rich and famous and the poor and needy. Suffering silently strikes a young mom who miscarries, an older dad in career transition, or a child captured by chronic illness. Some suffer from hunger, disease, persecution, finances, relationships, and mental and emotional sickness. It is only in surrender to the Suffering Servant that we learn how to suffer well. Indeed, in this life we have the potential to suffer many things, as Jesus suffered many things.

Therefore, see suffering as the process of dying to self and living for Christ. Let the Lord love you through this painful process as He produces His peace and His character. Learn what it means to be longsuffering and truly humble, and He will lift you up to inspire and encourage others. Do not waste pain in self-pity; rather, embrace it in intimacy with Jesus. As a suffering servant, stay focused on the loving cross and the glorious resurrection.

"Let us fix our eyes on Jesus, the author and perfecter of our faith, who for the joy set before him endured the cross, scorning its shame, and sat down at the right hand of the throne of God" (Hebrews 12:2).

How can I learn to suffer well? Who is suffering who needs my encouragement?

Related Readings: Isaiah 52:13–15; Isaiah 53:1–12; John 9:1–3; John 11:14–15

A SAD HEART

"So the King asked me, 'Why does your face look so sad when you are not ill? This can be nothing but sadness of heart.'" Nehemiah 2:2

Sadness can creep in like termites and over time erode the foundation of our joy. Or sadness can attack like a bandit and steal our gladness. Either way, it is not fun being sad. Sadness can have a variety of sources. It may be health related. You battle chronic pain that it is almost unbearable. Medication provides temporary relief, but you still struggle.

Sadness solicits when someone you love dearly is suffering and you feel there is nothing else you can do. Your sadness may come from disappointment, deep hurt and letdown, even betrayal. Perhaps your emotions are unstable. Discerning friends see it in your face. Your countenance is downtrodden, unable to mask the disappointment.

The loss of anything we value will contribute to sadness. It may be an opportunity, a friend, a death, money, or the injustice another is experiencing. None of us is immune to sadness. You can deny its reality, but it is lurking to lead us to despair. Dealing with sadness requires more than a mental exercise of trying to think positively. Jesus was in anguish just before His arrest in the garden. But He appealed to His heavenly Father and defaulted to the will of the One who eventually brought gladness.

So express your frustration, heartache, and grief to your heavenly Father. He already knows, but you need to be reminded of His unconditional love and grace. Jesus is there to understand and comfort. He feels your pain. Ask Him to make His joy your strength. This simple expression of humble dependence will not go unnoticed from your sympathizing Savior. Express how you feel to the One who is the creator of your emotions. He cares.

Another remedy for sadness is service to those in need. Visit an AIDS hospital, orphanage, cancer center, or nursing home. Suddenly your sadness seems irrelevant as you become caught up in helping others in their broken state. The smile of one crippled under the weight of disease will infuse your own soul with gratitude and hope.

Your service may find you helping in the church's preschool. You may encourage your spouse by serving together. The children's pure hearts and funny expressions will bring joy to your soul. You cannot help but smile around children, especially grandchildren. So reengage with God, people, or something bigger than yourself. Over time fear will be replaced with hope, frustration with joy, and sadness with gladness.

"Surely you have granted him eternal blessings and made him glad with the joy of your presence" (Psalm 21:6).

Am I seeking joy from Jesus in my sad state? Whom can I make glad who is sad?

Related Readings: Psalm 5:11; Psalm 69:32; Psalm 70:4; Psalm 100:2; Psalm 118:24; Luke 18:23; Revelation 19:7

THINGS OF GOD

"Jesus turned and said to Peter, 'Get behind me, Satan! You are a stumbling block to me; you do not have in mind the things of God, but the things of men.'" Matthew 16:23

The things of God contrast with the things of man. God says, "Trust me"; man says, "Can He be trusted?" God says, "Be patient"; man says, "I want it now!" God says, "Focus on the eternal"; man says, "Live for today." God says, "Give and get blessed"; man says, "Get and get more." God says, "Serve"; man says, "Be served."

But it is the things of God that become a building block, not a stumbling block, for belief. In fact, we play into the schemes of Satan when we think in the realm of the temporal and dismiss the eternal. This is an ongoing challenge, because one day we can fly high by faith and the next day live defeated in unbelief. Thus, be careful to think through the paradigm of Providence, and do not pander to the perspective of uninformed people.

"So we fix our eyes not on what is seen, but on what is unseen. For what is seen is temporary, but what is unseen is eternal" (2 Corinthians 4:18).

The things of God trump the things of man. So when you have the opportunity to offer a severance to a departing team member, be generous, not greedy. When your spouse or child reacts in emotion to your actions, be understanding, not defensive. When a financial issue surfaces unexpectedly, be prayerful and creative, not fearful and angry.

"Finally, brothers, whatever is true, whatever is noble, whatever is right, whatever is pure, whatever is lovely, whatever is admirable—if anything is excellent or praiseworthy— think about such things" (Philippians 4:8).

The things of God are time-tested and proven. So there is no need to try an unrighteous route when the righteous path is the road best traveled. Think on the things of God recorded in His Word, and you will flush out the things of man. Counterfeit beliefs are best exposed by authentic ideas from the Almighty. Jesus pushes the things of God in the forefront to be followed and respected. His favor rests where His things are revered most.

"O Sovereign LORD, you are God! Your words are trustworthy, and you have promised these good things to your servant" (2 Samuel 7:28).

How can I better trust the things of God over the things of man? What one thing can I change?

Related Readings: Deuteronomy 12:31; Job 37:5; Luke 5:26; Acts 14:15; 1 Corinthians 1:27

GOOD LISTENER

"While he was still speaking, a bright cloud enveloped them, and a voice from the cloud said, 'This is my Son, whom I love; with him I am well pleased. Listen to him!'" Matthew 17:5

What does it mean to listen well? Think of those you admire as good listeners. What are some of the traits they exhibit which mark them as excellent listeners? Perhaps it is their engaging eye contact, their warm conversation, or an empathetic ear. You feel understood and valued. Good listeners affirm what you say by repeating what you say with an illustration or an example from their life. They listen to learn, affirm, and instruct.

Those who learn good listening skills develop robust relationships. They embrace an "others first" way of thinking that places their own need to be heard down the priority list. Like a rare and exotic flower, they open themselves up in a beautiful way that invites you to smell the brilliant colors of their character. Indeed, good listeners are magnetic in the way they attract the good and the bad into their influence. If you are a good listener, be wise by investing in those who really want to change and follow after the Lord.

"Let the wise listen and add to their learning, and let the discerning get guidance" (Proverbs 1:5).

You can be assured that the Lord listens to you and the desires of your heart. He is not preoccupied with problems or people; instead, you have His full attention. He is always available to hear your cry for wisdom, healing, and direction. The Almighty's attention is focused on His children who come to Him by faith. His listening ear is near and dear.

"But God has surely listened and heard my voice in prayer" (Psalm 66:19).

Furthermore, make it a daily habit to listen well to your heavenly Father's heart. He sent His Son Jesus to teach us the truth about life and death, heaven and hell. We listen to the Lord Jesus because He was God speaking in the flesh. Why was the Almighty so pleased with His Son that He admonished us to listen to Him? Jesus modeled listening to His heavenly Father; so God have Him the words to speak on His behalf. The Lord is pleased with good listeners. He gives discernment and insight into His solutions to human needs.

So listen well by first listening well to the Lord. He will instruct and teach you in the way you should go. And once you have heard from Him, humbly listen to others, discern their needs, and then connect them to Christ and His ways. Indeed, good listeners lead others to love God and listen to His heart. Listen well, and watch God work!

"I will instruct you and teach you in the way you should go; I will counsel you and watch over you" (Psalm 32:8).

How can I be a good listener for Christ's sake? What is God telling me to do today?

Related Readings: Job 15:8; Proverbs 4:10; Proverbs 19:20; Ecclesiastes 7:5; James 1:19

FREEDOM IN FOCUS

"Because the Sovereign LORD helps me, I will not be disgraced. Therefore have
I set my face like flint, and I know I will not be put to shame." Isaiah 50:7

Focus brings freedom, because there is permission to say no to good, competing ideas and opportunities. It is out of focus that faith is forged. When Jesus Christ is the focal point for direction and discipline, all other priorities fall into place. Focus on Him brings to bear heaven's perspective and resources. A face like flint on Jesus creates freedom to trust and wait on Him. Keep your Savior the spotlight, and you will see clearly.

But how can I stay focused on the Lord when life's distractions tend to dominate my time? How do I remain a fruitful Christian and not be mired down in the mundane? It is essential to first master the fundamentals of honesty, humility, patience, and service to others. It is out of living the basic tenets of the Christian life that I can be trusted with more.

"Whoever can be trusted with very little can also be trusted with much, and whoever is dishonest with very little will also be dishonest with much" (Luke 16:10).

Focus brings freedom at work when you assess your activity around results and not busyness. Perhaps you do fewer things well instead of a lot of things mediocre. Average results are poor stewardship when you have above-average potential. We know we are too busy when we constantly run late for meetings and have a pattern of broken promises. So how can we break this crazy cycle of overcommitment? Where do we start?

Focus starts by gazing on God with a rare glimpse on your circumstances. Ask what Jesus would do and how He would reach the goal. When your identity is in the One who loves you most, you become most like Him. Confidence bubbles up for those who first focus on their heavenly Father. He gives you the ability and know-how to be the best for Him.

"One thing I ask of the LORD, this is what I seek: that I may dwell in the house of the LORD all the days of my life, to gaze upon the beauty of the LORD and to seek him in his temple" (Psalm 27:4).

Therefore, by faith focus on a few things, and do them well. Once you have mastered the basics, then explore other exciting opportunities. God opens additional doors once you have gone through the door of faith and obedience in being faithful where He has you. You will experience freedom by staying focused on the Lord and His calling for you.

Jesus was the master at staying focused on priorities: "I will drive out demons and heal people today and tomorrow, and on the third day I will reach my goal" (Luke 13:32).

What one or two relationships do I need to focus on the most? Is the Lord my focus?

Related Readings: Psalm 62:11; Luke 10:42; John 14:31; Galatians 3:2; Philippians 3:13

DON'T BE AFRAID

"But Jesus came and touched them. 'Get up,' he said. 'Don't be afraid.'
When they looked up, they saw no one except Jesus." Matthew 17:7–8

Fear is relentless in its pursuit to push peace from the heart of sincere followers of Jesus. No one is immune to its influence. You can be a new believer or a seasoned Christian of many years and still struggle with fear. Fear stalks us, when like a boxer we fall to one knee and wonder if we can get back up again. But it is in that point of weakness that we look up and see no one except Jesus. Fear flees when we appropriate faith in our Savior.

"Look unto me, and be ye saved, all the ends of the earth: for I am God, and there is none else" (Isaiah 45:22 KJV).

Fear sows doubt in our souls with "what ifs." What if I lose my job? What if we can't pay the bills? What if we can't retire? What if my child fails? What if he or she leaves me? What if the government takes over completely? What if I am rejected? What if I die? What if they die? What ifs are not healthy to obsess over because they only feed fear. Instead, think thoughts that anchor your hope in the certainty of Christ and His control. He's got you.

"Will he not much more clothe you, O you of little faith? So do not worry, saying, 'What shall we eat?' or 'What shall we drink?' or 'What shall we wear?' For the pagans run after all these things, and your heavenly Father knows that you need them. But seek first his kingdom and his righteousness, and all these things will be given to you as well" (Matthew 6:30–33).

Jesus expects us to get up from ungodly groveling in apprehension and worry and stand up by faith. Stand up by faith to Satan and his schemes to question God. Stand up by faith to emotions that forget the Lord's faithfulness. Stand up by faith to institutions or political systems that marginalize faith-based behavior. When we stand up by faith, we experience God's grace and assurance. Fear cannot coexist in the presence of faith.

Lastly, do not be afraid when the glory of God reveals itself in all its radiant splendor. The Lord's blessing may have burst upon you like cool, refreshing rain after days of drought and dryness. Do not wonder when it might be over; instead, enjoy Jesus and your window of opportunity to give Him glory for His gracious favor. The touch of Jesus is what is needed to trust Jesus. Bow before Him in awe and fear, but do not be afraid.

"Moses said to the people, 'Do not be afraid. God has come to test you, so that the fear of God will be with you to keep you from sinning'" (Exodus 20:20).

What fear of mine do I need to replace with faith? Do I invite the touch of Jesus?

Related Readings: Genesis 50:19–21; Judges 6:23; Luke 1:30; Hebrews 11:23

CHRIST'S SECOND COMING

*"For the Son of Man is going to come in his Father's glory with his angels,
and then he will reward each person according to what he has done." Matthew 16:27*

Jesus came the first time in a modest manger to save the people from their sin. He was not the king, but He threatened the king. Jesus is coming soon a second time with a grand entrance as King of Kings to judge the people for their sins and dead works. He rode the first time on a humble donkey. He will ride this second time on a brazen horse.

Christ's second coming must matter most to the church because we are His bride, the body of Christ. How can the church be ready to greet its godly groom, Jesus? Like any faithful wife whose husband is away traveling for work or waging war overseas, we want to greet Him with a holy kiss. A faithful church is not conformed by the culture; rather, it conforms the culture. The faithful bride of Christ is ready to rejoice at His glorious sight!

"'Let us be glad and rejoice and give Him glory, for the marriage of the Lamb has come, and His wife has made herself ready.' And to her it was granted to be arrayed in fine linen, clean and bright, for the fine linen is the righteous acts of the saints" (Revelation 19:7–8 NKJV).

When Christ comes back, He wants to catch the church evangelizing the lost and making disciples. He hungers for her disputes to be with the devil and not with each other. A humble church does not use finances to build man's kingdom but instead deploys resources to advance the kingdom of God. The church is ready for Christ's return when she serves the poor, ministers to the body of Christ, prays for the sick, and preaches the gospel!

"May the Lord make your love increase and overflow for each other and for everyone else, just as ours does for you. May he strengthen your hearts so that you will be blameless and holy in the presence of our God and Father when our Lord Jesus comes with all his holy ones" (1 Thessalonians 3:12–13).

Christ's coming is also compelling for individual Christians. We want to be about our Lord's business and not preoccupied with activities and assets that will burn up one day. The judgment seat of Christ is for Christians, not to be judged for salvation but to be judged for the quality of their works. You are wise when you invest in eternal matters with your time and money. Christlike character, missions, prayer, Bible teaching, corporate and individual worship, and service in the community all make Jesus smile.

When Christ comes, make sure He catches you about your Father's business. "And this is my prayer: that your love may abound more and more in knowledge and depth of insight, so that you may be able to discern what is best and may be pure and blameless until the day of Christ, filled with the fruit of righteousness that comes through Jesus Christ—to the glory and praise of God" (Philippians 1:9–11).

How can my church and I personally get ready for the second coming of Christ?

Related Readings: Ecclesiastes 12:14; Matthew 23:13; 1 Corinthians 3:9–15; 1 Corinthians 4:5

ONGOING GRATITUDE

"Give thanks in all circumstances, for this is God's will for you in Christ Jesus."
1 Thessalonians 5:18

It is God's will to give thanks in all circumstances. How can this be? Yes, in triumph and good things, but am I to be grateful in defeat and bad things? Often Christ's thoughts are counterintuitive to man's shallow assumptions. The Lord in His wonderful wisdom understands the advantage of thanksgiving in prosperity and adversity.

Perhaps we experience the marriage of a child and her fiancé who love the Lord, and we rejoice and give Him the glory. Conversely, we have the heartbreak of a child who cannot keep his or her marriage together, and it ends in divorce. It is in this dark day of disappointment that we still say to our Savior, "Thank you for working all things out for the good of those who love you." Thanksgiving governs our joy, peace, and contentment.

"And we know that in all things God works for the good of those who love him, who have been called according to his purpose" (Romans 8:28).

Gratitude and humility are first cousins. It is out of the fertile soil of thanksgiving that humility is able to grow and flourish. Gratitude says, "Thank you, God, for giving me salvation in Jesus." Humility says, "I want to go deeper in my intimacy with Jesus." Gratitude says, "Friends are a gift from God." Humility says, "How can I serve them?"

"I always thank my God as I remember you in my prayers, because I hear about your faith in the Lord Jesus and your love for all the saints" (Philemon 1:4–5).

Furthermore, gratitude gives you the positive energy to engage life and live it to the fullest. It is out of your thanksgiving that you are able to understand God's will and follow Jesus wholeheartedly. You can complain to Christ, just not about Christ. He wants more for you than you want for yourself; so be extremely grateful, ever rejoicing in Him.

"Do not be anxious about anything, but in everything, by prayer and petition, with thanksgiving, present your requests to God" (Philippians 4:6).

How has the Lord blessed my life? How can I express my gratitude to Him and others?

Related Readings: Psalm 118:28; Daniel 2:23; Colossians 3:17; Hebrews 12:28

LOST SLEEP

"That night the king could not sleep; so he ordered the book of the chronicles, the record of his reign, to be brought in and read to him." Esther 6:1

Sometimes life wakes us up in the middle of the night. The worries of the world can be heavy, even painstaking. Their severity can flush us out of bed like prey running from a predator. It is hard to sleep when fear grips our heart, but Christ calms our conscience. A good night's sleep is God's gift. He provides firm reassurance during fickle times.

Your heart may be heavy with financial worries, relational stress, and/or health issues. A child may be giving you fits. A teenager can add to your growing gray hair. Or a tragic accident can add fuel to your fears; a lawsuit may be looming. It is hard to sleep when your circumstances seem out of control. What are you to do? A full night's sleep has become as common as a snowflake in the desert. You lose heart when you lose sleep.

How can night interruptions be wisely interpreted? God speaks in the middle of the night. He may speak through the Bible. He may speak through a quiet prayer and contemplation. Either way, He has my attention, and He wants me to listen to Him. "On my bed I remember you; I think of you through the watches of the night" (Psalm 63:6).

Take the time to journal during this time of sleep deprivation. If you do not write down your "God thoughts," there is a good chance you will forget what He may be saying. The record of your engagement with God will become a future hope and encouragement. Your written word will serve as a reminder of God's personal care and direction.

The fear of the night will give way to the peace of the morning. Do not waste this time. Convert your late night pity party to a prayer party. Let God heal your soul and comfort your heart. He works twenty-four hours a day, seven days a week, even when we are unaware. "I will praise the LORD, who counsels me; even at night my heart instructs me" (Psalm 16:7).

Solicit your Savior Jesus to change you. Ask Him to make you more forgiving. Allow the unlimited forgiveness of God to flow through you. Be a channel of God's grace to those in your life who are undeserving and unloving.

Forgive your heavenly Father for allowing you to go through this hardship. He is here to walk with you through adversity, not to crush you under its weight. Christ's companionship will add hours to your sleep and maybe years to your life. Use this time of sleeplessness to grow your faith. The Lord's largeness looms over your opportunities like a fresh coat of morning dew over grass. He has you covered. He can be trusted. This situation did not sneak up on Him. Go back to sleep and rest securely in His arms.

"I will lie down and sleep in peace, for you alone, O LORD, make me dwell in safety" (Psalm 4:8).

Does my rest at night rest in the Lord? What is God trying to teach me in my unrest?

Related Readings: Genesis 2:21; Proverbs 3:24; Acts 12:6; 2 Corinthians 11:27

LEAVE AND CLEAVE

"'Haven't you read,' he replied, 'that at the beginning the Creator "made them male and female,"
and said, "For this reason a man will leave his father and mother and be united to his wife,
and the two will become one flesh"? So they are no longer two, but one. Therefore what
God has joined together, let man not separate.'" Matthew 19:4–6

It is hard for parents to give away their child in marriage. It is easy for parents to give away their child in marriage. These are mixed emotions that most fathers and mothers feel on the wedding day of their baby. I am happy the Lord brought the bride and groom together in holy matrimony, but I am sad to see them go. There is a hole in my heart.

But from the beginning our Creator made them male and female for the purpose of becoming one flesh. God's desire for oneness with married couples can only happen by leaving father and mother and cleaving to Christ and one another. It is sad to see them go, but there is gladness, knowing they will grow in grace and in love for one another.

"But grow in the grace and knowledge of our Lord and Savior Jesus Christ. To him be glory both now and forever! Amen" (2 Peter 3:18).

In fact, our children are limited in their understanding of the Lord if they remain under our roof. For their faith to become more real and robust, they must become their own man or woman. Faith is meant to flourish from the foundation of a Christ-centered marriage. They become one flesh in Christ so they can learn to passionately follow the Lord and serve others. Parents have the privilege of letting their children leave well and cleave well.

Therefore, trust God with the transition of your children into young adulthood. Do not hamper their growth by hovering, but hold them with an open hand, and watch the grace of God grow them into trophies of His truth. Let them go, and let them grow. The hole in your heart means you love them so much; so love large, and let the Lord fill your hole of sadness with His cup of gladness. Cleave to Christ as they leave and cleave to one another!

"But cleave unto the LORD your God, as ye have done unto this day" (Joshua 23:8 KJV).

Do I hold my child with an open hand? Am I cleaving to my spouse and Christ alone?

Related Readings: Deuteronomy 11:22; Judges 1:13; Acts 11:23; Romans 12:9–10

GOD'S PLAN

"'For I know the plans I have for you,' declares the LORD, 'plans to prosper you and not to harm you, plans to give you hope and a future.'" Jeremiah 29:11

God's plan is what is best. It is a good plan. It may not seem like a good plan right now, but God's plan is good. This apparent contradiction is where it gets confusing. A messy life is not always a fun life. Currently you may be experiencing heartache and hard times. His plan does not seem good in your current circumstance, but God is still good.

Perhaps your spouse has been unfaithful. God's plan seems to have taken a detour down a road of disappointment. You lost your home. God's plan seems wrong. You were asked to resign. God's plan does not seem fair. Your health is withering away. God's plan seems premature with its invitation for your homecoming. Every step you take, every choice you make, and every place you go seem to lead toward more confusion and chaos.

So how can God's plan be good, prosperous, and not harmful? This is a fair question. To answer this question accurately and fairly, we need to consider God's long-term plan. To walk wisely today requires a reminder of hope tomorrow. It is our future hope with God that inspires us to live for Him today. Wherever Jesus is, there hope resides. When we have Jesus, we have hope. Hope is heaven's righteous rope that lifts us out of our despair.

"Oh, that I might have my request, that God would grant what I hope for" (Job 6:8).

Therefore, you can look forward to a better day. But do not miss what God is teaching you today. Hope for tomorrow does not preclude learning from the Lord today. This is all a part of God's big plan. In the big scheme of God's plan, there is suffering. Your suffering may even last a lifetime, but this does not cancel out the goodness of God's plan. Suffering is our springboard into the depths of God's love and grace.

"Indeed, in our hearts we felt the sentence of death. But this happened that we might not rely on ourselves but on God, who raises the dead" (2 Corinthians 1:9).

Current challenges are preparation for His prosperity, His hope, and His future for you. On the other hand, you may be living large right now. Life looks good. God feels good. His plans seem to be rolling out flawlessly. Use this time to go deeper with Him, because the realities of His plan for you go much deeper than a surface, spiritual sentimentality.

His plan is robust and challenging. You can acquiesce to a plan of lesser consequence and miss His best. Or you can trust the Lord and follow hard after Him, even when His plan seems to have gone awry. Indeed, this is not your home. You are on assignment from heaven; so explore and enjoy His eternal exit plan. It is full of prosperity, hope, and a future. You can trust God's providential plan works out for the purpose of His will.

"In him we were also chosen, having been predestined according to the plan of him who works out everything in conformity with the purpose of his will" (Ephesians 1:11).

Is His plan what is best for me? Am I aligned with the Almighty's plan for my life?

Related Readings: Proverbs 21:30; Isaiah 14:24; 2 Corinthians 1:17; Hebrews 11:40

FINISHING WELL

"So they hanged Haman on the gallows he had prepared for Mordecai."
Esther 7:10

Some people do not finish well, and others do. Why? It comes down to our choices. The choices you make today determine how you finish tomorrow. You can live in very difficult circumstances and make wise choices. There is a great probability you will finish well. You can live in the best conditions and make unwise choices. Chances are you will not finish well. So does it mean we will have no regrets when we finish well? No.

God is not looking for perfection, but He does desire passion for Himself and obedience to His Word. People who do not finish well decide to take control. They act like they have a better plan than God. This type of decision-making process will have limited success, if any, in the Lord's eyes. How, then, does the Bible describe finishing well?

Hebrews 12:1–3 says, "Therefore, since we are surrounded by such a great cloud of witnesses, let us throw off everything that hinders and the sin that so easily entangles, and let us run with perseverance the race marked out for us. Let us fix our eyes on Jesus, the author and perfecter of our faith, who for the joy set before him endured the cross, scorning its shame, and sat down at the right hand of the throne of God. Consider him who endured such opposition from sinful men, so that you will not grow weary and lose heart."

Along the race of life you will encounter difficulty. You will have stretches of road that you run alone and feel like quitting. Other times the race will seem like an uphill battle with every muscle in your body screaming for attention. But thankfully, there are times of refreshment and rejuvenation. After you have run up a hill of hope, there is an opportunity to enjoy the righteous run down the other side. Indeed, some roads dead-end. You need to regroup and study the map (Scripture) of God's will.

Thus, finishing well thrives in the presence of God. Intimacy with Him positions you to hear His voice and obey Him. You want to please the one you love. And you want to please those who love you. Accountability from others who love you most facilitates finishing well. Listen intently to those who have your best interest in mind, who are finishing well themselves. We need mentors to help us refocus on the right priorities.

Lastly, finishing well means you live like you are dying because we all are terminal. There is a sense of urgency to live our life today for Christ, since tomorrow may not come. Thus, finish well today for your heavenly Father, family, friends, and future saints. A life well spent makes your Savior smile and say, "Well done, thou good and faithful servant" (Matthew 25:21 KJV).

What does it mean for me to finish well? Am I finishing well today?

Related Readings: Proverbs 20:28; Isaiah 26:2; Acts 27:25; 2 Timothy 4:6–8

TRAPPED BUT TRUSTING

"So the king gave the order, and they brought Daniel and threw him into the lions' den. The king said to Daniel, 'May your God, whom you serve continually, rescue you!' The king was overjoyed and gave orders to lift Daniel out of the den. And when Daniel was lifted from the den, no wound was found on him, because he had trusted in his God." Daniel 6:16, 23

Do you feel trapped by your circuslike circumstances? Have the jealous initiatives of another concocted your current rigmarole? Have your opportunities dried up like a lazy worm stuck on a sizzling summer sidewalk? Do outside forces threaten your faith? It is when we feel trapped that our trust in God releases His righteous reassurance.

I Am says, "I am with you through this trial where you feel on trial." The Lord lovingly reaches out with these words, "I have loved you from eternity past and I will not stop loving you now or forevermore." Jesus is our example, as we are reminded of His own pitlike experience on the cross when He announced to the world, "Father, forgive them, for they do not know what they are doing" (Luke 23:34). I feel trapped, but I will still trust.

Fear is what drives trapped animals. Unable to move or defend themselves, they are at the mercy of friends and foes. But the threats we receive from outside forces are a farce when our heavenly Father is orchestrating the outcome. He is not interested or intrigued by what the enemy expects. All He wants is what is best for His children. He is faithful.

"Be strong and courageous. Do not be afraid or terrified because of them, for the LORD your God goes with you; he will never leave you nor forsake you" (Deuteronomy 31:6).

Like the children of Israel's exodus from Pharaoh, your salvation is freedom from the slavery of sin and Satan. However, freedom by grace does not shelter you from occasions to wander in the wilderness with God. What seems like a circuitous trap is your righteous route to robust character that comes from abiding in Christ; so remain in Him.

It is in our confined quarters with Christ that He keeps us at close proximity. When you see entrapment as sanctioned by your Savior, you see the world differently. Your Master's matrix sees toothless, tame lions; unbelief sees fangs and ferocious ones. Unbelief coddles itself in the corner of the pit preoccupied by fear, but trust stands firm and courageously looks up toward heaven. Feeling trapped is meant to facilitate faith.

You are not in solitary confinement because He is with you. Indeed, look around you, and encourage prisoners of fear to embrace the grace of God in Christ Jesus. Your work or marriage is not a trap but an opportunity to remain faithful and display the glory of God. Man's trap becomes God's stage to show Himself faithful to all who fear and trust Him.

"Free me from the trap that is set for me, for you are my refuge" (Psalm 31:4).

Will I remain snared by Satan, or will I trust Jesus in my trap? Am I abiding in Christ?

Related Readings: Proverbs 11:6; Jeremiah 8:9; Luke 20:26; 1 Timothy 6:9; 2 Timothy 2:26

DIE TO MULTIPLY

"I tell you the truth, unless a kernel of wheat falls to the ground and dies, it remains only a single seed. But if it dies, it produces many seeds. The man who loves his life will lose it, while the man who hates his life in this world will keep it for eternal life." John 12:24–25

Christ's words can be counterintuitive and countercultural. What He says may not make sense on the surface, but with reflection the Holy Spirit reveals His intent. For example, Jesus instructs His followers to experience death in order to multiply life. Each day our Lord calls us to officiate by faith our own funeral of self-superiority and self-interest.

Indeed, death brings life. Christ's resurrected life brings life to disciples who die to self. We die to our old way of life to gain the Lord's new life. We die to carnal living and come alive to Spirit-filled living. We die to earthy affections and enthusiastically embrace heavenly affections. We die to mediocre living and engage in abundant living!

"The thief does not come except to steal, and to kill, and to destroy. I have come that they may have life, and that they may have it more abundantly" (John 10:10 NKJV).

If we want to multiply our leadership, we die to doing everything. If we want to multiply our influence, we die to selfish desires. If we want to multiply money, we die to greed. If we want to multiply our energy, we die to laziness. If we want to multiply disciples, we die to unfaithfulness. Jesus modeled the way by giving His life in service and sacrifice.

"For even the Son of Man did not come to be served, but to serve, and to give his life a ransom for many" (Mark 10:45).

If we want to multiply love, we die to lust. If we want to multiply our character, we die to sin. If we want to multiply our faith, we die to unbelief. Because of the death of Jesus for you, you die daily for Him. Because of the resurrection of Jesus for you, you come alive each day for Him. Your Master's multiplication tables are based on the calculus of trust in Him. Your death invites His life in you to reign!

"In him you were also circumcised, in the putting off of the sinful nature, not with a circumcision done by the hands of men but with the circumcision done by Christ, having been buried with him in baptism and raised with him through your faith in the power of God, who raised him from the dead" (Colossians 2:11–12).

What does my funeral of self-superiority look like? Is Christ's life released in my life?

Related Readings: Romans 6:11; 2 Corinthians 4:11; Colossians 2:13

PAINFUL WORSHIP

"At this, Job got up and tore his robe and shaved his head. Then he fell to the ground in worship."
Job 1:20

Are you struggling to understand? Are you stuck in a state of anger? Have you lost something or someone very precious? It may be the loss of your child's health or even the death of a child. A spouse has gone to heaven or left you for someone else. Your children are mad because they do not understand why you are divorced. They want their parents to work it out so they can have a mom and dad. You want to see the children, but your ex-spouse's anger has built a barrier between the two of you.

Is your heart hemorrhaging with hurt and animosity? In the middle of your ravished home, you also lost your job. You cannot afford to pay your child support because you do not have any income and your net worth has vaporized. This is a barren and lonely time for you. Everything you once held dear and took for granted is now gone.

You have no spouse, no children, no home, no job, and no money. One is a lonely number. Where are you to turn when the bottom falls out? God seems detached, and heaven seems a trillion miles away. Can you be forgiven? Yes, you can be forgiven. God is a God of second chances. Because He forgives you, you can also forgive yourself.

Invite back and serve those you have hurt, and watch God perform relational, emotional, and spiritual healing. Most of all, in the middle of your horrific loss, make the worship of Christ the centerpiece of your life. Worship fuels faith and heals.

Worship the Lord in your pain and loss. It is healing to focus on the greatness, holiness, and wonder of God. Praise Him with your voice, and praise Him with your heart and mind. Borrow or purchase worship songs that will lift you out of the depths of despair into the loving presence of Jesus. You may need to let a caring friend cradle you in his or her arms and sing softly in your ear, "Great Is Thy Faithfulness" and "Jesus Loves [You]."

You can become your own one-man band. Collect pots and pans from your kitchen and clang them together. Let these crude musical instruments become a fragrance of praise to your heavenly Father. Sing from the bottom of your heart.

Your praise to God will become a pillow of rest to your head. Our focus on the Lord's majesty through worship reminds us of our utter dependence on Him and His unconditional love for us. It is revolutionary, radical, redeeming, renewing. "Turn your eyes upon Jesus; look full into His wonderful face. And the things of earth will grow strangely dim in the light of His glory and grace."

Am I engaged in personal and corporate worship of my Lord Jesus?

Related Readings: 2 Samuel 12:20; 2 Kings 17:28; Psalm 100:2; Matt 4:10; Rev 15:4

FORGIVE YOURSELF

"Therefore, there is now no condemnation for those who are in Christ Jesus."
Romans 8:1

Have you forgiven yourself? Have you really forgiven yourself? We know we have forgiven ourselves if we are free from guilt and self-condemnation. Otherwise, we are stuck in the crazy cycle of reliving bad decisions that are done and cannot be changed. It is impossible to continually guilt our conscience in order to make up for past mistakes.

When we do not release ourselves from previous indiscretions, we try to make up for them by overcompensating in the present. Perhaps you neglected your children in their early years, and now that they are older teenagers, you have tried to make up for your absence by enabling their poor decisions. Instead, they need to experience the consequences of bad behavior while they are with you so they can learn and grow into responsible adults and citizens.

Jesus tells the story of a loving father who allowed his son to hit bottom. As a consequence, the son awoke to reality and took responsibility: "When he came to his senses, he said, 'How many of my father's hired men have food to spare, and here I am starving to death! I will set out and go back to my father and say to him: Father, I have sinned against heaven and against you'" (Luke 15:17–18).

Forgiving yourself begins by embracing the truth that your heavenly Father has forgiven you. The grace of God is in abundant supply. No one is beyond its reach. The Lord loves you unconditionally, and He forgives the objects of His love. Has the grace of God seeped deep into your soul so you know in your heart you are set free from the guilt and shame of sin? If not, forgive yourself, and trust the Lord to make up for lost time.

"In him we have redemption through his blood, the forgiveness of sins, in accordance with the riches of God's grace" (Ephesians 1:7).

When you forgive yourself, you are able to forgive others. Self-forgiveness is a key to unlocking real relationships. Authentic community with Christ and Christians comes from forgiveness from your heavenly Father, forgiveness from others, and forgiveness from you. What have you not released yourself from in forgiveness? Lay it at the altar of God's grace, and He will extinguish it with His eternal fire of forgiveness and love.

"This is the first and greatest commandment. And the second is like it: 'Love your neighbor as yourself'" (Matthew 22:38–39). When you love yourself—you forgive yourself!

How can I grow in my love and forgiveness of myself? How does God forgive me?

Related Readings: Psalm 130:3–5; 2 Corinthians 6:1; Colossians 1:14; 1 John 4:7–12

ARGUE WELL

"Let your conversation be always full of grace, seasoned with salt,
so that you may know how to answer everyone." Colossians 4:6

Mature followers of Jesus learn to argue well. But have you ever been frustrated in trying to communicate with someone you care deeply about? Yes, we all have. It is not uncommon to have conflict reflected in caring communication. So how can we learn to argue well? One way is to use language laced with grace and seasoned with sensitivity.

Like selective seasonings over a tasty meal, we want our words to be attractive and appetizing. To argue well requires unfiltered debate, but not unfiltered attitudes. It is a patient and respectful attitude that solicits the best response. So, for example, when a friend, coworker, child, or spouse speaks with concern, we listen with understanding. The goal is to win the relationship, not to outdebate the other in a defensive exchange.

Persuasive speech without prayerful preparation becomes manipulation. Thus, spirited discussions require a Spirit-filled engagement, not carnal combativeness. One of Job's friends asked a rhetorical question about a wise man's words: "Would he argue with useless words, with speeches that have no value?" (Job 15:2). No, wisdom measures words well.

Arguments are inevitable if couples care for each another. The goal is not to avoid arguments but to learn how to argue well. If you circumvent hard conversations, it will come back to hurt you more in passive-aggressive behavior. If, however, we first talk together to the Lord and then to each other, we converse with hearts aligned by the Almighty. Prayerful preparation injects grace into the flow of discussion. Like lubricant over metal gears, it keeps them running smoothly instead of grinding them to a halt.

"He who loves a pure heart and whose speech is gracious will have the king for his friend" (Proverbs 22:11).

Therefore, learn to argue well by listening well and comprehending the heart of those communicating with you. Pray, as they talk, for your patience and attentiveness to their needs and wants. Once they understand you know what they mean, then share your concerns with love and affirmation. Be direct, as the Holy Spirit directs you. Those who argue well grow in respect, love, trust, and understanding of each other. Everyone wins with these Christ-honoring outcomes. By faith be vulnerable, and initiate authentic conversation.

"A gentle answer turns away wrath, but a harsh word stirs up anger" (Proverbs 15:1).

How can I become a listener who responds with grace and understanding?

Related Readings: Isaiah 43:26; Proverbs 25:9; 2 Corinthians 8:7; 1 Peter 3:10

GET UP

"When the disciples heard this, they fell facedown to the ground, terrified.
But Jesus came and touched them. 'Get up,' he said. 'Don't be afraid.'
When they looked up, they saw no one except Jesus." Matthew 17:6–8

The world can get us down, but God gets us up. The cares of this world can choke out our motivation to move forward, but Christ is close by to release the pressure and resuscitate our resolve. What has you down? Is it finances, faith, family, foes? Is it a deal gone south or a relationship that has gone away? Whatever has you down, the Lord can lift you up!

"But you are a shield around me, O LORD; you bestow glory on me and lift up my head" (Psalm 3:3).

We bow down in humility and reverence to almighty God so we can get up, full of grace, to go on our way in quiet confidence. It is humble worship and praise that brings us back to the foot of the cross in gratitude to God for the gift of His only Son Jesus. We kneel at the cross overwhelmed by the forgiveness of our Savior Jesus, and we get up to forgive.

"But I, when I am lifted up from the earth, will draw all men to myself" (John 12:32).

If fear has you down, get up and walk by faith. If regret has you down, get up and go make restitution. If a relationship has you down, get up and initiate interest. If your job has you down, get up and go after excellence. If misunderstanding has you down, get up and clarify your concerns. If life in general has you down, get up and live a life for God.

Jesus gently admonishes us to lift our eyes off our circumstances and on to Him. So first get up and go to God in trusting determination. Ask Him for directions, and He will lead you in the way you should go. How do you get to your next destination in life? Ask the Lord. How do you solve your most pressing problem? Ask the dispenser of wisdom, holy God. It is from your humble posture in the low place that He lifts you up to see His face.

"Humble yourselves before the Lord, and he will lift you up" (James 4:10).

How can I humble myself before God? Where does He want me to get up and go?

Related Readings:1 Samuel 2:8; Psalm 30:1; Psalm 145:14; Luke 22:46; Acts 22:16; Acts 26:16

BELIEF BRINGS POSSIBILITIES

"He replied, 'Because you have so little faith. I tell you the truth, if you have faith
as small as a mustard seed, you can say to this mountain, "Move from here to there"
and it will move. Nothing will be impossible for you.'" Matthew 17:20

Belief brings possibilities, while unbelief limits possibilities. It is the prison of unbelief that locks up dreams and big visions. Why do we jail what Jesus could do through us? Why do we trust Him with our soul's salvation but not with our life's calling? It is forgetting the basic belief in God to do anything that limits the manifestation of grace.

What is the Lord asking you to do that seemed impossible in the past but is knocking on the door of your heart today? What will it take for you to open the door and walk through? Is it enough money? If so, can He provide in ways outside of the conventional system of the world? Yes, of course. Christ can be unconventional in His provision.

Jesus described the degree of His care by contrasting our needs with nature's nourishment. "If that is how God clothes the grass of the field, which is here today and tomorrow is thrown into the fire, will he not much more clothe you, O you of little faith?" (Matthew 6:30). The possibilities our heavenly Father offers are illustrated by His care of creation.

When faith falls short, we fail to see the extent of God's ability to engage opportunity. But when we believe with big thoughts, they transcend our meager offerings and latch on to what the Lord can accomplish. Defective faith dies for dread of what might happen, but effective faith thrives over the hope of what can happen. What is the object of your belief? Is it Jesus alone or Jesus plus what your mind can comprehend? Belief trusts Him.

A mind released by God's revelation is positioned for great things; so by faith ask Him to show you His grand plan for your next season of service for Jesus. Do not allow unbelief to hold you back; instead, embrace the possibilities from your heavenly Father's portfolio of opportunities. Be open to career transition, mission work, aggressive giving, writing, traveling the world, Bible study in your neighborhood, marriage, and graduate school. Yes, build a bigger business or church, but all for the glory of God. Belief in Him trusts Him.

"'You are my witnesses,' declares the LORD, 'and my servant whom I have chosen, so that you may know and believe me and understand that I am he. Before me no god was formed, nor will there be one after me'" (Isaiah 43:10).

What do I need to give over to God and trust Him with in exchange for eternal possibilities?

Related Readings: Psalm 106:12; Habakkuk 1:5; Mark 5:36; 1 Thessalonians 2:13

TEMPORAL TRUST

"What he trusts in is fragile; what he relies on is a spider's web. He leans on his web, but it gives way; he clings to it, but it does not hold." Job 8:14–15

Temporal trust is fleeting and deceptive. It looks like a safety net, but when you lean on it, it gives way. For example, you can trust in a good boss for your employment. However, your boss may receive a promotion, or he or she may leave the company altogether. Do not believe your job security revolves around a person or an institution. People may tell you something one day and do something entirely different another day.

Joseph experienced this when his boss believed an untrue accusation about his lack of integrity at work. "When his master heard the story his wife told him, saying, 'This is how your slave treated me,' he burned with anger. Joseph's master took him and put him in prison, the place where the king's prisoners were confined" (Genesis 39:19–20).

Trust in stuff is also vain, as metal cars cannot move mountains. Planes and homes cannot answer prayer. Stuff can provide leisure but cannot forgive your sins. Stuff can make life easier, but it cannot provide eternal life in heaven. Certainly money is not to be trusted; rather, it is to be given away and leveraged for God's kingdom. Trust in what you can see, and you will be disappointed. Trust in what you cannot see, and you will be fulfilled.

Trust in God is like being an instrument-rated pilot who flies through the night. The flickering lights that illumine the ground can be misleading. It is the accuracy of the pilot's instrument panel that can be trusted. Otherwise, you may talk yourself into landing on a well-lighted freeway instead of the safety of an airstrip.

So are the instruments of prayer, God's Word, and wise counsel. God uses these tools to provide you the coordinates to direct your life. Do not be in a hurry. Good things happen to those who wait on God. He gives you His coordinates for your life as you are ready to receive them. Whether they come one at a time or all at once, remain patient.

Refrain from moving forward until you know exactly the longitude and latitude of God's will. The last thing you want to do is land prematurely or, even worse, crash and burn. Trust in God. He is trustworthy. You cannot see Him, but you can see His evidence all around you—the marriage He healed, the body He made whole, the job He provided, the soul He saved, and His answered prayers. These shout of God's workings all around you.

Christ is at work around you and in you. He has not left you alone. Trust Him with your parent with whom you currently have no relationship. Trust Him with your prodigal child or with a friend who cannot seem to find his or her way. Give those you love space. Trust means you give God everything moment by moment, especially those things out of your control. "So we fix our eyes not on what is seen, but on what is unseen. For what is seen is temporary, but what is unseen is eternal" (2 Corinthians 4:18).

What temporal trust limits my trust in the Lord? How is He working around me?

Related Readings: Job 31:24–28; Psalm 20:7; Isaiah 31:1; John 12:35–36; Hebrews 2:13

NEWLYWED FOCUS

"If a man has recently married, he must not be sent to war or have any other duty laid on him.
For one year he is to be freed to stay at home and bring happiness to the wife he has married."
Deuteronomy 24:5

The first year of marriage is foundational for newlyweds. Our attitudes, actions, and habits define us for our entire marriage. If we start out with the habit of seeking to understand the other and quickly applying forgiveness when misunderstandings arise, chances are we will continue with this pattern. Love learns to forgive and start fresh.

Why not take the first year of marriage and really get to know one another? Limit your outside activities to church and close friends. Spend your time as a serious student of one another and what God's Word teaches about marriage. Discover what makes your spouse feel honored and loved.

Furthermore, make sure the first year you thoroughly leave your father and mother and cleave to one another. Talk with your husband first—not your mom—about how he has disappointed you. Talk with your wife first—not your dad—about how she has let you down. Learn to work through conflict. What are other helpful habits to develop year one?

First of all, pray together and attend Bible study together. Develop the discipline of a daily time with God by reading His Word and praying. Learn how to love God more than you love your spouse.

Secondly, enjoy each other sexually. Romance one another as you did while you were dating before marriage. Become comfortable with your own body and the body of your mate. Discover what is pleasing and pleasant to one another, and then serve each other selflessly. "The husband should fulfill his marital duty to his wife, and likewise the wife to her husband. The wife's body does not belong to her alone but also to her husband. In the same way, the husband's body does not belong to him alone but also to his wife" (1 Corinthians 7:3–4). Unselfishness in marriage facilitates sexual fulfillment.

Thirdly, take the time to listen and talk. Have focused moments daily to share your day or anticipate what the next week holds. Men, genuinely listen and ask, "What is she really saying?" Most of the time she just wants to be heard and held. Men, do not immediately go into fix-it mode!

Lastly, have a financial game plan. Agree on a budget, and stick to it. Live within your means. Avoid debt, tithe to your church, save ten percent, and live on the rest. Otherwise, you will never have enough, and you will live in perpetual frustration. Wise money management makes a marriage secure and satisfied.

Above all, focus on the Lord and your marriage the first year and throughout your marital relationship. Over time, the results will compound like invested money. You will be astounded at the depth and breadth of what God does through two surrendered souls!

What are the Lord's priorities for our marriage? How can we develop good habits?

Related Readings: Hosea 3:1; Malachi 2:15; 1 Corinthians 13:4–13; Ephesians 5:21–33

ETERNAL EXPECTATIONS

"My soul, wait silently for God alone, For my expectation is from Him."
Psalm 62:5 NKJV

What does God think? What does He expect of me? These are two questions I do not always default to in my thinking. I want to want what He wants, but sometimes my wants get in the way and cause me to get off course. However, it is the Lord's expectations that my soul craves for deep down. A soul is never satisfied until its expectations exceed earth. So how can we create expectations that lead our soul into an eternal perspective?

Soul care comes with a price of time, transparency, and truthfulness. Our soul will shrivel for lack of attention, or it will come alive with contemplation on Christ and honesty with ourselves. A busy, breakneck schedule without breaks for being only brings on spiritual fatigue. Without prayer to pace us, our decisions become earthbound and less wise.

Paul describes this tension: "Yes, and I will continue to rejoice, for I know that through your prayers and the help given by the Spirit of Jesus Christ, what has happened to me will turn out for my deliverance. I eagerly expect and hope that I will in no way be ashamed, but will have sufficient courage so that now as always Christ will be exalted in my body, whether by life or by death. For to me, to live is Christ and to die is gain" (Philippians 1:18–21).

It is in waiting on God that we come to understand His expectations. We acquiesce to the Almighty's outlook when we patiently sit at His footstool by faith. The soul rests between human comprehension and quiet unconsciousness, but it is in intimacy with our Maker that He enlivens our imagination. Eternal expectations engage a soul unleashed by belief that patiently waits on the Lord. It is here that we come to expect what Christ expects.

Are you disappointed by another's failure to meet your expectations? Probably; so shift your desires for fulfillment to Jesus, and He will not let you down. We need expectations of others, but only as they are filtered by faith into what our heavenly Father wants. Trust them with Him, and He will bring about His desired results. Eternal expectations extend our hope to heaven and the reward of waiting on God. So stay faithful to find Him first.

"Now devote your heart and soul to seeking the LORD your God" (1 Chronicles 22:19).

Have my expectations been filtered by the eternal? What does God expect of me now?

Related Readings:1 Chronicles 28:9; Proverbs 10:28; Luke 6:34–35; Hebrews 10:26–27

HUMILIATION'S HOPE

"I have become a laughingstock to my friends, though I called upon God and he answered—
a mere laughingstock, though righteous and blameless!" Job 12:4

Humiliation hurts. It is deeply painful. Humiliation comes when embarrassment is prolonged. Prestige and status are lost. It is a confusing state in which to live. People relate to humiliation like leprosy. Humility is admired, while humiliation is looked upon with suspicion—even disdain. At best, it receives pity. It is ominous to simply survive in shame.

People whom you thought would be at your side have walked away during this time of disgrace. Their excuse is they do not know what to say. This may be true, but beyond their speechlessness is a fear of association with failure. They are afraid others will think they are condoning your situation, or they are afraid others will see them afflicted with your same ailment. You are mortified. You feel abandoned by God and betrayed by people.

You are on the precipice of depression, and it is entirely possible you have fallen over its edge. You feel paralyzed—bewildered. But things may not be as bad as they seem. Do you have your health? Does the Lord love you? Are you still in business? Maybe you have blown it beyond belief, and to your chagrin you find yourself at the lowest point of your life. However, what humiliation tears down, humility can build back up in Christ.

God is our God of multiple chances. He understands, forgives, loves, and brings beauty out of pain. There is nothing you can do to erase the past or to clear up all the misunderstandings. What you can do is allow God to use this time of shame to bring Himself fame. He can be trusted, and He is faithful even through the depths of despair.

Let Him love you through this hard time. As Job lamented, "Though he slay me, yet will I hope in him" (Job 13:15). Our hope is in Jesus Christ. Every other pseudohope brings disappointment and delayed pain. Avoid these caricatures of peace, and cling to the Prince of Peace. Turn to your sympathizing Jesus, and He will soothe and heal your soul.

Lastly, we have an obligation to give hope to those hung up in humiliation. Do not try to diagnose their situation. Rather, pray for them. Be there to listen to them, while pointing them back to Jesus. Help transform their humiliation to humility by restoring them. Paul said it well, "Brothers, if someone is caught in a sin, you who are spiritual should restore him gently. But watch yourself, or you also may be tempted" (Galatians 6:1).

Have I allowed the Lord to transform my humiliation into humility? Whom can I humbly serve who has been humiliated?

Related Readings: Jeremiah 31:19; Malachi 2:9; Luke 14:8–10; 1 Corinthians 11:22

FORGIVENESS OF GOD

"In him we have redemption through his blood, the forgiveness of sins,
in accordance with the riches of God's grace." Ephesians 1:7

The forgiveness of God is far-reaching and without limitation to anyone who believes. He forgives the worst of sinners and the best of saints. Atheists, adulterers, murderers, liars, the hot-tempered, and the mild-mannered can all receive the free forgiveness of their heavenly Father. The good, the bad, and the ugly are all candidates for God's grace.

Jesus Christ's death on the cross bought us back or redeemed us from the penalty of sin. By faith in Him we no longer have to be burdened by our own indiscretions against almighty God. All sins of omission, commission, and ignorance can be laid at the foot of the cross and left for our Lord's pardon. Have you been freed by His forgiveness?

Will God forgive years of religious neglect? Yes. Will God forgive a life that lives for itself alone? Yes. Will the Lord forgive divorce, irresponsible living, and laziness? Yes. Will He forgive my chronic complaining, my bad attitude, and my tendency to gossip? And are my pride in my good works and my self-sufficiency covered by Christ's blood? Yes, God will forgive anything that is an enemy of His grace. His death gives peace.

"For God was pleased to have all his fullness dwell in him, and through him to reconcile to himself all things, whether things on earth or things in heaven, by making peace through his blood, shed on the cross" (Colossians 1:19–20).

Forgiveness is free to all who believe, but it came at a great cost in Christ's death. God gave His Son for our salvation from sin. So have you personally appropriated faith in Jesus Christ as your Savior and Lord? If so, since your salvation do you regularly bow to Him in confession for cleansing of your heart? Unconfessed sin clouds clear thinking.

Since you have believed, you are rich in God's grace and have a robust remedy for sin. Do you take advantage of your Lord's forgiveness? As a Christian, do you sit daily at the feet of your Savior and receive freedom through His forgiveness? At the cross you were set free from the eternal penalty of sin, and now His forgiveness frees you from the guilt of sin. Jesus said, "So if the Son sets you free, you will be free indeed" (John 8:36).

"Therefore, my brothers, I want you to know that through Jesus the forgiveness of sins is proclaimed to you" (Acts 13:38).

Have I trusted Jesus for the salvation of my sins? What hidden sins do I need to repent of and confess to Him?

Related Readings: Matthew 26:28; Acts 26:17–19; Romans 6:18–22; Hebrews 9:15

FORGIVENESS EMPOWERS

"And do not grieve the Holy Spirit of God, with whom you were sealed for the day of redemption.
Get rid of all bitterness, rage and anger, brawling and slander, along with every form of malice.
Be kind and compassionate to one another, forgiving each other, just as in Christ God forgave you."
Ephesians 4:30–32

Fullness of the Holy Spirit is facilitated by forgiveness, but unforgiveness grieves the Spirit of God. Resentment harbored in the heart of a child of God resists the work of the Spirit. If, however, forgiveness is fluid and forthcoming, the heart is free to be transformed by the Holy Spirit's influence. Forgiveness positions believers to be blessed.

God grieves when His children cannot get along and are encumbered and sometimes estranged by chronic unforgiveness. The Lord longs for the righteous to be reconciled, for He has given us the ministry of reconciliation. How can we call unbelievers to be reconciled when we are unable to be reconciled? Indeed, Spirit-filled followers of Jesus forgive.

"Therefore, if anyone is in Christ, he is a new creation; the old has gone, the new has come! All this is from God, who reconciled us to himself through Christ and gave us the ministry of reconciliation: that God was reconciling the world to himself in Christ, not counting men's sins against them. And he has committed to us the message of reconciliation" (2 Corinthians 5:17–19).

Who, by their unjust deeds, has imprisoned your heart in unforgiveness? Who are you unable to forgive—an absent parent, a prodigal child, an unethical partner, an evil boss, an insensitive sibling, an imperfect pastor, an unfaithful friend, or an abused individual? Perhaps you are waiting for them to change before you plan to forgive them.

But objects of unforgiveness can be oblivious to their hurtful actions. You may be waiting for others to repent who are unaware of what they have done, or they may be incapable of change. Why not forgive them as God, for Christ's sake, has forgiven you, trusting Him to change them? Release yourself from being responsible to do what only the Lord can do.

Once you forgive, then you are positioned to receive the fullness of the Holy Spirit. No longer is He grieved by your unforgiveness, but He empowers your forgiveness. The fruit of the Spirit flourishes in the fertile soil of forgiveness. Your act of unconditional forgiveness may be the very illustration of grace that God uses to draw your offender to Himself. So by faith forgive and trust the Holy Spirit to empower you and the forgiven.

"I ask you to forgive your brothers the sins and the wrongs they committed in treating you so badly" (Genesis 50:17).

Am I grieving the Holy Spirit by my unforgiveness? Whom by God's grace do I need to forgive?

Related Readings: Matthew 6:14–15; Luke 6:37; 2 Corinthians 2:7–10; Colossians 3:13

LEADERS ARE LEARNERS

"What do you know that we do not know? What insights do you have that we do not have?"
Job 15:9

Leaders who stay enrolled in God's school of learning are more the wiser. You have learned tremendous lessons over the years, but this is just the beginning. Stay in the educational process. We never arrive as learners. Teachability should only cease after our graduation into heaven. Indeed, great leaders want to follow leaders who are learners.

Effective leaders know that a growing leader will pass on his or her learning experiences. Great leaders grow leaders! And there is a good chance what you are currently learning as a leader is the same lesson someone else is struggling to conquer. Your ability to stay engaged in the learning process allows you to tutor other leaders facing the same issues.

When we stop learning we cease to be relevant, we become stale, and our influence begins to wane. Learning keeps us engaged with our team and with other leaders. Moreover, a wise leader understands the learning curve required to tackle new issues and problems. Every day there are opportunities that beg for attention and understanding. This means greater wisdom is required. Gratefully, the Lord gives wisdom liberally to those who ask. "If any of you lacks wisdom, he should ask God, who gives generously to all without finding fault, and it will be given to him" (James 1:5).

Furthermore, learn from everyone and everything around you. Educated and uneducated, rich and poor, young and old are all teacher candidates. God places people in our life daily as His teachers. Perhaps you study the lives of people from the past. You can read biographies, book reviews, and historical novels. Dead people are rich with life lessons to be harvested and stored in your barn of knowledge, both positive and negative examples.

Of course, feasting on the classics is imperative to the leader who is hungry to learn. Read books together and discuss them as a leadership team. Expose yourself to their timeliness, and you will find yourself lost in learning. Your mind and heart will travel to uncharted waters for you, where others have not feared to fail and succeed.

The classics will challenge you to become a critical thinker and look beyond the surface for great nuggets of truth. Why mess around with the milk of easy thinking when we can plunge into the meat of issues great thinkers have wrestled with over centuries? Most importantly, feed on the wisdom of God's Word. Holy Scripture is your number one source for truth. Wise leaders apply the practical principles for living found in the Bible.

"Do your best to present yourself to God as one approved, a workman who does not need to be ashamed and who correctly handles the word of truth" (2 Timothy 2:15).

What is God teaching me as a leader? Am I embracing and applying His wisdom?

Related Readings: Exodus 18:24–26; 1 Kings 4:29; John 12:42; Romans 12:8

KINDNESS AND COMPASSION

"Be kind and compassionate to one another."
Ephesians 4:32

Kindness and compassion are compelling commercials for Christians. When the misguided see manners from those who follow their Master Jesus, they are drawn to faith. So in the pressures of life, we who know the Lord know better, and we behave well. We are called to remain courteous when cursed and to stay cool when conversations heat up.

When slapped in the face by someone's disrespectful attitude, kind Christians "turn the other cheek" and offer respect. The disrespectful are disarmed by respect. There is no need to lower ourselves to the immature shenanigans of those spurred on by self-image control instead of Christ's control. What insecure person needs a kind word from you?

"Therefore, as God's chosen people, holy and dearly loved, clothe yourselves with compassion, kindness, humility, gentleness and patience. Bear with each other and forgive whatever grievances you may have against one another. Forgive as the Lord forgave you" (Colossians 3:12–13). Kindness is slow to anger and quick to forgive.

Do you have colleagues at work in need of compassion? Have you looked beyond their complaining to the hurt harboring in their heart? Perhaps you take them to lunch and learn more about their story. Fill in the blanks of what is behind their bad behavior. Is it an absent father or a smothering mother? Have they been abused, rejected, or unloved? Are they angry at God?

Compassion takes the time to care without compromising excellence in what is expected at work. If we drive others just to get results, we miss the riches of relational development. Everyone has a story that needs understanding and acceptance. Everyone needs compassion, as this puts a face on Jesus and the forgiveness that comes from Him.

"I will tell of the kindnesses of the LORD, the deeds for which he is to be praised, according to all the LORD has done for us—yes, the many good things he has done for the house of Israel, according to his compassion and many kindnesses" (Isaiah 63:7).

Because of the Lord's many kindnesses we have experienced and His rich compassion shown in our life, we are capable of representing Him well when we engage the world. It is an overflow of Christ's compassion for you that encourages others in your daily communications. It is the kindness of Jesus, exhibited in your actions, that draws others to Jesus. Indeed, clothe yourself daily as a kind and compassionate agent of almighty God.

Jesus modeled kindness when He replaced condemnation with compassion toward the woman caught in adultery. "'Then neither do I condemn you,' Jesus declared. 'Go now and leave your life of sin'" (John 8:11). Christ followers are known by their compassion.

Who needs an ongoing act of kindness or a compassionate conversation from me?

Related Readings: 2 Samuel 9:1–7; Isaiah 54:8; Mark 6:34; Acts 4:9; Romans 11:22

SELF-MADE MYTH

"You may say to yourself, 'My power and the strength of my hands have produced this wealth for me.' But remember the LORD your God, for it is he who gives you the ability to produce wealth, and so confirms his covenant, which he swore to your forefathers, as it is today."
Deuteronomy 8:17–18

Some are born into privilege, and others are first-generation wealth. The latter are commonly described as "self-made," "pulled up by their boot straps," or "new money." The flaw in this thinking is God can be completely left out of the equation or given credit after the fact—marginalized at best. However, God's will is at work above man's efforts.

The Lord determines what country and family we are born into and what stage in history we live life. Christ creates our physical appearance, He infuses our intelligence, and He gives us the drive and determination to work, live, and love. To take credit for our success is to ignore the glory of God, to worship our idol of achievement.

"And he is not served by human hands, as if he needed anything, because he himself gives all men life and breath and everything else. From one man he made every nation of men, that they should inhabit the whole earth; and he determined the times set for them and the exact places where they should live" (Acts 17:25–26).

The One who designed the intricateness of the human brain determines its intelligence quotient. The One who gave us the feelings of love, anger, compassion, and peace is the One who establishes our emotional intelligence. The Lord Jesus is Lord over all, or He is not Lord at all. So we all bow—the successful and unsuccessful—at the throne of God.

"Whenever the living creatures give glory, honor and thanks to him who sits on the throne and who lives for ever and ever, the twenty-four elders fall down before him who sits on the throne, and worship him who lives for ever and ever. They lay their crowns before the throne and say: 'You are worthy, our Lord and God, to receive glory and honor and power, for you created all things, and by your will they were created and have their being'" (Revelation 4:9–11).

Be careful not to substitute false humility as a veneer over the self-made myth. Authentic humility is able to keep Christ the focus over the fanfare others may create over what you have done. The foot of the cross is level for all who will linger there in adoration and thanksgiving. Gratitude and generosity govern a humble heart after God.

Humility prays like the ultrasuccessful King David: "Wealth and honor come from you; you are the ruler of all things. In your hands are strength and power to exalt and give strength to all. Now, our God, we give you thanks, and praise your glorious name" (1 Chronicles 29:12–13). Work smart and hard, and do your best, while giving God the glory!

Whom do I acknowledge as the giver of all good things? Is my humility authentic?

Related Readings: 1 Chronicles 29:10–11; Daniel 5:20; Luke 12:13–21; Philippians 3:4–11

s18

EXHAUSTIVE IMAGE CONTROL

"If anyone else thinks he has reasons to put confidence in the flesh, I have more: circumcised on the eighth day, of the people of Israel, of the tribe of Benjamin, a Hebrew of Hebrews; in regard to the law, a Pharisee; as for zeal, persecuting the church; as for legalistic righteousness, faultless. But whatever was to my profit I now consider loss for the sake of Christ." Philippians 3:4–7

What is image control? It is the motivation to make sure we appear as we want others to think about us. The exterior of who we are becomes more important than the interior of who we are in Christ. We are concerned, consumed, and in some cases obsessed over how we look, what we wear, what we drive, what school we attend, where we work, and where we live.

However, image control is exhausting because it is never quite satisfied. Jobs have to be a little more prestigious, cars a little more luxurious, homes a little more opulent, and status a little more admirable. The curse of image control is subtle because it can be confused with godly ambition, which is good. The difference is the first is about striving for self, while the latter is about dying to self. Godly ambition does its best and trusts the Lord.

Image control suffers from a sense of superiority prompted by pride. Jesus describes a religious leader afflicted by his condescending attitude and lofty self-image: "The Pharisee stood up and prayed about himself: 'God, I thank you that I am not like other men—robbers, evildoers, adulterers—or even like this tax collector. I fast twice a week and give a tenth of all I get'" (Luke 18:11–12). Humility lifts up Jesus, not self.

If we are not halted by humility, we become like Narcissus peering into a prideful pool, loving an image that is a figment of our imagination. Instead, as Spirit-filled followers of Jesus, we see ourselves as precious but peculiar people who are pilgrims just passing through on our way to heaven, not encumbered by the weights of worldly expectations. As we journey for Jesus, we want our simple life to point others to our Savior.

So who is in control of your image? Have you surrendered your self-image to your Savior Jesus Christ? Let go of the shallow sense of worth from the world, and embrace your eternal value in the Lord. Almighty God has already defined you as holy and acceptable to Him in Christ Jesus. Your inner beauty He admires most and celebrates.

"Your beauty should not come from outward adornment, such as braided hair and the wearing of gold jewelry and fine clothes. Instead, it should be that of your inner self, the unfading beauty of a gentle and quiet spirit, which is of great worth in God's sight" (1 Peter 3:3–4).

How much energy do I exhaust in image control? Do I trust Christ to control my image?

Related Readings: Genesis 37:23–28; Ephesians 1:5–6; Hebrews 11:9–13; I Peter 2:9-11

ACCORDING TO GOD'S WILL

"This is the confidence we have in approaching God: that if we ask anything according to his will, he hears us. And if we know that he hears us—whatever we ask—we know that we have what we asked of him." 1 John 5:14–15

Almighty God offers a friendly audience in the form of prayer, but not just any prayer. It is a prayer positioned in humility, offered by faith, and aligned with His will. Prayer rests on the platform of God's providence. It is this baseline belief that captures a heart for Christ's agenda. Prayer places people at the portal of His presence to discern His purpose.

So what does it mean to pray according to His will? It does not mean we ask flippantly or foolishly, but it does mean we ask boldly in humility. A prayer according to His will wills what God wills. We pray not our will but His will be done. My will submits to His will from a dependent heart and mind; then He defines His expectations.

Jesus modeled this for His followers in intense prayer: "He went a little farther and fell on His face, and prayed, saying, 'O My Father, if it is possible, let this cup pass from Me; nevertheless, not as I will, but as You will'" (Matthew 26:39 NKJV). His heavenly Father's will was death so others could be saved. God's will works out what is best for all.

We know we are praying according to the Lord's will when we hold the results with an open hand. Instead of willing a response in our own strength, we rely on His strength. One indicator is I am not stressed over the outcome from intercession but trust almighty God to govern my affairs accurately and according to His promises.

We know it is His will for men and women everywhere to be saved; so we intercede on their behalf. We can be confident that Christ's desire for His children is to love and forgive one another; so we approach His throne with this passionate petition. Scripture gives us plenty to pray about according to His will. In the unknown, we pray for His will. The Lord already knows what you need and will instruct you in the way you should go.

Jesus said, "Your Father knows what you need before you ask him. This, then, is how you should pray: 'Our Father in heaven, hallowed be your name, your kingdom come, your will be done on earth as it is in heaven'" (Matthew 6:8–10).

Am I praying according to God's will? Am I persistent in prayer over the unknowns, and then do I rest in Him for results?

Related Readings: 1 Kings 9:3; Nehemiah 1:11; Luke 1:13; John 15:7; Acts 10:5

LEADERS ADAPT

"To the weak I became weak, to win the weak. I have become all things to all men so that by all possible means I might save some." 1 Corinthians 9:22

Leaders adapt when people or circumstances change so they can more effectively execute their priorities. The temptation is to do nothing and then suffer the consequences of blind belief in inferior assumptions. For example, your customers may have purchased your product at a premium in the past, but competition now gives them an alternative.

Or perhaps a leader's style of arm's-length management has worked up to now, but current realities of cost cutting and change require him or her to be more hands on. The new normal in economics and people's psychology requires leaders to be discerning and nimble to adjust to raw realities. Agile leaders move wisely through relational and organizational obstacle courses. What reality obstructs progress and needs your attention?

The Lord uses disruptions to keep us dependent on Him. Financial pressures, employee turnover, and obsolete business models are a wake-up call that our Savior employs to shake up our stale thinking. Are you clinging to what made your company successful in the past, or are you openhanded with what needs to change to become profitable now?

"Forget the former things; do not dwell on the past. See, I am doing a new thing! Now it springs up; do you not perceive it? I am making a way in the desert and streams in the wasteland" (Isaiah 43:18–19).

Maybe it is time—by faith—to hit the refresh button on your leadership. Look for new and improved ways to walk with your team into cultural and organizational transformation. Pray profusely on the front end, gather all the pertinent data, and do the next right thing. Bold leadership assesses the situation and adapts under the Lord's leadership.

"When Pharaoh let the people go, God did not lead them on the road through the Philistine country, though that was shorter. For God said, 'If they face war, they might change their minds and return to Egypt.' So God led the people around by the desert road toward the Red Sea. The Israelites went up out of Egypt armed for battle" (Exodus 13:17–18).

Where do I need to adapt personally or professionally? How is the Lord leading?

Related Readings: Isaiah 48:6; Judges 7:16–18; Acts 3:16–18; Hebrews 13:7

PEACE OF MIND

"Peace I leave with you; my peace I give you. I do not give to you as the world gives.
Do not let your hearts be troubled and do not be afraid." John 14:27

Peace of mind begins with peace with God. Inner peace is only sustainable when the created has made peace with its Creator. This peace with Providence comes in surrender to the Lord. It is not a negotiation, compromise, or deal with Divinity. Tranquility comes from trust, a complete capitulation to Christ. Peace with God brings the peace of God.

"Therefore, since we have been justified through faith, we have peace with God through our Lord Jesus Christ" (Romans 5:1).

Peace of mind is a gift Jesus gives to all who will receive. He bequeathed His bountiful blessing of peace before He departed back to His heavenly home. Part of the legacy our Lord left was one of quiet confidence based on the belief of His sufficiency. When we have Jesus, we have all we need for genuine fulfillment. Peace accompanies His purposes.

There is a pseudopeace of mind the world offers, but its outside-packaging appeal quickly gives way to its destructive contents. It offers an alluring escape through artificial stimulants, busy schedules, material possessions, power, and control. However, these external facades of peace fade away; only the peace of Christ lasts with inner fortitude.

"May the God of hope fill you with all joy and peace as you trust in him, so that you may overflow with hope by the power of the Holy Spirit" (Romans 15:13).

It is this bond of peace that enables believers to come together with courage and conviction to accomplish Christ's plan. The enemy shrinks back when followers of Jesus forgo fighting each other and unify in prayer, love, spiritual warfare, the proclamation of the gospel, and making disciples. Peace of mind propels us forward by faith to serve Him.

"Whatever you have learned or received or heard from me, or seen in me—put it into practice. And the God of peace will be with you" (Philippians 4:9).

Above all, allow the peace of Christ to rule your heart. Then trouble and fear will tremble in the face of peace because they lose their grip to God's grace. No longer are you whipped around by the cares of this world because your compass is Christ. You have peace of mind because you have Jesus. Submission to His Spirit produces real peace.

"Let the peace of Christ rule in your hearts, since as members of one body you were called to peace. And be thankful" (Colossians 3:15).

Is my peace based on external circumstances or my internal intimacy with Jesus?

Related Readings: Numbers 6:25–26; 1 Thessalonians 5:13; 2 Thessalonians 3:16

BENEFITS OF BROKENNESS

"My spirit is broken, my days are cut short, the grave awaits me."
Job 17:1

Brokenness is a prerequisite to God's thorough usefulness. Before brokenness we were still self-sufficient and self-dependent. There was no authentic humility. It was either false or nonexistent. Before brokenness anger lurked behind the corner of every situation that did not go our way. Then it pounced on our unsuspecting victims.

Before brokenness prayer was a routine rather than a necessity. Our fellowship was not sweet and refreshing. Before brokenness our life could be explained by our own efforts. There was no resurrection power harvesting results; rather, results were rooted in our limited strength. Before brokenness there was a subtle spiritual pride that intimidated or impressed others by our "wisdom" instead of pointing them to the Author of wisdom.

Brokenness is the rite of passage to blessing. It is a bridge across—into the depths of God's love and intimacy—but it is not without discomfort, even pain. Brokenness seems on the surface to be failure, but, on the contrary, it positions us for success. A sleek, stubborn, and strong-willed stallion must be broken before it can benefit its riders. Otherwise, its unfocused energy ravages its environment and terrorizes those with whom it comes in contact. Our full potential cannot be unleashed without heaven's taming. The "choking point" in spiritual maturity is not from outside forces. Let God break your will before it breaks you.

There is an important distinction between a broken will and a broken spirit. God's desire is not to chronically crush your spirit but to break your will. His goal is to tame your stubbornness. Do not buck God. He will eventually have His way, one way or another. We can work with Him, or we can work against Him. A bridle is not comfortable, but it is necessary to get the required results. God's bridle will lead you into His eternal benefits.

We miss the Lord's best without brokenness. It is a lifelong process of three steps forward and two steps backward. We will repeat some mistakes, and sometimes it takes a protracted time for us to "get it." However, some of us need brokenness to come upon us with God's loving intensity. Without Him arresting our attention, we tend to move nonchalantly through our Christian life.

Your life should be markedly different from the world. If there is no fruit of the Holy Spirit, there is no brokenness. Pray for God to break your will, not your spirit. Your spirit is where hope resides. Your spirit communes with God. Your tamed spirit trusts in Him. Let go, and let God break you and make you into the image of His Son Jesus Christ. What He breaks, He makes. And what God makes is beautiful! "He heals the brokenhearted and binds up their wounds" (Psalm 147:3).

Have I experienced true brokenness? Have I allowed the Lord to heal my heart?

Related Readings: Psalm 34:18; Psalm 51:17; Isaiah 61:1; Luke 4:18

WISDOM'S WEALTH

"But where can wisdom be found? Where does understanding dwell?
Man does not comprehend its worth.... And he said to man, 'The fear of the Lord—
that is wisdom, and to shun evil is understanding.'" Job 28:12–13, 28

Wisdom is like money, as its value compounds over time. When we regularly add wisdom to our life, we become wealthy in the ways of God. What is wisdom? Why is it so valuable? It is the ability to discern right from wrong and to understand what is true and lasting. It exposes the devil's deceptions and lies. Wisdom frees us to know God's ways.

Furthermore, a life built on the foundation of wisdom can withstand the winds of change and the waves of adversity. Wisdom keeps you engaged with God's perspective. It is a life preserver for the drowning, a compass for the lost explorer, and a light in a dark and perplexing situation. However, there is a price to pay in the process of its discovery and acquisition. But once wisdom lodges in a mind and heart, it grows wise, humble leaders.

Its value does not fluctuate with the stock market; instead, it consistently increases over time. Gray hair does not guarantee wisdom, but examined experience does position you to obtain wisdom. It is possible to be an old fool or to be wise beyond your years. Youth or aged, smart or an average intelligence quotient, you can gain wisdom. Seek out the wisdom of God, and you will find it. This eternal intentionality with holy aggression pays divine dividends.

Wisdom begins and ends with the fear of God. The truly enlightened engage God in the equation of life. Indeed, you fly life solo without your Savior's insights. The fear of God means you involve Him in your attitude and actions; you meditate on His ways and His truth. As followers of the Lord, "We have the mind of Christ" (1 Corinthians 2:16).

By God's grace, wisdom allows you to synthesize multiple options into the best course of action. Wisdom can take a complex situation and offer simple solutions. It has the uncanny ability of cutting through the layers of agendas and motives to the real issues. Wisdom is a no-nonsense defender of common sense and truth. It is very practical.

However, wisdom resides with God. He owns the trademark and the patent. Anyone who attempts to take credit for its effectiveness could lose the rights of its use. So seek out wise individuals who humbly depend on God and who give Him the credit for the wisdom entrusted to them. Humility mixed with wisdom builds relational and eternal wealth.

"To God belong wisdom and power; counsel and understanding are his" (Job 12:13).

Am I intentionally seeking out the wisdom of God in my daily life and work?

Related Readings: 1 Kings 3:28; Ezra 7:25; Luke 2:40; 1 Corinthians 1:20–30

SELFLESS PRAYER

"And the LORD accepted Job's prayer. After Job had prayed for his friends, the LORD made him prosperous again and gave him twice as much as he had before." Job 42:9-10

Friends snared by sin need our prayers, not our prognosis. God's part is conviction and life change, while our part is prayer. There is definitely a time and place to confront a believer in disobedience. However, we are not the judge—God is. Other-centered praying is freeing for both the person praying and the person being prayed for. As we pray for others, we are freed from preoccupation with our own problems.

Indeed, the severity of another's needs tends to dwarf our own. It is through the posture of praying for another that our perspective becomes healthier. Our gratitude grows through selfless prayer. We learn to count our many blessings and be content. Of course it is okay to ask God's favor on our life, but not at the expense of excluding prayer for others.

"Isaac prayed to the LORD on behalf of his wife, because she was barren. The LORD answered his prayer, and his wife Rebekah became pregnant" (Genesis 25:21).

Authentic Christianity results in love for people. Is prayer a meaningful way to love? Of course, and the greatest test may be to pray for those who do not pray for you. This is truly unselfish praying. Your only reward may be a clear conscience before God. Pray for your adversaries, and trust the Lord to accomplish His purpose in their life, in His time. Jesus said, "Love your enemies and pray for those who persecute you" (Matthew 5:44).

An exciting part of praying for others is the change you experience. Prayer for people cultivates an attitude of love and forgiveness in the person praying that no human counselor can provide. Prayer places you face-to-face with your heavenly Father.

Talk with God often about the needs of others, but be careful; you may become an answer to your own prayer. Pray for a friend in financial need, and the Lord may lead you to assist. Pray for a relative whose heart is hard, and God may lead you to soften this person with kindness. Pray for a child who has lost a parent, and you may become his or her parent. Pray for the leadership needs at the church, and by faith you may step into that leadership role. Be keenly aware of what you pray, as you may become the answer to your own prayer.

Most importantly, pray for those outside of faith in Christ. You can pray this boldly, knowing it is God's will. Pray God will use you, circumstances, and other believers to draw another to Him. A stubborn heart is no match for prayer. Satan's deception is no match for prayer. Prayer can travel behind enemy lines and accomplish more in a moment than a lifetime of worry and work. Pray for sinners to be saved and glorify God.

"Brothers, my heart's desire and prayer to God for the Israelites is that they may be saved" (Romans 10:1).

How can I regularly pray for the needs of family, friends, and foes to be met in Christ?

Related Readings: Exodus 8:8–9; 1 Kings 13:6; 2 Corinthians 13:7–9; Ephesians 1:15–23

TEMPTATION'S ALLURE

"When the woman saw that the fruit of the tree was good for food and pleasing to the eye,
and also desirable for gaining wisdom, she took some and ate it. She also gave
some to her husband, who was with her, and he ate it." Genesis 3:6

Temptation is not ugly. It is pretty. It dresses in seductive clothing, and it smells good. Temptation can be a man who is kind, gentle, sensitive, tall, dark, and handsome. Or it can be a smiling and bubbly woman who brings energy and excitement to a relationship. Temptation baits our appetites for food, sexual pleasure, and knowledge, to name a few.

We cannot feed our body poor quality food or large quantities of food and not be unaffected. Thus, eat to live; do not live to eat. Good health is a gift from God. Steward it well and wisely. Budget your diet as you do your money. Your physical well-being is one of your best investments. Better to pay a personal trainer now than a surgeon later.

The same goes for your optical intake. Do not allow your eyes to feast on someone or something that you cannot have. Why place yourself in a position of compromise? If you travel, hire an intern of the same sex for accountability and apprenticeship. You may need to remove your television and/or computer from your home for a season so you are not bombarded by temptation. Appreciate the beauty your eyes behold, but do not desire or crave the object. Unbridled curiosity can easily cripple your commitment to Christ.

Furthermore, knowledge is designed for God's purposes. Keep your motive for wisdom pure. Make it your goal to attain wisdom so you can obey God precisely and wholeheartedly. Let your understanding of information be used to the advantage of serving and loving God and people. Temptation never goes away until we go to glory.

It started in the garden of Eden, and it continues today. Even in the best of environments, like sinless paradise, temptation still crouches at the door. There is no completely encapsulated "temptation-free" zone. However, you can still be smart and not place yourself in a position that feeds and facilitates temptation. You may need to break off that "friendship," or quit confiding in a coworker about your marital problems. (Seek professional help instead.) Innocent flirting can easily lead to not-so-innocent infidelity.

Temptation is a fire waiting to destroy. Do not go close to its flickering flames. Instead, draw closer to the warmth of God's love and to those who love you the most. Yes, indeed, frustrations feed falling into temptation, but reject this excuse. Invite the Holy Spirit to douse temptation's fires. Let people who care know what you are thinking and doing. We do better when others are watching. The consequences of giving in to temptation are crushing. The fruit of following Jesus is rich, rewarding, and satisfying. Reject the tempter, and accept your Savior Jesus. Never forget—the bait has a hook!

Heavenly Father, lead me away from temptation and into trust in You.

Related Readings: Matthew 4:1; Matthew 26:41; Luke 11:4; 1 Corinthians 10:13; James 1: 13-15

RUSH GOD

"So she said to Abram, 'The LORD has kept me from having children. Go, sleep with my maidservant; perhaps I can build a family through her.' Abram agreed to what Sarai said."
Genesis 16:2

Do not rush God. He can be trusted. What He says, He will do. He will accomplish His will, His way—in His time. This is difficult because we cannot wait to experience God's promise. But the anticipation is supposed to be part of the process. The joy of looking forward to God's blessing is rivaled by few emotions and experiences. He has allowed us to see His future vision for our edification, not our consternation. Trust—do not rush Him.

Because of a crisis and overwhelming needs, we are tempted to help God make things happen. But is this His timing? Be patient. God is not rushed. How audacious of us to think we can accelerate the Almighty's timeline. It is His grace pace that is best for believers. It is not about striving to impose an issue or creating circumstances that force His will. "Woe to him who strives with his Maker!" (Isaiah 45:9 NKJV).

He has a plan. You can be content as His plan unfolds, or you can remain frustrated trying to facilitate twisted means to reach good goals. Do not allow the compelling issue to manipulate you into doing anything and everything to meet the necessary need. It may be a crisis of belief, but it is not a crisis that demands frantic reactions. You may feel rushed, but Jesus is patient. Take a step back, and breathe in God's fresh air of faith.

God's timing and God's methods may seem unnatural to you, even impossible. But they are all for a purpose. His purposes prevail. You may be tempted to laugh at the Lord's methods, but He is counterintuitive. The level of faith required for this phase of your journey seems unrealistic. Yes, at times there is a fine line between foolishness and faith.

But what the world sees as foolish, God sees as wise. And what the world looks on as wise, God sees as foolish. So it may seem foolish to give more time and money to the kingdom of God, but He is pleased with your step of faith. Indeed, your return on investment of peace, joy, and contentment will far outweigh your meager sacrifice.

How is your family? It is a big deal to trust your children or siblings with God. It should not be, but it is. Leave them in their Creator's hands. They may need to suffer the current consequences of their choices to recognize and understand their need for God. Be there for them, but do not rush what Christ is up to in their faith development.

Yes, you can rush ahead of the Lord and get short-term results, which ultimately lead to long-term distractions and disappointments. Or you can wait on God's plan to unfold and experience unprecedented peace, fulfillment, and significance. Then you know He did it, and you were part of His bigger plan. No one likes to be rushed, especially God!

Heavenly Father, teach me to wait on You and Your amazing works.

Related Readings: Psalm 37:7; Proverbs 6:18; Jeremiah 5:4; 1 Corinthians 1:18–27

ROCK OF GOD

"As for God, His way is perfect; the word of the LORD is flawless. He is a shield for all who take refuge in Him. For who is God besides the LORD? And who is the Rock except our God? It is God who arms me with strength and makes my way perfect." Psalm 18:30–32

God is rock solid—always dependable—ever present. There are no storms of life or surges from sin that dislodge the Lord's foundation of faithfulness. Christ is a cleft in the rock and the Rock of ages. He protects, provides, and perseveres. Skeptics cannot shove Him aside or ignore His works of salvation. He is the righteous Rock for all who believe.

"When my glory passes by, I will put you in a cleft in the rock and cover you with my hand until I have passed by" (Exodus 33:22).

Some days our weary souls feel like giving up and giving in to the enemy's enticements. But we have One greater, who goes with us the extra mile and fights our battles for us. The rock of God cannot be penetrated with arrows of apathy or bullets of unbelief. He stands strong, ready to defend His children and give them victory in His Son Jesus.

"With bitterness archers attacked him; they shot at him with hostility. But his bow remained steady, his strong arms stayed limber, because of the hand of the Mighty One of Jacob, because of the Shepherd, the Rock of Israel, because of your father's God, who helps you, because of the Almighty, who blesses you with blessings of the heavens above, blessings of the deep that lies below" (Genesis 49:23–25).

How is your foundation of faith? Is it built on the solid rock of Jesus Christ or on the shifting sand of circumstances? Circumstantial belief depends on outside forces, while true faith relies on the unchanging inner peace of God. Choices based on obedience to Christ result in outcomes that honor Him and others. Because you have confidence in the foundational principles found in God's flawless Word, you find His perfect way by faith.

So praise the Lord, your everlasting and unchanging Rock of righteousness. He is worthy to receive all glory and gratitude you offer Him. There is none other like your lofty and lifted up Lord of glory. Exalt His holy name, and rest in the cleft of your reassuring Rock. As a follower of Jesus, build on His reliable rock of character—faith, hope, and love.

"The LORD lives! Praise be to my Rock! Exalted be God, the Rock, my Savior" (2 Samuel 22:47).

Does my faith rest on the unchanging Rock of God or on my ever-changing circumstances?

Related Readings: Psalm 19:14; Psalm 40:2; Isaiah 26:4; Matthew 7:24; 1 Corinthians 10:4

FORGETFUL FRIENDS

"The chief cupbearer, however, did not remember Joseph; he forgot him."
Genesis 40:23

Sometimes friends forget. They forget birthdays, anniversaries, commitments, and what is important to their friends. The forgetfulness of friends facilitates frustration and disappointment. After all, some of these friends have been past recipients of your help and encouragement. You have been there for them during their days of discouragement. Now when the tables have turned and you are in need, they do not seem to be near.

Maybe they are too busy with life, maybe they are buried in their own troubles, or maybe they have simply forgotten you. Unfortunately, some friendships are tentative and unpredictable. When adversity strikes, you are able to filter out false friends from forever friends. Fair-weather friends will fly in and out of your life. Some friendships are expedient for the moment, while others compound in loyalty and love as the years pass.

However, be careful not to place expectations on your friends. Expectations increase the chances for disappointment. Friends will let you down if you hold lofty expectations over them. If your friends feel the pressure to perform a certain way, they will push back in fear or resentment. Friendships are meant for release—not control.

Companions are a gift from Christ. Steward them well so you can be trusted with more. It is tempting to take our friends for granted, especially long-term friendships, because they are low maintenance and tend to get the least attention. But, in reality, even old friends need nurturing. They need a phone call, a visit, or written correspondence. They need time. Friendships grow or atrophy, but care and attention fertilize a friendship.

Moreover, make it a goal for your spouse to become your best friend. You and your spouse sleep and eat together. You raise children together. You manage the home together. You budget money together. You hurt and laugh together. You are growing old together. Since you spend so much time together "doing life," it is imperative you fortify your friendship. Your goal is to become best friends, so when the children move out, you are not bored and relationally bankrupt. Fun friendships are intentional.

The marriage relationship is a friendship not to forget. If you ignore this friend, you will wake up one day with regrets. Remember your spouse's birthday, your anniversary, and all those little things that make him or her feel special. When you remember a friend, you honor a friend. When you remember a friend, you feed a friendship. Friendships fatigue for lack of attention. Remember a friend today. Remind this friend how special he or she is to you and to God. Love this friend, and expect nothing in return. Be a friend, and you will have friends. "A man who has friends must himself be friendly, but there is a friend who sticks closer than a brother" (Proverbs 18:24 NKJV).

Am I a friend worthy of friendship? What friend do I need to love and encourage?

Related Readings: 1 Samuel 20:42; Job 16:20–21; Proverbs 27:10; John 15:13–15

FILLED WITH GRIEF

"When they came together in Galilee, he said to them, 'The Son of Man is going to be betrayed into the hands of men. They will kill him, and on the third day he will be raised to life.' And the disciples were filled with grief."   Matthew 17:22–23

Every minute a baby is born who fills family and friends with joy. Simultaneously, a person dies who fills loved ones left behind with grief. Grief is a God-given emotion that everyone experiences when something valuable is lost, especially loss of life. An unborn child lost to miscarriage, a middle-aged woman's terminal cancer, or an old man's heart failure all result in grief for those who long to love them again. Grief hurts deeply.

So how are followers of Jesus to process severe sorrow? How do we keep on living when a child, parent, grandparent, or friend is now among the dead? Indeed, we let them down if we linger too long in despair, living as if there is no future hope after life. One way to honor the dead is to live well until we die. The loss of a loved one is a wake-up call that our existence on earth is finite. We are called by God to live purposely for Him.

"Come now, you who say, 'Today or tomorrow we will go to such and such a city, spend a year there, buy and sell, and make a profit'; whereas you do not know what will happen tomorrow. For what is your life? It is even a vapor that appears for a little time and then vanishes away. Instead you ought to say, 'If the Lord wills, we shall live and do this or that'" (James 4:13–15 NKJV).

Furthermore, when friends or family are grieving, be patient and give them space to be with Christ in His compassionate consultation. It is your loving-kindness and care that warm them to reengage with life responsibilities. Some people snap back quickly, while others require a long length of time to process through their enormous emptiness.

Ultimately, only Jesus can fill the void of human attachment. When deep-felt love is vacated to heaven, you need heaven's help. Grief is not to be processed alone but with almighty God and those who love you dearly. Open your hurting heart to genuine love, but be wise to not succumb to a greedy or self-serving "friend" seeking to take advantage of your vulnerability. Guard your heart in your grief, but give yourself fully to God.

Remember grief is momentary, but heaven is forever. Life is like a drop of water in time, but eternity with Jesus is a sea of hope, healing, and happiness. Through Christ you will soon be reunited with your spouse, son, daughter, mom, dad, brother, sister, and friend. Use your grief to grow closer to God and those who love you most. Grief gets us to God.

"Saul and Jonathan—in life they were loved and gracious, and in death they were not parted" (2 Samuel 1:23).

Am I allowing the Lord to love me through my grief? Who is grieving and hurting whom I can comfort with God's Word?

Related Readings: Deuteronomy 32:39; Isaiah 38:10; John 5:24; 2 Timothy 1:10

HOLY SPIRIT COMPELLED

"For I am full of words, and the spirit within me compels me."
Job 32:18

God wants us to live a life compelled by His Spirit. When the Spirit within us says yes, we are obliged to follow His lead. It may interfere with our comfort. It may cause us to say no to other good opportunities, and it may require us to sacrifice. But because Christ compels us, we come alive to live for Him and to unselfishly serve others.

If it is to speak, then speak with grace and boldness. If it is to teach, then teach with accuracy and relevance. If it is to make deals, then make deals with those you trust and within your area of expertise. If it is to share the gospel, then share the gospel with love and acceptance. If it is to mentor others, then mentor others with humility and wisdom.

If it is to invest in your family, then invest in your family with energy and abandon. Time is short—so do not waste it on people and projects that are not compelling to you. It may compel others, but not you. Go after those things that motivate you to excellence. You are compelled by the Spirit of God inside you to influence the world outside you.

"These men began to argue with Stephen, but they could not stand up against his wisdom or the Spirit by whom he spoke" (Acts 6:9–10).

A compelling life compels others. Your compelling life lifts others out of their apathy and hesitation. You are a force field of hope and courage. Your life becomes more compelling the deeper you go with God. Your character overflows with the fruit of the Spirit. People can taste the fruit of the Spirit through your life, and it tastes delicious.

So what does it look like to be compelled by the Holy Spirit? Certainly you are comfortable with God's purpose for your life. Maybe you broker people for kingdom purposes. You may be a homemaker, a lawyer, a secretary, a salesman, a software developer, a banker, a mechanic, a teacher, or a politician. Your vocation is not ministry, but your ministry is your vocation. Wherever God has called you, do it in a compelling fashion, or do not do it at all. A Spirit-compelled life compels others to follow Jesus.

Barnabas was a Spirit-led man of God. "He was a good man, full of the Holy Spirit and faith, and a great number of people were brought to the Lord" (Acts 11:24).

Where is the Spirit leading me to serve the Lord? Does my life compel others to Christ?

Related Readings: Acts 16:6–7; Romans 5:5; Romans 15:13–30; 1 Corinthians 2:4–15

o1

INFANT CHRISTIANS

"Anyone who lives on milk, being still an infant, is not acquainted with the teaching about righteousness. But solid food is for the mature, who by constant use have trained themselves to distinguish good from evil." Hebrews 5:13–14

Some have been saved by the Lord but not sanctified by the Lord. Fulfilled followers of Jesus not only have their "fire insurance" from hell, but they are learning how to live for heaven. We are saved by grace through faith; then we grow in grace by faith. Mature believers desire the meat of God's Word and are not satisfied with sipping on milk alone.

Like an infant, some Christians cannot take care of themselves, much less the needs of others. They have never advanced beyond the basic teachings in righteousness and have avoided training themselves to discern good and evil. Those who fail to grow in grace miss the blessing of experiencing the fullness of God's grace. Infant Christians are needy.

"Like newborn babies, crave pure spiritual milk, so that by it you may grow up in your salvation, now that you have tasted that the Lord is good" (1 Peter 2:2–3).

It is okay to be a babe in Christ, but it is not okay to remain a babe in Christ. So has your faith flourished beyond your initial confession of faith? Are you growing or backsliding? It is a sin and a shame for a child of God to not put away childish traits and embrace the truth of Scripture. It hurts the Christian brand when Christians fail to move forward in their faith.

"When I was a child, I talked like a child, I thought like a child, I reasoned like a child. When I became a man, I put childish ways behind me" (1 Corinthians 13:11).

Infant Christians draw attention to themselves; mature Christians point people to Jesus. Infant Christians are enamored by earthly rewards; mature Christians store up heavenly rewards. Infant Christians obsess over their needs; mature Christians serve the needs of others. Infant Christians forget God and worry; mature Christians remember God and pray. So seek the Lord and learn from Him how to grow in grace. Maturity wants more.

"Epaphras, who is one of you and a servant of Christ Jesus, sends greetings. He is always wrestling in prayer for you, that you may stand firm in all the will of God, mature and fully assured" (Colossians 4:12).

How can the understanding and application of Scripture become a routine in my faith?

Related Readings: Isaiah 28:23–29; Ezekiel 37:23; Luke 8:14–15; 1 Corinthians 3:1–3

REDEEMING THE TIME

"See then that you walk circumspectly, not as fools but as wise, redeeming the time, because the days are evil. Therefore do not be unwise, but understand what the will of the Lord is." Ephesians 5:15–17 NKJV

What does it mean to redeem the time? It is an attitude that values every minute as a gift from God to be stewarded well. Redeeming the time trades distrust for trust in the Lord because He has given His children more than enough time to transact His will. It is tapping into the Lord's reservoir of wisdom and understanding in how His ways work.

For example, I can remain in a job beyond my time of full usefulness. Good things are still happening, the mission is being accomplished, but I am just biding my time. Is this the best use of God's time and resources? Maybe it is the season to transition into a situation that is a better use of everyone's time, money, and attention. Am I investing my time well?

Without being watchful in how we prioritize our time, we drift into unwise living and miss living out the perfect will of God. It is easier to execute the expedient rather than the eternal. What does Jesus think about how you spend your time? Does it fulfill His will for you? If no, then reconsider how to better honor Christ in your career and in your choices.

What open door is before you that invites your entrance? What opportunities has the Lord given you that are waiting for your attention? By faith walk through the open door, and prayerfully plan a process to better manage your Master's opportunities. Fools complain and remain frustrated, while the wise rise to the occasion with fresh faith and fulfilling work. When you use your gifts for God, time will fly in fruitful living for Him.

Time is short, as we are only alive a short time. We make the most of our time when we are mindful and intentional with those outside faith in Jesus Christ. Evil days engulf our life in noneternal outcomes. So take the time to influence the lost with the message of God's redeeming love. Time is earthbound until you have a heavenly transaction of faith in Jesus. Indeed, those redeemed by God have the capacity to wisely redeem the time.

"Walk in wisdom toward those who are outside, redeeming the time. Let your speech always be with grace, seasoned with salt, that you may know how you ought to answer each one" (Colossians 4:5–6 NKJV).

Has God through Jesus Christ redeemed me? Am I wisely redeeming the time?

Related Readings: Deuteronomy 7:8; Psalm 78:35; Titus 2:14; 1 Peter 1:17–19

WELCOME CHILDREN

"Therefore, whoever humbles himself like this child is the greatest in the kingdom of heaven.
And whoever welcomes a little child like this in my name welcomes me."
Matthew 18:4–5

When we welcome a child in the name of Jesus, we welcome Jesus. A child's traits of humility, trust, and purity are the greatest in the kingdom of heaven. Humility brings down pride, trust defeats distrust, and purity flushes out impurities. So welcomed children are a reminder of almighty God's attributes. They show us what is good.

Loving acceptance is attracted to humility, and the humility of a child is refreshing. Children are dependent because they have yet to enter the work force and earn a wage. Like believers need their heavenly Father's wisdom and direction, children need their parents' instruction and guidance. A humble child honors his or her mom and dad by listening and obeying. Likewise, Christ is honored when we understand and apply His commands.

The Lord says, "Those who honor me I will honor" (1 Samuel 2:30).

Do your children feel welcomed in your home? Do they really feel accepted, or is it a conditional acceptance based on how they behave? Remember humility accepts, and pride rejects. Yes, children can bring joy or grief to a parent. They can break hearts or mend hearts. But whether they are estranged or engaged, be there for them so they can see and feel an example of their heavenly Father's love. Humility loves unconditionally.

Perhaps there is a child you have never met who is orphaned or adrift in the foster care system and needs your love and acceptance. God has given you the capacity and compassion to care for an additional little one. Is the Lord leading you to open your emotional, physical, spiritual, and financial resources for society's outcasts?

Where the culture marginalizes the disenfranchised, Christians capitalize by offering wholeness in a healthy home environment. So sincere followers of Jesus honestly ask: "Are we leveraging our assets for the Lord or just ourselves? Is our church engaged in the --culture or deaf to the children's cries for help?" Helping the helpless welcomes Jesus.

"Be imitators of God, therefore, as dearly loved children and live a life of love, just as Christ loved us and gave himself up for us as a fragrant offering and sacrifice to God" (Ephesians 5:1–2).

What child needs my loving care? Is God calling me to adopt or become a foster parent?

Related Readings: Psalm 103:17; Proverbs 3:9; Philippians 2:28–30; 2 John 1:1

EVIDENCE FOR GOD

"Have you comprehended the vast expanses of the earth? Tell me, if you know all this."
Job 38:18

What we do not know about creation is as much evidence for God as what we do know about creation. Our knowledge limitations point to the probability of God within the information we have not yet comprehended. How can we dismiss the existence of God when all is not yet known? If the proof of God cannot be dismissed, why dismiss Him?

If the nonexistence of God is inconclusive, why declare Him not here? We do not dismiss other areas of life as nonexistent or irrelevant if we are unable to fully comprehend them. We enjoy the fruits of electricity, though we are severely limited in understanding its origin and makeup. But we enjoy the light, heat, comfort, and security it generates.

Most of us do not understand aerodynamics, but we like the option of traveling quickly and safely across land or sea by airplane. The physics of tons of steel floating on water are not one hundred percent comprehendible to the average seafaring person, but most of us invite the opportunity to relax on a cruise ship. We accept what we do not fully know.

The truth is, evidence for God continues to stream into our knowledge banks. We are rich with informational deposits for God. Every time the sun rises in the east and sets in the west, it is evidence for the unchangeableness of God. Every time we experience multicolor flowers and the vast array of insects, both large and miniscule, it is evidence for the creativity of our Creator. Every time a prayer is answered, it is evidence of God.

Every time a wayward life is rescued and put on the narrow path of Christ's righteousness, it is evidence for the all-powerfulness of God. Every time the human body is explored in all its intricacies, it is evidence of God's sophistication and attention to detail. The mountains point heavenly to His majesty, and the ocean waves clap for His glory and praise. The Lord God is the beginning of creation and the sustainer of creation.

And one day He will recreate a new creation, much like His original paradise with Adam and Eve. He is a creative, masterful artist and brilliant beyond the imagination of man. We are a dot on His canvas of creation, though we are a very important dot. God does not create anything insignificant. You are very, very important to your Creator. You are the pinnacle of His creation. Enjoy Him in what you comprehend about His creation, and trust Him with what is incomprehensible.

"Then I saw a new heaven and a new earth, for the first heaven and the first earth had passed away, and there was no longer any sea. I saw the Holy City, the new Jerusalem, coming down out of heaven from God, prepared as a bride beautifully dressed for her husband. And I heard a loud voice from the throne saying, 'Now the dwelling of God is with men, and he will live with them. They will be his people, and God himself will be with them and be their God'" (Revelation 21:1–3).

What evidence is around me that points to the existence of God? Do I really believe?

Related Readings: Psalm 19:1; Psalm 98:8; Isaiah 66:22; Zechariah 12:1; John 6:29–31

PURSUED BY GOD

"What do you think? If a man owns a hundred sheep, and one of them wanders away,
will he not leave the ninety-nine on the hills and go to look for the one that wandered off?
And if he finds it, I tell you the truth, he is happier about that one sheep than about
the ninety-nine that did not wander off. In the same way your Father in heaven
is not willing that any of these little ones should be lost." Matthew 18:12–14

The Lord's great love is not passive in its pursuit of people. He longs for every last, lost soul to be saved from the snares of sin, the devil's deceptions, and the world's allure. The Lord Almighty is personally engaged in engaging a human heart with heaven. Christ's love crosses all cultures and socioeconomic levels. He is in humble, hot pursuit of those He loves. Have you yielded to the Holy Spirit's tender wooing of your heart to God?

Left to our own whims and desires, we are prone to wander away from the Lord. Our culture competes with our heavenly affections until we grow indifferent to eternal matters. But Jesus does not quit His traversing for our heart's allegiance. Even during our darkest days, He is a light of hope that hovers over our head as a reminder of His love.

"I will lead the blind by ways they have not known, along unfamiliar paths I will guide them; I will turn the darkness into light before them and make the rough places smooth. These are the things I will do; I will not forsake them" (Isaiah 42:16).

Like wandering sheep, bad things distract us, and good things attract us. When we lose our way, we have a loving Shepherd ever present to show us the way. We are never out of His sight or out of reach from His sympathetic staff. The Lord looks for us and looks out for us because He loves us unconditionally. No one is too far from the love of God.

"May the God of peace, who through the blood of the eternal covenant brought back from the dead our Lord Jesus, that great Shepherd of the sheep, equip you with everything good for doing his will, and may he work in us what is pleasing to him, through Jesus Christ, to whom be glory for ever and ever. Amen" (Hebrews 13:20–21).

When Jesus found you, how did you feel? Was it forgiven, grateful, relieved, and ready for heaven? You probably felt these few emotions and many more. If you have not given in to God's good intentions, you can come to Christ now. Turn and look to Him. He loves you as none other can love you. Heaven rejoices when the pursued are persuaded by God.

"'Rejoice with me; I have found my lost sheep.' I tell you that in the same way there will be more rejoicing in heaven over one sinner who repents than over ninety-nine righteous persons who do not need to repent" (Luke 15:6–7).

How is God pursuing me? How does Christ want me to respond to His compelling love?

Related Readings: Job 19:22; Isaiah 41:2–4; Luke 19:20; John 10:3

EMOTIONAL OVERHEAD

"Drive out the mocker, and out goes strife; quarrels and insults are ended."
Proverbs 22:10

Are you consumed by conflict with someone at work or in a personal relationship? Have you tried to appease them, confront them, and pray for them to no avail? Unfortunately, no amount of cajoling or arguing can change the heart of a mocker. Until this person comes face-to-face with brokenness from God, he or she will not truly change for Christ's sake.

Like a lease or mortgage creates financial overhead, so does a person intent on disrupting the culture of a company or a family. Mockers are made up of insecure individuals full of a grandiose self-image. Pride and jealousy drive them to discredit anyone who gets in the way of their man-made agenda. Mockers angrily attack even the most loving heart.

"Whoever corrects a mocker invites insult; whoever rebukes a wicked man incurs abuse" (Proverbs 9:7).

It is not worth carrying this type of emotional overhead on the books of your brain. You wake up in the middle of the night fearful of what may happen next if you do not walk the fine line of pleasing this person at work. Your preoccupation with meeting his or her expectations has caused you to neglect other important relationships. Continual drama from the same source is a recipe for confusion and contempt from the team.

"Blessed is the man who does not walk in the counsel of the wicked or stand in the way of sinners or sit in the seat of mockers" (Psalm 1:1).

After confronting a mocker, things very likely will get worse. It is because a scorner does not receive a rebuke or seek wisdom. "A mocker resents correction; he will not consult the wise" (Proverbs 15:12). Some relationships are a black hole of wasted time and energy. You may have to make the bold move to remove this person before his or her path of destruction continues its course. Let the disloyal go for the sake of the loyal whole.

You can still pray for those who are mockers and love them from a distance. Indeed, overwhelming emotional overhead is not a cost you can afford with your own emotional budget. Yes, we bear the burdens of those who are broken before God, but not those trying to break others. The Lord extends His grace to the humble, but mocks the proud who are consumed in their mockery.

"He mocks proud mockers but gives grace to the humble" (Proverbs 3:34).

Whom in my life do I need to let go for the sake of the whole?

Related Readings: 2 Kings 16:3; Job 17:2; Isaiah 29:20; Mark 9:28–29; 1 John 4:18

REWARD OF FAITHFULNESS

"To the faithful you show yourself faithful, to the blameless you show yourself blameless."
Psalm 18:25

Faithfulness is doing what I said I would do. It is an integrity issue. Commitments are not to be taken lightly. For example, a verbal commitment is an unwritten contract. However, these can be the most risky and misunderstood. If we make a verbal commitment, it behooves us to make sure it is plain with all parties involved.

If there is not a clear understanding, there is a good chance for miscommunication and a perception of unfaithfulness. The burden of responsibility is on the communicator. If we are moving fast and overcommitted, our communication skills and follow-through suffer. We may assume others understand us and know what is going on, but this is risky.

Slow down, communicate more, and show up on time for appointments. Less is more. Most of us would be much better off if we focused on fewer commitments. Take a relational audit, and ask others if they perceive you as being faithful to your commitments to them. Do not blame others for unfaithfulness if this is a chronic problem in your own life. Fortunately, as followers of Christ we have Him as our faithful model.

The Lord has been faithful even in our unfaithfulness. God says what He does and does what He says. He is faithful to forgive our sin and lead us to forgive. He is faithful to convict us of sin and to lead us into righteousness. He is faithful to flood our souls with peace, joy, and contentment. God understands what it means to keep a commitment, even at great cost—the death of His only Son. Indeed, the Lord is faithful to the faithful.

Unfaithfulness will catch up with us if not quickly remedied. Adultery is an example of marital unfaithfulness. Yet how many of us go to bed with other conflicting relational commitments. Do not let work, hobbies, children, or money become your "mistress." Faithfulness begins and ends with follow-through with our commitments to God.

After our conversion, we made a commitment to follow Christ. Following Jesus requires fidelity of faith. There are no equals to our love for Him. When He says in His Word to let our yes be yes and our no be no, we follow through because we want to be faithful to Him and others. Yes, the Lord defines your faithfulness and rewards your faithfulness.

Your faithfulness does not go unnoticed or unrewarded. One of the greatest rewards is the gift of trust. Faithfulness births and grows trust; so over time you earn the reputation of a trustworthy person. Those who can be trusted with a little can be trusted with much. Thus, be faithful so you can be trusted. Above all, be faithful because He is faithful!

How is the Lord faithful to me? To what commitment do I need to remain faithful?

Related Readings: Deuteronomy 7:9; Deuteronomy 11:13; Psalm 37:28; Matthew 5:37; 1 Timothy 1:12

CONFRONTATION NOT GOSSIP

"If your brother sins against you, go and show him his fault, just between the two of you.
If he listens to you, you have won your brother over." Matthew 18:15

It is easier to talk about others than it is to talk with them. I struggle with this because I do not like confrontation; however, if I really care for others, I will take the time to discuss with them their indiscretion. The temptation is to "confide" in another of the need to "pray" for a friend without first being direct with him or her in a loving conversation. "A perverse man stirs up dissension, and a gossip separates close friends" (Proverbs 16:28).

Love seeks to sit down and sort through misunderstandings and discuss the dangers of remaining on a path of destruction. Perhaps your friend is neglecting family or harming his or her health. Your role is to provide a safe environment for your friend to see the error of his or her ways. Hard discussions may not immediately bear fruit, but they plant good seeds. "I planted the seed, Apollos watered it, but God made it grow" (1 Corinthians 3:6).

There is always the risk of becoming like the one we are confronting. For example, if you challenge an angry man, be forgiving lest you become angry. If you face a lustful woman, be pure lest you become lustful. If you expose a lie, be honest lest you become a liar. If you stand up to a proud person, be humble lest you become proud.

"Brothers, if someone is caught in a sin, you who are spiritual should restore him gently. But watch yourself, or you also may be tempted" (Galatians 6:1).

Confrontation without grace prolongs graceless living, but confrontation with grace attracts Spirit-filled living. Sin squirms in its dark state when exposed by the light of a loving conversation. Be direct with a humble heart, and you cannot be accused of harshness. Take the time to prayerfully help someone see his or her sin; then trust Jesus.

"Everyone who does evil hates the light, and will not come into the light for fear that his deeds will be exposed" (John 3:20).

Make sure God's Word is the foundation of your concerns because it carries the weight of Christ's authority. Do not be a self-righteous Bible thumper but a meek Bible believer. Our opinions may or may not be helpful, but the whole counsel of God's Word resonates within a soul seduced by sin. So speak the truth in love, and watch the Holy Spirit work.

"Speaking the truth in love ... each of you must put off falsehood and speak truthfully to his neighbor, for we are all members of one body" (Ephesians 4:15, 25).

Whom do I need to talk to with a humble heart instead of proudly talking about them?

Related Readings: Proverbs 26:20; Zechariah 8:16; 1 Corinthians 2:13; 3 John 1:10

GOD'S SIGNATURE

"Let them know that it is your hand, that you, O LORD, have done it."
Psalm 109:27

God's signature is all over a surrendered life. Sometimes He writes with small letters, sometimes with bold expression, and other times with the invisible ink of His intimacy. He only autographs what He is proud of, and He is extremely proud of His children. He is proud of your faithfulness when everything around you screams unfaithfulness.

He is proud of the beautiful family you have loved and nurtured over the years. He is proud of the way you steward your finances with generosity and frugality. He is exceedingly proud of the passion and love you have for Him and people. Whatever God touches becomes very valuable because its worth can be traced back to Divinity.

His appraisal of an obedient life is of great value. So submit to Jesus, and people will recognize and acknowledge the touch of God on your life. Indeed, His touch can be tough and tender at the same time. It is God's favor on your life that causes others to say, "The LORD has done this, and it is marvelous in our eyes" (Psalm 118:23).

The hand of God is comforting, but its absence is foreboding. When His hand signs off on you and your activities, there is confidence. God's notary in the presence of two or three witnesses is heavenly validation. You can move forward. Do not delay. God has validated your ideas, your motives, and your actions. You can totally trust Him when He has orchestrated the circumstances; so now you can move forward with abandonment.

Others are drawn to you because of the Lord's hand on your life. But, if well-meaning people try to elevate you to a pedestal, step down and kneel at the foot of the cross. It is at the foot of the cross we lay selfish ambition and every fiber in our being that wants to take credit for God's blessing. It is at the foot of the cross that God's ownership of everything is confessed. It is at the foot of the cross the ground is level for all, so none are exalted other than Jesus. When He is raised up, all people are drawn to Him.

"But I, when I am lifted up from the earth, will draw all men to myself" (John 12:32).

Because we are a conduit for Christ's blessings, we give Him the glory. A beautiful painting always points to a brilliant artist. It is the originator of the beauty who deserves credit for his or her work of art. God will proclaim His presence, power, and purpose with or without our acknowledgement. However, His hand is on a life that declares Him. God's signature is His guarantee. He guarantees He is the one and only true God!

"Humble yourselves, therefore, under God's mighty hand, that he may lift you up in due time" (1 Peter 5:6).

Am I surrendered under the mighty hand of God? Do I glorify Him with my life?

Related Readings: Exodus 32:11; Ezra 8:31; Nehemiah 2:8; Romans 8:34

EFFECTIVE RADICAL PRAYER

"Again, I tell you that if two of you on earth agree about anything you ask for,
it will be done for you by my Father in heaven. For where two or three
come together in my name, there am I with them." Matthew 18:19–20

Effective radical prayer engages the hearts of men and women, teenagers and young adults, boys and girls. Solo prayer invites the ear of the Lord, but group prayer purifies prayer. In a group of devoted disciples, God's will is established and boldly petitioned to heaven. Prayer support from a small group gives confidence, direction, and determination.

For example, the righteous one who fervently prays for those outside the faith is effective to draw them within the faith. There is no doubt hell shudders when heavenly supplications seek to snatch lost souls from eternal damnation. The Holy Spirit hovers over prayer meetings motivated to glorify the Lord and save sinners. Group prayer ignites eternity.

"After they prayed, the place where they were meeting was shaken. And they were all filled with the Holy Spirit and spoke the word of God boldly" (Acts 4:31).

We pray and praise God, but Christ converts. The pressure is not on Christians to make Christians, but to pray for hearts to be pricked by God's Spirit, converted, and born into the kingdom of God. The Lord uses prayer to soften sinners so the soil of their heart moistens and seeds of truth take root. Pray without ceasing for Jesus to save lost souls.

"Every day they continued to meet together in the temple courts. They broke bread in their homes and ate together with glad and sincere hearts, praising God and enjoying the favor of all the people. And the Lord added to their number daily those who were being saved" (Acts 2:46–47).

The local church is a natural location to lean into the Lord in small group prayer. Our homes can also be a sanctuary of supplication to Christ, with other like-minded believers. So begs the question, "Are you engaged in effective prayer with other followers of Jesus?" Prayer is a team sport. It is not meant for us to only linger alone with the Lord.

We all need prayer, and we need to pray for others. It is a Holy Spirit-initiated prayer movement that moves cultures and communities toward God. Perhaps we complain less to each other and pray more with each other. When we humble ourselves together before God, He hears, He answers, and He heals. Effective prayers mobilize the body of Christ.

"You will have complete and free access to God's kingdom, keys to open any and every door: no more barriers between heaven and earth, earth and heaven. A yes on earth is yes in heaven. A no on earth is no in heaven" (Matthew 16:19 MSG).

Does Christ capture my heart in radical prayer with a small group of believers in Jesus?

Related Readings: 2 Chronicles 5:13; 2 Chronicles 7:14; 1 Corinthians 5:4; James 5:16

HOLY DESIRE

"As the deer pants for streams of water, so my soul pants for you, O God.
My soul thirsts for God, for the living God. When can I go and meet with God?"
Psalm 42:1–2

Holy desire has to hear from heaven. There is a devotion and determination to know God in the splendor of His holiness. A soul captured by holy desire is not satisfied until it sees Jesus and the glory of His grace. It is an inner interest in the eternal that is not content with the earthly. Things of earth grow dim as holy desire reverently reaches for heaven.

Jesus says blessing comes when holy desire is the motivation of a life surrendered to Him. "Blessed are those who hunger and thirst for righteousness, for they will be filled" (Matthew 5:6). Am I willing to miss a meal so my heart and soul can first be fed by faith? When our soul's thirsty affections are consecrated to Christ, it has to drink from the fountain of faith and be hydrated by heaven. Holy desire must meaningfully meet God.

Where can we go to meet the Lord? We can meet Him in the privacy of our home or in the public arena of worship at church. We can meet Him in the outdoor sanctuary of His incredible creation or in an indoor prayer meeting. Jesus can be found in a hospital's intensive care unit, in the maternity ward, or in the humble care of hospice at home.

Meetings with God are only limited by a mind that categorizes Christ into the sacred and the secular. This is why during an intense time of meetings at work you can pray and ask the Lord to give you the love and discipline to serve people well. In your responsibilities at home, you can play worship music and transform your domestic duties into a sacrifice of service to heaven. Holy desire is meant to be integrated into our faith and work life.

The heart of a devoted disciple is captured by divine desire and holy intent. You want to know Him better so you will follow Him better. You want to love Him better so you will love people better. You want to serve Him unselfishly so you will serve others selflessly. You only want Him because you know in your heart this is all you need.

Holy desire is the need to know Christ in the middle of suffering, in the mundane activities of everyday life, and on the mountaintop of happiness. Paul expressed it perfectly. "I want to know Christ and the power of his resurrection and the fellowship of sharing in his sufferings, becoming like him in his death, and so, somehow, to attain to the resurrection from the dead" (Philippians 3:10–11).

Are all my desires captured by the one desire to know Christ?

Related Readings: Deuteronomy 10:12; Psalm 37:4; Luke 24:32; Romans 12:11

A FRUITFUL FAMILY

"Blessed are all who fear the LORD, who walk in his ways. You will eat the fruit of your labor; blessings and prosperity will be yours. Your wife will be like a fruitful vine within your house; your sons will be like olive shoots around your table. Thus is the man blessed who fears the LORD." Psalm 128:1–4

The fruit from a family who fears the Lord is tasty and delicious. However, this type of fruit does not happen immediately but is cultivated over time. A fruitful wife sets the tone for the home. By God's grace she weeds out criticism and replaces it with creativity. The home is her "pride and joy." It is a reflection of her, as it is her nest.

A home to the wife is like an office to the husband. Things need to be just right, or she feels violated. Indeed, be grateful for a conscientious wife who wants to express herself through the home. The fruit of a clean, decorated, and ordered home is calming. It provides an environment of stability and frees family members to focus on each other and people. A husband is free to do what he does best at work with a supportive wife at home.

A mother's influence spreads like a lovely vine throughout the house. No area is left untouched. The children are nurtured and encouraged by her sensitivity. When instilled from birth, the fruit from children becomes obedience to God and love for the Lord. Their heart for God grows when parents read Bible stories to them as they wait in the womb.

The warm embrace of their little arms around your neck is the fruit of trust. The look of their kind and trusting eyes is the fruit of consistent love from mom and dad. Their bent toward love for God and people is fruit from their parents' example of following Jesus.

Furthermore, family fruit flourishes when the man of the house models faithfulness. A husband's intentional effort to follow the Lord ignites faith at home. A fruitful wife has no problem submitting to a husband who submits to God. A God-fearing man is quick to confess sin to his heavenly Father and to his family. It is not uncommon for him to say, "I am sorry" or "I was wrong." Authentic confession encourages confession in others.

Confessed hearts are family fruit. It is probable the family will pray, read their Bible, and go to church if the leader of the home does the same. Family fruit has a direct correlation to the faithfulness of the family head. Family fruit flourishes when the man fears God. Regardless of the circumstances, he is committed to doing what God expects.

Therefore, your home becomes a hothouse of character. The fruit threatens to burst through the glass panes for all to see. People are encouraged when they visit your hospitable home. Sinners need a safe environment, as acceptance comes from the fruit of Christ's acceptance. Heaven's dew and rainfall keep the fruit coming to a home submitted to Christ. Jesus says, "This is to my Father's glory, that you bear much fruit, showing yourselves to be my disciples" (John 15:8). Fruit is proof of faithful families.

Does my character cultivate fruit that glorifies God in my family?

Related Readings: Genesis 7:1; Proverbs 31:15; Mark 5:19; Acts 10:2

HEARTFELT FORGIVENESS

"This is how my heavenly Father will treat each of you unless
you forgive your brother from your heart."
Matthew 18:35

As a follower of Jesus, I know in my head I am to perpetually forgive, but this truth does not always migrate to my heart. It is a struggle to be patient with, much less pardon, those who are reckless with their words and angry in their attitude. My heartfelt forgiveness does not catch up with my head knowledge until I truly take to heart the depth and breadth of God's forgiveness. "In him we have redemption through his blood, the forgiveness of sins, in accordance with the riches of God's grace" (Ephesians 1:7).

Christ's clemency on the cross for mankind is unconditional for all who believe. "Everyone who believes in him receives forgiveness of sins through his name" (Acts 10:43). The reminder that we are sinners saved by grace grows humility and dismisses pride. Indeed, a prideless person is able to offer perpetual forgiveness to offenders.

However, those who behave like they are unforgiven (by their unmerciful actions) will be treated as if they were unforgiven by their heavenly Father. A more severe judgment awaits followers of Christ who withhold the grace and forgiveness they have received from God. True forgiveness offers a permanent pardon, not a temporary reprieve.

Have you been treated unjustly and accused unfairly? Has someone you really respected let you down? Has a friend gossiped about you, or has a church member lied to you? If you stay stuck in self-pity and anger, you will miss an opportunity to model mercy, grace, and forgiveness. Jesus says it is easy to love those who love us; even the world does this.

"Do to others as you would have them do to you. If you love those who love you, what credit is that to you? Even 'sinners' love those who love them. And if you do good to those who are good to you, what credit is that to you? Even 'sinners' do that" (Luke 6:31–33). Thus, heartfelt forgiveness goes the extra mile to extend grace to the undeserving.

Therefore, by God's grace grant bold forgiveness to bad deeds against you and your family. Let go of the emotional debt another owes you, who can never repay you. Heartfelt forgiveness opens the door of pride's prison and releases the offender and the one offended. Extend Jesus' gift of perpetual forgiveness, and enjoy its freedom forever.

"For I will forgive their wickedness and will remember their sins no more" (Hebrews 8:12).

Is my forgiveness of others heartfelt and Christ centered?

Related Readings: 1 Kings 8:39; Ecclesiastes 4:1; Matthew 11:20; Luke 7:47

GOOD INTENTIONS

"There is a way that seems right to a man, but in the end it leads to death."
Proverbs 14:12

Good intentions need to be governed by God's wisdom, or they lead down the wrong path. My sincerity does not make up for incorrect assumptions or foolish choices. For example, I can talk myself into trusting someone who has questionable character because of his potential to bring in business. But if I rush and hire the wrong person, it sets back the organization and threatens the morale of the team. Wisdom first clarifies God's choice.

Good intentions in marriage occur when a husband or wife thinks they are helping their partner, but in reality they are hurting them. A surprise large purchase by one spouse that was not in the budget can become a nightmare of worry in financial liability. Well-meaning intentions that are irresponsible do damage to those who are there to help.

What decisions are you facing—a move, a purchase, a gift? Have you vetted your decision-making process with wise counsel? Ignorance and naïveté are not protected from producing wrong results. If you rush into a relationship or a deal without taking time to test your assumption, it may very well lead to regret and a waste of time and money.

"The way of a fool seems right to him, but a wise man listens to advice" (Proverbs 12:15).

However, you can find the right way by first following the way of Jesus Christ. He said, "I am the way" (John 14:6). With the ways of Jesus as our beginning point, our self-delusion is replaced by His divine revelation. And we read, "He who walks with the wise grows wise" (Proverbs 13:20), and then we submit to wise advisors. Wisdom puts us on the path of constructing Christ's will, thus moving toward a productive outcome.

Above all else, test your good intentions about God. You may think He is all love without standards for living, or you may assume He is all judge without love. Either extreme causes you to miss the real thing. Yes, the Lord requires a personal relationship through His Son Jesus to exit hell and enter heaven. And the beauty of knowing God is the ability to follow God. The path of death is paved with good and bad intentions, but the path of life is paved with wise ones. So seek not what seems right but what is right.

"Learn to do right! Seek justice, encourage the oppressed. Defend the cause of the fatherless, plead the case of the widow" (Isaiah 1:17).

Am I objective and teachable in my pursuit of truth and the best path to follow?

Related Readings: Isaiah 45:19; Isaiah 58:2; Zephaniah 2:3; Hebrews 12:11; 1 Corinthians 7:35

EYES ON GOD

"In the year that King Uzziah died, I saw the Lord seated on a throne,
high and exalted, and the train of his robe filled the temple." Isaiah 6:1

Kings and queens rule for a season and are then deposed or die, but the Lord is alive and reigns eternally. The shepherds of God's flock lead and care for the sheep, but some pastors stumble and fall. However, the Great Shepherd God is without sin and is always looking out for the least of His wandering flock. So we look only at the Lord to secure our faith.

Did you have someone on a pedestal who has let you down by his or her immoral or fickle behavior? Has a Christian celebrity taken advantage of his or her freedom and power to exploit naïve and trusting followers? When we place our expectations of a leader above the Lord, we set ourselves up for disappointment, even rejection of our faith.

Therefore, keep your eyes on Jesus for He will never let you down. Look beyond the disappointments of sinful men and women, and set your gaze on the glory of God. He is the only one worthy of our worship and one hundred percent worthy of loyalty and affection. He is high above hypocrisy and lifted up over lies and deceit. His throne is high and holy, trustworthy and true. Go to God in your grief over sinful acts disguised by - religion. He heals hurt hearts.

The Lord will judge those who use their position of public trust to abuse their authority. "'Woe to the shepherds who are destroying and scattering the sheep of my pasture!' declares the LORD" (Jeremiah 23:1). Those who represent God must genuinely submit to and obey God. There is a greater accountability for those who teach the Word of God.

"Not many of you should presume to be teachers, my brothers, because you know that we who teach will be judged more strictly" (James 3:1).

Above all else, keep the eyes of your faith fixed on King Jesus, the ruler of your life. His crown of compassion glistens with glory. His scepter of selfless love dispenses endless decrees of grace and mercy. His righteous robe of holiness causes us to bow down in awe and fear of His judgment. While the angels praise Him, you adore Him. Fix your eyes on the Eternal. Today you see the unseen by faith, but that day you will see Him face-to-face.

"See, the Lord is coming with thousands upon thousands of his holy ones" (Jude 1:14).

Are my eyes set on the clay feet of men or on the unchanging Christ?

Related Readings: Psalm 25:15; Psalm 123:2; Psalm 141:8; Hebrews 12:14; Revelation 4:8

CONSTRUCTIVE COMPLAINTS

"I cry aloud to the LORD; I lift up my voice to the LORD for mercy.
I pour out my complaint before him; before him I tell my trouble." Psalm 142:1–2

Christ invites constructive complaints. He does not expect His children to have a complaint-free life. It is okay to express our heavy hearts to the One who created our heart and emotions. Our complaints are an opportunity to intersect our anxieties with God's compassion and faithfulness. Complaints are meant for us to regroup with Jesus.

David expressed his humble complaint to the Lord. "Hear me, O God, as I voice my complaint; protect my life from the threat of the enemy" (Psalm 64:1).

However, complaints should not evolve into a gripe session with God without any redeeming outcomes. The purpose is not to spew out frustrations and continue to live a cynical life. The reason for our expression of fear, doubt, anger, or jealousy is to deal with this negative energy in a safe environment.

God listens and loves you; He wants to lead you into a better way. He receives your complaints like a fair and caring judge in a court of law. Here a prepared attorney presents a plaintiff's complaint of injustice. Your lawyer is Jesus, and He pleads your complaint to your heavenly Father. "For there is one God and one mediator between God and men, the man Christ Jesus, who gave himself as a ransom for all men—the testimony given in its proper time" (1 Timothy 2:5–6). Christ frees us from chronic complaining.

Moreover, learn from the Lord how to receive complaints from others. Be patient and understanding with complainers in your life. See them not as an annoyance but as those who are hurting and in need of relief. You may not know how to fix them or their situation, but you can listen with care and lend a helping hand. People do not want to be fixed, but they do want to be heard with empathetic ears.

Complainers can become a nuisance, or their pent-up energy can be channeled into productivity. Your biggest complainers can become your most effective managers and leaders. But they require coaching and leading on your part. People are where you have led them. Anyone can ignore or isolate a complainer, but skilled leaders know how to appreciate and capitalize on those who boldly express themselves.

Listening to complaints may save you a lawsuit or be the springboard for improving a process or policy. There is normally a better way to do something; so listen to those who are in the middle of the work. Grassroots ideas are usually the best ideas. Bad news needs to travel fast; so encourage rapid complaints from those around you. Let complaints become a catalyst for change. Let them draw you closer to God, and learn from Him.

"Those who are wayward in spirit will gain understanding; those who complain will accept instruction" (Isaiah 29:24).

Am I prayerful and teachable in my complaints to Christ? To whom do I need to listen?

Related Readings: Job 7:11–13; Jeremiah 12:1; Acts 6:1; Acts 18:14

APPEARANCE OF EVIL

"Abstain from all appearance of evil."
1 Thessalonians 5:22 KJV

Perception is reality in the eyes of the beholder; so what does the world see in me? Am I known as a committed Christian on Sunday and someone who is somewhat shady the other six days of the week? Where I go, what I do, and with whom I spend time give the appearance of good or bad behavior. The Lord calls us to abstain from unseemly activity.

Corrupt affections cause us to pervert what God intended as good, while a pure heart cannot help but love as the Lord loves. It is in our autonomy that temptation raises its appealing head and causes us to deceive ourselves. What seems an innocent flirtation appears as an invitation to unfaithfulness. What looks like a sloppy expense report appears to lack integrity. What resembles inconsistency communicates hypocrisy.

So we have to ask ourselves, "Is our testimony for Christ trustworthy and true?" Do we represent Him well in the world, or have we diluted the Christian brand with bad associations? Jesus prayed for us, "My prayer is not that you take them out of the world but that you protect them from the evil one. They are not of the world, even as I am not of it" (John 17:15–16). So Jesus followers are to be in this world but not of this world.

There is always a risk of being branded "a friend of sinners," but it is a compliment to be labeled like our Lord was labeled. "The Son of Man came eating and drinking, and they say, 'Here is a glutton and a drunkard, a friend of tax collectors and "sinners."' But wisdom is proved right by her actions" (Matthew 11:19). Jesus loved relationally.

Evil appearances attract a heart comfortable with sin, but not a heart adverse to sin. We are commanded to love the sinner without being soiled by his or her sin. Like Jesus we are called to get our hands dirty in the messiness of life while bringing hope, holiness, and wholeness to recipients of God's grace. Life motivated by true love is a good appearance.

So how do we embrace good appearances and avoid bad appearances? We pray, we set standards based on the wisdom of God's Word, and we seek accountability from trusted friends. Believers snared by certain behaviors in the past are wise to avoid them in the present. Abstain from those attitudes and actions that dilute your fidelity to faith in Jesus.

"You were taught, with regard to your former way of life, to put off your old self, which is being corrupted by its deceitful desires; to be made new in the attitude of your minds; and to put on the new self, created to be like God in true righteousness and holiness" (Ephesians 4:22–24).

Am I above reproach in my money management, sexual purity, and truthfulness?

Related Readings: Proverbs 3:4; Proverbs 13:20; Proverbs 16:6, 17; 1 Timothy 3:2; 1 Thessalonians 5:22

HEART HEALING

"He heals the brokenhearted and binds up their wounds."
Psalm 147:3

Like our physical heart, our emotional heart can suffer from neglect. Without a proper diet of truth and the exercise of forgiveness, a wounded heart will eventually break. Was your childhood an emotional wasteland? Have you been emotionally starved, or have you exhausted your emotions on others? If so, you are a candidate for Christ's healing.

Maybe your parents deeply disappoint you. They are unable to connect at a deeper heartfelt level. This wounds your heart. Maybe a physical aliment or lack of training in social skills has crushed your confidence. Does insecurity dominate your self-image? This hurts your heart. Have you wept at night crying out to God for relief, but heaven is silent? Indeed, a heart burdened with emotional baggage longs for the Lord's love, grace, and healing.

Your heart may be crushed under the weight of unmet expectations. The cumulative effect of multiple wounds to your heart has led to a broken heart. You mask these deep hurts in hyperactivity. You work harder, but your heart needs to be softened by Jesus. A heavy heart yearns for healing to avoid angry outbursts and impatient attitudes. "A soft answer turns away wrath, But a harsh word stirs up anger" (Proverbs 15:1 NKJV).

God is our heart specialist. He has never lost anyone on His surgical table of love. To some degree we are all candidates for a divine coronary bypass of forgiveness and truth. Truth is medicinal. It is one of God's most potent drugs that He administers to a broken heart. He loves you and has a grace-filled plan for your life. He loves you right where you are. He loves who you are. Believe it, and let God begin healing your heart.

The truth is, as a follower of Christ, you are a child of the King. You can be grateful because as a believer, you come from the blue bloodline of King Jesus. Hold your head high, and walk with a bounce in your step because you matter to God. You are extremely valuable to your heavenly Father. Believe it, and allow Him to heal your heavy heart.

The truth is, we can forgive those who have deeply wounded us because Christ has forgiven us. We have the capacity to forgive dwelling within us in the person of the Holy Spirit. "The spirit is willing, but the body is weak" (Mark 14:38). So we forgive, especially when we do not have the energy to emotionally engage. We trust Him to heal.

The truth is, you can seek first the kingdom of God, and you do not have to clamor after the approval of people. Believe it, apply it, and let God begin healing your heart. He is your heart specialist. Invite Him to perform heart surgery today with the scalpels of truth and forgiveness. "You will know the truth, and the truth will set you free" (John 8:32).

What areas of my heart need the healing touch of my heavenly Father?

Related Readings: Proverbs 15:30; Isaiah 6:10; Isaiah 30:26; Matthew 9:22; Acts 9:34

TOO-FAMILIAR LEADERS

"Obey your leaders and submit to their authority. They keep watch over you as men who must give an account. Obey them so that their work will be a joy, not a burden, for that would be of no advantage to you." Hebrews 13:17

Leaders can become so familiar with their team that they dilute their effectiveness to lead. They are not one of the boys or one of the girls—they are the leader. Parents have to learn this. They are not the child or teenager's friend—they are first the dad or mom. Friendship can come later with adult children; in the meantime, they need leadership.

So how familiar are you to those you lead? Are you respectful of others so you invite their respect? Do you lift them up with commendation or tear them down with coarse kidding? Joking around on the job is not a pattern great leaders model. This may have been your behavior in the past, but in the present your role requires more maturity.

Does this mean leaders are not transparent about their weaknesses? No, because humble leaders are the first to confess their struggles and blind spots. But it does mean that wise leaders approach their God-given role with solemn responsibility and a serious resolve. People need leaders they can trust and look up to as the Lord's leaders for this season.

We do not want those we lead to pray as David did: "May his days be few; may another take his place of leadership" (Psalm 109:8). Followers want to be led by a wise leader.

Moreover, when we become too close to a team member, it creates jealousy, rivalry, and resentment. This happens with children. If we play favorites with a child, other siblings will notice and spew out their frustrations on the parent's pet. We can reward good behavior and praise obedience, but we should not overdo it by crossing the line of becoming too familiar.

Leadership can be lonely, but we are not alone as followers of Jesus. Wise leaders keep their emotions under the Spirit's control in the presence of their team, but in the presence of the Lord they bare their soul. You cannot become too familiar with your heavenly Father. He already knows more about you than you do. Pour out your frustrations and fears to Him, and He will listen, forgive, and lead you in the way you should go.

"My tears have been my food day and night, while men say to me all day long, 'Where is your God?' These things I remember as I pour out my soul: how I used to go with the multitude, leading the procession to the house of God, with shouts of joy and thanksgiving among the festive throng. Why are you downcast, O my soul? Why so disturbed within me? Put your hope in God, for I will yet praise him, my Savior and my God" (Psalm 42:3–5).

Do I look to the Lord to lead me? How can I lovingly lead with honesty and respect?

Related Readings: Exodus 18:13–16; Zechariah 12:5–6; John 12:42; Hebrews 13:7

PROSPERITY GOSPEL

"All these people were still living by faith when they died. They did not receive the things promised; they only saw them and welcomed them from a distance. And they admitted that they were aliens and strangers on earth." Hebrews 11:13

The promises of God are not all fulfilled on earth but have their grand expression in the eternal. He promises to take care of His children, but He does not promise to prosper them financially. The godliest, Christ-loving Christian may be the poorest of the poor or one who has been blessed materially. But the gospel of Jesus Christ is about giving, not getting. "For even the Son of Man did not come to be served, but to serve, and to give his life as a ransom for many" (Mark 10:45). Unfeigned faith looks out for the interests of others.

Preachers do parishioners a disservice when they equate faithfulness with financial gain. They especially do harm when they justify their opulent lifestyle with their obedience to God. How can we teach this when our Lord Jesus had nowhere to lay His head? The Holy Spirit grieves when the church becomes an ecclesiastical pyramid scheme instead of His house of prayer. Paul expressed clearly the proper motive of a pastor:

"Unlike so many, we do not peddle the word of God for profit. On the contrary, in Christ we speak before God with sincerity, like men sent from God" (2 Corinthians 2:17).

Furthermore, affluence can be an impediment to our intimacy with the Almighty. Stuff can get in the way of serving people. A cluttered life can compete with a simple life of service. Are we mentoring young men and women, or are we too busy making a living or traveling for fun? The gospel is meant to prosper people's lives, not their pocketbooks.

So what is the application of the gospel? The Lord calls us to get up from our lap of luxury and get down our knees in humble prayer. He expects us to willingly and joyfully give away our excess abundance. He asks us to rightly divide His truth—the promise of the riches of His grace and not the riches of wealth—to people. Jesus Christ's gospel is prosperous to set free all who believe from earthly expectations, replacing them with heavenly hope.

"Some faced jeers and flogging, while still others were chained and put in prison. They were stoned; they were sawed in two; they were put to death by the sword. They went about in sheepskins and goatskins, destitute, persecuted and mistreated—the world was not worthy of them. They wandered in deserts and mountains, and in caves and holes in the ground. These were all commended for their faith, yet none of them received what had been promised" (Hebrews 11:36–39).

Am I allowing the gospel to prosper my soul in service and generosity to others?

Related Readings: Luke 9:58; Luke 18:18–30; Luke 19:46; Acts 8:18–24; Revelation 3:14–22

GOD'S GIFTS

"Moreover, when God gives any man wealth and possessions, and enables him to enjoy them, to accept his lot and be happy in his work—this is a gift of God." Ecclesiastes 5:19

God gives multiple gifts over the course of a lifetime. Wealth, relationships, enjoyment of possessions, contentment in life, and fulfilling careers are significant gifts of God. No one can outgive God because generosity is one of His passions, and He has unlimited capacity. Not only does He give, but He also gives the ability to enjoy His blessings.

"Every good and perfect gift is from above, coming down from the Father of the heavenly lights, who does not change like shifting shadows" (James 1:17).

Access to money and possessions without the ability to enjoy them is meaningless. If wealth has you trapped in a perpetual maze of worry, then look to the gift giver. He did not give you possessions to obsess over. Fixation on money marginalizes faith. If you are unable to relax and enjoy money, God, and friends, then money may be your master.

We cannot enjoy what we cling to for ourselves. When money steals our peace of mind, it may have become an idol. It soon replaces Christ as our number one loyalty for attention and worship. Keep money in its proper place, or it will wear you out. It will wear you out in worry, and it will wear you out in trying to amass more. "Do not wear yourself out to get rich; have the wisdom to show restraint" (Proverbs 23:4).

Our work is another gift from God, and our ability to enjoy it is from Him. Even if we do not have to work, we need to work. Our Creator designed us for work. If you have no joy in your career and see no relief on the horizon, then make a move. God does not expect you to be miserable in your work. Toil for the Lord, and you will never lack purpose.

It is not so much the quantity of your wages as it is the quality of your work environment. It is a gift from God when you are privileged to work alongside people who value excellence, teamwork, innovation, results, faith, and family. Recognize often this gift from God, and thank Him. Are you "salt and light" for Christ at your work? Jesus said, "You are the salt of the earth.... You are the light of the world" (Matthew 5:13-14).

Do not wear your Christianity on your sleeve; instead, roll up your sleeves, and do excellent work. As you enjoy work, people will ask how you can be so joyful and content in all work environments. God's gifts glorify Him. "But in your hearts set apart Christ as Lord. Always be prepared to give an answer to everyone who asks you to give the reason for the hope that you have. But do this with gentleness and respect" (1 Peter 3:15).

Do I enjoy to the fullest God's gifts of wealth, work, and relationships?

Related Readings: 1 Chronicles 29:11–12; Ezra 1:5–7; Luke 11:13; 1 Corinthians 15:57

CHRISTIAN BRAND PROMISE

"A new command I give you: Love one another. As I have loved you, so you must love one another. By this all men will know that you are my disciples, if you love one another." John 13:34–35

What is the Christian brand promise? How do followers of Christ need to be remembered? Jesus spoke very clearly and compellingly when He said love identifies His disciples. It is not just any love, but a love that is born from above, a love that is covered with the Lord's fingerprints. Indeed, Christ's love expressed by Christians is irresistible.

He did not say we might love one another or we can love one another if we feel like loving. He most emphatically stated, "You must love one another." Just like the sun rises in the east and sets in the west, Christians have no choice but to love one another. Love the unlovely, love carnal Christians, and love infant and mature Christians alike.

It is love that is expressed in the laboratory of Christian community to which those outside the faith are attracted. So our salvation in Jesus places us on the stage of love with an audience of unbelievers looking on in wonder. What do they see? Do they see church members who fight or forgive? Do they see Christians who sacrifice for each other or who ignore each other? It is Christians who truly love who learn to honor others above themselves. "Be devoted to one another in brotherly love. Honor one another above yourselves" (Romans 12:10).

Where does this top-grade love reside? It is the work of the Holy Spirit in the human heart. Before our conversion to Christ, we were unable to love at the Lord's high level of expectation. But God's Spirit transforms the Christian's heart with regular doses of truth mixed with a humble heart to create a loving believer in Jesus. It is foundational that the first fruit of the Spirit is love. "But the fruit of the Spirit is love, joy, peace, patience" (Galatians 5:22). Spirit-filled followers of Christ naturally default to radical love.

Above all else, allow the Lord to love you compassionately and completely. It is out of your love relationship with Jesus that you have the capacity to love others unconditionally. An unloved soul is unable to love, but the overflow of a loved soul streams into the thirsty hearts of those it encounters. "Let the morning bring me word of your unfailing love, for I have put my trust in you. Show me the way I should go, for to you I lift up my soul" (Psalm 143:8). The lover of your soul empowers you to love large for the Lord.

The human heart longs to be loved, really loved. The world wants something to calm its fears, soothe its sorrow, and forgive its sins. As the chorus from the old hymn reminds us, "They'll know we are Christians by our love, by our love, yes, they'll know we are Christians by our love." The most effective evangelistic strategy is unconditional love.

Do others know I am a Christian by the love I have for other Christians?

Related Readings: Romans 13:8; Galatians 5:13; Ephesians 4:2; Hebrews 10:24

YOUTH DISCIPLESHIP

"Remember your Creator in the days of your youth, before the days of trouble come and the years approach when you will say, 'I find no pleasure in them.'" Ecclesiastes 12:1

The heart of a child, student, and young adult is impressionable. Like moist clay in the hands of an artist, it is pliable and moldable. This is the time to train and teach a youthful heart in the ways of Christ. It is on the solid foundation of the Lord's precepts and principles that life and death make sense. A young memory of God remembers God.

His hope is alive and everlasting for the young at heart. We need young people who are world changers, who believe they can make a difference. Those of us who have been around a while need to encourage their zeal for living and their optimism for engaging opportunities and people. Commission them to travel the globe while being undergirded by the Word of God. The Lord looks to the young of heart to ignite a revival of prayer.

Your opportunities as a young person are staggering. Your greatest leverage will come as you dive deep in your relationship with God and people. Channel your youthful energy and passion toward an intimate love relationship with your heavenly Father. Your earthly father may be distant or nonexistent, but not God. He is there for you twenty-four hours a day, seven days a week. He longs to walk with you through these days of multiple transitions, challenges, and growth.

Do not miss God. Your relationship with Him sets the pace for other relationships. If you want relational security, learn how from the lover of your soul—Jesus. If you want peace in your relationships, then become a student of the Prince of Peace. If you desire to better understand people, then hang out with their Creator who fully understands them. Youth is your asset, not your liability. Do not be ashamed, but be confident in Christ.

As an adult, you have tremendous influence on youth. It may be formal education, like paying tuition to a school that aligns with your values and beliefs. Maybe you can volunteer at church, educating the children and youth. Graduate beyond babysitting to instilling the truth of God at all levels of childhood and teenage development.

Disciple young people early on so they can be examples for Christ. Their spiritual growth will not happen by accident. Help them to understand "why" they believe "what" they believe. Move them way beyond sterile religion to a robust relationship with Jesus. If the young remember their Creator and follow His ways, everyone is successful. Therefore, remember your Creator, and lead the youth to do the same. God memories matter most.

"They remembered that God was their Rock, that God Most High was their Redeemer" (Psalm 78:35).

Do I often remember my Creator? In what young person can I invest the ways of God?

Related Readings: Proverbs 22:6; Isaiah 46:9; Ephesians 2:11–13; Titus 2:4

A PRUDENT WIFE

"Houses and wealth are inherited from parents, but a prudent wife is from the LORD."
Proverbs 19:14

A prudent wife is a gift from the Lord. Jesus is the perfect matchmaker who brings together husbands and wives who need each other. A wife assigned by the Almighty is a good thing that brings godly gain. "He who finds a wife finds what is good and receives favor from the LORD" (Proverbs 18:22). Wise is a husband who receives this gift from God and does not resist her unique qualities but invites her as a complement to his character.

She is a gift who reflects the glory of God in her attitude and actions. She is wise to watch out for her husband's well-being by advising him to only take Spirit-led risks. Her noble character is a reminder of Christ's blessing that comes from obeying His commands. "A wife of noble character is her husband's crown, but a disgraceful wife is like decay in his bones" (Proverbs 12:4). A husband is proud to present his faithful wife.

So where does a man look for a wife from the Lord? Start with a prayer: Heavenly Father, who is the woman you have for me and where do I find her? When we wait on a helpmate endorsed by heaven, we receive God's best. But if we rush into a relationship driven by selfish desires, we risk missing the right mate. Wisdom waits on God's choice.

Wisely you pray for a woman who has experienced a father and mother who love each other unconditionally—parents who are slow to speak harshly and quick to forgive. Look for a young lady whose dad has dated her and given her confidence and love. Growing up in a grace-filled family is a strong foundation for a new marriage secured by heaven.

A discerning wife has been trained in the wise ways of God. She had the benefit of being brought up in a God-fearing family who worshiped regularly at a Bible-teaching church. You take an unnecessary chance when you cling to a future wife who is away from the Lord. So seek out a wise woman who loves the Lord more than she loves you, who is your best friend, and who makes your heart flutter. A woman of faith is found in places of faith.

Receive the Lord's wife for you, and you receive His favor—favor in your work, in your emotional stamina, in your physical health, and in your spiritual well-being. Thank God for His gift of your wife. Let Christ reign and change you, and trust Him with her. Love and enjoy one other. "Enjoy life with your wife, whom you love" (Ecclesiastes 9:9).

Do I thank the Lord often for the gift of my wife and for His favor in and through her?

Related Readings: Genesis 24:12–27; Malachi 2:15; Acts 18:1–3; 2 Corinthians 6:14

A PRUDENT WIFE - PART TWO

"A wife of noble character who can find? She is worth far more than rubies."
Proverbs 31:10

Prayer is the most potent process for finding a prudent wife. God's choice for a lifetime mate in marriage is discerned by seeking His character qualities for a bride as He defines in Scripture. Like the businessman who sought out and discovered the finest of pearls, so is a faithful man who follows the Holy Spirit's lead in looking for a precious wife.

"Again, the kingdom of heaven is like a merchant looking for fine pearls. When he found one of great value, he went away and sold everything he had and bought it" (Matthew 13:45–46). One secret to success in life is selecting a woman of character as your wife.

So where do we look for the Lord's best to love in sickness and in health, for richer or for poorer? It may be a lady who was blessed to grow up in a God-fearing home, or it may be a woman of God who did not experience the joy of parents who knew Jesus. Because of her broken home, she became broken before the Lord and came to know Christ by faith. The genealogy of Jesus is defined by those like Tamar who learned to trust God in trials.

A woman of faith who looks to her heavenly Father to replace her absent earthly father is a wise choice for a wife. Her security and value come from Christ and His unconditional love and acceptance. She is emotionally whole because the Lord has healed her soul by His amazing grace. Look for a woman of deep faith among those who found Jesus in the fires of adversity. Her inner beauty of peace and gratitude is a trophy of God's grace.

"Your beauty should not come from outward adornment, such as braided hair and the wearing of gold jewelry and fine clothes. Instead, it should be that of your inner self, the unfading beauty of a gentle and quiet spirit, which is of great worth in God's sight" (1 Peter 3:3–4). The inner beauty of character makes the outward beauty most attractive.

Lastly, once the Lord has led you to the "one," be ever grateful of His gift to you of a godly wife. Do not take her for granted; instead, treat her like the daughter of King Jesus that she is. Love her more each day—show her and tell her. Listen to her tender heart for God, and welcome the words He speaks through her. Praise her in public, and confront her in private. Pray with her, and pray for her. Pursue her, protect her, and thank God for your wise wife. "Daughters of kings are among your honored women" (Psalm 45:9).

Do I trust the Lord with His choice of a wife for me? Do I value her like He does?

Related Readings: Genesis 12:18; 1 Samuel 19:11; Matthew 1:1–16; 1 Corinthians 7:11

A HUMBLE HUSBAND

"Husbands, in the same way be considerate as you live with your wives,
and treat them with respect as the weaker partner and as heirs with you of
the gracious gift of life, so that nothing will hinder your prayers." 1 Peter 3:7

A humble husband has a hungry heart for the Lord and seeks to follow Christ's commands. He submits to His Savior Jesus before he expects submission from his wife. A humble husband hears from God before He seeks to direct his family. It is from a position of humility that his prayers are not hindered; indeed, heaven hears and answers.

Furthermore, a husband who walks in humility is considerate and caring of his wife. He makes her feel special daily, especially on her birthday, wedding anniversary, and special days in between. Humility is respectful and loving, always watching for ways to honor God's gift—his wife. Love and respect are twin traits of humility that tower over pride.

A humble husband is quick to admit he does not know everything; thus, he values his wife's opinion and advice. Before a major decision, he leads his bride in prayer to their heavenly Father for His wisdom and direction. She is comforted knowing that he, as the spiritual leader of the home, is accountable to almighty God. Humility invites trust.

A humble husband sees Jesus as his model of humility that leads to obedience. "And being found in appearance as a man, he humbled himself and became obedient to death—even death on a cross!" (Philippians 2:8). Humility follows Jesus wherever He leads.

Powerful prayers flow from the heart of a humble husband. On his knees he engages the enemy on behalf of his family. He understands his responsibility in the home to represent God well. His attitude toward almighty God strongly influences his wife and children's attitude toward the Lord. He totally trusts the Lord and leads his family to do the same.

How is your heart? Is it haughty or humble under Christ's authority? Have you accepted your role as the spiritual leader of your home? If so, engage with your wife as joint heirs of God's gracious gift of life. Learn to love her like the Lord loves her. Admit your wrongs, ask her forgiveness, and serve her well—so your prayers will prosper for God's glory.

"The LORD said to me, 'Go, show your love to your wife again.... Love her as the LORD loves'" (Hosea 3:1).

Do I humble myself daily before the Lord and my wife? Does she normally feel love and respect from me?

Related Readings: Genesis 24:67; Deuteronomy 8:3, 16; Luke 18:14; Colossians 3:19

TOTAL TRUST

"'Surely God is my salvation; I will trust and not be afraid. The LORD, the LORD is my strength and my song; he has become my salvation.' With joy you will draw water from the wells of salvation."
Isaiah 12:2–3

Total trust in God means total confidence in Christ's character, which is available to every faithful follower of Jesus. Total trust means we give up total control. It is a wise trade that reaps radical results. Christ's control replaces fear with peace. We do not have to figure it all out; instead, we trust God. We are not capable of knowing all, but we do have capacity to totally trust Him. Do I utterly trust Him with everything? "Trust in the LORD with all your heart and lean not on your own understanding" (Proverbs 3:5).

If Christ is who He claimed to be—He can be trusted. Jesus said, "Anyone who has seen me has seen the Father" (John 14:9). If we can trust Him with the eternal salvation of our soul, we can trust Him with the temporal control of our life. If we can trust Him with the big things like faith in Jesus, we can trust Him with the small things like fear of man.

If He leads you to a new career, He will give you the wisdom, finances, and relationships to be successful. If He leads you to be a missionary, He will build bridges across the cultural barriers to allow you to serve and love the people. If He leads you to have children, He will provide the needed resources to be successful parents.

Wherever God leads, He provides. What God initiates, He completes. His part is provision, and our part is trust. Do not fall into the trap of trusting Him with some things and not trusting Him with others. Distrust in God is distasteful. It is an insult to His integrity. How can God not be big enough to handle any situation? Health issues, war, teenagers, money, conflict, prosperity, relationships, and uncertainty can all be placed into God's hands—not to be taken back. Total trust means we leave it in the Lord's care.

God can be trusted because He is trustworthy. The waters of His salvation bubble up from an infinitely deep well so our thirsty souls can always drink and be satisfied. Without the support of a sympathetic Jesus, you will be immobilized—even crushed—under the weight of worry, but Jesus is there to outsource your anxiety. Be with Him.

"Come to me, all you who are weary and burdened, and I will give you rest. Take my yoke upon you and learn from me, for I am gentle and humble in heart, and you will find rest for your souls. For my yoke is easy and my burden is light" (Matthew 11:28–30).

Trust in Christ means to prayerfully walk with Him in your choices. Slow down, look up, trust Him, and watch Him create extraordinary results. Partial trust leads to frustration and worry, but total trust leads to contentment and calm. Joy occupies fully trusting the Lord. Your soul sings in thanksgiving, and an inner peace from Jesus strengthens your faith.

Jesus said, "Peace I leave with you; my peace I give you. I do not give to you as the world gives. Do not let your hearts be troubled and do not be afraid" (John 14:27).

Do I trust Christ only when it is convenient, or do I totally trust Him at all times?

Related Readings: Exodus 14:31; 2 Samuel 7:28; Acts 14:23; Revelation 22:6

PERSONAL SAVIOR

"The LORD is my shepherd, I shall not be in want."
Psalm 23:1

In a similar way, Jesus Christ shepherds the souls of His sheep. The Lord is large and in charge, but He also knows the names and feels the emotions of His followers. He is the Great Shepherd, but He is also the Good Shepherd. He rules the world, but He also rules over individual hearts. The Lord personally shepherds saved souls with patient love.

"'You my sheep, the sheep of my pasture, are people, and I am your God,' declares the Sovereign LORD" (Ezekiel 34:31). He knows His sheep, and His sheep know Him.

Is the Lord my Shepherd? By faith, have I entered into a personal relationship with my God? Or am I a lone sheep who has wandered from the flock of faith? If He is not your Shepherd, or if you have drifted away, your Savior Jesus is waiting to bring you into the fold of His faithfulness. Let the Lord lift you onto His secure shoulders and carry you into His caring community. To survive, sheep need each other and a trustworthy shepherd.

"We all, like sheep, have gone astray, each of us has turned to his own way; and the LORD has laid on him the iniquity of us all" (Isaiah 53:6). Jesus saves us from sin.

There are no healthy desires your Shepherd does not fulfill. Do you need forgiveness? He forgives you. Do you long for love? He loves you. Do you wish not to worry? He gives you peace. Are you afraid? He protects you. Are you confused? He clarifies with godly counsel and His Holy Word, the Bible. Are you alone? He walks with you forever.

"I am the good shepherd; I know my sheep and my sheep know me—just as the Father knows me and I know the Father—and I lay down my life for the sheep" (John 10:14–15).

Therefore, listen intently to the voice of your sensitive Shepherd Jesus. He longs to lead you along His providential path. There will be tests and unknowns along the way, but fear only God and rest in His reassuring presence. He will lead you to His best, to the destination He has determined for you. Follow your Shepherd and personal Savior Jesus.

"Jesus answered, 'I did tell you, but you do not believe. The miracles I do in my Father's name speak for me, but you do not believe because you are not my sheep. My sheep listen to my voice; I know them, and they follow me'" (John 10:25–27).

Is Jesus my personal Savior? Do I trust and follow Him as the Shepherd over my life?

Related Readings: Psalm 100:3; Ezekiel 34:11–15; Romans 8:35–37; 1 Peter 2:25

SPIRITUAL RESOURCES

"A shoot will come up from the stump of Jesse; from his roots a Branch will bear fruit.
The Spirit of the LORD will rest on him—the Spirit of wisdom and of understanding,
the Spirit of counsel and of power, the Spirit of knowledge and of the fear of the LORD—
and he will delight in the fear of the LORD." Isaiah 11:1–3

God provides spiritual resources for His children. All we need is in Christ. The same Spirit of the Lord that indwelled and empowered Jesus is the One who does the same for His followers. The Son of God indwells us by faith. The Spirit of God rests on us and in us. The Holy Spirit provides all the spiritual resources needed to carry out His will.

You need wisdom; He provides good judgment. You need understanding; He provides discernment. You need counsel; He provides advice. You need power; He provides strength. You need knowledge; He provides information. You need the fear of God; He provides holy awe. However, resources without reception are without results.

I can offer to take my daughter shopping, but if she chooses to attend a movie with her friend instead, she will miss her daddy buying her some cute clothes. It is a moment in time that God offers you His resources. Do not be so wrapped up in your plan that you miss His provision. Every day the resources you need are a prayer away.

Wisdom, understanding, and His godly counsel are all there for the asking. The same Spirit of God who indwelled and empowered Jesus does the same for you. The Holy Spirit is at your side to convict, comfort, and guide. "But the Counselor, the Holy Spirit, whom the Father will send in my name, will teach you all things and will remind you of everything I have said to you" (John 14:26). Thus, solicit the Spirit to lead you.

Jesus is our friend and Savior. God is our father and Lord. The Spirit is our guide and counselor. The Holy Spirit will guide you in truth and righteousness. You cannot see the Spirit of God, but you can experience His affects. The Spirit puts a check in your spirit to protect you from an unwise choice. The Spirit empowers your spirit to faith and courage. Allow the Holy Spirit to congeal with your spirit.

This is where unremarkable religion can become a rejuvenated relationship. If your relationship with God is in a rut, then let the Holy Spirit fall fresh on your life. Start by allowing the fruit of the Spirit to mold your character. Be accountable to fruit inspectors in your life. Let these honest, more mature friends help you purge fruitless attitudes and actions. Prune the bad to make room for the good. Unpack and use the Spirit's gifts.

God has gifted you uniquely. Allow His gifts to develop and come to full fruition. If you are gifted to teach, teach. If you are gifted to write, write. If you are gifted to mentor, mentor. If you are gifted to give, give. By faith, allow the Spirit to develop your character and competence into bushels of fruit.

Do I daily invite the fullness of the Spirit to fill me with faith, hope, and love?

Related Readings: Genesis 41:38; Exodus 35:31; Galatians 5:16–26; 1 John 4:2–3

BOLD GOING

"Then I heard the voice of the Lord saying, 'Whom shall I send?
And who will go for us?' And I said, 'Here am I. Send me!'" Isaiah 6:8

Bold going responds to God's invitation to join Him in going to unlikely places. These are countries that need the love of Christ—where people smell different, look different, talk different, and act different. But they all have the same need for a Savior. Their hearts are hungry for God. Some do not even realize why their thirsty soul longs for heaven.

They are waiting for someone to tell them the truth about Jesus. These cross-cultural encounters are not always romantic or noble. Sometimes they are hard and grueling. It becomes difficult when our body rejects the foreign food and water. However, a little bit of discomfort is well worth the salvation of souls who are lost.

Your position as a follower of Jesus Christ is availability. Be available to the world on behalf of God. With ninety-five percent of the globe's population outside the borders of America, how can we only share the gospel here? When Jesus instructs us to make disciples, we have to engage with the world. It may be a short-term or long-term mission trip overseas. Either way, join God in this great adventure. Do not be afraid to travel. Trust the Lord!

Yes, give money to missions, but this is just a start. Move way beyond your money to showing up on the ground with the Holy Spirit in your heart and the Word of God on your breath. Show up to serve. Show up to learn. Show up to give. Find those who are teachable, and teach them the Word of God. Find those who want to lead, and train them to be servant leaders. Seek out the gifted evangelists, and help them evangelize.

Build buildings, create jobs, birth businesses, start ministries, feed the hungry, clothe the orphans, and love the widows. Do whatever it takes to bridge the cultural gap to Christ. Just be available. Do not feel like you have to have all the answers. Do not be fearful of the unknown or of illness. This is God's opportunity to grow your faith, love, and joy.

Your investment will make you a much better husband, wife, employer, employee, and Christian. Your theology becomes more balanced and robust. You discover that some of your beliefs have become westernized and unbiblical. You have inadvertently limited God because of your own cultural restraints and conceit.

God wants you to partner with Him to unleash your faith and the faith of others. Let Him send you to a nation temporarily or for a lifetime of relational investment. Do not be shy, but be brave in the power of the Holy Spirit. Partner with God, and watch Him work. Believe and go boldly! Jesus said, "Go and make disciples of all nations" (Matthew 28:19).

Am I willing to get out of my cultural comfort zone for Christ and a lost world?

Related Readings: Jonah 1:1–17; Acts 10:1–48; Acts 13:1–52; Revelation 5:9

FORCED REST

"He makes me lie down in green pastures, he leads me beside quiet waters."
Psalm 23:2

Sometimes the Lord makes His children create margin in their life. He understands that a life without real rest can become graceless and grumpy. It may be physical illness, emotional overload, spiritual fatigue, or ruptured relationships that begin to scream for attention. The flesh thinks it can continue with little or no rest, but the spirit knows better.

We may work through our fatigue and fake it for a while, but eventually we hit an unscalable wall without anything to give anymore. Jesus knows we are extra vulnerable during these tired times, and He makes a way of retreat and rest. His gentle and loving care calls us to come away with Him. It is much better to heed His invitation for intimacy than to move down the road without Him. Resting in the Lord invigorates and inspires.

Does rest have to be mandated by our Master, or can it be done willfully? A wise man or woman understands the need for rhythms of rest in his or her schedule. This is why a good night's sleep and occasional naps are necessary. Weekends, especially Sundays, are made for rest, reflection, and rejuvenation. If we are intoxicated by activity, we run the risk of living in a restless hangover. Real rest allows us to recover and unwind in His presence.

Like green pastures are pleasant and fulfilling for any animal dependent on the earth, so God's heavenly resources feed our soul, fill our mind, and hydrate our heart. Are you tired and overwhelmed? Do you feel alone and deplete of any energy to engage with others? If so, take the time to get away with God. Say no to the unnecessary and yes to the necessary. The most productive life accomplishes more by doing less. It rests in Him.

Most importantly, allow the Lord to lead you by faith into a quiet place. Sit by the soothing silence of still waters, and drink in the majesty of God's creation. You know Jesus is leading you when you intentionally engage in solitude for the purpose of hearing His voice. Lie on His green grass, and look up so your gaze is on God. Do not resist His required rest. Instead, cease and desist activity, embrace and celebrate His rest.

"When I consider your heavens, the work of your fingers, the moon and the stars, which you have set in place, what is man that you are mindful of him, the son of man that you care for him?" (Psalm 8:3–4). The grandeur of God's glory comes down to care for you.

Do I voluntarily engage with eternity in quiet places? Does my life rhythm require rest?

Related Readings: Exodus 31:13; 2 Samuel 22:33–34; Zechariah 10:1; Romans 9:11

RESTORATION AND GUIDANCE

"He restores my soul. He guides me in paths of righteousness for his name's sake."
Psalm 23:3

Restoration and guidance come from the righteous One, Jesus Christ. Sin stains a soul like time tarnishes an old piece of furniture. But the Lord's grace and forgiveness restore a soiled soul to its intended image of God. A Christian occasionally needs a renewal of faith, hope, and love. There is a deep longing in us to be the children He purposed us to be. "Then God said, 'Let us make man in our image, in our likeness'" (Genesis 1:26).

A saved soul is meant to sit at the feet of its Savior Jesus and be revived with a radical faith. It is when our belief becomes stale and moldy with mediocrity that we miss making a difference in the lives of the lost. Christ is the Bread of Life; so He expects no less of an appetizing life from His children. Is my life enticing, or does my soul need realignment?

"But thanks be to God, who always leads us in triumphal procession in Christ and through us spreads everywhere the fragrance of the knowledge of him. For we are to God the aroma of Christ among those who are being saved and those who are perishing" (2 Corinthians 2:14–15). A restored soul is attractive and inviting to those with whom it connects.

Furthermore, our loving Shepherd Jesus guides us on the right path of His purposes. He does not harshly drive us like cattle; rather, He lovingly leads us like sheep. Curiosity or ignorance can cause us to miss the way, but Jesus is the Way. So when His long and sensitive staff seeks to pull us back on the path, we are wise to follow His lead.

Guidance from God is a necessity for us to know we are doing His will. Building His kingdom, not our kingdom, is the real issue. If I pray, "Your kingdom come," but focus on building my kingdom, then I need to surrender to my King Jesus. Thus, is your business or family about building His kingdom, or is it an idol that represents your kingdom?

It is for His name's sake that you are a husband, wife, parent, child, leader, and friend. In Christ you are His namesake; therefore, you are motivated to love and serve in His name. Living for the Lord means you make choices, like modifying your lifestyle, so you can better promote Him. Perhaps you replace a vacation with a mission trip so you can proclaim His name. Or maybe you simply serve a neighbor in Jesus' name. "Since you are my rock and my fortress, for the sake of your name lead and guide me" (Psalm 31:3).

Has my soul been fully restored by my righteous God? Do I serve for His name's sake?

Related Readings: Psalm 85:6; Isaiah 38:16; Romans 12:12; Colossians 3:10

SHADOW OF DEATH

"Even though I walk through the valley of the shadow of death, I will fear no evil, for you are with me; your rod and your staff, they comfort me." Psalm 23:4

Everyone walks through life in the long shadow of death. There is no place on the globe it can be avoided and no physical condition that can escape. Death constantly knocks on the door of all demographics, all cultures, and all classes of people. There are those who try to delay death's effects with surgery, medicine, diet, and exercise, but all eventually die.

Death for the dying can be a shadow of discomfort, discouragement, and even despair. It is in death's valley that faith is tested, families are stressed, and friends rally in prayer. How do you serve those who are in their last months or days on earth? First you live before them a life of faith. Dying loved ones need love from those who know the Lord so they can come to know the Lord. Life in a valley needs care, comfort, and heaven's hope.

Like Saul and Jonathan, allow death to bring you together as a family. "Saul and Jonathan—in life they were loved and gracious, and in death they were not parted" (2 Samuel 1:23). Death is God's reminder that we need Him and each other.

We all walk toward death, but in Christ it is a passage to eternal life. It is hard when believing parents begin to lose their ability to think clearly, but we patiently listen to their irrational words, knowing one day they will speak with tongues of angels. It is even harder when unbelieving parents begin to lose their faculties because we wonder if they truly know Jesus. So we pray and trust that the reality of death brings them to the Lord.

"'Where, O death, is your victory? Where, O death, is your sting?' The sting of death is sin, and the power of sin is the law. But thanks be to God! He gives us the victory through our Lord Jesus Christ" (1 Corinthians 15:55–57).

Our faith in Jesus triumphs over death and comforts us on the way to death. The destination of this life is death, but when traveled with the Lord, there is no need to fear evil or the unknown. His presence is all we need to persevere in righteous living. Hope, peace, and love are the outflow of walking with Jesus through the lonely valley of death.

Because of the passion of Christ, death's shadow is a pass to paradise. The cross is a comfort to the dying, and it is a bridge to heaven for those who believe in Jesus' death for their sin and His resurrection for their abundant life on earth and their eternal life in heaven. Jesus assured His disciples at His death, "Now is your time of grief, but I will see you again and you will rejoice, and no one will take away your joy" (John 16:22).

Am I walking with Jesus in my valleys? Whom can I walk with through their valleys?

Related Readings: Psalm 56:13; Proverbs 14:27; Isaiah 38:10; John 5:24; Romans 8:38

PEACEFUL TRUST

"You will keep in perfect peace him whose mind is steadfast, because he trusts in you. Trust in the LORD forever, for the LORD, the LORD, is the Rock eternal." Isaiah 26:3–4

Peace and trust are best friends. Normally we do not see one without the other. Where peace resides, trust is close by, and where trust abounds, there is peace. Their goal is to stamp out fear and doubt.

Our mind can cause us to well up with courage because our focus is on God. Or our mind can cause us to wilt in the face of adversity because our focus is on our circumstances. Peace melts away in the heat of distrust, and trust shudders in the face of fear. So as we trust the Lord, He gives us peace that passes all understanding. Trust leads to peace.

"And the peace of God, which transcends all understanding, will guard your hearts and your minds in Christ Jesus" (Philippians 4:7).

Thus, fill your mind with the truth of God, and let it lodge in your conscience. Truth releases peace and trust when you are pressured. Your mind is a school for study; so make sure your faculty members flow from the character of God. If you are preoccupied with the faulty teachers of fear and pride, you will wallow in the energy of worry. What you think about Christ's capabilities determines your level of peace and trust.

Your thoughts, perceptions, emotions, will, memory, and imagination are all wrapped up in your human consciousness called the mind. This is why your mind is like the rudder of your life. Wherever your mind takes you, your behavior will follow. "For as he thinks in his heart, so is he" (Proverbs 23:7 NKJV). If thoughts take you toward the rocks of fear, you will act fearful. If they take you toward the shore of peace, you will act calm.

But a mind latched onto the Lord trusts Him when circumstances beg for you to cower in fear. Thus, keep your perspective on the horizon of heaven. Like a ship surging through the open sea, you have the wind of the Holy Spirit moving you forward, with the compass of truth leading you toward the ultimate destination of God's will.

Make peace and trust a staple of your spiritual diet, as they nourish your soul like food and water invigorates your body. Like a security detail, they will escort you through good and bad times. They will protect you from lashing out in anger when you have been deeply hurt. A steadfast mind is one that stays focused on Jesus and His expectations.

Cultivate your brain for more creative ways to apply His peace and trust. Do not analyze God out of the equation; rather, draw Him into your conclusions. A steadfast mind on the Lord will erupt like a volcano in perfect peace. Trust Him today, and enjoy the lava of His hot love and warm embrace. A peaceful trust comes from our perfect God!

Jesus said, "I have told you these things, so that in me you may have peace. In this world you will have trouble. But take heart! I have overcome the world" (John 16:33).

Do I embrace the peace of Jesus daily? Does my thinking default to peace and trust?

Related Readings: Job 22:21; Psalm 85:8; Isaiah 52:7; Luke 2:14; Romans 16:20

GOD'S PREPARATIONS

"You prepare a table before me in the presence of my enemies.
You anoint my head with oil; my cup overflows." Psalm 23:5

The Lord is a bountiful benefactor to all who believe. Christ consistently looks ahead and anticipates the needs of those who love Him. Are you in need of education? He is aligning the necessary resources. Are you praying for a husband or wife? He is orchestrating relationships. Are you seeking a career transition? He is preparing the way.

Like a seasoned chef, the Lord prepares a table of provision that is customized to our circumstances. His appetizers, entrees, sides, and desserts are all beautiful to behold. The spread from our Savior provides a variety of spiritual and physical nourishment; so when we leave the Lord's Table of provision, we are full and content. He provides opportunities.

There are naysayers who are enemies of faith-filled living. They have to explain the unexplainable and take personal credit for any results they experience. But it is in the presence of unbelievers that the Lord can make believers. How do you define a life that lives for the Lord and in service to others? God's preparation produces faith followers.

"If anyone serves, he should do it with the strength God provides, so that in all things God may be praised through Jesus Christ. To him be the glory and the power for ever and ever. Amen" (1 Peter 4:11).

The expectations of others can fall short, but the Lord never disappoints. His preparations and provisions are thorough and thought through. He anoints us with love and respect, and our cup of joy runs over in gratitude to our great God. In the presence of Jesus there is no prejudice, just provision. Thus, bow in worship, and receive His beautiful blessings.

Jesus said to Simon, "'You did not put oil on my head, but she has poured perfume on my feet. Therefore, I tell you, her many sins have been forgiven—for she loved much. But he who has been forgiven little loves little.' Then Jesus said to her, 'Your sins are forgiven'" (Luke 7:46–48).

The Lord's last preparation for His people is the marriage supper of the Lamb. This grand and glorious celebration is for all who have embraced Christ as their Savior and Lord. Have you opened your invitation from Jesus for forgiveness and grace, intimacy and provision? Have you by faith sent your confirmation to this gala with God? He has prepared the way for those He loves; so follow by faith, and enjoy the journey with Jesus.

"Then the angel said to me, 'Write: "Blessed are those who are invited to the wedding supper of the Lamb!"' And he added, 'These are the true words of God'" (Revelation 19:9).

Am I pleased with the Lord's preparations for my life? Am I prepared to meet Him?

Related Readings: Psalm 68:10; Jonah 4:6–8; 1 Corinthians 10:13; 1 Timothy 6:17

AUTHOR OF CHANGE

"Forget the former things; do not dwell on the past. See, I am doing a new thing!
Now it springs up; do you not perceive it? I am making a way in the desert
and streams in the wasteland." Isaiah 43:18–19

God is the original change agent. The past is past, as He is interested in new things. New relationships, new life, new endeavors, new learning, new languages, new cultures, new methods, new character, and new ways of doing things are on the heart of God. He never changes, but what He does transforms. "I the LORD do not change" (Malachi 3:6).

His Spirit is on the move, initiating all the time. His work is never totally complete. God is a master at taking nothing and making something. He can take raw talent and craft it into a Christ-honoring home or career. The grim times of yesterday He replaces with the potential of today. Do not be afraid to start over with our God of second chances.

He can take your desert experience and build beautiful aqueducts of grace. He wants to do a new work in your life. He wants you to change. Christ is your change agent. The old habits of anger and unforgiveness can and will be changed by the work of the Holy Spirit in you. A surrendered life is always under the influence of righteous transformation.

"And we, who with unveiled faces all reflect the Lord's glory, are being transformed into his likeness with ever-increasing glory, which comes from the Lord, who is the Spirit" (2 Corinthians 3:18).

God is the father of change, but He wants to use you as a change agent as well. You can become God's representative for change—a revolutionary for righteousness. There are new things that need to happen in your family, work, and church. You have been a spectator long enough. It is time you engaged as a participant. You have properly prepared; now others look to you for leadership. Prayerfully make wise changes.

You will lead your family through this valley. Your response to adversity will be their response to adversity. If you are calm and trusting, then they will be calm and trusting. If you embrace change, then they will embrace change. Change can shake the members of your family out of their complacency and move them forward in Christ. Embrace and celebrate change.

You may be the change agent for your church. The church needs to change from irrelevant methods to ones that captivate the culture. And lastly, your work needs an extreme makeover. It is through your humble influence that change is taking place. Submit to Christ's changes in your life so you can be His change agent in the culture.

"But now, by dying to what once bound us, we have been released from the law so that we serve in the new way of the Spirit, and not in the old way of the written code" (Romans 7:6).

Am I allowing my unchanging Savior Jesus to change me? Am I a catalyst for change?

Related Readings: 1 Samuel 10:9; Psalm 55:19; 1 Corinthians 11:25; Hebrews 10:20

FOREVER WITH GOD

"Surely goodness and love will follow me all the days of my life,
and I will dwell in the house of the LORD forever." Psalm 23:6

Faith in Jesus is a forever engagement with eternity. His dwelling—which is not made with human hands—invites us into intimacy and eternal security. It is reassuring beyond earthly inconsistencies to know that once we place our faith in Jesus, we are always with Jesus. We enjoy His goodness and love now and forevermore in heaven.

"Now we know that if the earthly tent we live in is destroyed, we have a building from God, an eternal house in heaven, not built by human hands" (2 Corinthians 5:1).

But to dwell in the Lord's house is not a life of ease and self-focus. It is just the opposite. It is an opportunity to follow the directives and fulfill interests for the Master of the house. We dwell with the Lord, to serve the Lord, for the Lord's glory. Just as the owner of the house left strict instructions to his managers left behind, so we are to boldly obey Jesus.

Jesus described serving in His kingdom: "Again, it will be like a man going on a journey, who called his servants and entrusted his property to them" (Matthew 25:14).

There is a reoccurring blessing of goodness and love that follows those who dwell well in the Lord's presence. Instead of bitterness and resentment nipping at our heels, God's goodness and love are our righteous rearguard. Bitterness is a poison we drink, thinking it will kill another, but when we drink forgiveness, it gives life to everyone. Goodness and love are an annuity from almighty God waiting for us to receive and apply liberally.

"But you, O Sovereign LORD, deal well with me for your name's sake; out of the goodness of your love, deliver me. For I am poor and needy, and my heart is wounded within me" (Psalm 109:21–22). He heals us so we can administer healing on His behalf.

Above all, your Savior and Lord Jesus Christ is in preparation for your eternal dwelling place. No house on earth (ever how grand it may be) can come close to comparing with your righteous residence in heaven. Its architect is almighty God, its designer is divine, and it is engineered for eternity. It is better to be in a shack with Jesus than a mansion without Him. By faith in Jesus, you are with Jesus now and forevermore. Amen.

Jesus said, "Do not let your hearts be troubled. Trust in God; trust also in me. In my Father's house are many rooms; if it were not so, I would have told you. I am going there to prepare a place for you. And if I go and prepare a place for you, I will come back and take you to be with me that you also may be where I am. You know the way to the place where I am going" (John 14:1–4).

Do I dwell well in the presence of Jesus? Do I receive and give His goodness and love?

Related Readings: Exodus 29:46; 1 Kings 8:12–49; Psalm 15:1–5; Revelation 21:3

RESPONSIBLE CHRISTIAN CITIZENS

"Then the commander said, 'I had to pay a big price for my citizenship.' 'But I was born a citizen,'
Paul replied. Those who were about to question him withdrew immediately. The commander
himself was alarmed when he realized that he had put Paul, a Roman citizen, in chains."
Acts 22:28–29

Citizenship in a free country means something, especially for Christian citizens. Citizens who are followers of Christ have a platform to live out the teachings of Jesus. A responsible Christian citizen modestly models his values and principles that are based on the Bible. Beliefs lived out are truly beliefs, while those unapplied are not real beliefs.

"You were taught, with regard to your former way of life, to put off your old self, which is being corrupted by its deceitful desires; to be made new in the attitude of your minds; and to put on the new self, created to be like God in true righteousness and holiness" (Ephesians 4:22–24).

This applies to our political beliefs as Christian citizens. We can endorse an independent political party, but we are not autonomous from the Almighty's influence. Paul was persecuted for his faith, but he still spoke the truth with humble boldness. If we say we believe in the sanctity of life, then we elect congressmen or women who do the same.

If we say we believe in a government that spends less and balances a budget, then we elect leaders who will make hard choices and implement fiscally conservative changes. If we say we believe in free enterprise, then we elect statesmen and women who support the system, even if it requires businesses to fail. Responsible Christian citizens care more.

Because our citizenship is in heaven, we always keep an eye on eternity's expectations while we deal with earthly issues. It is not creating an entitlement-motivated government that becomes the savior of the masses. On the contrary, it is a political system that ensures the freedoms and liberties of its citizens are not threatened and removed. A diverse people can only be truly unified around common values and principles espoused by God.

"For through him [Jesus] we both have access to the Father by one Spirit. Consequently, you are no longer foreigners and aliens, but fellow citizens with God's people and members of God's household, built on the foundation of the apostles and prophets, with Christ Jesus himself as the chief cornerstone" (Ephesians 2:18–20).

Am I a responsible Christian citizen who expresses my convictions at the voting booth?

Related Readings: Ecclesiastes 9:14–16; Acts 23:1–11; Ephesians 2:11–13; Titus 3:1

STEWARDS OF GRACE

"For this reason I, Paul, the prisoner of Christ Jesus for the sake of you Gentiles—Surely you have heard about the administration of God's grace that was given to me for you." Ephesians 3:1–2

Stewards of God's grace have unlimited resources to manage on behalf of their Master Jesus Christ. Like Paul and Stephen, when full of grace we are in a better position to allocate its riches. God gives His children grace to dispense to needy hearts. Jew or Gentile, believer or unbeliever, agitator or encourager—all need God's matchless grace.

"Now Stephen, a man full of God's grace and power, performed great wonders and signs among the people" (Acts 6:8). Indeed, the grace of God is evidence for the works of God.

Grace stewards give grace, especially to those who are the most different. Diverse cultures, races, religions, opinions, and giftedness are great candidates for grace. How do you handle someone who challenges your ideas? Do you listen with grace or react with a proud defense? Grace is slow to speak, quick to listen, and responds in the Spirit's power. Mercy withholds punishment; grace does the same and extends favor. It is proactive.

"Our conscience testifies that we have conducted ourselves in the world, and especially in our relations with you, with integrity and godly sincerity. We have done so, relying not on worldly wisdom but on God's grace" (2 Corinthians 1:12).

So we ask, "What is our capacity for Christ's grace?" The larger our grace quotient, the more gracious we become. Like knowledge expands the mind and food the stomach, so grace enlarges our soul's capacity for the Lord. The more He has of us, the more we want of Him. Faithful stewards of God's grace use its influence in service to others.

"Each of you should use whatever gift you have received to serve others, as faithful stewards of God's grace in its various forms" (1 Peter 4:10).

It is out of the overflow of grace-based living that we are able to seek out and serve the ungracious on behalf of Jesus. The grace of God goes where no man can go. It heals the heart of a hurting friend. It softens the heart of an angry parent. It warms the heart of a distant boss. Grace extended never disappoints. It melts fear, calms concerns, and receives sinners back. Steward well the grace of God, and watch Him work wonders.

"The grace of the Lord Jesus be with God's people. Amen" (Revelation 22:21).

Do I prayerfully steward God's grace toward all people? Am I a gracious Jesus follower?

Related Readings: Romans 5:15; 2 Corinthians 6:1; Philippians 1:7; Colossians 1:3–7

ETERNAL ENERGY

"Even youths grow tired and weary, and young men stumble and fall; but those
who hope in the LORD will renew their strength. They will soar on wings like eagles;
they will run and not grow weary, they will walk and not be faint." Isaiah 40:30–31

There is a good weary. We can be weary in the Lord's work and not be weary of the Lord's work. Sleep is sweet knowing we have exhausted our efforts toward the will of God. Trust and hope in the Lord send us into a real rest. We grow weary, but our fatigue is bolstered by faith. Our smile may be faint, but our heart is full of God's grace.

In contrast, there is an unhealthy type of weariness that strives in the power of the flesh. It is the result of misguided motives. Perhaps we become driven by the fear of people. We are preoccupied with not wanting to let someone down. Our fear of people transcends our fear of God. We default into performance-based living. It saps our energy and leaves us feeling depleted. Worry is wearisome, and fear is fatiguing. "The mind governed by the flesh is death, but the mind governed by the Spirit is life and peace" (Romans 8:6).

Indeed, the Lord is your hope and strength. Even as you experience accomplishments, you can quickly lose faith because you have not cultivated a hopeful heart. It is present practitioners of hope who can extend hope to other fainthearted souls. "Hope deferred makes the heart sick, but a longing fulfilled is a tree of life" (Proverbs 13:12).

An eagle soars somewhat effortlessly. He cannot create or direct wind, but he greatly benefits from its silent effect. He is hopeful that the wind will blow again tomorrow. But if it is boisterous or too mild, he may wait in his nest, positioned in the cleft of the rock. He experiences rest and renewal while he anticipates the energizing power of the unseen wind. In the same way, the Holy Spirit lifts those who wait to be empowered by Him.

You can run God's race with patient endurance, but it comes through the process of hope and renewal. Hope in God expands your capacity. You can run harder and farther in the renewed strength of the Holy Spirit. This is eternal energy that comes from God. Hope in the Lord renews your strength in your weariness. Thus, rest in God. Let the wings of your faith carry you as you wait on the wind of the Holy Spirit to empower you.

"The wind blows wherever it pleases. You hear its sound, but you cannot tell where it comes from or where it is going. So it is with everyone born of the Spirit" (John 3:8).

Does hope in the Lord renew my strength? Do I engage with eternity's energy?

Related Readings: 1 Samuel 30:6; Psalm 42:5; Micah 7:7; Romans 5:5; Galatians 3:3

COMFORT AND JOY

"Shout for joy, O heavens; rejoice, O earth; burst into song, O mountains!
For the LORD comforts his people and will have compassion on his afflicted ones."
Isaiah 49:13

God is aware of our suffering, and He wants His children to discover relief in Him. Our affliction may be self-inflicted or from outside sources. Regardless, His compassion is more than empathy. It is active and far-reaching. No matter how deep and severe our wounds, He cares. He comforts the afflicted and afflicts those who are too comfortable.

He understands your hurt. He understands your rejection. He understands your humiliation. He understands your fears. Jesus walked through the hurt of humanity on His way to the hallelujahs of heaven. He will never leave you or forsake you. It is for you and others that He lived and died. His mercies, love, and grace are new every morning. "Because of the LORD's great love we are not consumed, for his compassions never fail. They are new every morning; great is your faithfulness" (Lamentations 3:22–23).

Christ is a catalyst for community as He invites you to join Him and His church. The compassion of Christ and others is a healing balm; so seek out the comfort and compassion of God's people. The body of Christ is there to administer healing and support. A wounded body part will eventually die if left unattended, but will recover and thrive with the support of other members. Christians are interdependent on one another.

Pride resists receiving help, but humility seeks help. Pride and humility cannot coexist. Pride says, "I can buck up and go this alone." Humility says, "Alone I will fail, but with others I will succeed." Our perception becomes skewed under the onslaught of affliction. We lose sight of the spiritual battle that is raging. Humility battles on its knees in prayer.

But your brothers and sisters in Christ help you fight the enemy, like loyal comrades in a crisis. So let God's comfort and the comfort of others administer grace to your wounded heart. Trust Him to fight the good fight on your behalf. Let Jesus love you. Let people encourage you and hold you accountable. One day you will be able to comfort others with the same comfort you have received. Indeed, your compassion will be much deeper, broader, and Christlike. Therefore, rejoice because of His great comfort and compassion!

"Praise be to the God and Father of our Lord Jesus Christ, the Father of compassion and the God of all comfort, who comforts us in all our troubles, so that we can comfort those in any trouble with the comfort we ourselves receive from God" (2 Corinthians 1:3–4).

Do I rejoice in the comfort of Christ? Am I extending His comfort to the uncomfortable?

Related Readings: Psalm 119:50–52; Isaiah 12:1; 2 Corinthians 7:7; Philippians 2:1–3

BOASTING GOD BLESSES

"This is what the LORD says: 'Let not the wise man boast of his wisdom or the strong man boast of his strength or the rich man boast of his riches, but let him who boasts boast about this: that he understands and knows me, that I am the LORD, who exercises kindness, justice and righteousness on earth, for in these I delight,' declares the LORD." Jeremiah 9:23–24

There is beneficial boasting, and there is destructive boasting. My self-promotion and bragging are distasteful and rejected by God and people. Insecurity and fear may be the culprits as excessive pride causes me to speak in a self-glorifying way. My talk becomes self-admiring rather than Christ-adoring. In a moment of weakness, I feel like I have to prove my worth. Yet it is in my weakness that I can point to Him and rely on His power.

"Therefore I will boast all the more gladly about my weaknesses, so that Christ's power may rest on me" (2 Corinthians 12:9).

Bragging can be clothed in our prayer requests as a way to spiritualize insecurities. We can offer up prideful prayers that are meant in some strange way to impress God and our prayer partners. Ironically, prayer is the last place to parade our accomplishments. Prayer is reserved for humility, brokenness, and dependence on God.

Boasting driven by spiritual pride may be the worst form of bragging. The world feeds our pride by pointing to our achievements and says, "Look at your education, look at your net worth, and look at your physical prowess." However, those who are sober-minded and mature understand that any good gift comes from their heavenly Father.

He is the originator and sustainer of blessings. Your wisdom is a gift from God. Your wealth is a gift from God. Your health is a gift from God. Your only response can be gratitude marinated in humility. Then your life is appetizing and tasteful. Then any boasting comes only reluctantly, always reflecting faith in God and His character.

"My soul will boast in the LORD; let the afflicted hear and rejoice" (Psalm 34:2).

You are overwhelmed in gratitude for the opportunity to know God. Not only have you met Him, but He has also afforded you the occasion to know and understand Him. You trust the character of Christ. His character has become your confidence. You have grown to trust Him exclusively. Indeed, the Lord is dependable when others are undependable.

His goodness is not to be exploited but experienced for His glory. When people ask about your peace and serenity, you can tell them it comes from God through His Son the Lord Jesus Christ. This is beautiful boasting that God blesses. It is not always understood, but it is always helpful. Reflect credit off yourself, and give it to Christ. He deserves it!

"Therefore, as it is written: 'Let him who boasts boast in the Lord'" (1 Corinthians 1:31).

How can I better boast in the Lord and not in my own accomplishments?

Related Readings: Judges 7:2; Psalm 44:8; 2 Corinthians 12:5–10; Galatians 6:14

WORK OF ART

"So I went down to the potter's house, and I saw him working at the wheel. But the pot he was shaping from the clay was marred in his hands; so the potter formed it into another pot, shaping it as seemed best to him…. 'Like clay in the hand of the potter, so are you in my hand.'"
Jeremiah 18:3-4, 6

We are God's work of art. If we are a follower of Jesus Christ, God owns us. He is the - potter, and we are the clay. Our life is destined to be a masterpiece in the hands of our Master Jesus. It requires a lifetime of molding and shaping, but our life after experiencing the grace of God is more attractive than before God's grace governed our life.

There are at least two prerequisites to a life masterpiece molded by God. One is a masterful artist, and the other is moist clay. One without the other is doomed for failure. A gifted artist can be motivated and available, but without a subject he only works in his imagination. A person can long to be the object of an artist's inspiration, but there must first be a relationship in order for him or her to benefit.

God is the artist, and you are His subject. His part is to mold and create. Your part is to be available and teachable. This is how your Master works. He needs your life coupled with your undivided attention and your moldable heart and mind. Dry and brittle clay is useless in the hand of the potter. It cracks under pressure and gives in to discomfort.

However, clay that is moist and moldable is full of potential. In the beginning, the sticky mire is unpleasing to the eyes and uninviting, but over time it begins to take shape. The molding process is not easy. Sometimes you feel discombobulated and shapeless. You know God is in control, but your circumstances have you feeling upside down and spiraling out of control. This is God's wheel of wisdom. Uncertainty and dizziness are God's opportunity to grip the dampened clay of your heart and form dependence on Him.

Sometimes it is the water of adversity that keeps the clay moist. Other times it is success that dampens the dirt. Whatever God is using to mold your character, do not resist. Let Him process your life through His caressing and caring hands. It is better to be in the hands of God, spinning in uncertainty, than to be on our own, riskless and restless.

Feel His fingers of compassion, hope, and holiness. He not only comforts you but also conforms you into the image of His Son Jesus. He has the big picture in mind as He looks down on the potter's wheel. Your perspective is limited as you look up from the clay-soaked wheel, peering up into the faithful face of the potter.

"But who are you, a human being, to talk back to God? 'Shall what is formed say to the one who formed it, "Why did you make me like this?"' Does not the potter have the right to make out of the same lump of clay some pottery for special purposes and some for common use?" (Romans 9:20–21).

Do I willingly submit to my Master's molding me into the character of Christ?

Related Readings: Isaiah 29:15–16; Isaiah 45:9; Isaiah 64:8; Matt 10:29–31; Phil 3:20–21

SERVANT SHEPHERD

*"'I will place shepherds over them who will tend them, and they will no longer
be afraid or terrified, nor will any be missing,' declares the LORD."*
Jeremiah 23:4

Shepherding the flock of God can be hard, frustratingly difficult, and demanding. It is a challenge to serve one boss, much less dozens or even hundreds of bosses. The servant shepherd is expected to teach God's Word with new insight and relevant application. He is to attend every meeting, raise capital campaign funds, kiss the babies, relate to the youth, and have a perfect, pretty, personable, and passionate wife who can play the piano.

His children are instantly obedient. He is engaging in conversation, easy on the eyes, physically fit, and intelligent. He rushes to the hospital for the sick, mediates conflict, counsels couples, marries, buries, baptizes, and is available at anyone's beck and call. The loving pastor loves the lost. He comforts the afflicted and afflicts the comfortable.

Even Jesus did not do all of this, as He placed limitations on His life. He had down time. He took retreats. He prepared. He focused on a few. He taught with authority because He had been in communion with His heavenly Father. Indeed, having super servant shepherd expectations is sinful. The servant shepherd may need to repent of chasing these never-to-be-fulfilled demands, and the flock need not expect a messiah as a minister.

The true servant shepherd is called and appointed by God. It is a divine placement. A new minister is more than likely unlike your last pastor. He looks differently, acts differently, leads differently, and speaks differently. Do not be cruel and hold the positive qualities of the last minister over him. He will never be just like the last pastor but will mature into the leader God has uniquely gifted him to be; so give him space to grow.

As a servant shepherd, stay close to Christ. Get your marching orders from Him, and lead with humility and grace. Fear God only, and serve people patiently. There are times to make hard decisions that may cost you money and people. And there are times to die to your desires and trust God with the consensus of other Spirit-led leaders.

The heart of a servant shepherd seeks God's will first and foremost and then validates the Lord's will with godly counsel. Your hope and acceptance are in Christ. People will let you down, but not Jesus. It is a heavenly honor to shepherd the flock of God; so do not take it lightly or too seriously. God and His people want you, love you, and pray for you.

Moreover, as parishioners, love your servant shepherd. Shower him with prayers and written notes of gratitude. Make him rest. Do not think too highly of him or too lowly of him. Love his wife. As a servant shepherd, you are God's man; so lead the sheep by serving the sheep. Churchmen and women, follow the shepherd with trust and respect. Most of all, let everyone focus his or her undivided devotion on the Great Shepherd—the Lord Jesus Christ!

Do I regularly pray for my pastor to be encouraged in the Lord by His Word?

Related Readings: Psalm 78:71; Isaiah 40:11; Matthew 9:36; Revelation 7:17

GOD'S REFRESHMENT

"I will refresh the weary and satisfy the faint."
Jeremiah 31:25

God refreshment is required; without it we risk living a dull and sad life. Like bread gone stale, our hearts can become crusty and hard. God's refreshment softens our hearts and shaves away the rough edges. He understands the need to break from work and responsibilities. He created times of refreshment for refinement and rest.

We think too much of our capabilities when we have no time for Him. We work hard and play hard, but where is God in the equation? His desire is to be at the core of our concentric circles of marriage, children, work, ministry, and leisure. When we place Christ in the center of our priorities, He influences us from the inside out.

He moves from being another life compartment to permeating all aspects of your life. It is not just a Sunday routine that brings refreshment, though the Lord's Day is crucial for corporate worship, prayer, and teaching from Holy Scripture. It is taking time to pause daily and receive refreshment from the Word of God and the Bread of Life.

"The law of the LORD is perfect, refreshing the soul. The statutes of the LORD are trustworthy, making wise the simple" (Psalm 19:7).

Jesus is there to refresh. You cannot bear your current burden alone, but He can. You cannot fix the other person, but He can. You cannot save the world, but He can. The refreshing love of Christ energizes and rejuvenates. Take time, and observe Him in His creation. The chirping of the birds, the crashing of the waves, the changing of the leaves, and the transformation of lives are all soul refreshers. Jesus satisfies.

"Then Jesus declared, 'I am the bread of life. Whoever comes to me will never go hungry, and whoever believes in me will never be thirsty'" (John 6:35).

People are also an important part of the refreshment process. Let people love you. Receive their kind words like drops of cool water on a parched tongue. For example, learn to enjoy the presence of your children. Their honesty, purity, energy, and naivety are all meant to refresh, not frustrate. Do not wish them away, for they will empty the nest soon enough. Enjoy every moment with them. Let them refresh you, not upset you.

We can enjoy the refreshment of others when we first learn to accept it from those who love us the most. You become a more effective giver as you grow in the grace of receiving. You are then able to refresh others as you are refreshed by God and people. And as a bonus, your refreshment of others even refreshes you! "A generous person will prosper; whoever refreshes others will be refreshed" (Proverbs 11:25).

Do I allow the Lord to regularly refresh me so I can refresh others in Christ?

Related Readings: Psalm 23:3; Psalm 68:9; 1 Corinthians 16:18; Philemon 1:7, 20

FALSE ACCUSATIONS

"'You are deserting to the Babylonians!' 'That's not true!' Jeremiah said.
'I am not deserting to the Babylonians.' But Irijah would not listen to him; instead,
he arrested Jeremiah and brought him to the officials." Jeremiah 37:13–14

False accusations are like daggers to the heart. They cut deeply and hurt profoundly. False accusers have a variety of origins. They can be friends who are misinformed or confused over the nature of the circumstances. Their warning to you may even be wise counsel, in general, but does not apply to your situation. False accusers invite a defense.

However, the Lord and the facts will vindicate your position. In the meantime, deal with false accusations with truth, grace, and pure motives. Be careful not to falsely accuse your assailants, and let others become your defenders. The banner of truth will be held high as those who know the details of the situation stand by your side. It may be many, or it may be a few. Regardless of the size of your support, stay focused on God.

"Do not turn me over to the desire of my foes, for false witnesses rise up against me, spouting malicious accusations" (Psalm 27:12).

Pray that your life under fire will be a blaze of blessing for the many others who have suffered under the burden of injustice. It is imperative that you are consumed with Christ and not your false accusers. Feel empathy for them, yes. Pray for them, yes. Forgive them, yes. Fear them, no. Fear God only, and forgive your false accusers.

Jesus walked this lonely road of false accusations. He forgave because He knew they really did not know what they were doing. He gave them over to God and trusted Him with vindication in His timing. This road of injustice is not an easy one to travel; so travel with Jesus. Let him drive the process, and trust Him with the results. "Jesus said, 'Father, forgive them, for they do not know what they are doing'" (Luke 23:34).

So much is out of your control, except your attitude. Be grateful for your ever-enduring advocate Jesus who stands by your side. He is your defense and your refuge as the rain of false accusations beats down on your life. Do not give up on Him; He has not given up on you. He will see you through this very difficult time. Adversity with Jesus is much better than smooth sailing without Him. Your prayers and His peace will sustain you.

"At the king's command, the men who had falsely accused Daniel were brought in and thrown into the lions' den" (Daniel 6:24).

Am I consumed by Christ or my accusers? Do I trust God and have I forgiven them?

Related Readings: Psalm 38:20; Isaiah 12:2; Mark 11:25; Acts 26:2

AUDIENCE OF ONE

"I love the Father and do exactly what my Father has commanded me."
John 14:31

I struggle playing to an audience other than almighty God. I create an unnecessary tension by asking myself, "What will they think? How will they respond?" Yet the heart of Jesus asks, "What does my heavenly Father want? How can I obey Him with my whole heart?" It is an audience of one with my heavenly Father that requires my focus.

So I ask myself, "Whom do I love more? Do I love my Savior more, or do I love the praise of people more?" If I truly love the commendation of Christ more than the approval of people, then I will obey His commands, even when I am misunderstood and mistreated. A life that loves God longs to grow in a relationship that faithfully follows His ways.

Caution is required to not become proud in our obedience. In a distorted way, a disciplined life can play into impressing people instead of pleasing God. It is false humility to be proud of our humility and wish others could attain our level of maturity. False humility on the stage of life acts out its spirituality for the world's accolades.

"These rules, which have to do with things that are all destined to perish with use, are based on merely human commands and teachings. Such regulations indeed have an appearance of wisdom, with their self-imposed worship, their false humility and their harsh treatment of the body, but they lack any value in restraining sensual indulgence" (Colossians 2:22–23). True humility seeks only to deflect glory back to God's glory.

However, when all is said and done, living for an audience of one insists on intense intimacy with Jesus Christ, so that we naturally follow His lead. It is like an eloquent dance rendition, where He leads and we follow. Some steps are new and awkward, while other moves are comfortable and unconscious. If we dance with Jesus before others, He will amuse them most, as He leads us into His will. True humility follows Christ's lead.

Lastly, learning to live for an audience of one means to give away recognition and resist taking credit. For example, at work give the team credit for success, and take responsibility for failure. At home quietly serve behind the scenes without a worry about who gets the recognition for the household chores. Most of all, minister for Christ's kingdom, so your kingdom fades away and His becomes full center. An audience of one pleases the One.

Joseph revealed his devotion to an audience of one with the Lord when he declared, "How then could I do such a wicked thing and sin against God?" (Genesis 39:9).

Do I live unashamedly for an audience of one? What competing audience can I dismiss?

Related Readings: 2 Chronicles 32:12; Isaiah 65:16; John 17:1–5; Colossians 2:18

RESTLESS RUMORS

"Do not lose heart or be afraid when rumors are heard in the land; one rumor comes this year, another the next, rumors of violence in the land and of ruler against ruler." Jeremiah 51:46

Rumors can be relentless and can drive us to restlessness. This is why it is imperative to listen to the Lord. The shifting sentiment of society is unpredictable, but God is the same. Rumors are the sport of people with too much time on their hands. They are the economic driver for some industries like the media, but do not be deceived or distracted by them.

The discerning choose to reject rumors outright or selectively listen only to the soft murmur of truth that may be represented. Jesus said we would become a rumor-crazed culture in the last days. "When you hear of wars and rumors of wars, do not be alarmed. Such things must happen, but the end is still to come" (Mark 13:7).

There are rumors of possible terrorist attacks. There are rumors of government corruption. There are rumors of someone's infidelity. There are rumors of layoffs. There are rumors of job creations. There are rumors of mass firings. There are rumors of mergers. There are rumors of forced retirement. There are rumors that God is dead. Rumors relentlessly rain down on us, creating fear and worry.

We seem to enjoy rumors because they are tantalizing to the tongue. We want to know the juicy details, even though it is none of our business. Rumors feed our pride and get us focused on issues which are either out of our control or even nonexistent. Instead, rest in the "rumor" of Christ's return. Though we do not know the day or hour, we can prepare for His glorious return.

"But about that day or hour no one knows, not even the angels in heaven, nor the Son, but only the Father. Be on guard! Be alert! You do not know when that time will come" (Mark 13:32–33).

Your conscience can be clear while you wait for the Lord's return. He may return today, tomorrow, or in the distant future. It is contingent on fulfilled prophecy, and ultimately it is at God's discretion. But you can rest in the reassurance of Christ's return. Indeed, His imminent return has been rumored over the past two thousand years. "With the Lord a day is like a thousand years, and a thousand years are like a day" (2 Peter 3:8).

The Lord's return is a righteous rumor that will occur. When other worthless rumors assail you, rest in the certainty of Christ's return. Be ready for Him. Live like He might come tomorrow. Spend your money and time in preparation for the return of our reigning King Jesus. Rest in the Lord, not in restless rumors. Be ready for the rumor of His return.

"So you also must be ready, because the Son of Man will come at an hour when you do not expect him" (Matthew 24:44).

Do I live as if the Lord's return is imminent? Do I rest in Him in spite of other rumors?

Related Readings: Luke 21:9; 1 Timothy 1:4; Revelation 20:4

GROW OLD TOGETHER

"Even to your old age and gray hairs I am he, I am he who will sustain you.
I have made you and I will carry you; I will sustain you and I will rescue you."
Isaiah 46:4

There is a relational richness that comes from growing old together. It may be parents, a spouse, children, siblings, friends, church acquaintances, or a work associate who contributes to a caring community. Regardless of the source of relational fulfillment, it brings to life the Lord's creative design of intentionality in doing life together.

We are not created by our heavenly Father to be isolated and insecure. His plan for us is to engage with each other in meaningful conversation, patient prayer, loving service, and relaxing recreation. Families and friends who grow old together are able to work through conflict, overcome obstacles, serve unselfishly, and celebrate God's faithfulness.

"I will sing of the LORD's great love forever; with my mouth I will make your faithfulness known through all generations" (Psalm 89:1).

Perhaps you and your spouse pray for three other couples with whom you can invest intentional time in fun, fellowship, and going deeper with the Lord. They are in a similar season of life as you; so you are able to walk together with empathetic understanding and genuine prayer support. Consider a monthly dinner with games, a Bible study, and annual trips together. It is important to grow old with those whose company you enjoy.

Above all else, grow old with God. The Lord longs to be there for you in the ups and downs of life. His strength sustains you, His compassion carries you, and His righteousness rescues you. Every day with Jesus grows sweeter than the day before for the Christian who grows old with grace. God does not give up on you, and neither should you.

"The LORD rewards everyone for their righteousness and faithfulness" (1 Samuel 26:23).

Enjoy the Lord's ever-growing influence in your life. Each season of service for your Savior is meant to draw you into more intense intimacy and love. Understanding and accepting Christ's unconditional acceptance and love gives you peace and security to relax in His righteous arms. His aging process gives you permission to be yourself. Relational richness comes from growing old with Christ and with His trusted friends.

"Therefore, my brothers and sisters, you whom I love and long for, my joy and crown, stand firm in the Lord in this way, dear friends!" (Philippians 4:1).

Am I intentional in growing old well with the Lord, friends, and family?

Related Readings: Psalm 92:14; Ecclesiastes 4:12; Acts 2:46; 3 John 1:14

LOVE, COMPASSION, FAITHFULNESS

"Because of the LORD's great love we are not consumed, for his compassions never fail.
They are new every morning; great is your faithfulness. I say to myself,
'The LORD is my portion; therefore I will wait for him.'" Lamentations 3:22–24

The love of Christ keeps us from being consumed. His love is a healer to the hurting heart. Our sorrows can overwhelm us, but He is there as our loving heavenly Father to see us through our sadness. The love of God is a peacemaker when we become consumed with conflict. His love mediates and works out solutions for all willing parties. Conflict melts under the loving influence of God. We are not consumed because of Christ.

Worry is consuming until it comes under the direct influence of God's love. His love exudes peace. Thus, the peace of God and the worry of the world cannot coexist. We are not consumed. Fear can be all consuming. However, the love of God flushes out fear and replaces it with trust. Fleeting fear must be replaced by faith, or it will return to occupy your heart and mind. The love of God floods our souls with rock-solid faith.

Therefore, because of God's great love, we are not consumed. The Lord's love is served daily on the silver platter of His compassion. God has a deep awareness and concern for your heartache. This awareness is the beginning of His compassion. His compassions provide the relief of companionship and care. Indeed, they have never recorded a failure.

"LORD, you are my God; I will exalt you and praise your name, for in perfect faithfulness you have done wonderful things, things planned long ago" (Isaiah 25:1).

People will fail you, but God is still faithful. Work will fail you, but God is still faithful. Your health will fail you, but God is still faithful. Finances will fail you, but God is still faithful. Circumstances will fail you, but God is still faithful. You will fail, but God is still faithful. Great is His faithfulness! God does what He says—now and forevermore.

You do not ever have to second-guess Jesus. Take Him at His Word. He is there for you. He is there for your family. He is there for your friends. He is there for your enemies. He is faithful. He cannot not be faithful. For God to not be faithful would be like the sun not rising in the east. It is not possible, and so it is impossible for God to be unfaithful.

Therefore, wait on Him. He is worth the wait. He is faithful. He will do what He says in His time. You can rest and relish in His faithfulness. He will be faithful to lead you to the right spouse, the right career, and the right friends. Because He is faithful, He can be trusted. Let go of your inhibitions, and trust Him. You can trust Him with your future, health, and eternity. We serve a great God full of love, compassion, and faithfulness.

"He is the Rock, his works are perfect, and all his ways are just. A faithful God who does no wrong, upright and just is he" (Deuteronomy 32:4).

Do I rest in the faithfulness of almighty God? Do I extend His love and compassion?

Related Readings: Isaiah 30:18; Joel 2:23; 2 Corinthians 1:3; Jude 1:21

MEANINGFUL MARRIAGE

"'Haven't you read,' he replied, 'that at the beginning the Creator "made them male and female,"
and said, "For this reason a man will leave his father and mother and be united to his wife,
and the two will become one flesh"? So they are no longer two, but one flesh.
Therefore what God has joined together, let no one separate.'" Matthew 19:4–6

Marriage means something, because God says it means something. He invented marriage and as the inventor is very proud of His creation. The Lord's primary purpose for a man and a woman coming together in holy matrimony is to glorify Him. Thus, a marriage built on Christ points people to His character and His perspective on relationships.

For example, God's definition of love is active and other centered; so when we read "love is kind" (1 Corinthians 13:4), we express a kind and caring attitude toward our spouse. There is a culture of humility in meaningful marriages that is quick to put the other person's needs before our own. A fulfilling marriage first follows Christ's commands.

"It does not dishonor others, it is not self-seeking, it is not easily angered, it keeps no record of wrongs" (1 Corinthians 13:5). Love looks for ways to love like God loves.

Moreover, a meaningful marriage is made up of a man and woman who are intentional in their investment in each other. A husband cherishes his wife when he prays for her to grow in God's grace and when he seeks her counsel and advice. A wife honors her husband when she prays for him to grow in God's wisdom and when she sees him as the spiritual leader. A marriage of significance is one that plans and prepares on purpose.

"But the plans of the LORD stand firm forever, the purposes of his heart through all generations" (Psalm 33:11).

Wise are the woman and man who learn and discern the Lord's purpose for marriage and then plan to live it out. So with bold humility, hitch your marriage to heaven's tractor of trust. The ride is not always smooth and easy, but it is a great adventure with Jesus and your best friend. Ride out the rough spots in faith and forgiveness, and celebrate God's goodness along the way. A meaningful marriage is fun and fulfilling for Christ's sake.

"It always protects, always trusts, always hopes, always perseveres. Love never fails" (1 Corinthians 13:7–8).

How can I make my marriage more meaningful? Have I surrendered to the lordship of Christ?

Related Readings: Joshua 15:16–17; Nehemiah 13:26; Ephesians 5:33; Philippians 2:13

GRATITUDE GENE

"Do not get drunk on wine, which leads to debauchery. Instead, be filled with the Spirit, speaking to one another with psalms, hymns, and songs from the Spirit. Sing and make music from your heart to the Lord, always giving thanks to God the Father for everything, in the name of our Lord Jesus Christ." Ephesians 5:18–20

A heart controlled by the Holy Spirit is grateful, as the gene of gratitude is in the DNA of a disciple of Jesus Christ. Once the Spirit of God vaccinates the soul with gratitude, it prevents the virus of discontentment and complaining to control a life. Gone is murmuring, and it is replaced with an appreciative attitude that is helpful and hopeful.

"Those who belong to Christ Jesus have crucified the flesh with its passions and desires. Since we live by the Spirit, let us keep in step with the Spirit. Let us not become conceited, provoking and envying each other" (Galatians 5:24–26).

Anyone can define the obvious of a difficult situation, but a positive problem solver is able to bring prayerful and thoughtful solutions to bear. So in the work environment, it is imperative we engage associates who are able to bring new information to the discussion and share fresh insights and deep discernment with other team members. Gratitude grows those around it to be thankful and intentional in developing valuable and creative ideas.

Gratitude is able to navigate around relational ruts and get to the bottom of real issues. We want to be around people grateful to God because it is infectious. You can see it in the calm of their countenance, you can hear it in their soothing speech, and you can feel it in the positive energy of their emotions. Indeed, gratitude governs people to serve people.

"Let the message of Christ dwell among you richly as you teach and admonish one another with all wisdom through psalms, hymns, and songs from the Spirit, singing to God with gratitude in your hearts" (Colossians 3:16).

Worship to God bursts forth from a grateful heart captured by Christ. When you reflect on the richness of your salvation in Jesus, your heart and soul lift praise and thanksgiving to the Lord. It may be a joyful noise, but you need not worry because almighty God looks at the heart, not your harmony. A melody of grateful praise to your Master Jesus brings joy. So sing out in worship with a smile on your face and a song in your heart.

"But I, with shouts of grateful praise, will sacrifice to you. What I have vowed I will make good. I will say, 'Salvation comes from the LORD'" (Jonah 2:9).

Am I controlled by the Holy Spirit or by the enemy's lies? Am I a grateful worshiper?

Related Readings: Psalm 100:1; Psalm 147:7; Acts 24:2–4; Romans 16:4

GRATEFUL TO GOD

"But thanks be to God, who always leads us in triumphal procession in Christ and through us spreads everywhere the fragrance of the knowledge of him." 2 Corinthians 2:14

Gratitude to God is a guarantee for an attitude of humility and happiness. It is hard to be grateful and not be full of joy and contentment. When we reflect on His salvation and grace in Jesus Christ, we are left awestruck that almighty God would freely give us the gift of His only Son. Indeed, grateful Christians never get over the forgiveness and freedom they have in Christ Jesus. Gratitude gives us the right attitude!

How can we renew our thinking each day to be appreciative when so many negative thoughts assault our minds? What is a wise process to keep us praising God for His provision? One way is to recount His blessings by writing them in a journal. Take the time to pen what the Lord has done for you, and your sorrow will turn into a smile of satisfaction. Your glow comes back when you remember Christ's incredible love and acceptance. When was the last time you spent your entire prayer time just praising and thanking God?

"Praise him for his acts of power; praise him for his surpassing greatness" (Psalm 150:2).

Perhaps you praise Him in the morning for life and love. Praise Him midmorning for fulfilling work. Praise Him at the noon hour for health and happiness. Praise Him midday for forgiveness and faith. Praise Him at dinner for family and friends. Praise Him before bed for His Word and the wonder of His grace. Praise God, and gratitude will follow.

Your gratitude goes a long way in leading others to be grateful. A grateful life is like a sea of thanksgiving that buoys all boats with hope. Appreciation attracts great people. Your thanksgiving to God for His favor and blessings and for the incredible people in your life sets you up for success. Gratitude is a self-fulfilling prophecy for peace, joy, and love.

"And whatever you do, whether in word or deed, do it all in the name of the Lord Jesus, giving thanks to God the Father through him" (Colossians 3:17).

Do I regularly express gratitude to God? Whom can I honor by showing sincere appreciation and thanksgiving?

Related Readings: 1 Chronicles 16:9; Daniel 4:34; 1 Corinthians 1:4; 1 Timothy 4:4

REMEMBER THANK YOU

"One of them, when he saw he was healed, came back, praising God in a loud voice.
He threw himself at Jesus' feet and thanked him—and he was a Samaritan."
Luke 17:15-16

A culture of entitlement is slow to say thank you, but the grateful are honored to express appreciation. Ungrateful people expect, even demand, good things with no gratitude in return. But grateful men and women are humbled and give God the glory for His blessings. The most gratefulness comes from those who least expect the Lord's lavish love. It is the mercy of God that heals our heart and causes us to exclaim, "Praise the Lord!"

Is it your regular routine to sincerely thank God for His healing power? Do you bow at the feet of Jesus when the body of a friend or family member was cured by God's work through the miracle of modern medicine? Have you celebrated Christ's blessing of keeping your body whole from a debilitating disease? Humility is a thank you waiting to happen.

Listen to David's prayer for healing, "Be merciful to me, LORD, for I am faint; O LORD, heal me, for my bones are in agony" (Psalm 6:2). You can pray boldly for your physical healing. Pray depending on God, and with great faith ask the Great Physician to bring His healing power on your body. Your Creator understands how to bring wholeness to His creation. It is not a question of if He can, but if He will.

However, whether He heals in this life or in the life to come, give Him thanks. "Pray continually; give thanks in all circumstances, for this is God's will for you in Christ Jesus" (1 Thessalonians 5:17–18). Furthermore, gratitude to God expresses gratitude to people. Make it a goal to write a thank you note before you cash the check. Look a friend in the eye and express your thankfulness for his or her friendship. Show your gratitude to your server with a generous gratuity. Appreciate others, and you invite appreciation into your life and work.

Mostly, thank the Lord Jesus Christ for His death on the cross for your sin and salvation. Jesus came from living with sinners to die for sinners. "The Lord Jesus, on the night he was betrayed, took bread, and when he had given thanks, he broke it and said, 'This is my body, which is for you; do this in remembrance of me'" (1 Corinthians 11:23–24).

Do I thank God often for His incredible gift of grace and forgiveness? Do I thank Him during the bad times as well as the good times? Am I quick to appreciate others?

Related Readings: Proverbs 3:8; Proverbs 17:22; Romans 14:6; 1 Corinthians 15:57

THANKFUL PRAYERS

"For this reason, ever since I heard about your faith in the Lord Jesus and your love for
all the saints, I have not stopped giving thanks for you, remembering you in my prayers."
Ephesians 1:15–16

How often do you offer a prayer of thanksgiving for the saints of God who have great faith and lavish love? Who comes to mind when you think of those who have persevered with God through pain, sorrow, joy, and abundance? Perhaps you think of career missionaries, ministers, or a successful businessperson. Maybe your mind locks onto a loved one who has kept the faith in the middle of fiery trials or a complicated health condition. These are quality human beings you can honor by thanking God for them with powerful prayers.

God expects prayer for missionaries; however, make it more personal by placing their pictures in a prominent place in your home. When you walk by them or at a designated time, intercede on their behalf to almighty God. It is those with great faith who foster a flaming fire of faith within your soul. Thanking the Lord for His faithful followers bolsters your faith to be more like those for whom you are exceedingly grateful.

Your children need to hear you pray, thanking God for the faith of your forefathers and other living family members who love Jesus. It is this attitude of respect for committed Christians that builds commitment into your sons and daughters. Gratitude to God for those who are serious about their Savior Jesus builds a generation of God followers.

Furthermore, thank the Lord for their love, for as their faith grows, love is not far behind. "We ought always to thank God for you, brothers, and rightly so, because your faith is growing more and more, and the love every one of you has for each other is increasing" (2 Thessalonians 1:3). Those with great faith love great!

Indeed, pray for those with great faith who love to finish well. This is the testimony of those we admire the most: "All these people were still living by faith when they died" (Hebrews 11:13). Mature Christians still need encouragement and accountability to remain faithful. Your prayers compel them to move forward with Christ.

Whom do I know, who is solid in his or her faith, whom I can thank God for often in prayer?
Who is a missionary couple my family can pray for weekly?

Related Readings: 2 Chronicles 30:27; Nehemiah 1:6; 1 Thessalonians 1:3;
Hebrews 11:39–40

A GRATEFUL NATION

"In that day you will say: 'Give thanks to the LORD, call on his name; make known among the nations what he has done, and proclaim that his name is exalted."
Isaiah 12:4

A nation born out of the womb of religious liberty has much to thank almighty God for. We can thank Him that man's tyranny lives oceans away and that we are free to worship, vote, and treat our fellowman with civility and respect. "With your hand you drove out the nations and planted our fathers; you crushed the peoples and made our fathers flourish" (Psalm 44:2). He is the initiator and sustainer of our nation's freedom; without the Lord, we lose.

A large lump fills our throats with the memory of men and women whose blood saturated the soil of foreign fields to preserve our freedom. A nation like ours that encourages free enterprise, free speech, free press, and free worship comes with a severe sacrifice. When was the last time you thanked the Lord for those on the front lines who risk their lives for your liberty? His blessing remains where gratitude is retained; so thank Him often.

Indeed, it is a country with character that positions itself for God's blessing. Therefore, do not just ask God to bless America, but in addition thank Him for already blessing America. "With praise and thanksgiving they sang to the LORD: 'He is good; his love to Israel endures forever'" (Ezra 3:11). A grateful nation gives God the glory for His goodness. Out of our national appreciation, the world wonders what God can do for them.

So when the United States of America appreciates almighty God, we become a shining light from shore to shore as men and women around the globe take notice of our humble dependence on Him. Jesus described the collective role of God-fearing people: "You are the light of the world. A city on a hill cannot be hidden" (Matthew 5:14).

If we extinguish our light by abandoning the faith from where we came, He will raise up other nations to take our place. However, He smiles when He sees a nation acknowledge Him as Lord and Savior. It sets a standard for those who admire our freedoms to see where they originate. Thanksgiving Day is the Lord's Day to privately and publically give Him the glory and gratitude for His incredible favor and blessing on our nation.

How can I lead our extended family in a sincere prayer of thanksgiving to the Lord? What are some specific freedoms I can thank God for in blessing my country? How can I pray for our president to be an example of a Christian leader the world will follow?

Related Readings: Psalm 102:15; Malachi 1:14; Acts 10:34–36; Revelation 15:4

GRATEFUL CHILDREN

"I have no greater joy than to hear that my children are walking in the truth."
3 John 1:4

Gratitude is a wonderful gift we can give to our children and our children to us. It brings overwhelming joy to the heart of parents when they witness an appreciative child. It is music to their ears when they hear "Thank you," "You are welcome," and "How can I help?" Moms and dads long for their loved ones to grow into grateful adults.

Thankfulness is a vaccine against selfishness and discontentment. Children and teenagers who understand and apply appreciation are quick to serve others, not demanding their needs or wants to be met. They take to heart what God expects of His sons and daughters. "Do nothing out of selfish ambition or vain conceit, but in humility consider others better than yourselves. Each of you should look not only to your own interests, but also to the interests of others" (Philippians 2:3–4). Gratitude leads to a Christlike attitude.

So how can you help your children learn to live a life of thanksgiving and gratitude? What does it take for teenagers to meet the needs of others before addressing their own needs? One thought is to begin teaching your children the value of hard work early. Assign them chores, and pay them when the job is completed with excellence. Train them to divide their money into the categories of save, give, and spend. When they invest time and energy into a meaningful outcome, they are much more appreciative of the money.

Perhaps you accompany them to feed the homeless, care for a family in financial distress, or visit those confined to jail. You may decide on a family mission trip overseas. It may be a construction project, evangelism outreach, or loving orphans. Contentment and gratitude will erupt from the heart of your children when they engage people who smile in the face of ugly circumstances. They see firsthand that joy comes from Jesus, not stuff.

Therefore, be intentional about modeling appreciation in front of your offspring. Be quick to thank God and others, while slow to complain. Grateful children are attractive and pleasant to be around. Their appreciative attitude will serve them well the rest of their lives.

"Your attitude should be the same as that of Christ Jesus: Who, being in very nature God, did not consider equality with God something to be grasped, but made himself nothing, taking the very nature of a servant, being made in human likeness. And being found in appearance as a man, he humbled himself and became obedient to death—even death on a cross!" (Philippians 2:5–8).

How can I model an attitude of gratitude in front of my children? What can we do as a family to learn appreciation and experience contentment?

Related Readings: Deuteronomy 4:9–10; Psalm 34:11; Proverbs 22:6; Ephesians 6:4

GRATEFUL GIVER

"In the midst of a very severe trial, their overflowing joy and their extreme poverty welled up in rich generosity. For I testify that they gave as much as they were able, and even beyond their ability. Entirely on their own, they urgently pleaded with us for the privilege of sharing in this service to the Lord's people." 2 Corinthians 8:2–4

Christians give because they have so much to be grateful for. Our gratitude starts with salvation in Jesus, as He saves us from our sin and saves us from eternity without God. New life in Christ creates an abundance of grace that gives us the faith, love, joy, and hope to represent Jesus to a wandering world. Gratitude begins with God's goodness.

"What shall I return to the LORD for all his goodness to me? I will lift up the cup of salvation and call on the name of the LORD" (Psalm 116:12–13).

Those who are grateful are not concerned about what they can get but only what they can give. As gratitude makes its way into the fabric of our faith, we voluntarily engage the needs of others. Perhaps a work associate needs help reaching a deadline, a mission trip to dig a well for the poor needs help, an unwed relative needs a baby shower, or foster parents need a weekend break. Grateful service to the needy grows our faith.

"If you spend yourselves in behalf of the hungry and satisfy the needs of the oppressed, then your light will rise in the darkness, and your night will become like the noonday" (Isaiah 58:10).

Furthermore, grateful men and women see their service on behalf of God as a privilege. Like a patriotic serviceman, they do not wait to be drafted; rather, they enthusiastically enlist in the Lord's army. A grateful child of God proudly represents heaven (his home country) in battle against the enemy and in care for the bedridden and walking wounded.

Gratitude gives us a pure motivation to pour our lives into the lives of those seeking God. So we aggressively give because the Lord has abundantly given to us. He gives us peace; so we extend peace. He gives us more money; so we generously give money. He freely gives forgiveness; so we offer perpetual forgiveness. Gratitude actively gives God glory.

"This service that you perform is not only supplying the needs of the Lord's people but is also overflowing in many expressions of thanks to God" (2 Corinthians 9:12).

What is the depth of my gratitude to God? Is my giving motivated by gratitude to Him?

Related Readings: Genesis 47:11–12; Psalm 142:7; Philippians 2:25; Titus 3:14

ALWAYS GIVING THANKS

"Always giving thanks to God the Father for everything, in the name of our Lord Jesus Christ."
Ephesians 5:20

It is easier to give thanks to God when things are going well but much harder when circumstances are not going the way I think they should go. Can I still thank Jesus when my body aches or when a child is away from the Lord? Can I remain grateful to God when people act strange, hurtful, unloving, and disrespectful? Can I remain grateful when work is laborious?

Can I be content to thank my heavenly Father for the manna He has provided for today and not be fraught with worry about how He will provide in the future? Thankfulness for the Lord's provision is His remedy for not rushing ahead of His will and wondering how everything will work out. Wise are we to settle down and settle into our Savior's rest.

"Then the LORD said to Moses, 'I will rain down bread from heaven for you. The people are to go out each day and gather enough for that day. In this way I will test them and see whether they will follow my instructions'" (Exodus 16:4).

It may be in suffering that we are most tempted to not thank God but complain to God. After all, why would a loving heavenly Father allow us to struggle and hurt? In His great wisdom, He knows it is in our adversity that we feel the greatest need for Him. So we can see our challenging circumstances as an opportunity to draw close to Christ. Thankfulness to God during difficulty builds humility and wisdom for the better times.

"We also glory in our sufferings, because we know that suffering produces perseverance; perseverance, character; and character, hope. And hope does not put us to shame, because God's love has been poured out into our hearts through the Holy Spirit, who has been given to us" (Romans 5:3–5).

So are you grateful to God even when a friend or your spouse has let you down? Are you thanking Him right now for His blessings beyond what you could have ever imagined? Gratitude to God gives you an attractive attitude toward others and their shortcomings. It is out of an appreciative heart that the Lord is able to capture your heart. Thankfulness to Jesus Christ incubates humility, creates contentment, purges pride, and looks to love.

"Thanks be to God, who delivers me through Jesus Christ our Lord! So then, I myself in my mind am a slave to God's law, but in my sinful nature a slave to the law of sin" (Romans 7:25).

How can I express gratitude to God in my current situation? How can I bless others?

Related Readings: Psalm 136:26; Daniel 6:10; 1 Corinthians 1:4; 2 Timothy 1:3

THANKFUL LEADERS

"To Timothy, my dear son: Grace, mercy and peace from God the Father and Christ Jesus our Lord.
I thank God, whom I serve, as my ancestors did, with a clear conscience, as night and day
I constantly remember you in my prayers." 2 Timothy 1:2–3

Thank the Lord for past leaders who proclaimed a day of thanksgiving to God for His blessings and provision. Men and women worth following are not afraid to publically profess their dependency on almighty God. Political correctness is not a part of their persona because they are more concerned about pleasing Jesus than people.

Am I a leader who models thanksgiving to God for my associates? Are others drawn to my appreciation for them, or am I avoided for fear of my ungrateful attitude? Thankfulness is infectious and encouraging. Grateful leaders have the potential for greatness, while those stuck in an unappreciative mindset muddle through mediocrity.

"I always thank my God as I remember you in my prayers, because I hear about your love for all his holy people and your faith in the Lord Jesus" (Philemon 1:4–5).

At work and home it is more than words of affirmation and appreciation—though this is a good start. A community of thankful people creates a culture of gratitude. There is not a day that goes by that God is not thanked for food to eat, a place to work, or air to breathe. Children observe mom and dad, modeling what they see and hear. Is your home full of thanksgiving to Jesus and for each other? Is your family infected with grateful hearts?

Perhaps you write a note of thanksgiving to your spouse for his or her unwavering love for you and your children. Pen a poem of gratitude to your children for their unique gift to your family. Thank your parents for their patient love. E-mail or call a friend and express thanks for his or her loyal friendship. Mostly, get on your knees and thank your heavenly Father.

Thankful leaders learn the power of grateful prayers. They approach heaven with sincere supplications full of thanksgiving and praise to God for sending His Son Jesus to save them from their sins. Prayers of thanksgiving are light on personal petitions and heavy on gratitude to God for the faith of family and friends. Be a thankful leader, and watch Christ grow an army of thankful followers. Grateful leaders show appreciation above and below.

"Therefore, since we are receiving a kingdom that cannot be shaken, let us be thankful, and so worship God acceptably with reverence and awe, for our 'God is a consuming fire'" (Hebrews 12:28–29).

Am I a thankful leader who inspires gratitude in those I serve and influence?

Related Readings: Psalm 106:47; Daniel 2:23; 1 Timothy 4:4; Revelation 7:12

LITTLE IS MUCH

"'Truly I tell you,' he said, 'this poor widow has put in more than all the others. All these people gave their gifts out of their wealth; but she out of her poverty put in all she had to live on.'"
Luke 21:3–4

Little becomes much when the Lord is factored into the equation. He takes a little money and multiplies ministries. He receives a little faith and moves mountains and heals sick bodies. He applies a little forgiveness and restores relationships. He blesses a little sacrifice from leadership and saves a business. Christ takes a little courage and fulfills a grand vision. Thus, do not despise your small contribution. It makes a huge difference.

Jesus exhorted His disciples regarding the potential of a little faith: "Truly I tell you, if you have faith as small as a mustard seed, you can say to this mountain, 'Move from here to there,' and it will move. Nothing will be impossible for you" (Matthew 17:20).

You may be the only person at work or in your extended family who stands up for Christian values. It is tempting to ease into the status quo and blend in with a complacent culture. However, with humility and love, stay the course of unselfish service, and you will see Christ work. Exceptions become exceptional with eternal favor and persistence.

"One of them [a leper], when he saw he was healed, came back, praising God in a loud voice. He threw himself at Jesus' feet and thanked him—and he was a Samaritan" (Luke 17:15–16).

Do the right thing, even if the majority does not take seriously the Lord's expectations. Your quiet service is not unnoticed by Jesus. Keep thanking God when others take Him for granted. Persevere in your prayer closet when it seems like prayerless people are progressing. Remain faithful in gift giving, especially when money is tight and uncertain.

A little is much when you lay it at the altar of obedience and the Holy Spirit's fire ignites it for God's glory. So lay before the Lord your gifts, talents, and faith, and watch Him forge you into a faithful disciple of Jesus. Lay your plan before almighty God, and trust Him to lead you through a prayerful process of implementation and adjustment. A little faith and obedience go a long way in God's game plan.

Joshua brought his army to Jericho expecting a brutal battle, but the Lord simply had him march around the wall and worship! "When the trumpets sounded, the army shouted, and at the sound of the trumpet, when the men gave a loud shout, the wall collapsed; so everyone charged straight in, and they took the city" (Joshua 6:20).

Have I laid before the Lord my little faith for Him to multiply and grow for His glory?

Related Readings: Leviticus 14:21–22; 1 Kings 17:13–16; Matthew 6:4–6; Luke 10:21

ACTIVE ACCOUNTABILITY

"But if you do warn the righteous man not to sin and he does not sin, he will surely live because he took warning, and you will have saved yourself." Ezekiel 3:21

Effective accountability partners are not passive. Once someone invites a friend into his or her life for accountability, it is a serious responsibility. Accountability is active, engaging, and encouraging. The giver and the receiver of accountability have entered into a trusting relationship. Indeed, wisdom listens to the warning of its accountability partner or group.

Authentic accountability requires caring confrontation. A little bit of short-term discomfort and embarrassment will save you a lot of long-term regret. Thus, when you encounter emotional situations, you keep a level head. Accountability facilitates objectivity. When you are under pressure, you have an objective team that gives you wise perspective. Your accountability group is there as a buffer to unwise decision making.

"Better a poor but wise youth than an old but foolish king who no longer knows how to heed a warning" (Ecclesiastes 4:13).

Accountability provides much needed courage for another to do the right thing. Sometimes it is hard decisions that paralyze us into nonaction. However, avoiding a difficult decision today will compound its inevitable consequences in the future. Accountability encourages you not to procrastinate when you are afraid. It relieves your fears and bolsters your faith.

For example, team members may need to be terminated for the good of the company and for their individual betterment. Prospective church volunteers may need to be told no because their character is not fitting for a leadership role. Your young adult children are not prepared for marriage because they need to first move out from home and experience independent living. Accountability helps everyone move forward in God's will.

Above all else, live like you are accountable to almighty God, as one day we all give an account to Him for our actions. "They are surprised that you do not join them in their reckless, wild living, and they heap abuse on you. But they will have to give account to him who is ready to judge the living and the dead" (1 Peter 4:4–5).

Am I truly accountable to others, and do I provide effective accountability to friends?

Related Readings: Proverbs 7:1–27; Jonah 3:6; Luke 17:1–4; Hebrews 4:13

SECRET TO HAPPINESS

"Praise the LORD. Blessed are those who fear the LORD, who find great delight in his commands."
Psalm 112:1

Praise to the Lord and fear of the Lord are foundational for a fulfilling life. This is the focus of a child of God in love with and loyal to his or her heavenly Father. Worship of Jesus causes the eyes of faith to see Him in His Shekinah glory. His great love secures the soul, and His hallowed holiness pierces the heart, resulting in joy and reverence for God.

Moses encountered God at the burning bush: "'Do not come any closer,' God said. 'Take off your sandals, for the place where you are standing is holy ground.' Then he said, 'I am the God of your father, the God of Abraham, the God of Isaac and the God of Jacob.' At this, Moses hid his face, because he was afraid to look at God" (Exodus 3:5–6).

When Christ is the core of a belief system, the natural outcome is peace, joy, and happiness. Jesus gives His children His promises so we can walk by faith, trusting that He will do what He said He would do. For example, lasting peace and calm come only from Christ. Jesus gives us peace of mind when others angrily give us a piece of their mind. Happiness comes from resting in eternal expectations, not craving earthly ones.

Jesus said, "Very truly I tell you, you will weep and mourn while the world rejoices. You will grieve, but your grief will turn to joy…. Now is your time of grief, but I will see you again and you will rejoice, and no one will take away your joy" (John 16:20, 22).

It is in the presence of Jesus that joy wells up in our inner being. Circumstances and other menacing culprits cannot take away His happiness. We bow our heads in fear of the Lord and then lift our eyes toward heaven in worship of the Lord. In worship, as we are overwhelmed by His majestic glory, we are delighted to follow Christ's commands.

Blessed, happy, fortunate, prosperous, and enviable is the one "whose delight is in the law of the LORD, and who meditates on his law day and night" (Psalm 1:2).

What is the secret to happiness in this life? It is holding with an open hand the temporal and grasping with a firm hand of faith the eternal. It is an unwavering focus on God and not being disillusioned by other well-meaning, and not so well-meaning, Christians. If your joy is gone, replace your fears with the fear of the Lord. Joy follows submission to Jesus.

"As Jesus was saying these things, a woman in the crowd called out, 'Blessed is the mother who gave you birth and nursed you.' He replied, 'Blessed rather are those who hear the word of God and obey it'" (Luke 11:27–28).

Am I happy over what brings happiness to the Lord's heart? Do I joyfully obey Jesus?

Related Readings: 1 Samuel 12:14; Psalm 119:166; John 16:33; 3 John 1:1–4

HAPPINESS IN HUMILITY

"Blessed are the poor in spirit, for theirs is the kingdom of heaven."
Matthew 5:3

The poor in spirit may understand their need for God in their deepest conscience, but what they need is to experience an emptying of self and a filling of the Holy Spirit. It is this recognition of spiritual poverty that enables them to receive the riches of Christ's grace. The humble are also in position to enrich their knowledge and understanding of God's ways. Before they knew the Lord they were void of everything, but in Christ they are in need of nothing. He makes the humble heart happy.

"For you know the grace of our Lord Jesus Christ, that though he was rich, yet for your sake he became poor, so that you through his poverty might become rich" (2 Corinthians 8:9).

How is humility developed in the attitude and heart of a follower of Jesus? It begins with a recognition and understanding of our utter dependence on God. Then there is a willful surrender to Jesus Christ where we give over everything to Him. So in marriage there need not be any negotiation regarding mutual submission to the Lord and to each other. The humble are intentional in their service of meeting the needs of others above their own interests and desires.

"In your relationships with one another, have the same mindset as Christ Jesus: Who, being in very nature God, did not consider equality with God something to be used to his own advantage; rather, he made himself nothing by taking the very nature of a servant, being made in human likeness. And being found in appearance as a man, he humbled himself by becoming obedient to death—even death on a cross!" (Philippians 2:5–8).

Furthermore, concerning money and material goods, the Lord is the owner, and we are the managers. Like Job we still bless the Lord, even when He takes away our possessions. "'Naked I came from my mother's womb, and naked I will depart. The LORD gave and the LORD has taken away; may the name of the LORD be praised.' In all this, Job did not sin by charging God with wrongdoing" (Job 1:21–22). We cannot lose what we never owned to begin with. Happiness comes by humbly trusting God with His possessions.

The outstanding outcome of the poor in spirit is the riches of God's kingdom. The kingdom of heaven is within all who acknowledge Jesus as the King and the Lord of their lives. Servants of the Lord Almighty are blessed with salvation and have all the benefits of being a son or daughter of the King. Followers of Jesus have access to His presence for peace, security, and direction. True humility facilitates a happy and contented heart in Christ.

"But seek first his kingdom and his righteousness, and all these things will be given to you as well" (Matthew 6:33).

Is my happiness based on walking with Christ in humility?

Related Readings: 1 Samuel 2:7; Matthew 19:14; 2 Timothy 4:18; Revelation 2:9

VISION FULFILLMENT

"The days are near when every vision will be fulfilled."
Ezekiel 12:23

God delights in vision fulfillment because what He initiates—He completes. A God-sized vision is what wakes us up in the morning. The reality of engaging in something much bigger than we ourselves is humbling and, at the same time, compelling. The greater the vision—the greater the faith required. Our capacity to trust needs to keep pace with the expansion of the vision. If not, we begin to feel overwhelmed, anxious, and defeated.

This is why it is critical to follow God's vision for your life and not your own contrived one. God's vision for you will always have the tension between trust and terror. His vision will wake you up in the middle of the night in wonder. "I wonder if there will be enough money." "I wonder if this will work." "I wonder." "I wonder." Do your wonders worry you?

Moreover, let the wonder of Christ's provision consume you, and these other wonders will pale in comparison. Say in your heart, "God, because your provision is wonderful, I will wait on you to provide. I will not force things to happen in my timing." It is the wonder of God and His timing that you can trust. The Lord is never late and rarely early; therefore, He can be trusted. His vision is fulfilled in His way and in His will.

Furthermore, His will is not a half-baked vision. It is one that comes to full fruition in all of its facets. He already has the people, money, and resources needed to fulfill your vision. Perhaps He is waiting on your character to grow and mature. You need a makeover from the Master. Your current character may lack the capacity to handle the success and responsibility awaiting His great vision. Let Christ mold you into His vision bearer.

Hold your vision with an open hand, and pray. Your big idea may need to be expanded beyond a small scenario. Do not base your vision of what has been done in the past. Define your vision by what God can do in the future. Heaven's infinite resources are the only limitations for the man or woman wholly submitted and obedient to the Lord.

You may need to keep your vision between you and God. Others may not be ready yet or may try to talk you out of following this God-sized assignment. Pray about it. Stay focused by faith on what needs to happen next. Do not get stuck in the inertia of what needs to happen in the end. Be faithful today, and tomorrow will take care of itself.

Patience and faith are two key ingredients in a vision's recipe. Over time, glimpses of what is to come will compel you forward. Stay tethered to trust in Jesus. Be humble and bold in the power of the Holy Spirit. Vision fulfillment is His expertise. In God's mind the vision is already fulfilled. So trust Him, enjoy the process, and see the vision unfold.

Is my vision God-sized, and will I remain faithful even when the vision seems dead?

Related Readings: Genesis 15:1; Joel 2:28; Acts 16:6; Acts 18:9

HAPPINESS IN GRIEF

"Blessed are those who mourn, for they will be comforted."
Matthew 5:4

Life is a series of gains and losses. We gain friends, and we lose friends. We gain confidence, and we lose confidence. We gain money, and we lose money. We gain a position, and we lose a position. We gain weight, and we lose weight. We gain perspective, and we lose perspective. Many times it is the transition between our loss and our gain that we grieve. Grief follows loss. But it is in our grieving that God gets our attention.

Whom or what do you miss? Is it a loved one who graduated to heaven, a career that you enjoyed, or child who has left the nest and started his or her own family? Perhaps your heart still aches from time to time, anger may well up occasionally, or your mind plays tricks on you with "what if" scenarios, causing you to doubt your decisions. However, it is in this contemplative process that we learn to listen to the Lord, trust, and be loved by Him.

There can be no comfort from Christ without grief from a loss. We all live in a house that contains rooms of mourning. We avoid these areas, but eventually we have to visit them. And we learn—the greater the grief, the greater the potential for gladness. God's goodness becomes the glue for our fractured faith. Job experienced the Lord in his loss. "The lowly he sets on high, and those who mourn are lifted to safety" (Job 5:11).

Spiritual grief comes when we are separated from God by our sin; thus, we mourn over broken fellowship. There is a godly sorrow that is sensitive to sin and quick to repent. Spiritual mourners lament when their sin isolates them from intimacy with Christ. So do not linger long in grief over letting down the Lord. Freely receive His forgiveness.

"Have mercy on me, O God, according to your unfailing love; according to your great compassion blot out my transgressions. Wash away all my iniquity and cleanse me from my sin" (Psalm 51:1–2).

Lastly, look for those around you who silently suffer or who may be grieving unknowingly. Followers of Jesus sympathize by mourning with those who mourn. Take the time to come alongside them, and offer care, comfort, and Christ. Weep with those who weep, while the Lord's love wipes away their tears. Jesus ministered to the grieving while on earth, and He still comforts and makes hearts happy through the Holy Spirit.

"But the Comforter, which is the Holy Ghost, whom the Father will send in my name, he shall teach you all things, and bring all things to your remembrance, whatsoever I have said unto you" (John 14:26 KJV).

Is Christ my comfort during times of grief? Whom can I comfort who is grieving a loss?

Related Readings: Nehemiah 1:1–10; Ecclesiastes 3:4; Acts 8:2; Romans 12:15

HAPPINESS IN MEEKNESS

"Blessed are the meek, for they will inherit the earth."
Matthew 5:5

The meek are marked by the same quality as their gentle Savior Jesus. Before Christ our meekness is considered weakness; after Christ it is admired as strength. The meek can be happy and content because their quiet confidence is in Christ. Meekness is meant to make men and women of God more like their Lord Jesus. It invites God's blessing.

Jesus described His character: "Take my yoke upon you and learn from me, for I am gentle and humble in heart, and you will find rest for your souls" (Matthew 11:29).

What does it mean to be gentle like Jesus? It is a disposition that does not always have to be right. It is patient to let wisdom prove itself over time. Gentleness has the unique ability to confront injustice and lies boldly and directly—all with respect and honor. The recipient of its reproof feels loved and is captured by its grace-filled demeanor. Indeed, the gentle are happy. They feel no need to prove themselves, only to promote Jesus.

Do you strive to force your opinion, or do you patiently persuade in prayer? Meekness is what makes a marriage beautiful to behold. It attracts friends, solicits respect, and invites admirers from a distance. It is not high-minded, nor does it seek revenge. Meekness on the surface seems easy to take advantage of, but its secret is resting in the Lord's might.

For example, Scripture teaches that husbands are won over by "the unfading beauty of a gentle and quiet spirit, which is of great worth in God's sight" (1 Peter 3:4). Nagging him gets a short-term, guilt-motived response, but bragging on him gets a long-term, grace-motivated response. Men respond to gentle women because they communicate respect.

Women are attracted to gentle men because they communicate care and sensitivity. Loving her conditionally gets a guarded response, but loving her unconditionally gets an unrestrained response. "But the fruit of the Spirit is love, joy, peace, forbearance, kindness, goodness, faithfulness, gentleness and self-control" (Galatians 5:22–23).

Lastly, your meekness qualifies you to enjoy the beauty and provision of God's good earth. Just as He gave the land of Canaan to the broken Israelites and the new world to the persecuted Puritans, so He gives you what you need from the earth's resources. Happy are the meek because they are in a position to steward well the Lord's provisions.

"A little while, and the wicked will be no more; though you look for them, they will not be found. But the meek will inherit the land and enjoy peace and prosperity" (Psalm 37:10–11).

How can I apply gentleness in my life and work? Who needs a gentle word from me?

Related Readings: Zephaniah 3:11–13; 2 Corinthians 10:1; Titus 3:1–2; 1 Peter 2:19–22

GOD SPEAK

"They say, 'This is what the Sovereign LORD says'—when the LORD has not spoken."
Ezekiel 22:28

Be careful what you attribute to the Lord; make sure He is speaking and not ego, greed, or pride. Watch out for spiritually sounding souls, as they can be the culprits of Christless advice. They may talk about God and even invoke His will into discussions. Be wary of someone who assigns God's will arbitrarily—on a prayerless whim.

Make sure what others are suggesting, even commanding, is not self-serving for them. God speaks through generous givers, not tawdry takers. God normally communicates through humility, faith, and accountability. If others have it all figured out for you, this is a flag. They may have a wonderful plan for your life and have missed God's plan entirely. Avoid people who throw around God's endorsement aimlessly.

Pseudospirituality is nauseating to our Lord. How can He speak clearly, consistently, and with creditability through someone infiltrated with compromised character? This type of "God speak" creates a dysfunctional faith. It is faith built on man's persuasion and persistence rather than God's will. What starts out as a pure word from the Lord can evolve into a perverted word from man. Listen first to God; then validate it with man.

God does speak through His Word. Holy Scripture does not need any help as it stands on its own, tall and glistening in the glory of God. While you read and digest His Word, by faith you know He has spoken. He speaks loudly, precisely, and clearly from Scripture. "Jesus answered, 'It is written: "Man shall not live on bread alone, but on every word that comes from the mouth of God"'" (Matthew 4:4).

Use the New Testament as a filter for the Old Testament. This is the Jesus method of Bible interpretation. Seminary can be a good form of learning, but sitting at the feet of Jesus is better! As He speaks to you through His Word, validate it through wise counsel.

God speaks loudly and precisely every day. He speaks through authorities, He speaks through our spouse, He speaks through our health, He speaks through our calendar, He speaks through friends, He speaks through strangers, and He speaks through circumstances, but most of all He speaks through His Word.

Obey what you know, and over time what you are unsure of will become clear. Listen intently to the Lord and submit. Do not use or abuse this Christian privilege of hearing, knowing, and understanding God's voice. He speaks; so humbly listen and obey.

"The LORD came and stood there, calling as at the other times, 'Samuel! Samuel!' Then Samuel said, 'Speak, for your servant is listening'" (1 Samuel 3:10).

Is the Bible my primary resource for discerning God's will?

Related Readings: Exodus 20:1; Psalm 62:11; Acts 11:9; Hebrews 1:1–3

HAPPINESS IN PASSION

"Blessed are those who hunger and thirst for righteousness, for they will be filled."
Matthew 5:6

Passion precedes a hungry heart for God, as determined disciples of Jesus are not satisfied until they get to the Lord for love and direction. What does it mean to hunger and thirst for righteousness? It is a deep desire within the believer's inner being to not only want to participate in righteousness but also possess it. It craves more of Christ.

"Listen to me, you who pursue righteousness and who seek the LORD: Look to the rock from which you were cut and to the quarry from which you were hewn" (Isaiah 51:1).

A faith-focused frame of mind is filled with God thoughts. When I give in to doubtful thinking, I am susceptible to believing lies, but when my mind is set on things above, the world's allure loses its luster. Like a rock climber, we can look up and see the beauty of our destination, or we can look down and become dizzy with doubt and fear. "You come to the help of those who gladly do right, who remember your ways" (Isaiah 64:5).

Happiness results when we pursue righteousness with a passion. Does this drive your behavior? Do you try to get by with what is least expected from the Lord, or do you seek to exceed His eternal expectations? What if we pursued righteousness like we pursue unrighteous mammon—money? Economics, politics, and religion would all benefit. "In the way of righteousness there is life; along that path is immortality" (Proverbs 12:28).

Sinners seek Jesus for salvation, and then they continue to seek their Lord for sanctification. Our pursuit of righteousness was enabled by Christ's purchase of righteousness on the cross. Hunger and thirst are appetites that return frequently. So we daily feast by faith before our heavenly Father. God gladly fills and satisfies our soul.

What hinders your race for righteousness? Are you in the race or sitting on the sidelines? Perhaps you once sought the Lord. It is not too late to return to a righteous rhythm of life. Do not allow the hypocrisies of others to become an excuse for your inconsistent living. Jesus Christ is the standard bearer for righteousness. So make Him the goal for goodness.

Constant meals of grace are merited for a hungry heart and a thirsty soul. So take time to take in His hearty meat of forgiveness and to drink His delicious love. His banquet table of peace, joy, holiness, wisdom, faith, hope, and happiness satisfies to the uttermost. A life filled with the righteousness of God has no room for other meaningless morsels. It is full.

"You have loved righteousness and hated wickedness; therefore God, your God, has set you above your companions by anointing you with the oil of joy" (Hebrews 1:9).

Is my heart hungry for Jesus and Jesus alone? Am I in pursuit of righteousness?

Related Readings: Psalm 11:7; Psalm 106:3; Matthew 5:20; 1 Timothy 6:11; Hebrews 10:38

PRAY ABOUT THAT

"Pray that the LORD your God will tell us where we should go and what we should do."
Jeremiah 42:3

There is wisdom in praying about "that," whatever "that" may mean. It may mean waiting on marriage because one parent has yet to bless the engagement. "That" could represent a check in your spirit over a business deal or an additional financial obligation. Praying about "that" is the Lord's way to protect, preserve, and provide for His children.

What are you currently facing that needs your prayerful attention? Perhaps it is a career transition—pray about that, considering changing churches—pray about that, tempted to quit school—pray about that, or weighing an opportunity to volunteer—pray about that. Prayerfully ask, "What does the Lord want for my life and what is best for His kingdom?"

"Then you will call on me and come and pray to me, and I will listen to you. You will seek me and find me when you seek me with all your heart" (Jeremiah 29:12–13).

It is in the discipline of waiting that we discern the best course of action. Consider cloistering yourself with Christ for twenty-four hours just to listen and learn. It is rare that prayer is a waste of time; indeed, it saves time. When you pray about "that," you allow the Holy Spirit to tap on the brakes of your busy life. Slow down and listen to Him.

Prayer positions you to be productive in the ways of God. Abraham's senior servant experienced this. "Then he prayed, 'LORD, God of my master Abraham, make me successful today, and show kindness to my master Abraham'" (Genesis 24:12).

When you, your family, your church, your company, or your ministry prays about "that," you receive liability insurance for your life from the Lord. Where He leads, He commits to provide. Where He reroutes, He creates the necessary resources. Where He shuts doors, He opens another with greater kingdom possibilities. So pray about that knot in your stomach, and watch Him free you in effective service for your Savior Jesus.

"Lord, let your ear be attentive to the prayer of this your servant and to the prayer of your servants who delight in revering your name. Give your servant success today by granting him favor in the presence of this man" (Nehemiah 1:11).

What am I facing that needs my patient prayers? Whom can I engage to pray with me?

Related Readings: Ezra 8:23; Daniel 9:20; Luke 22:40–46; Acts 4:23–31

DIO

D10

POOR AND NEEDY

"Now this was the sin of your sister Sodom: She and her daughters were arrogant, overfed and unconcerned; they did not help the poor and needy." Ezekiel 16:49

The poor and needy abound, and poverty can be their gateway to God. It is a chronic ministry opportunity on behalf of Jesus Christ. Whether it is down the street or across eight time zones, the poor and needy are in need of food, jobs, and spiritual nourishment. Our own abundance can inoculate us from the hunger of others, and we forget the poor.

We enjoy so much delicious food that it is not uncommon for leftovers to be thrown in the trash—a feast for the poor and needy. Food is a daily necessity that needs to remind us to thank God and to feed the hungry. The blessing over meals is an expression of gratitude to God for His provision. Perhaps our mealtime prayer, as we enjoy life and the Lord, can also include a prayer for those who are starving to death without Jesus.

We can ask the Lord to use us to become agents on behalf of the poor and needy. This may mean sponsoring a child overseas, or it may mean working in a soup kitchen for the homeless. It could be as simple as an anonymous delivery of groceries to a struggling family. A little bit of love in action goes a long way with the Lord's favor.

James, the half brother of Jesus, said it well: "Religion that God our Father accepts as pure and faultless is this: to look after orphans and widows in their distress and to keep oneself from being polluted by the world" (James 1:27). A compelling distinctive of the early church was its love and compassion toward the poor and needy.

The church of Jesus Christ must be a lighthouse, a refuge, and a rescuer for the displaced and disenfranchised. As you take care of the hungry and homeless in your community, you may also be led by God to help the poor and needy internationally. Use your medical skills, your home building experience, or your homemaker expertise to serve for Jesus.

With a fraction of money and business training on your part, hundreds of economic enterprises could be birthed within the ranks of the poor and needy. Perhaps you place a Bible verse on the dash of your car to remind you to pray for the poor. Give your time and money generously. As everyone does a little, a tsunami of relief will flood the poor and needy with life's necessities. Then some will embrace by faith the Jesus you are personifying by your good works. The gospel lived will lead to the gospel believed!

"Let your light shine before others, that they may see your good deeds and glorify your Father in heaven" (Matthew 5:16).

Am I intentional in my prayers and gifts for the poor? Who is in need I can serve today?

Related Readings: Deuteronomy 24:14; Psalm 40:17; Proverbs 14:31; Mark 10:21

D11

HAPPY ARE THE MERCIFUL

"Blessed are the merciful, for they will be shown mercy."
Matthew 5:7

Merciless men and women lack the joy of Jesus. You can see it in their hard face that is reflected by their hardened heart. Indeed, mercy is meant to mold us into the image of our Savior Jesus. He was a man of mercy who looked into the eyes of sinners with mercy and over His complacent and corrupt city with tearful mercy. "As he approached Jerusalem and saw the city, he wept over it" (Luke 19:41). Mercy cares and cries.

Tormented is the soul of those who seek to judge others for juvenile behavior, when they have experienced the mercies of their Lord Jesus Christ. How can we stay bitter when we enjoy the betterment of God's blessings? Mercy does not obsess over what others get away with; instead, it pities the poor soul who is blind to true freedom found in grace.

Jesus said, "Do not judge, and you will not be judged. Do not condemn, and you will not be condemned. Forgive, and you will be forgiven" (Luke 6:37).

Has someone wronged you? Are you mad for being left out? Mercy extends to intentional and unintentional offenses. Tension and hard feelings fester where mercy has vacated, but grace and forgiveness flourish where mercy is at home. We give mercy when we look back and see mercy received and when we look forward to anticipate the mercy we need.

Who needs mercy? The poor do; when you show them mercy, it is like giving to the Lord. "Whoever is kind to the poor lends to the LORD, and he will reward them for what they have done" (Proverbs 19:17). God rewards mercy with mercy. You really do not desire what you deserve. A child of the living Lord really wants His reward of grace and mercy.

So enter often through the quiet vestibule of prayer into the sanctuary of your heavenly Father's presence. Bow in humble worship and adoration. Thank Him for the certitudes of His promises, confess your sin, repent, and receive His mercy and grace. His mercy is sudden and sure. Do not delay its deployment to your circle of influence. Mercy horded does not help anyone, but it hurts everyone. It is meant to activate your actions to love.

Mercy loves, not expecting to be loved; serves, not expecting to be served; and gives, not expecting to receive. Mercy raises the conversation beyond itself to Christ. It asks, "What does Jesus want?" Mercy educates the ignorant, cares for the careless, instructs the immature, and snatches sinners from hell. Happiness is mercy given and mercy received. "And you must show mercy to those whose faith is wavering. Rescue others by snatching them from the flames of judgment. Show mercy to still others, but do so with great caution, hating the sins that contaminate their lives" (Jude 1:22–24 NLT).

Do I actively receive and give God's mercy? Am I merciful to myself?

Related Readings: Job 6:14; Micah 6:8; Matthew 18:23–35; James 2:12–13

D12

GOD'S BREATH

"This is what the Sovereign LORD says to these bones:
I will make breath enter you, and you will come to life." Ezekiel 37:5

Without Christ we are dead in our sins, but in Christ we come alive. He breathes life into our souls. Sin is a drag on life—Christ is fuel for life. Sin is a wall between God and man—Christ is a bridge between God and man. Sin bleaches the bones of life and causes them to become brittle and lifeless—Christ is vitamin D for the bones of life and causes them to become robust and resilient. Sin crushes us—Christ builds us up.

Sin kills—Christ makes alive. Sin takes—Christ gives. Sin destroys—Christ creates. Jesus is the antithesis to sin. What sin is, He is not. Sin is bad news—the gospel is good news. A family without the foundation of God is like a ship without a rudder. There is no moral compass to keep you moving in the right direction. The reefs of sin are subtle and promise to rip the hull of your home. You are responsible as the spiritual leader to navigate your family around these perilous pitfalls. Lead them to follow the Lord.

The breath of God is sweet, pleasant, and life-giving. He knows when you feel claustrophobic by the stale air of sin. Jesus is one hundred percent pure oxygen, like the uncontaminated air of a hyperbaric chamber. Let Him breathe on you. Anger may have an asthmatic hold on your relationships. If they are choking, receive the Lord's inhaler of forgiveness and love.

"But it is the spirit in a person, the breath of the Almighty, that gives them understanding" (Job 32:8).

If you are deep into extramarital sex, your air tank of love has been replaced with lust. Thus, exchange your lust with God's unconditional love before your spiritual lungs explode. You have violated the sacred trust of marriage. Only the breath of God can build back the trust. Pray with your spouse, and ask Him to breathe life into your marriage. "In his hand is the life of every creature and the breath of all mankind" (Job 12:10).

Let God breathe life into your work, your kids, your finances, your relationships, your health, and your future. Pray the old hymn, "Holy Spirit, breathe on me, until my heart is clean; let sunshine fill its inmost part, with not a cloud between. Breathe on me, breathe on me, Holy Spirit, breathe on me; take Thou my heart, cleanse every part, Holy Spirit, breathe on me." Inhale the fresh breath of heaven, and exhale the stale air of sin.

"Again Jesus said, 'Peace be with you! As the Father has sent me, I am sending you.' And with that he breathed on them and said, 'Receive the Holy Spirit'" (John 20:21–22).

Do I daily inhale God's breath of faith for my soul and exhale doubt and fear?

Related Readings: Genesis 2:7; Job 33:4; Isaiah 42:5–6; Acts 17:25; 2 Timothy 3:16

HAPPINESS FROM PURITY

"Blessed are the pure in heart, for they will see God."
Matthew 5:8

Purity comes from the perpetual cleansing of Christ. It begins at conversion and continues in consecration. And there is joy that results from a right relationship with Jesus. Guilt is gone, fear flees, peace rules, and hope encourages the heart. Purity in its profound simplicity places us at the feet of Jesus for forgiveness, love, and direction. Pureness applies to pure thoughts, pure motives, pure conversations, and pure behaviors.

"'Come now, let us settle the matter,' says the LORD. 'Though your sins are like scarlet, they shall be as white as snow; though they are red as crimson, they shall be like wool'" (Isaiah 1:18).

Our Savior Jesus scrubs our soul like a holy body wash that leaves us smelling sweet and attractive to a soiled and smelly society. We stay clean so we can offer a pure alternative to those stuck in the muck and mire of self-centered living. Purity of heart places you on the solid rock of Christ's righteousness with the ability to lift others up to a secure place.

"He lifted me out of the slimy pit, out of the mud and mire; he set my feet on a rock and gave me a firm place to stand" (Psalm 40:2).

The Lord lifts us up so we can lift others up, and this is a happy place. Helping others brings happiness. The happiness of heaven comes to earth when purehearted followers of Jesus see people as God sees them—lost, needy, poor, hurting, deceived, and dying. Moral purity and a single-minded spirit give us a clear vision of God and His interests.

You see God in the glory of His holiness. You see the Lord high and lifted up, and you worship Him. You see the love and compassion of Christ. You see the Almighty ever ready to intervene as an advocate on your behalf. You see your heavenly Father full of wisdom and grace. You see your Savior dying and coming alive for you. You see Jesus as King of Kings and Lord of Lords, and you bow in humble submission and service to Him.

Holiness and happiness go together like romance and love. True holiness woos happiness into its presence. It is pure hands and a clean heart that we lift to the Lord in joyful worship. He cleanses us from the filthy lucre of covetousness to be generous. He washes our dirty deeds so we are free to serve others unselfishly. Purity expunges the pollutants of pride, lust, and lying. Pureness allows you to see Jesus, enjoy Jesus, and be like Jesus.

"Let us draw near to God with a sincere heart and with the full assurance that faith brings, having our hearts sprinkled to cleanse us from a guilty conscience and having our bodies washed with pure water" (Hebrews 10:22).

Are my motives and actions pure before God?

Related Readings: Psalm 24:4–5; Acts 15:9; Hebrews 12:14; 1 Timothy 1:5; 1 John 1:7

RADICAL TRUST

"If we are thrown into the blazing furnace, the God we serve is able to save us from it, and he will rescue us from your hand, O king. But even if he does not, we want you to know, O king, that we will not serve your gods or worship the image of gold you have set up." Daniel 3:17–18

Radical trust means you trust God even when He does not come through. You are not pregnant, but you still trust God. You do not have a job, but you still trust God. You have been betrayed, but you still trust God. You are sick, but you still trust God. You are lonely, but you still trust God. You are afraid, but you still trust God.

Your wise decision making is based on God's trustworthiness. You know He is able, but it is still about His timing. And you will not compromise your convictions because you trust Him. It does not seem fair or right. But God has a bigger picture in mind. Do not be held captive by your finite knowledge and understanding. You can still trust the One with infinite wisdom and understanding. You are not alone in your current fire of adversity.

The Lord is with you. Your faith has been bolstered and is not extinguished because you know God is walking with you. Your faith is fireproofed by the Holy Spirit. The flames of hell are no match for fire from heaven. Your Savior defeats Satan in every encounter. But even when you are denied acceptance and physical comfort, you can still trust God.

Trust in God is not just for the good times, though there is a radical trust required as prosperity pelts your faith. But radical trust is much needed when things heat up. When you lose something precious or you are refused something you deserve, this is the time to ratchet up your radical trust. It is for times like this that God has molded your faith.

What if God has not come through? Radical trust means you stay focused on His past faithfulness. The mundane of everyday life is a link in the chain between life's transitions. Today's link is as important as tomorrow's transition. Hope for the transition to come, but trust God with today. You cannot handle more than today's troubles and triumphs. Do not worry about matters in the future over which you have no control.

Trust God with today, and do not worry about the uncertainty of tomorrow. If you obsess over fear of the future, you most certainly will define the ambiguity with negative consequences. Then unwittingly you create a self-fulfilling prophecy. You worry yourself sick. You worry others sick. Or you are of no use for today because you are worried about tomorrow. You are stuck in the inertia of distrust.

But the Lord can be trusted. Meditate on His faithfulness instead of what might happen. Unleash the radical trust that resides within you. Reignite that passion for Jesus. Lay aside the sins of disbelief and worry. Trust God even if He has not or does not come through. He is still trustworthy; so be radical in your trust!

Do I radically trust the Lord with past events and decisions? How is He trustworthy?

Related Readings: Psalm 28:7; Isaiah 12:2; John 8:26; Romans 15:13

PRIDE HUMBLED

"Now I, Nebuchadnezzar, praise and exalt and glorify the King of heaven, because everything
he does is right and all his ways are just. And those who walk in pride he is able to humble."
Daniel 4:37

Pride will eventually give way to humility. It may not happen overnight. It may have to follow a painful process, because pride can be very, very stubborn. Like an embedded splinter deep in the flesh of your foot, it is hard to remove. You cannot remove it alone, and there is constant throbbing and pain until it is extracted.

This is the plight of pride. Pain and suffering are its cohorts. Pride provides a false sense of security. Spiritually minded people know it is only a matter of time until a fall, as pride will catch up with you. Humility was once a staple in your spiritual diet, but success has squelched your humility and subtly replaced it with pride.

The more authority you possess, the more you must submit to accountability. Otherwise, you cannot handle this freewheeling power. Your behavior defaults to pride without the checkmate of humility. This is true in relationships, business, and ministry.

Paranoia is an application of pride. You are fearful of losing control. It is better to hand over control than to lose control. Humility gives control, while pride grasps for it. So be open and humble about your insecurities. We are all insecure to some degree. Humility builds security, and pride tears it down. The humble have nothing to hide. So root out pride, and replace it with humility.

The process of pride's removal begins with submission to Christ. It is acknowledging His lordship and ownership over your life. He is in control. He is large and in charge. Nothing in your life has sneaked up on God. He can be trusted. He holds your life, family, health, and career in His hand. You start by humbly bowing to God.

You have the awesome opportunity to worship and adore Him. When you walk with God, you walk in humility. Pride cannot coexist in a growing relationship with Jesus Christ. Pride is extinguished in the presence of Jesus. Pride is like a roach lurking in the dark recesses of your heart. The Holy Spirit's light reveals pride and convicts you during times of prayer and Scripture meditation.

The second offense to pride is prayer. Ask people to pray for humility to infiltrate and occupy your life. You want the occupation of humility on the soil of your heart and mind.

Humble yourself, and trust God to humble others. It is easy to recognize pride in others while it is still looming in your spirit. Run from spiritual pride. It is the worst kind. It is insidious. It is pharisaical in nature, and it chokes the Holy Spirit. Humility grows in an environment of honesty, openness, prayer, and change. Humble pride!

Heavenly Father, help me walk in humility of heart and mind.

Related Readings: Exodus 10:3; 2 Kings 22:19; Romans 12:3; Philippians 2:1–11

PROCESS ANGER PRAYERFULLY

"A gentle answer turns away wrath, but a harsh word stirs up anger."
Proverbs 15:1

Anger is a God-given emotion, but when it becomes self-serving, it is a relationship killer. Does anger bubble just below the surface of your emotions? Do you justify your anger as an excuse to spew your disappointment at the expense of bruising another? Has a volatile attitude become normal behavior? If so, anger has become a sin that needs serious prayer.

Men and women alike can be afflicted with anger's self-absorbing curse. We can blame it on our hostile home environment growing up, which may have given us a bad example of anger management. But the Christian's process for dealing with sin is not management, but prayerful confession and repentance. I take responsibility for my selfish anger and ask God and others to hold me accountable to walk in humility and patience.

"Mockers stir up a city, but the wise turn away anger" (Proverbs 29:8).

Is anger your method for motivating work associates or intimidating your family? Just because it works does not make it right. Behaviors created by fear do not last. They only contribute to resentment and a dysfunctional environment. If you find yourself being mad, or if anger has become an addiction, seek out help.

Seek the Lord, and admit your need for His grace and forgiveness to flood your heart and mind. Replace your selfish wants with selfless giving. Prayerfully ask the Lord to create a clean heart of patience and contentment; trade your demanding, proud heart. A life full of the Holy Spirit is gentle, loving, and forgiving. There is no room for selfish anger.

"Get rid of all bitterness, rage and anger, brawling and slander, along with every form of malice" (Ephesians 4:31).

Lastly, seek out other followers of Christ who are honest about their struggles with anger, and become accountable to each other. Meet for transformation and truth dealing in the power of the Holy Spirit. Learn how to process anger in a productive way that energizes work against injustice and serves the poor, widows, and orphans. Anger channeled for Christ's purposes is productive and redemptive; thus, prayerfully process your anger.

"My dear brothers and sisters, take note of this: Everyone should be quick to listen, slow to speak and slow to become angry, because human anger does not produce the righteousness that God desires. Therefore, get rid of all moral filth and the evil that is so prevalent and humbly accept the word planted in you, which can save you" (James 1:19–21).

Do I use my anger to control others? If so, will I release my anger to Christ's control?

Related Readings: Proverbs 27:4; Jonah 4:1–3; Colossians 3:8; 1 Timothy 2:8

ORIGIN OF WISDOM

"It is because of him that you are in Christ Jesus, who has become for us wisdom from God—
that is, our righteousness, holiness and redemption." 1 Corinthians 1:30

Where does wisdom originate? The genesis of wisdom is God through His Son Christ Jesus. He is wisdom from God. When He speaks, His wise words resonate eternal truth. Thus, wisdom begins and ends with the Lord Jesus Christ. Ignorant and unwise is the individual whose calculus for wise thinking circumvents Christ—for He is wisdom.

Why did our heavenly Father send us His Son as wisdom from Him? Because God's providential plan begins with righteousness, holiness, and redemption through Jesus. Heavenly wisdom starts in a human heart with belief in Christ as the Son of God. By faith we trust His death on the cross and His resurrection from death to give us life eternal.

Intelligence is frustrated and grossly incomplete without embracing the transcendent and true wisdom of Christ. This is why unbelieving elites attempt to marginalize Jesus. He does not fit into their man-made, man-focused, and man-controlled box. The wisdom of God blows up the world's wisdom and replaces it with humble trust in Jesus. Even some who do not receive God's wisdom will recognize it in other wise leaders they respect.

"And you, Ezra, in accordance with the wisdom of your God, which you possess, appoint magistrates and judges to administer justice to all the people of Trans-Euphrates— all who know the laws of your God. And you are to teach any who do not know them" (Ezra 7:25). Wisdom wisely administered is even admired by unbelievers.

Foolish are those who think their thinking alone is any match to almighty God's algorithms for living. How can a life be fulfilling and focused without faith in the Lord as the underpinning for understanding life and death? It may seem surreal that our Savior Jesus rose from the grave, but this is validation of God's wise plan of salvation, "so that your faith might not rest on human wisdom, but on God's power" (1 Corinthians 2:5).

Therefore, thank the Lord for His infinite wisdom and understanding. Give Him the glory and credit for sending His Son Jesus to earth so you could know and understand Him. And in the process of applying faith in Christ, you acquired the wisdom and knowledge necessary to follow God's will for your life. Praise the Lord—He is the origin of wisdom!

"Amen! Praise and glory and wisdom and thanks and honor and power and strength be to our God for ever and ever. Amen!" (Revelation 7:12).

How can I prayerfully and creatively seek out the wisdom of Christ?

Related Readings: Job 12:13; Job 15:8; Romans 11:33; 1 Corinthians 2:7

GODLY ADVICE

"Then King Rehoboam consulted the elders who had served his father Solomon during his lifetime. 'How would you advise me to answer these people?' he asked. They replied, 'If today you will be a servant to these people and serve them and give them a favorable answer, they will always be your servants.'" 1 Kings 12:6–7

Where can godly advice be found? The source, of course, is Christ, but beyond the creator of wisdom, who can be trusted to dispense counsel that represents God's wisdom? There are godly men and women the Lord has blessed with His insight and discernment of what is right and wrong. Thus, pray for access to people with a wise heart for God.

In addition, look for and engage older mentors who are not afraid to speak the truth clearly and lovingly. It may be a parent or grandparent seasoned in the ways of his or her Savior Jesus who wants you to follow His productive path. Godly advice could come from your pastor, a wise writer, a teacher, or a friend who follows Jesus Christ. Like Job, look for godly wisdom, listen to understand, and then validate its legitimacy.

"Then he looked at wisdom and appraised it; he confirmed it and tested it. And he said to the human race, 'The fear of the Lord—that is wisdom, and to shun evil is understanding'" (Job 28:27–28).

You can be surrounded by godly wisdom and miss the advantage of accessing its availability. Yes, the process of acquiring wisdom is prayerful and takes more time than just finding friends to encourage what you want to do, but the results are worth the wait. A quick decision can be expedient but ineffective. A wise decision requires patience and is extremely effective. So take your time. Do not be rushed into regretting your decision.

For example, you can decide to serve the people you lead, or you can demand that they serve you. Godly leaders will tell you it is not what you demand that results in long-term sustainability but what you model in humble service. For a man it can be unloading the dishwasher, vacuuming, and taking out the trash at home. For a woman it can be planning a budget and living within the budget. Godly behavior grows out of godly examples.

Paul modeled this way of life: "Therefore I urge you to imitate me. For this reason I have sent to you Timothy, my son whom I love, who is faithful in the Lord. He will remind you of my way of life in Christ Jesus, which agrees with what I teach everywhere in every church" (1 Corinthians 4:16–17). Look for godly advice from godly people.

Avoid the temptation to dismiss those who are gifted in discerning your needs just because you know what they will say. Truth needs repeating, and when you expose your mind and heart to repetitive godly advice, God begins to penetrate pockets of pride. Humility asks the godly for prayer and wise counsel; so stay humble, and seek wisdom.

What godly example has the Lord placed in my life from whom I need to learn?

Related Readings: 2 Samuel 20:14–22; Proverbs 12:15; Proverbs 19:20; Romans 16:19

WISE LIVING

"Who is wise? He will realize these things. Who is discerning? He will understand them.
The ways of the LORD are right; the righteous walk in them, but the rebellious stumble in them."
Hosea 14:9

Wise living keeps the realization and understanding of God in the vortex of your thinking, as His awareness is centerpiece. What Jesus would do becomes a way of life. His desires, His motivations, His thoughts, and His character become paramount in your thinking. This leads to wise living because it is based on Christlike living.

God's ways are the path to wisdom. The wisdom of God is unfathomable, and He is willing to share. In fact, His preference is to shower His children with raindrops of wisdom. He delights in imparting His game plan for living. However, it takes a regular realization on our part for the wisdom of God to penetrate our thinking.

Wise living defaults to a biblical worldview of thinking. The ways of God are revealed as you understand and apply the Bible. The Bible teaches that you serve and worship a personal God. There are no details of your life of which He is not aware. He knows how many hairs are on your head, which may not be as many as when you were younger!

This understanding of His personal concern invites security and confidence in Him. This is wise living based on the character of God. There are right ways and wrong ways to live life. The ways of the Lord are right. Furthermore, His desire is for His followers to treat others as He treats them. This is a high standard, but this is the road of wisdom.

This level of love and respect for others is wise living. What goes around comes around. When we are too busy for people, we are too busy. Do not let your success shelter you from people, as they are objects of God's affection. Jesus gave His life on the cross for people. Your accessibility to people is wise living.

Wise living includes the ability to discern right from wrong and good from best. Why settle for God's crumbs when you can feast at His banquet table of wisdom? Therefore, present your insights with grace and humility.

What God changes stays changed. What we change has a tendency to revert back to its old way of doing things. Indeed, you see what needs to be done, but be patient.

This leads to wise living for all involved. Above all, seek out wisdom. Ask God first, and then listen to others. Be humble and teachable. Understanding and discernment will - follow. This is wise living!

Am I wise to listen to the Lord with an open and understanding heart?

Related Readings: Proverbs 11:30; Proverbs 13:14, 20; Proverbs 15:31

WORTH THE WAIT

"Now there was a man in Jerusalem called Simeon, who was righteous and devout. He was waiting
for the consolation of Israel, and the Holy Spirit was upon him. It had been revealed to him
by the Holy Spirit that he would not die before he had seen the Lord's Christ." Luke 2:25–26

The first Christmas was an exercise in waiting for God, as His people had been anticipating the arrival of Messiah for hundreds of years. They longed and looked for their Lord to come as sovereign ruler and king, but instead God's Son entered earth in a humble manger, secured by a simple stable.

His parents were not royal or regal, but righteous, and a little rough around the edges. The ethos of Jesus' birth was unexpected, but He arrived at just the right time to redeem the souls of men. The Bible says, "But when the fullness of the time had come, God sent forth His Son, born of a woman, born under the law" (Galatians 4:4 NKJV).

God is worth the wait because He is never late, but seldom is He early. What are you waiting for right now? Is it a job, a wedding, a class, forgiveness, peace, or love? Whatever your situation, wait for the Lord to lead you into His opportunities, and by faith you will find fulfillment. Waiting for God is worthwhile.

God is worth the wait because He gets you where you need to be without relying on the delay of human hassle. People are pawns in the hand of Providence; so do not trust in them for peace or progress. God will bring just the right relationships and resources into place in His perfect timing. Trust Him to be your provision. He will provide what you need in the nick of time. You can stare down fear with the inner strength of the Holy Spirit.

Confide in Christ as your confidant. He will counsel you in the wise way to walk. Wait for God's best; in retrospect you will have no regrets. Look for Him in humble people and simple situations, as pride and sin seem to overcomplicate circumstances. Jesus was worth the wait at His first coming, and He will be worth the wait at His second coming. In the meantime, practice His presence in the present.

Prayerfully follow the Holy Spirit's leading during times of waiting, and you will walk in the ways of the wise. The Bible says this about a saint who profoundly understood waiting for God: "Noah was a righteous man, blameless in His time; Noah walked with God" (Genesis 6:9 NASB). This Christmas, wait on Christ to show you His next steps for life.

Where do I need to be patient and wait on God to fulfill His purpose in His timing?

Related Readings: Lamentations 3:25; Acts 1:4; Acts 10:2–22; Titus 2:11–14

EXPECTING A BABY

"He [Joseph] went there to register with Mary, who was pledged to be married to him and was expecting a child. While they were there, the time came for the baby to be born, and she gave birth to her firstborn, a son. She wrapped him in cloths and placed him in a manger, because there was no room for them in the inn." Luke 2:5–7

An expecting wife needs extra sensitivity and a strong, supportive husband. She is emotionally vulnerable and physically overwhelmed at times. As with Mary, there may be some uncertainty of the ultimate outcome, but she trusts the Lord to care for her and her baby. The circumstances are challenging when you are away from the comforts of home and its familiar feel. Pregnancy is a transition that requires trust in the Lord.

Husbands, your expecting wife needs you to step up like Joseph and provide leadership. This is not the time to lose faith or become frightened. Perfect love casts out fear; so overcome any apprehension with the Christlike love that dwells in your mind and heart. See pregnancy as a prayerful process to accomplish the plan of almighty God, as expecting moms and dads can expect great things from Him. Hannah and her husband Elkanah gave God the glory for the blessing of their son Samuel.

"Early the next morning they arose and worshiped before the LORD and then went back to their home at Ramah. Elkanah made love to his wife Hannah, and the LORD remembered her. So in the course of time Hannah became pregnant and gave birth to a son. She named him Samuel, saying, 'Because I asked the LORD for him'" (1 Samuel 1:19–20).

Furthermore, a husband's leadership needs to provide protection for his wife. Accompany her, as Joseph did, to new places and people who might take advantage of your sweet-spirited spouse. It makes your woman feel safe and secure when you buffer her from bad people or strangers with unseemly motives. Stay with her, and see her through stressful situations, like family members who can be awkward and insensitive toward your bride.

Intervene and defend your wife if your children, parents, or siblings show disrespect, however subtle it might be. God made you one flesh in marriage; so if she is offended, you are offended. Of course, prayerfully confront all parties in a spirit of grace and humility, but with clarity. An expecting wife is beautiful to behold as she brings forth an innocent infant woven in her womb by God. Be there for her labor of love for the Lord and for His gift of a precious little one to love. Mary gave God the glory for her baby Jesus!

"The LORD has done this, and it is marvelous in our eyes" (Psalm 118:23).

Whom can I support and pray for who is expecting a baby? How can I thank my heavenly Father for His gift of baby Jesus to me and to mankind?

Related Readings: Isaiah 7:14; Micah 5:2; John 16:21; 1 John 4:18

CHRIST IN CHRISTMAS

"Today in the town of David a Savior has been born to you; he is Christ the Lord."
Luke 2:11

Christ in Christmas is like memorial in Memorial Day, mother in Mother's Day, father in Father's Day, labor in Labor Day, independence in Independence Day, and thanksgiving in Thanksgiving Day. However, in our attempt to not offend other religions and to become politically correct, we have diluted and desecrated the true meaning of Christmas.

Indeed, Jesus is the reason for the season. He is the explanation for eternal life. He is the answer from almighty God for grace and truth incarnate. He is the beginning and the end, a bright light in the darkest darkness. He is our hope on earth as we prepare for our home in heaven.

If Christ is not in Christmas, then churches can convert to corporate offices and missions can morph into humanitarian agencies. Christ in Christmas creates a tension for those who have yet to trust, but to us who have been saved, it is the most significant celebration.

"But when the set time had fully come, God sent his Son, born of a woman, born under the law, to redeem those under the law, that we might receive adoption to sonship" (Galatians 4:4–5).

Christ in Christmas means you live for a purpose much grander than merchandise and commerce. Your children have a legacy of love for God and country and service to others. You work as unto the Lord and give generously out of gratitude for God's bountiful blessings.

Christ in Christmas motivates you to live like you were dying and to die like you were living, all in a spirit of faith, hope, and love. By God's grace you promote a Christian worldview populated by praying people and full of eternal opportunities, while on guard in Spirit-led discernment to Satan's schemes and evil's deceptive intentions.

Christ in Christmas compels you to exclaim, "He was born so we would believe, He died so we would live, and He rose so we would rise!" Therefore, in humility and with pride, boldly keep Christ in Christmas. His birth is your excuse to brag about Jesus.

The Bible says, "For to us a child is born, to us a son is given, and the government will be on his shoulders. And he will be called Wonderful Counselor, Mighty God, Everlasting Father, Prince of Peace" (Isaiah 9:6).

How can I keep Christ in Christmas with my church and family traditions and in my everyday life and conversations?

Related Readings: Isaiah 19:20; Malachi 3:1; Acts 2:36

PEACE ON EARTH

"Glory to God in the highest heaven, and on earth peace to those on whom his favor rests."
Luke 2:14

Peace on earth begins with peace in the human heart. It is the result of an inner transformation that affects external conditions. For example, if a home is conflicted with angry adults, then peace will come when hearts have been captured by peace with God. When Jesus enters the arena of life, He brings peace to those who submit to Him.

"Therefore, since we have been justified through faith, we have peace with God through our Lord Jesus Christ, through whom we have gained access by faith into this grace in which we now stand" (Romans 5:1–2).

Are you stressed out over meeting everyone's expectations? Is the pressure of buying gifts, planning menus, and making year-end financial decisions pushing your patience to the edge? If so, inhale the peace of God, and exhale the expectations of others. Be careful not to miss the joy of Jesus during this celebration of His birth. Focus on His desires.

Peace on earth does not mean all wars will cease, as our Savior taught, "When you hear of wars and rumors of wars, do not be alarmed. Such things must happen, but the end is still to come" (Mark 13:7). In fact, many times following Christ means a clash with the mores of society, a discomfort with family members, and conflict with your work culture.

However, in the middle of our unrest, we can rest in the Lord. The calming presence of Jesus was illustrated as He lay in swaddling clothes as the world's Savior. His peace pursues impure hearts—He came to "seek and to save the lost" (Luke 19:10). So begin by surrendering to your Master Jesus, who began His reign in a humble manger.

Worship the glory of God in all of His goodness, mercy, and grace. Wise men and women still seek Him because He is the originator of wisdom and peace. His favor rests on those who rest in Him, love and obey Him, and follow Him all the days of their lives. So settle down and see Jesus. Replace your frantic pace with calm faith and loud noise with quiet silence. Invite the peace of God to enter into your hurried heart. His peace settles stress.

Lastly, use this season of celestial celebration to celebrate your salvation in Christ. Bake a birthday cake for Jesus, and sing happy birthday to your Savior. Dress up in His honor, and read the Christmas story. Encourage the children and grandchildren to take on Bible character roles and act out that special day in Bethlehem. Most of all, by grace model for a world without peace—the world of peace Jesus gives you.

Have I made peace with God? How can I rest in His peace under stressful situations?

Related Readings: Job 22:21; Psalm 85:8; Isaiah 9:6; 1 Corinthians 14:33; Philippians 4:7–9

PROPHECY FULFILLED

"All this took place to fulfill what the Lord had said through the prophet: 'The virgin will be with child and will give birth to a son, and they will call him Immanuel'—which means, 'God with us.'"
Matthew 1:22–23

Prophecy predicted Christ's birth, His life, and His second coming. Hundreds of years before His entrance into earth, heaven directed men of God to describe His declaration of salvation for mankind. Christmas celebrates God being with us in the person of Jesus Christ. He is Immanuel, and He invites the human race to learn of His everlasting love.

The purpose of prophecy is not to chart out every intricate detail of how and when Christ will return the second time. Jesus said only His heavenly Father is privy to these predictions, "No one knows about that day or hour, not even the angels in heaven, nor the Son, but only the Father" (Matthew 24:36). The purpose of prophecy is to validate what Jesus has done and will do in the future. The unknown of His exact return gives us a sense of urgency to prepare for His second coming, by doing His will while we wait.

Prophecy predicted Jesus would be born in Bethlehem, and He was. "But you, Bethlehem Ephrathah, though you are small among the clans of Judah, out of you will come for me one who will be ruler over Israel, whose origins are from of old, from ancient times" (Micah 5:2). He was to be born of a virgin and called Immanuel, and He was. "Therefore the Lord himself will give you a sign: The virgin will be with child and will give birth to a son, and will call him Immanuel" (Isaiah 7:14). Prophecy affirms your faith in Christ.

Christmas is your opportunity to celebrate the accuracy of almighty God's words spoken through His humble and obedient servants. Use this merry moment to bring joy to the hearts of those yet to believe and experience their heavenly Father's grace and forgiveness. Be there for your family and friends, especially those who struggle to see themselves as precious in the Lord's eyes. Christmas reminds us His best is yet to come!

Jesus predicted His death. "He then began to teach them that the Son of Man must suffer many things and be rejected by the elders, chief priests and teachers of the law, and that he must be killed and after three days rise again" (Mark 8:31).

Do I understand the significance of the prophecies Christ has and will fulfill? Whom can I extend joy to in the name of Jesus during this celebration of His birthday?

Related Readings: Genesis 3:15; Galatians 4:4; Isaiah 11:10; Romans 15:12

GOD DRAWING NEAR

*"In the beginning was the Word, and the Word was with God, and the Word was God.
The Word became flesh and made his dwelling among us. We have seen his glory,
the glory of the One and Only, who came from the Father, full of grace and truth."*
John 1:1, 14

God came near us on Christmas in the birth of Jesus so we could draw near to Him for eternity by a spiritual birth based on belief in Christ. The Son of God became the Son of Man so we could become children of God. It is an inspiring image to see the Lord leave His throne in heaven to be laid in a manger on earth. "Who, being in very nature God, did not consider equality with God something to be grasped, but made himself nothing, taking the very nature of a servant, being made in human likeness" (Philippians 2:6–7).

How can this be that God would leave glory to bring His glory to earth? Can the human mind fully comprehend His depth of love and outpouring of compassion? The sacredness of our Savior's birth can easily get lost in the commercialism of the Christmas season. He dwelt with us on earth so we could dwell with Him now and forevermore in heaven.

Are you grateful that the Almighty draws near to His creation even when the created ones avoid His advances? Indeed, His holy love is relentless in reaching out to those who reject Him and to those who have been rejected. He draws near to the nobodies, the some-bodies, the atheists, the almost Christians, the new Christians, the backslidden Christians, and the Christians who are growing in grace. However, distance brings distrust. "She obeys no one, she accepts no correction. She does not trust in the LORD, she does not draw near to her God" (Zephaniah 3:2). So draw near, and your faith will flourish.

The simple act of drawing near to the Lord does what the law never could. "The former regulation is set aside because it was weak and useless (for the law made nothing perfect), and a better hope is introduced, by which we draw near to God" (Hebrews 7:18–19). God replaces guilt with hope and performance with acceptance. Close proximity to Christ produces enduring faith, patient love, and encouraging hope.

So are you drawing near to your heavenly Father as He draws near to you? Do you allow Him to get up close and personal in your character, your choices, and your convictions? There is no downside to drawing near to God. He has your back, your front, and both sides. There is no fear when you draw near. There is peace and forgiveness when you draw near. You draw near and get the sense that everything is okay because He is okay and in control.

"Let us draw near to God with a sincere heart in full assurance of faith, having our hearts sprinkled to cleanse us from a guilty conscience" (Hebrews 10:22).

*Do I allow the Lord to draw near to my heart, mind, and soul? Do I reciprocate by -
drawing near to Him in faith, worship, confession, repentance, and thanksgiving?*

Related Readings: Isaiah 7:14; Isaiah 51:5; Luke 21:28; Hebrews 10:1

FINDING GOD

"Jesus said to him, 'Today salvation has come to this house, because this man, too, is a son of Abraham. For the Son of Man came to seek and to save the lost.'" Luke 19:9–10

The Christless human condition is lost and in need of a Savior. An unsaved soul is in search of peace, forgiveness, and eternal life in heaven. Along the way a soul's search may take detours into the pleasures of sin for a season, but when awakened it comes back to the narrow road looking for the Lord. Faith is found in a humble and sincere search for God.

"Enter through the narrow gate. For wide is the gate and broad is the road that leads to destruction, and many enter through it. But small is the gate and narrow the road that leads to life, and only a few find it" (Matthew 7:13–14).

Finding God is educational as the Bible contains sixty-six textbooks in the University of Truth. Upon a quick read, Jesus is the main character, ever looking to give glory to His heavenly Father. He is truth personified, and His promise is the only way to God. Faith in Jesus as the Son of God is the bridge from an endless hell to eternal salvation in heaven.

"Thomas said to him, 'Lord, we don't know where you are going, so how can we know the way?' Jesus answered, 'I am the way and the truth and the life. No one comes to the Father except through me'" (John 14:5–6).

Not only does our inner being initiate an audience with almighty God, His great love is out to get us. Righteousness out-romances the soul from sin; it just depends on which voice we follow. Listen for the Lord, and you will hear His tender calling for you to come home. Listen to sin, and it leads to sorrow. Listen, learn, and come to Christ in faith.

"No one can come to me unless the Father who sent me draws them, and I will raise them up at the last day. It is written in the Prophets: 'They will all be taught by God.' Everyone who has heard the Father and learned from him comes to me" (John 6:44–45).

Therefore, look for the Lord by faith, and you will find Him. Submit to the seducing and convicting power of the Holy Spirit in your heart. No one has ever regretted receiving the Lord Christ into his or her life, but many have wished they had not waited so long. A joyful, heavenly party awaits the ones who come to their senses and go home to their Savior Jesus!

"'My son,' the father said, 'you are always with me, and everything I have is yours. But we had to celebrate and be glad, because this brother of yours was dead and is alive again; he was lost and is found'" (Luke 15:31–32).

Am I sincerely searching for God in worship, Bible study, prayer, and obedience?

Related Readings: Deuteronomy 4:29; Job 8:4–6; Acts 17:27; Hebrews 11:6

THE LORD'S NAME

"And everyone who calls on the name of the LORD will be saved."
Joel 2:32

The name of the Lord can be trusted, and His name is much more than great riches. His name is wonderful. His name is beautiful. The name of the Lord is full of grace and truth. His name is the object of salvation. The weary sinner who cries out to the Lord will be saved. Trust in the name of the Lord, and you will be saved. The Lord is your salvation.

He saves us from our sins. He saves us from utter ruin and damnation in hell. He saves us from ourselves. His salvation is boundless and all encompassing. His name is a refuge for the refugee, a shelter for the homeless, and a retreat for the restless. The name of the Lord is not soiled or tarnished. His name represents the glory of God.

The name *Lord* conjures up emotions of comfort, joy, peace, holiness, fear, freedom, and gratitude. Candidates for Christ around the world know His name intellectually, and His name is known experientially by almost two billion believers globally. His name is above every name. At His name every knee will eventually bow and every tongue will eventually confess that He is Lord. (See Philippians 2:10–11.)

The Lord's name remains a symbol of holiness, humility, and hope, at best, unless we truly trust Him by calling on His name. An emergency call is useless unless someone phones for help. In a time of need or uncertainty, you default to a name you can trust. You can call on Him because He has already called you—yours is a return call.

Softly and tenderly Jesus is calling lost sinners to come home. He has already reached out. He reached out on the cross with the ultimate expression of love and sacrifice. And still today He has reached out through the prayers of friends and family. He has reached out by giving you breath to breathe and another day to become alive.

Do not let another day pass without calling on the name of the Lord. Your fears will subside when you call on the name of the Lord. Your strength will increase when you call on the name of the Lord. Your faith will bolster when you call on the name of the Lord.

Humility invites you to call on the name of the Lord. Your prosperity compels you to call on the name of the Lord. Your need for wisdom implores you to call on the name of the Lord. Call on Him boldly and often; you cannot call too much. God does not have voice mail or a receptionist. He has a direct line and accessibility twenty-four hours a day, seven days a week. Do not delay. Bow in humble prayer, confession, and repentance. Call on the name of the Lord and be saved!

"If you declare with your mouth, 'Jesus is Lord,' and believe in your heart that God raised him from the dead, you will be saved" (Romans 10:9).

Have I called on the Lord for salvation? Do I call on the name of the Lord for help?

Related Readings: Genesis 4:26; 1 Chronicles 16:8; Acts 15:26; 2 Thessalonians 1:12

SAVED TO SERVE

"Let us not become weary in doing good, for at the proper time we will reap a harvest if we do not give up. Therefore, as we have opportunity, let us do good to all people, especially to those who belong to the family of believers." Galatians 6:9–10

An affluent society can easily succumb to selfish Christianity. An inward-focused behavior feels it is entitled to be served rather than to serve. It happens at home, with work, at school, with government, in local communities, and, sadly, even at church. Affluence provides the expedient option of giving money but not precious time.

Yet the heart of Jesus Christ is selfless in service—doing good for others without expecting anything in return. So as seasoned followers of our Savior Jesus, we have to ask ourselves, "Is my desire to be served or to serve?" "Am I volunteering at church to serve fellow believers?" "Do I give my time in ministry to care for those outside the faith?" The example of Jesus is to be a servant of all—even the ultimate sacrifice of death.

"And whoever wants to be first must be slave of all. For even the Son of Man did not come to be served, but to serve, and to give his life as a ransom for many" (Mark 10:44–45).

Death to our self-centered motivations makes us a candidate in the Lord's service business. Customers of Christ constantly call in with complaints, needs, and fears. Their rent or house payment may be past due, their electricity about to be cut off, their daughter pregnant out of wedlock, or their son addicted to drugs and alcohol.

You do not have to be an expert to listen and pray with someone who is confused and hurting. It only takes availability and the ability to care. Faith is a verb, or it is not real faith at all. If my behavior does not back my beliefs, I really do not believe. I only say I believe. However, faith in action looks for opportunities to serve in the name of Jesus.

What is your personal ministry? Is it a ministry of prayer? Has God called you to short-term or long-term missions? Perhaps you can volunteer one day a week at a nursing home or tutor inner-city children afterschool. Do for one what you would like to do for everyone. Quality service affects one person at a time for God's glory. He gave us His matchless grace so we might magnify His glory in selfless service to the saved and the unsaved.

"Because of the service by which you have proved yourselves, others will praise God for the obedience that accompanies your confession of the gospel of Christ, and for your generosity in sharing with them and with everyone else" (2 Corinthians 9:13).

What is my personal ministry to others on behalf of Jesus Christ?

Related Readings: Joshua 22:5; 1 Samuel 12:24; Psalm 116:16; Ephesians 6:6–8

AGREED EXPECTATIONS

"Do two walk together unless they have agreed to do so?"
Amos 3:3

Sometimes it is difficult to agree upon expectations, and, in reality, we deal daily with expectation management. We are expected to do certain things at work, at home, and in friendships. We also project expectations on others. We know God expects faithfulness from us, and we have our expectations of Him, but expectations can get us into trouble.

We can expect the wrong things. Our expectations can be unclear or unrealistic or unrighteous. The same can be said of what others expect of us. At work you thought one outcome was expected while your supervisor expected something different. Even after the goals were put into writing, there were still different interpretations of the facts.

Indeed, it is easier to corral expectations of simple tasks. I can expect or even require my children to complete their homework. This is not unreasonable, and I would be an unfit parent if I did not provide some framework of expectations for my children. However, I would be an equally ineffective parent if I had expectations of my children but did not communicate them with grace and understanding. Clarifying expectations takes time.

"Fathers, do not exasperate your children; instead, bring them up in the training and instruction of the Lord" (Ephesians 6:4).

Furthermore, the more your trust grows in a relationship, the fewer the expectations. Trust precludes the need for expectations. Trust causes many expectations to expire. When you place your total trust in God, you default to character expectations. You expect His love to be unconditional. You expect His forgiveness to be infinite. You expect to avail yourself to His wisdom. Your expectations are character driven rather than cynical driven.

It becomes about God's will, not our wants. Healthy expectations revolve around God and His desires. The focus is off me but on God and others. He orchestrates the concert of life; so the goal is to discover His role for me and follow His lead. Then the motive with people becomes one of serving them in order to carry out God's plan for their lives.

How can you facilitate understanding God's will for your spouse, child, or work associate? This is not always easy to discern, but character-driven expectations can get to the point of their true need, and you can help meet that need. Focus on building trust in the relationship, and communication will flow more clearly and compassionately.

Focus on fewer expectations and more on trust. Allow your expectations to begin and end with the character of God. Expect less, and you will receive more. You can expect His faithfulness. Agree to expect what God expects, and allow your expectant desires to birth God's will.

What does the Lord expect of me in the life roles He has assigned to me?

Related Readings: Job 29:21; Psalm 5:3; Matthew 20:1–16; Philippians 1:20

TRUTH TELLERS

"I was neither a prophet nor a prophet's son, but I was a shepherd, and I also took care of sycamore-fig trees. But the LORD took me from tending the flock and said to me, 'Go, prophesy to my people Israel.'" Amos 7:14–15

Surround yourself with truth tellers—those who define reality for you. They are not intimidated to speak the truth with grace and directness. Their only fear is God. Pray for gifted truth tellers who have a God-given innateness to discern situations, people, and a wise course of action. Sometimes their counsel will not be what you want to hear.

However, if you are wise, you will listen anyway. Do not allow your ego or pride to run rough shod over truth tellers. Do not marginalize them because what they have to say makes you uncomfortable or even upset. Make sure you value, and even celebrate, truth tellers in your life. They are few and far between; so latch on to the one the Lord sends.

Even when the spirit of a truth teller is not stellar, still listen. Get beyond your hurt feelings, and learn from the truth. "Wounds from a friend can be trusted, but an enemy multiplies kisses" (Proverbs 27: 6). It is better to receive a slight injury from the truth early on than to be bludgeoned by it later. Receive truth tellers into your life, and you will be better positioned to receive the blessings of God.

Moreover, make sure you hear truth from someone steeped in the Word of God, as it is penetrating and life changing. You cannot be confronted with God's Word and stay the same. You will either recoil in apathy or respond in humility and growth. Do not be satisfied to stay the same. Hold the plumb line of God's standards against your morals and ethics. Then conform your behavior into those eternal patterns of living.

Pitiful are the men and women who are surrounded only by those who tell them what they want to hear instead of wisely surrounding themselves with those who will tell them what they need to hear. Take an inventory of your close personal advisors. Have you created an environment of openness and confrontation by giving them permission to hold you accountable? Is there fear of reprisal, or are they rewarded for challenging your thinking and/or behavior? Truth tellers are a gift from God; so cherish and value them.

Look for ways to enhance their abilities even more. Maybe there is a need to engage a personal coach who has no agenda other than God's best for you and who can help you define your God-given priorities and hold you accountable to execute them in a wise and systematic way. Receiving truth leads to liberty; so enjoy your freedom in obedience!

"Jesus said, 'If you hold to my teaching, you are really my disciples. Then you will know the truth, and the truth will set you free'" (John 8:31–32).

Whom do I need to listen to and learn from who is telling me the truth?

Related Readings: Genesis 21:12; Job 33:31–33; John 18:37; James 1:22–24

LEARNING TO SAY NO

"But let your 'Yes' be 'Yes,' and your 'No,' 'No.' For whatever
is more than these is from the evil one." Matthew 5:37 NKJV

With whom do you need to communicate a firm answer of no? What opportunity is staring you in the face to which you know in your heart you have to say no? Hesitation or delay only creates an expectation of commitment. It is better to say no early on than to let silence send a message of yes. Learning to say no comes with mature faith in Christ.

God's game plan requires us to go deeper with fewer opportunities and fewer people so that we are able to give them the quality time and attention they desire and deserve. If we halfheartedly say yes without the conviction of truly caring, then we dilute our effectiveness and the overall success of the project or the team. An active answer of no is better than a passive yes.

Children are a good example of regular opportunities to lovingly say no. They do not have the context or experience to discern between what they want and what they need. For example, is it wise to give them a cell phone without it costing them anything? It probably is not, even if they say, "Everyone else has one." Your no helps them to mature.

In the same way, the Lord tells us no for our own good. Our heavenly Father is in a much better position to understand what is best for us. You may not understand today why He shut a relational or career door, but in the days ahead it will become abundantly clear. Do not listen to Satan's temptation to lead you to question where God has already said no to you.

"Now the serpent was more crafty than any of the wild animals the LORD God had made. He said to the woman, 'Did God really say, "You must not eat from any tree in the garden"?'" (Genesis 3:1). The devil is a master at causing us to doubt what Jesus knows is best for us.

The better you are at trusting and obeying the Lord's noes, the better equipped you are to say no. It is a faith journey that never ends until we are promoted to our eternal home in heaven. When you say no to a nice attraction, you have the energy and emotional margin to say yes to God's best. Say no now, by faith, and become free from the fear of rejection.

"Before I was afflicted I went astray, but now I obey your word" (Psalm 119:67).

Who needs to hear my loving no, and what no do I need to accept from the Lord?

Related Readings: Job 22:27; Psalm 119:168; Isaiah 50:10; James 3:1–12

How to Become a Disciple of Jesus Christ

Then Jesus came to them and said, "All authority in heaven and on earth has been given to me. Therefore go and make disciples of all nations, baptizing them in the name of the Father and of the Son and of the Holy Spirit, and teaching them to obey everything I have commanded you. And surely I am with you always, to the very end of the age." Matthew 28:18-20

Holy Scripture gives us principles related to becoming a disciple and to making disciples:

1

BELIEVE: That if you confess with your mouth, "Jesus is Lord," and believe in your heart that God raised him from the dead, you will be saved. Romans 10:9

Belief in Jesus Christ as your Savior and Lord gives you eternal life in heaven.

2

REPENT AND BE BAPTIZED: Peter replied, "Repent and be baptized, every one of you, in the name of Jesus Christ for the forgiveness of your sins. And you will receive the gift of the Holy Spirit. Acts 2:38

Repentance means you turn from your sin and then publicly confess Christ in baptism.

3

OBEY: Jesus replied, "If anyone loves me, he will obey my teaching. My Father will love him, and we will come to him and make our home with him." John 14:23

Obedience is an indicator of our love for the Lord Jesus and His presence in our life.

4

WORSHIP, PRAYER, COMMUNITY, EVANGELISM, AND STUDY: Every day they continued to meet together in the temple courts. They broke bread in their homes and ate together with glad and sincere hearts, praising God and enjoying the favor of all the people. And the Lord added to their number daily those who were being saved. Acts 2:46-47

Worship and prayer are our expression of gratitude and honor to God and our dependence on His grace. Community and evangelism are our accountability to Christians and compassion for non-Christians. Study to apply the knowledge, understanding, and wisdom of God.

5

LOVE GOD: Jesus replied: "'Love the Lord your God with all your heart and with all your soul and with all your mind.' This is the first and greatest commandment." Matthew 22:37-38

Intimacy with almighty God is a growing and loving relationship. We are loved by Him, so we can love others and be empowered by the Holy Spirit to obey His commands.

6

LOVE PEOPLE: "And the second is like it: 'Love your neighbor as yourself.'" Matthew 22:39

Loving people is an outflow of the love for our heavenly Father. We are able to love because He first loved us.

7

MAKE DISCIPLES: And the things you have heard me say in the presence of many witnesses entrust to reliable men who will also be qualified to teach others. 2 Timothy 2:2

The reason we disciple others is because we are extremely grateful to God and to those who disciple us, and we want to obey Christ's last instructions before going to heaven.

Meet the Author
BOYD BAILEY

Boyd Bailey, the author of **Wisdom Hunters Devotionals,**™ is the founder of **Wisdom Hunters, LLC**, an Atlanta-based ministry created to encourage Christians (a.k.a. wisdom hunters) to apply God's unchanging truth in a changing world. By God's grace, Boyd has impacted wisdom hunters in over 86 countries across the globe through the Wisdom Hunters daily devotionals, wisdomhunters.com devotional blog, and devotional books.

For over 30 years, Boyd Bailey has passionately pursued wisdom throughout his career in full-time ministry, executive coaching, and mentoring. Since becoming a Christian at the age of 19, Boyd begins each day as a wisdom hunter, diligently searching for truth in Scripture, and by God's grace, applying it to his life. These raw, unedited, "real time" reflections from his personal time with the Lord are now impacting over 106,000 people through the **Wisdom Hunters Daily Devotional e-mails.**

In addition to the daily devotionals, Boyd has authored devotional books: **Seeking Daily the Heart of God**, a 365-day devotional; three 90-day devotional books including **Infusion, Seeking God in the Psalms**, and **Seeking God in the Proverbs**; as well as several 30-day devotional books on topics such as **Wisdom for Fathers, Wisdom for Mothers, Wisdom for Work, Wisdom for Graduates**, and **Wisdom for Marriage.**

In addition to Wisdom Hunters, Boyd is the cofounder and CEO of **Ministry Ventures**, a faith-based, non-profit ministry. He has trained and coached over 1000 ministries in the best practices of prayer, boards, ministry models, administration, and fundraising. Prior to Ministry Ventures, Boyd was the national director for **Crown Financial Ministries** and an associate pastor at **First Baptist Church of Atlanta**. Boyd serves on the boards of **Ministry Ventures, Wisdom Hunters, Atlanta Mission, Souly Business**, and **Blueprint for Life.**

Boyd received his bachelor of arts degree from **Jacksonville State University** and his master of divinity degree from **Southwestern Seminary**. He and his wife of over 30 years, **Rita**, live in Roswell, Georgia, and are blessed with four daughters and three sons-in-law who love Jesus, two granddaughters, and a grandson. He and Rita like to hike, read, travel, invest in young couples, work through their bucket list, watch college football, serve in missions, and hang out with their kids and grandkids whenever possible.

Wisdom Hunters resources by
BOYD BAILEY

DAILY DEVOTIONAL
Sign up for free Daily Devotional emails at **WisdomHunters.com**

E-BOOKS & PRINT BOOKS
available at **WisdomHunters.com**

   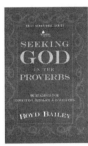 

New Wisdom Hunters App
for iPhone and iPad on iTunes.

Free Download at iTunes!

SCRIPTURE INDEX

TITLE INDEX

TITLE INDEX

TITLE INDEX

TITLE INDEX

RELIGION THAT GOD OUR FATHER
ACCEPTS AS PURE AND FAULTLESS IS THIS:
TO LOOK AFTER ORPHANS AND WIDOWS
IN THEIR DISTRESS...

JAMES 1:27

Family Christian Stores Foundation, The James Fund, is a nonprofit organization dedicated to meeting the needs of orphans and widows around the world. God's direction and purpose for this mission is defined in James 1:27: "Religion that God our Father accepts as pure and faultless is this: to look after orphans and widows in their distress..."(NIV) Along with other ministry partners, **The James Fund** is privileged to be a voice for the fatherless and a means for others to enter into God's work on behalf of the orphan and the widow.

To learn more and donate today, visit www.jamesfund.org.

The James Fund is a 501(c)(3) nonprofit organization founded by **Family Christian** Stores in 2003 to meet the needs of orphans and widows around the world.

Be a part of God's plan for the orphan and the widow.

Explore adoption assistance opportunities, or start an Orphan Care or Widow Care Ministry in your church.

Visit **www.JamesFund.org** to help you get started.